# Impact within the Human Rights Framework

# Impact within the Human Rights Framework

*Edited by*


Yves Haeck

*Professor of International Human Rights Law, Director of the Programme for Studies on Human Rights in Context, Faculty of Law and Criminology, Ghent University, Belgium*

Clara Burbano Herrera

*Professor of International Human Rights Law, Principal Investigator of the ERC Consolidator Grant IMPACTUM, and Director of the Programme for Studies on Human Rights in Context, Faculty of Law and Criminology, Ghent University, Belgium*



Edward Elgar PUBLISHING

Cheltenham, UK • Northampton, MA, USA

Published by

Edward Elgar Publishing Limited
The Lypiatts
15 Lansdown Road
Cheltenham
Glos GL50 2JA
UK

Edward Elgar Publishing, Inc.
William Pratt House
9 Dewey Court
Northampton
Massachusetts 01060
USA

Authorised representative in the EU for GPSR queries only: Easy Access System Europe – Mustamäe tee 50, 10621 Tallinn, Estonia, gpsr.requests@easproject.com

A catalogue record for this book is available from the British Library

Library of Congress Control Number: 2025951277

This book is available electronically in the **Elgar**online
Law subject collection
https://doi.org/10.4337/9781035360307

MIX
Paper | Supporting responsible forestry
FSC® C013604

ISBN 978 1 0353 6029 1 (cased)
ISBN 978 1 0353 6030 7 (eBook)
ISBN 978 1 0353 9664 1 (ePub)

Printed and bound by CPI Group (UK) Ltd, Croydon, CR0 4YY

# Contents

# List of contributors

**Yves Haeck,** Professor of International Human Rights Law, Director of the Programme for Studies on Human Rights in Context, Ghent University, Belgium

**Clara Burbano Herrera,** Professor of International Human Rights Law, Principal Investigator of the ERC *IMPACTUM* Project, Director of the Programme for Studies on Human Rights in Context, Ghent University, Belgium

**Carolina Bejarano Martínez,** Research Fellow Max Planck Institute for Comparative Public Law and International Law, Heidelberg, Germany

**Bruno Boti Bernardi,** Professor Universidade Federal da Grande Dourados, Dourados, Brazil

**Daniel Cerqueira,** Director Climate Justice and Human Rights program Due Process of Law Foundation, Washington DC, United States

**Par Engstrom,** Professor Institute of the Americas, University College London, London, United Kingdom

**Mariela Morales Antoniazzi,** Senior Research Fellow Max Planck Institute for Comparative Public Law and International Law, Heidelberg, Germany

**Laura Alessandra Nocera,** Professor Università degli Studi di Milano, Italy

**Oscar Parra Vera,** Justice, Chamber for Acknowledgment of Truth and Responsibility of the Special Jurisdiction for Peace, Colombia.

**Sabrina Ragone,** Professor, University of Bologna, Bologna, Italy.

**João Roriz**, Professor and Sérgio Vieira de Mello Chair, Universidade Federal de Goiás, Goiãna, Brazil

**Mónica Trespalacios-Leal,** Adviser Special Jurisdiction for Peace, Colombia

**René Urueña,** Professor Universidad de Los Andes, Colombia

**Alberte Verwohlt-Hansen,** Researcher Human Rights in Context, Ghent University, Belgium

**Stephania Yate Cortes,** Research Fellow Max Planck Institute for Comparative Public Law and International Law, Heidelberg, Germany

# Preface

The Inter-American Human Rights System (IAHRS) has distinguished itself as an important framework in the promotion and protection of human rights across the Americas, providing avenues for justice and redress in societies where democratic institutions and the rule of law have often been fragile or contested.

This volume is a response to the growing need for a comprehensive analysis of the impact of the IAHRS beyond traditional compliance studies. While compliance remains an essential component of human rights analysis, it offers an incomplete view of the ways in which regional human rights institutions shape legal, political, and social dynamics at both national and international levels. The chapters in this book seek to expand the analytical lens by integrating theoretical, methodological, and empirical insights to better understand how human rights decisions impact multiple layers of society.

The contributors to this volume bring together diverse perspectives that reveal the complex interactions between regional human rights bodies, domestic institutions, civil society actors, and individuals. By engaging with the concept of impact as a complex, multidimensional phenomenon that extends beyond compliance, this book underscores the importance of examining the role of human rights systems in fostering legal, institutional, social, and normative transformations, influencing judicial reasoning, and empowering human rights advocacy. In doing so, the volume highlights the critical dialogues and exchanges that occur between the Inter-American Commission on Human Rights (IACHR), the Inter-American Court of Human Rights (IACtHR), and domestic actors striving to uphold human rights.

The structure of this book reflects its dual emphasis on conceptual rigor and empirical analysis. The first part provides a theoretical and methodological foundation, addressing key debates surrounding the notion of impact and offering frameworks for its assessment. The second part delves into case studies that illustrate the diverse ways in which the IAHRS has influenced legal and political landscapes in specific national contexts. By bridging theory and practice, this volume seeks to contribute to ongoing scholarly debates and provide valuable insights for those engaged in human rights advocacy.

This book would not have been possible without the generous support of several institutions and individuals. We are deeply appreciative of the contributing scholars, whose thought-provoking analyses have greatly enriched this academic endeavour. Their collective efforts have advanced our understanding of the impact of the IAHRS, offering valuable insights into its significance and complexity in contemporary human rights governance. We also express our profound gratitude to the Programme for Studies on Human Rights in Context (Ghent University, Belgium) and the European Research Council (ERC) for their support in the development of this research. Finally, our heartfelt thanks go to researcher Ms Luna Lanckvrind and Mr Peter Low, whose dedication and editorial support have been instrumental in bringing this volume to fruition.

It is our hope that this book will serve as a useful resource for scholars seeking to deepen their understanding of the role of regional human rights systems and will contribute to a more critical engagement with the impact of human rights within the Inter-American system and beyond.

Yves Haeck and Clara Burbano Herrera

# Acknowledgments

This research work has been funded by the European Union (ERC Consolidator Grant, IMPACTUM 101044852) and Research Fund Ghent University (Belgium). Views and opinions expressed are, however, those of the authors only and do not necessarily reflect those of the European Union, the European Research Council Executive Agency or Ghent University. Neither the European Union nor the granting authority can be held responsible for them.

We wish to express our heartfelt appreciation to Edward Elgar Publishing for facilitating the publication of this work, and especially to Amber Watts, Jonathan Cailes, Mark Griffiths, and Ben Booth for their thoughtful guidance and generous support throughout the process.

# 1. Introduction: Impact within the human rights framework

**Yves Haeck and Clara Burbano Herrera**

## 1 IMPACT WITHIN THE HUMAN RIGHTS FRAMEWORK

The purpose of this volume is to provide a diverse array of analytical perspectives to facilitate a deeper understanding of the impact of the Inter-American human rights system (IAHRS). This regional human rights system has gained increasing significance, not only with regard to the types of human rights it protects and its evolving and expanding interpretation of these rights, but also in terms of what it demands from states.[1] The importance of the IAHRS is evident in its various functions of documenting human rights violations, ensuring justice for victims of severe human rights abuses, and safeguarding the human rights enshrined in international legal instruments, particularly in contexts where the rule of law is fragile or under threat. Despite its critical role, the legal framework of human rights at the regional level has largely been overlooked in discussions concerning the impact of the IAHRS and its interactions with domestic stakeholders. Research to date has predominantly concentrated on the study of state compliance with the decisions of human rights bodies.[2]

[1] This research work has been funded by the European Research Council (ERC) as part of the ERC project *IMPACTUM* (Grant Agreement No 101044852), and the Research Fund of Ghent University (Belgium). Views and opinions expressed are, however, those of the author(s) only and do not necessarily reflect those of the European Union, the European Research Council Executive Agency, or Ghent University. Neither the European Union nor the granting authority can be held responsible for them.

[2] For literature on compliance see: R. Grote, M. Morales Antoniazzi and D. Paris (eds), *Research Handbook on Compliance in International Human Rights Law* (Edward Elgar, Cheltenham, UK and Northampton, MA 2021); Timothy Meyer, 'How Compliance Understates Effectiveness' (2014) 108 *Proceedings of the ASIL Annual Meeting* 93; Robert Howse and Ruti Teitel, 'Beyond Compliance:

Therefore, it is essential to develop a deeper academic understanding of the impacts of this regional system that encompasses its relationships with domestic actors, as well as its influence on local human rights law and policy.

The contributors to this volume agree that the human rights system must be analyzed beyond the confines of a compliance-led assessment. As Bernardi and Roriz in Chapter 7 articulate, 'The analysis of compliance with human rights bodies in specific cases evaluates whether states and their relevant organs have upheld or neglected the resolutive aspects of international human rights decisions, often employing a checklist approach to the implementation of individual rulings and recommendations. In contrast, impact analysis—such as the one developed in this chapter—encompasses a broader scope, examining the far-reaching consequences of international decisions within processes that extend beyond the designated institutional actors and specific recommendations or resolutive points.' By employing the concept of impact as an expanded analytical framework, this volume seeks to offer a more comprehensive understanding of the dynamics shaping human rights protections in the Americas. The volume covers a wide range of topics, including advancements in these protections within the IAHRS, the methods by which states implement Inter-American human rights decisions, and the ways in which domestic actors—such as those from civil society, judges, and victims—utilize Inter-American standards to further the protection of human rights. A key focus is the dialogue between regional human rights bodies and domestic tribunals, as well as other domestic actors, regarding the most effective means of safeguarding victims' rights.

The Inter-American human rights bodies, in essence the Inter-American Commission on Human Rights (IACHR) and the Inter-American Court of Human Rights (IACtHR), have consistently engaged with various domestic actors, including judges, non-governmental organizations (NGOs), scholars,

---

Rethinking Why International Law Really Matters' (2010) 1 *Global Policy* 128; M. Peter Haas and Richard B. Bilder, 'Compliance Theories: Choosing to Comply—Theorizing from International Relations and Comparative Politics' in Dinah Shelton (ed), *Commitment and Compliance: The Role of Non-binding Norms in the International Legal System* (Oxford University Press, Oxford 2003; online edn, Oxford Academic, 1 January 2010); Kal Raustiala and Anne-Marie Slaughter, 'International Law, International Relations and Compliance' in Walter Carlsnaes, Thomas Risse and Beth A. Simmons (eds), *Handbook of International Relations* (SAGE, London 2002) 553; Benedict Kingsbury, 'The Concept of Compliance as a Function of Competing Conceptions of International Law' (1998) 19 *Michigan Journal of International Law* 345; George W. Downs, David M. Rocke, and Peter N. Barsoom, 'Is the Good News About Compliance Good News about Cooperation?' (1996) 50 *International Organization* 379.

victims, and their families. The dynamics of these interactions must be understood and analyzed within the specific political and legal-normative contexts of the continent as a whole, as well as those of the individual countries. Indeed, the Americas are characterized by a complex political landscape that is marked by a history of repressive regimes alongside contemporary fragile democracies that face significant challenges in upholding human rights. Within this context, the legal-normative framework, particularly the American Convention on Human Rights and its interpretation by the IACHR and the IACtHR, has facilitated substantial opportunities for these actors to engage with and implement human rights decisions. This engagement has evolved from passive to more active involvement with human rights monitoring bodies since 1959, utilizing a variety of methods and strategies.[3]

The objective of this volume is to contribute to the ongoing debates in the literature regarding the impact of the organs of the IAHRS.[4] To that end, the book seeks to engage in a scholarly dialogue on the concept of impact, from both a conceptual and empirical standpoint. It aims to draw insights from the current academic discourse, while pursuing a more comprehensive and contextual analysis of impact within the human rights framework. This volume presents the latest developments in the analysis of impact through three distinct perspectives: (i) the impact of human rights decisions; (ii) the impact of human rights bodies; and (iii) the impact of the Inter-American human rights system itself. These perspectives are explored by providing a theoretical examination of impact that goes beyond mere compliance and by applying this theoretical framework to specific case studies and countries.

---

3 C. Burbano Herrera and Y. Haeck, 'The Historical and Present-Day Role of Non-Governmental Organisations Before the Inter-American Human Rights System in Documenting Serious Human Rights Violations and Protecting Human Rights and the Rule of Law Through Ensuring Accountability' (2021) 17 *Utrecht Law Review* 8–24. See also M. Morales Antoniazzi and V. Krsticevic, 'NGOs: A Critical Link to Understanding and Strengthening Compliance of International Decisions' in R. Grote, M. Morales Antoniazzi, and D. Paris (eds) *Research Handbook on Compliance in International Human Rights Law* (Edward Elgar, Cheltenham, UK and Northampton, MA 2021).

4 Literature on impact: A. von Bogdandy, E. Ferrer Mac-Gregor, M. Morales Antoniazzi and F. Piovesan (eds), *The Impact of the Inter-American Human Rights System: Transformations on the Ground* (Oxford University Press, Oxford 2024); E. Gonzalez-Ocantos and W. Sandholtz, 'Constructing a Regional Human Rights Legal Order: The Inter-American Court, National Courts, and Judicial Dialogue, 1988–2014' (2021) 19 *International Journal of Constitutional Law* 1559–1596; C.S. Gibson, 'Legal Impact Analysis: The Ideal and the Practicable' (1982) 24 *Journal of the Indian Law Institute* 837–847. http://www.jstor.org/stable/43950844.

The book comprises an introduction, eight chapters, and a conclusion. The main body of the volume is divided into two parts: Part I consists of four chapters that focus on theoretical and methodological frameworks, outlining the impact model, exploring various conceptualizations of impact, and clarifying its components, promises, and limitations, as well as the challenges associated with its measurement. Part II includes four chapters that reflect on the impact of human rights bodies through the analysis of specific countries and case studies.

The first part of the book starts with a chapter authored by Par Engstrom. His contribution, titled 'Inter-American human rights experimentalism', critically examines the IAHRS with the aim of defining and conceptualizing its human rights impact. This chapter puts forward a theory of institutional effectiveness that is centred on patterns of interaction and highlights the potential for long-term impact through dynamic causal pathways that emerge over time. The central argument is that the normative and institutional evolution of the IAHRS since its establishment has progressively intensified interactions between the IAHRS and domestic legal orders, political processes, and actors. Consequently, the IAHRS has effects that extend beyond those traditionally associated with enforcement and rule compliance models. The analytical model developed in this chapter is based on experimentalist accounts of human rights governance, and it posits that impact is conditional on the dynamically evolving relationships between international and national human rights standards, norms, institutions, and political practices. The chapter has two sections. The first explores the transnationalization of the IAHRS, mapping its institutional and normative development against five key features of experimental human rights governance. The second section develops a nuanced understanding of the IAHRS's impact, emphasizing the pivotal role of domestic actors as the driving force behind the system's effectiveness. It presents a dynamic, iterative, and interactive process through which IAHRS impact unfolds. In conclusion, Engstrom argues that conceptualizing the IAHRS as an experimental governance framework provides a deeper and more nuanced understanding of its practical functionality. This framework highlights the dynamic interactions among diverse actors, the centrality of dialogue and flexibility, and the ongoing experimentation with strategies for effective human rights implementation.

The second chapter, authored by Sabrina Ragone and Laura Alessandra Nocera, is titled 'Tools to understand the impact of human rights systems from a comparative perspective'. This chapter provides methodological and definitional tools for identifying various types of impact resulting from the case law of the Inter-American and European human rights systems, approached through the lens of comparative law. The authors consider the differences between these two human rights systems, particularly in terms of their respective contexts, instruments, resources, and organizational structures.

Specifically, they identify three types of impact stemming from the case law of two regional human rights bodies:

1. *Ordinary impact* (or natural impact), which refers to the influence exerted by decisions of the IACtHR and/or the European Court of Human Rights (ECtHR) on all national judges and courts within the respective regions. This type of impact is characterized by its physiological nature, remaining within the dialogue among judicial bodies without transcending the system.

2. *Conformative impact* on non-judicial institutions, which pertains to the influence of both the ECtHR and the IACtHR on state non-judicial institutions, with a particular focus on the interaction with parliaments and legislative bodies. As national parliaments are the principal bodies responsible for regulating human rights within their respective states—regardless of the specific models of state and forms of government—this is a critical consideration. Domestic legislatures are obliged to pass the necessary legislation when national laws conflict with international human rights standards.

3. Finally, they suggest the term *systemic-transformative impact*, which refers to the impact on actors outside of public organizations—those that are neither judicial nor institutional, but part of broader society. To understand this impact, scholars must examine a range of factors and connections that may influence the acceptance of human rights doctrines. This analysis should also consider the transformative role that these doctrines play in shaping societal norms and values. Indeed, every case decided by either the IACtHR or the ECtHR affects societal debates and sparks new legal interpretations, extending the impact beyond the specific region in question.

Overall, both the Inter-American and European courts have significantly influenced institutional and non-institutional actors at the domestic level, contributing to a heightened awareness of human rights and fostering a form of constitutional pluralism. The authors affirm that each legal system tends to construct a sphere of influence that differs from that of its usual intended recipients. This phenomenon is particularly evident in legal systems designed to protect human rights. Modern international courts, in particular, are institutions whose systemic function extends beyond merely settling disputes between two or more parties. In this regard, the activity of international human rights systems cannot be confined to the resolution of judicial disputes alone. These systems also encompass a variety of activities, the nature and analysis of which are far more complex than a purely judicial perspective could reveal.

The third contribution, by René Urueña and Stephania Yate Cortes, titled 'Impact through aesthetics: narrative, perception, and justice in the Inter-American Court of Human Rights', contributes to the discussion of impact by conceptualizing it as a constantly evolving description of reality performed by the IACtHR. The authors emphasize that impact itself is manifested through narratives that shape how human rights realities are interpreted. They assert that the narratives constructed by the IACtHR shape not only legal reasoning but also perceptions of reality, thereby also shaping the particular ways in which human rights violations are seen and experienced. By using aesthetics in this analysis, the authors argue that representations of reality can be created and transformed by narrative. In their chapter, the authors examine how the IACtHR constructs and modulates representations of violence, victims, and justice, and how this influences how these realities are understood and internalized by the community of practice. They emphasize that the role of aesthetics in the IACtHR's narratives is crucial in shaping both the perception and impact of human rights discourse. These narratives have an aesthetic dimension in that they engage readers not only through legal argumentation but also by immersing them in a particular representation of events. They explain three distinct types of images that are consistently shaped by the narratives present in the jurisprudence of the IACtHR. The first type concerns the representation of violence, which shifts from an 'atrocity aesthetic' (i.e. highlighting specific harms that produce horror, a way of focusing on 'spectacular' acts of physical violence) to a 'structural aesthetic' (i.e. considering the multifactorial causes that lead to human rights violations, thus shifting the focus from physical harm to the broader structural conditions that perpetuate systemic injustices). The second type pertains to the representation of victims, which goes beyond the traditional notion of an 'ideal victim' (the victim is perceived as inherently vulnerable) to introduce the image of an empowered subject. Finally, the third type involves the conceptualization of justice, transitioning from 'distant justice' (where justice refers to practices where courts are geographically, politically, or culturally distant from the communities affected by human rights violations) to 'embedded justice' (where justice resonates locally, encourages participation, and challenges the perception of international justice as distant or detached). These dynamics are illustrated through an analysis of three IACtHR cases: *Villagrán-Morales et al. v. Guatemala ('street children case'), Miguel Castro Castro Prison v. Peru*, and *Villamizar Durán et al. v. Colombia*.

The final contribution in the first part, Chapter 5, is titled 'A theoretical model for measuring the impact of urgent measures aimed at protecting at-risk detainees in Latin America', and is authored by Clara Burbano Herrera, Yves Haeck, and Alberte Verwohlt Hansen. This chapter introduces a theoretical framework for understanding and evaluating the impact of urgent measures (UMs) within the context of detention in Latin America. The proposed model employs a mixed-methods approach, integrating desk research with qualitative research methodologies to assess the impact of such measures. It also emphasizes the necessity of incorporating the perspectives of those deprived of liberty, their social environments, state authorities, and members of human rights bodies into the analysis. The authors also call for the adoption of decolonial methodologies throughout the research process, particularly in light of the unique human rights challenges posed by various prison systems and governmental regimes in Latin America. They argue that the solutions, initiatives, and conceptual frameworks developed within Latin America regarding crime and detention offer critical insights, contributing to a non-Western, decolonial understanding of human rights violations in contexts of deprivation of liberty. The authors conceptualize impact as the outcomes resulting from the implementation of UMs, affecting both the direct beneficiaries and broader society. They underscore the challenges of measuring impact, noting that its assessment is inherently variable and contingent upon the specific context of each case. Recognizing the impracticality of capturing all potential dimensions of impact, the authors instead propose a comprehensive and adaptable theoretical framework. Additionally, they identify several key factors that could enhance the analytical process. The authors present a multifaceted approach to impact assessment, recognizing that impact may differ across societal levels and from diverse perspectives. They distinguish between direct, indirect, and symbolic impacts and propose a tiered framework encompassing micro-, meso-, and macro-level analyses. Furthermore, they acknowledge that the nature of impact may evolve over time, manifesting itself in the short, medium, and long term, and that its characteristics may shift depending on the temporal context in which it is evaluated.

The second part of the book is devoted to case studies, beginning with Chapter 6, titled 'Impact of Inter-American jurisprudence on the fight against impunity in Colombia: the case of the Special Jurisdiction for Peace', authored by Oscar Parra and Mónica Trespalacios-Leal. This chapter offers a sophisticated analysis of the influence of Inter-American jurisprudence within the framework of transitional justice in Colombia, with Engstrom's theoretical framework serving as the primary reference point. The study provides an in-depth examination of how Inter-American jurisprudence has shaped the decisions of the Colombian Constitutional Court (CCC) and the Special Jurisdiction for Peace (JEP) regarding the most effective ways to safeguard the rights of victims of systemic violence. It emphasizes the design, implementation, and evolution of strategies aimed at identifying, prosecuting, and holding accountable those responsible for human rights violations in the context of the transitional justice system established in Colombia following the peace agreement. The authors examine how the JEP has adopted and operationalized the standards of justice and the fight against impunity developed by the jurisprudence of the IAHRS as a form of impact. These standards can be categorized as follows: (i) the prohibition of full amnesties and judicial pardons in cases of gross violations of human rights; (ii) the macro criminal investigation as a development of the logic lines of investigation; and (iii) the robust participation of victims within the JEP, which has paved the way for restorative moments within judicial procedures. The authors argue that the jurisprudence of the IAHRS compelled the negotiators of Colombia's peace agreement to prioritize the maximization of justice, while the CCC established a condition that all benefits be contingent upon the satisfaction of victims' rights. To support their argument, the authors provide a detailed analysis of two of the eleven macro-cases initiated by the JEP, namely Case 1, concerning kidnappings, and Case 3, addressing the criminal phenomenon known as 'false positives'. They contend that the Inter-American standards laid the groundwork for victims to be prioritized in the judicial process, culminating in the establishment of infrastructure and services that have enabled significant participation in the JEP. Moreover, by amplifying the voices of victims who had not been heard within the ordinary justice system, the JEP has fostered restorative dialogues between victims and perpetrators, thereby redefining the parameters of justice for heinous crimes within the context of a peacebuilding process.

The second contribution to Part 2, by Bruno Boti Bernardi and João Roriz, Chapter 7, titled 'Behind the scenes of impact in the Yanomami Case (1980–85): civil society and bureaucratic politics in the Inter-American Commission on Human Rights', provides a comprehensive analysis of the case *Yanomami v. Brazil.* Drawing on historical institutionalism and using the Yanomami case as its focus, the authors argue that impact analysis should incorporate an examination of the micro-dynamics of decision-making, focusing on the specific bureaucratic politics within human rights bodies and their interactions with civil society groups. Such dynamics are critical for explaining the content and nature of decisions made by human rights bodies. They propose an impact analysis that accounts for the broader consequences of international decisions in other processes, extending beyond the designated institutional actors and specific recommendations or resolutions. In addition to examining how international human rights decisions are received and implemented locally within specific countries, the authors content that it is essential to 'open the black box' of human rights bodies themselves in order to understand how and why they act in the manner they do. The authors conclude by asserting that the IACHR's final recommendation in favour of the demarcation of indigenous lands was the result of several factors, including: (i) the civil society complainants being highly motivated and technically well prepared; (ii) civil society's ability to utilize its transnational connections, alongside its US-based members and institutions, to intervene systematically before the IACHR, thereby leveraging its direct political and legal advocacy with the Commissioners and IACHR staff; (iii) the Commission's reinterpretation and implementation of its rules and standards in new and innovative ways, using the data and legal formulations proposed by civil society; and (iv) the IACHR's increased political space, legal tools, and reasoning capacity, which enabled it to explore the ambiguity of its norms and adopt new positions regarding indigenous issues. All subsequent impacts were not only related to the concrete case, but also to the future jurisprudence of the Inter-American human rights system.

The third chapter of this part, Chapter 8, was authored by Mariela Morales Antoniazzi and Carolina Bejarano Martínez. Their contribution is titled 'Towards the consolidation of the *Ius Coonstitutionale Commune* in Latin American LGBTIQ+ rights: the transformative impact of Advisory Opinion OC-24/17'. The authors use the term 'impact' as a broader analytical lens than 'compliance' to explore the dynamics of human rights protection in the Americas. They analyze the various ways in which Inter-American law influences practices, structures, and social outcomes, both within and beyond the Inter-American human rights system. The chapter is divided into two sections. The initial section introduces the concept of *Ius Constitutionale Commune* in Latin America (ICCAL) as a framework for impact analysis. This framework underscores the Inter-American human rights system's context-sensitivity and responsiveness concerning human rights, democracy, and the rule of law. The authors argue that this context enables a more comprehensive understanding of the circulation, appropriation, and application of inter-American standards within the Latin American human rights community of practice. Taking a regional approach to transformative constitutionalism, the chapter argues that a set of common standards reflects the emergence and consolidation of an *ius constitutionale commune* in Latin America. These common standards are driven by three key factors: (i) the primary treaties of the international human rights systems and their incorporation into national constitutions; (ii) the transformative jurisprudence of the IACtHR and the broad mandate of IACHR; and (iii) the legal practices of states and the active participation of a Latin American community that includes judges, politicians, social movements, academics, national human rights institutions, and civil society. In the second section, as a concrete example to apply the concept of impact within the ICCAL framework, the authors examine regional standards on LGBTIQ+ rights as established by Advisory Opinion No. 24 of the IACtHR. This section provides an in-depth analysis of the IACtHR's Advisory Opinion OC-24/17 on gender identity and equality and non-discrimination in respect of same-sex couples, to illustrate the multiple ways in which inter-American law impacts practices, structures, and social outcomes. The section discusses innovative mechanisms by which a Latin American *ius commune* has influenced LGBTIQ+ rights in Brazil, Mexico, and Colombia, offering an illustrative, though not exhaustive, example of the constellation of LGBTIQ+ human rights protections. The authors demonstrate how this advisory opinion has had the potential to impact a variety of spheres, including judicial rulings, national policies, and civil society practices, such as those of LGBTIQ+ social movements. Furthermore, it is asserted that the advisory opinion has contributed to the broader academic discourse.

The final contribution, 'Urgent measures and Indigenous peoples' territorial rights in the Inter-American system', written by Daniel Cerqueira, provides a detailed examination of the institutional and normative framework related to the urgent measures adopted by the IACHR and the IACtHR to protect Indigenous territories and natural resources. The author elucidates how political, rather than legal, constraints have negatively impacted the protection of Indigenous territorial rights through the adoption of urgent measures. It is evident that the safeguarding of Indigenous territorial rights has been excluded from these measures since 2011, undoubtedly due to the prevailing political context. Cerqueira argues that the jurisprudence of the organs of the Inter-American system concerning urgent measures can be divided into two distinct phases: one in which Indigenous rights were clearly protected, and another, from 2011 onwards, in which this protection diminished under pressure from certain states, notably Brazil, which disagreed with the decisions issued by the IACHR. This disagreement has led to substantial reforms in the Commission's Rules of Procedure, particularly Article 25, which addresses urgent measures. Notably, Article 25 has undergone significant changes, including the introduction of additional procedural requirements and stricter criteria for the approval of such measures. The author asserts that the 'strengthening process' initiated in 2011 has had a profound impact on the IACHR's practices. This process has led the IACHR to refrain from issuing precautionary measures to suspend large-scale projects in Indigenous and tribal territories, even when such projects are related to contentious cases that allege foreseeable, serious, and irreparable harm. As a result, hundreds of individuals and communities have been deprived of a vital tool for the protection of their territorial rights within the IAHRS. Cerqueira contends that, despite the IAHRS embodying some of the most advanced standards for Indigenous territorial rights, the current practices of its organs make it virtually impossible to safeguard these rights through urgent measures. In his concluding remarks, the author proposes two recommendations for enhancing the protection of Indigenous territorial rights within the Inter-American system. The first is the reinstatement of the urgent measures mechanism in exceptional circumstances, and the second is the prioritization of the processing of contentious cases based on allegations of significant and irreparable harm to Indigenous and tribal lands.

By way of conclusion, it is our hope that this edited volume will serve as a valuable tool for facilitating a deeper understanding and critical examination of the impact of human rights systems. In particular, we trust that it will provide readers with a deeper insight into the role of human rights systems, extending beyond states' compliance with their decisions, even in contexts where the rule of law and respect for human rights are under significant threat.

# PART I

# Laying out the impact model

# 2. Inter-American human rights experimentalism

**Par Engstrom**

## 1 INTRODUCTION[1]

This chapter develops a distinct analytical perspective on understanding and evaluating the impact of the regional human rights system in the Americas. The Inter-American human rights system (IAHRS) – consisting of the Inter-American Commission on Human Rights (IACHR) and the Inter-American Court of Human Rights (IACtHR) – has been at the forefront of normative and institutional developments in international human rights. The IAHRS has responded to evolving human rights conditions in ways that underline the potential of institutional change and adaptation in human rights governance. The system has become increasingly ambitious not only in terms of the types of human rights challenges it deals with, but also in terms of what it demands from states. The IAHRS is pushing normative boundaries, not least beyond the liberal minimalist definitions of human rights as well as in its continually evolving and expanding interpretation of the scope of state obligations.

There is a pressing need, however, to develop a better understanding of the effects of regional human rights institutions, such as the IAHRS. Despite its importance, *regional* human rights governance remains neglected in the study of the interplay between international and local human rights law and politics.[2] This relative oversight is regrettable, given the substantial human rights activity taking place at the regional level. While the United Nations (UN)

[1] The author gratefully acknowledges the assistance of Edward Pérez with the production of the figures included in the chapter, and for comments on a previous draft. The author also thanks two anonymous reviewers for their observations and suggestions that helped to improve this chapter.

[2] Alexandra Huneeus and Mikael Rask Madsen, 'Between Universalism and Regional Law and Politics: A Comparative History of the American, European, and African Human Rights Systems' (2018) 16 *International Journal of Constitutional Law* 136.

human rights system has advanced human rights standard-setting, progress has been much slower at the global level with regard to the development of effective monitoring mechanisms to ensure the implementation of increasingly ambitious norms and standards.[3] Similarly, while there is an extensive scholarly literature examining the impact of international human rights norms and the efficacy of international advocacy efforts, assessments of the role of international *institutions*, specifically, remain relatively scant.[4]

It is against this background that this chapter examines the IAHRS with the objective to define and conceptualize its human rights impact. The analytical model developed in the chapter builds on experimentalist accounts of human rights governance[5] to argue that impact is dependent on the dynamically evolving relationships between international and national human rights standards, norms, institutions, and political practices. The perspective here on human rights impact emphasizes the iterative interactions between international actors and institutions (such as the IAHRS) and local actors and institutions, and the human rights outcomes they generate. Unlike conventional enforcement models that prioritize clearly defined and specific norms, the approach in this chapter emphasizes the value of gradual interpretations and ongoing interactions. Through this iterative process, shared understandings of human rights norms are more likely to be fostered over time. Instead of focusing on the perceived weaknesses of institutional enforcement mechanisms, this chapter proposes a theory of institutional effectiveness centred on patterns of interaction and highlighting the potential for long-term impact through dynamic causal pathways that emerge over time. Similarly, in contrast to many compliance-focused human rights models, this chapter highlights how the IAHRS operates in practice, turning our analytical gaze away from the dominant focus on top-down imposition of human rights standards. Instead, the IAHRS's institutional strength lies in its ability to generate continuous engagement and interaction between local and international actors and institutions.

Building on these insights derived from human rights experimentalism, this chapter pays particular attention to the politically contentious character

---

3 Rainer Grote, Mariela Morales Antoniazzi and Davide Paris, 'Conclusion: Moving beyond Compliance without Neglecting Compliance in International Human Rights Law' in Rainer Grote, Mariela Morales Antoniazzi and Davide Paris (eds), *Research Handbook on Compliance in International Human Rights Law* (Edward Elgar, Cheltenham, UK and Northampton, MA 2021) 510–522.

4 Alejandro Anaya-Muñoz, Hector M. Nuñez and Aldo F. Ponce, 'Setting the Agenda: Social Influence in the Effects of the Human Rights Committee in Latin America and Central and Eastern Europe' (2018) 17 *Journal of Human Rights* 229.

5 Gráinne de Búrca, 'Human Rights Experimentalism' (2017) 111 *American Journal of International Law* 277.

of human rights impact. The basic argument developed is that the normative and institutional evolution of the IAHRS since its creation has gradually increased interactions between the IAHRS and domestic legal orders, political processes, and actors. Most notably, the IAHRS has developed transnationalized structures of regional human rights governance. This can be seen in the expansion and widening scope of regional human rights norms and legal standards. It is also evident in the expanding array of actors now involved in human rights implementation, each with distinct interests, identities, and power capabilities, creating a complex web of transnational dynamics shaping the realization of rights. The chapter develops an actor-oriented approach to understanding IAHRS impact, by explaining how different actors within and outside the system shape its impact, both in terms of advancing and resisting human rights. Additionally, the system itself has developed practices of decentralized modalities of human rights implementation. As a result, the IAHRS has effects beyond those traditionally associated with enforcement and rule compliance models.[6]

The chapter is divided into two main parts. The first part examines the transnationalization of the IAHRS, mapping its institutional and normative development onto five key features of experimental human rights governance. The second part develops a specific understanding of IAHRS impact that emphasizes the role of domestic actors as the driving force behind the system's effectiveness, advancing an understanding of IAHRS impact through an iterative, interactive, and dynamic process. This approach signifies a shift away from one-off compliance and enforcement models and underscores the growing importance of decentralized human rights implementation. The conclusion highlights the analytical and normative benefits of framing the IAHRS as an experimental governance framework compared to alternative approaches.

## 2 TRANSNATIONALIZING HUMAN RIGHTS: THE NORMATIVE AND INSTITUTIONAL DEVELOPMENT OF THE IAHRS

Since its creation, the IAHRS has developed from a government-run diplomatic entity to a highly institutionalized and legalized regime with formal authority to hold governments to account for their human rights records. Following the establishment of the IACtHR in 1979, an independent regional human rights court together with an autonomous commission are now regularly monitoring regional states' human rights performance. The system has developed an

6 Par Engstrom (ed), *The Inter-American Human Rights System: Impact beyond Compliance* (Palgrave Macmillan 2019).

increasingly extensive set of human rights norms and practices that legitimize international concern for the general welfare of individuals and action regarding internal human rights practices of states.[7] The access of individuals and human rights organizations to the IAHRS has strengthened over time as the system has become increasingly judicialized with a procedural focus on legal argumentation and the generation of regional human rights jurisprudence. Undeniably, these are all extensive normative and institutional changes hardly envisaged by the state representatives responsible for the initial creation of the IAHRS.[8]

Most notably, the IAHRS has developed features associated with experimental governance frameworks. The literature on experimental governance highlights five distinctive features.[9] First, effective experimental governance requires an initial *recognition and agreement on a shared understanding* of a common problem by the diverse participating actors. A second key feature of experimental governance involves establishing a framework with *clear but open-ended goals*, and that outlines a set of rights in broad, flexible, and general terms, allowing participating actors to reach agreement. Third, experimental governance frameworks emphasize the importance of the implementation of broadly defined goals by actors at the local level or those directly affected by the issue. This approach encourages *active participation from key stakeholders* who possess local understanding, knowledge, and the flexibility to adapt the framework to specific contexts. A fourth feature emphasizes *continuous feedback* from local contexts and stakeholders to a central body, allowing for monitoring, reporting, and continuous review processes. A final key characteristic of experimental governance is the need for *continuous re-evaluation*. This involves regularly assessing both the initial goals and the current practices employed, informed by the ongoing review process and the shared objectives established at the outset. In this section, the chapter will develop these five dimensions to assess the extent to which the IAHRS broadly conforms to a regional experimental human rights governance framework.

---

[7] David Harris, 'Regional Protection of Human Rights: The Inter-American Achievement' in David Harris and Stephen Livingstone (eds), *The Inter-American Human Rights System* (Clarendon Press 1998).

[8] Par Engstrom, 'The Inter-American Human Rights System and US–Latin American Relations' in Juan Pablo Scarfi and Andrew R. Tillman (eds), *Cooperation and Hegemony in US–Latin American Relations: Revisiting the Western Hemisphere Idea* (Palgrave Macmillan US 2016).

[9] Búrca, 'Human Rights Experimentalism' (n 5).

## 2.1 Formal State Commitment

Considering the undeniable heterogeneity of states and societies across the Americas, there is a remarkable level of support for a regional human rights system. There is a high degree of formal normative commitment by states in the region to the basic principles and fundamental values of international human rights generally, and to the IAHRS specifically. Over time, as indicated in Figure 2.1, there has been an increasing level of ratification of international legal instruments developed by the IAHRS, indicating the strengthening of formal state commitment to international human rights.

States across the region have also signalled their agreement to the IAHRS through their participation in, as well as their decisions to allocate resources towards, supporting the activities of the IAHRS. States also continue to engage with the system through routine participation in IAHRS proceedings, whether in response to contentious litigation of individual rights violations or as part of public hearings on pressing human rights challenges. It is in this sense that there is a broadly shared perception of the value of human rights and a basic acceptance across the diverse range of participating states in regional human rights governance in the Americas, reflecting a declared regional consensus among signatory states.

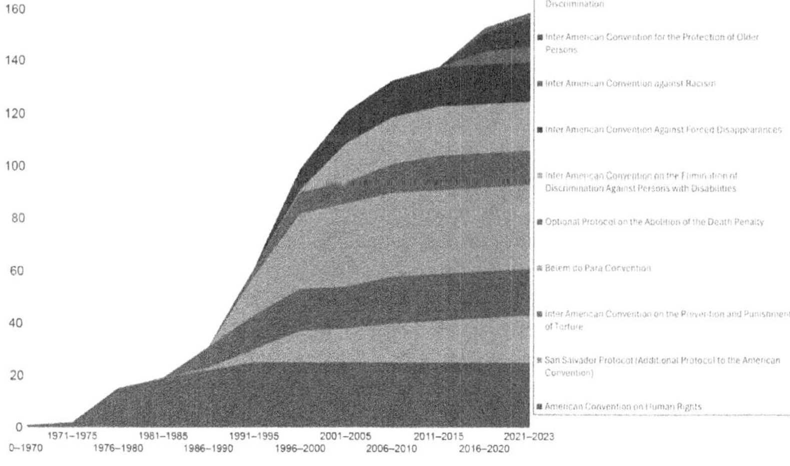


*Figure 2.1* *Cumulative state ratifications of Inter-American human rights treaties*

Recognizing these basic forms of state recognition is not to deny or overlook the contentious politics that permeate the system. States regularly display strident criticisms of the IAHRS. There is a continuing reluctance by Organization of American States (OAS) member states to fully fund its activities, making the IAHRS financially dependent on extra-regional donors for a broad range of its regular activities. There are continuous efforts to rein in the reach and influence of the system, whether in the form of ad hoc negative responses to individual adverse rulings against governments or more systematic attempts to cut its wings.[10] These various forms of backlash against the IAHRS represent, for some, existential challenges to its future existence.[11] However, formal state withdrawals from the IAHRS have historically been rare, and in some cases, they have also been reversed following a change in government (the case of Peru following the fall of Alberto Fujimori comes to mind). Even in the recent instance of Venezuela's departure from the IAHRS and the OAS, it is conceivable to imagine that one of the initial symbolic gestures of a future Venezuelan government after Nicolás Maduro, aiming to demonstrate its dedication to democratic and rights-oriented governance, might involve rejoining the IAHRS.[12] In other words, there is a detectable consensus, however superficial and fragile, amongst signatory states that an international human rights system is an important part of the regional order in the Americas, reflecting a broadly shared commitment to the basic principles of human rights.

---

[10] Gabriela Kletzel, 'The Inter-American Commission on Human Rights' New Strategic Plan: An Opportunity for True Strengthening' (2018) 22 *The International Journal of Human Rights* 1249; Jorge Contesse, 'Resisting the Inter-American Human Rights System' (2019) 44 *Yale Journal of International Law* 179.

[11] Ximena Soley and Silvia Steininger, 'Parting Ways or Lashing Back? Withdrawals, Backlash and the Inter-American Court of Human Rights' (2018) 14 *International Journal of Law in Context* 237.

[12] Indeed, the Venezuelan 'interim government' of Juan Guaidó deposited a 're-ratification' of the American Convention. Available at: https://www.oas.org/es/sla/ddi/docs/B-32_venezuela_RA_7-31-2019.pdf. The Commission has also argued before the Court that the 2019 re-ratification by the then interim Venezuelan government grants the Court jurisdiction over cases concerning Venezuela, including with respect to alleged violations, as if the treaty denunciation had never occurred. See, *José Luis Parada* (2024), available at https://www.oas.org/es/cidh/decisiones/Corte/2024/VE_14.174_NdeREs.PDF; *Oscar Pérez (Junquito Massacre)* (2023), available at https://www.oas.org/es/cidh/decisiones/corte/2023/VE_14.178_NdeREs.PDF; and *Henrique Capriles* (2022), available at https://www.oas.org/es/cidh/decisiones/corte/2022/VE_13.834_NdeREs.PDF.

## 2.2 Normative Expansion

The IAHRS has articulated a broad set of human rights standards, agreed to by states. Over time, the system has developed an expanding set of rights in general terms on which states in the region have been able to reach a degree of consensus. As illustrated in Table 2.1, the expansion of human rights standards and norms is reflected in the broad range of issues formally enshrined in regional human rights instruments. Moreover, the Court has developed progressive human rights jurisprudence through its rulings, and it has pioneered a unique reparative approach to human rights violations.[13] The Commission also significantly contributes to soft law development through, for example, its thematic reports and elaboration of policy guidelines.

Once more it is important to recognize that there is regular contention, even rejection of specific norms and standards. States frequently resist the IAHRS's interpretation of human rights standards and the obligations these impose on states. There is even the occasional normative backlash against the IAHRS in particularly sensitive political and public policy issue areas (a recent example includes ongoing contention with respect to reproductive rights).[14] There is also sustained criticism of the IAHRS for its allegedly inflexible and overly prescriptive approach to human rights implementation and state obligations. Some critics argue that the IAHRS prioritizes punitive legal norms.[15] Others contend that the system disregards local democratic processes in favour of imposing its own standards,[16] thereby lacking sufficient deference to locally determined solutions and political preferences.[17]

These critiques notwithstanding, the IAHRS continues to articulate rights that provide a regional normative framework that is to a significant degree open-ended and continually evolving in light of regional conditions.[18]

---

[13] Thomas M. Antkowiak, 'Remedial Approaches to Human Rights Violations: The Inter-American Court of Human Rights and Beyond' (2007) 46 *Columbia Journal of Transnational Law* 351.

[14] Contesse, 'Resisting the Inter-American Human Rights System' (n 10).

[15] Ezequiel Malarino, 'Judicial Activism, Punitivism and Supranationalisation: Illiberal and Antidemocratic Tendencies of the Inter-American Court of Human Rights' (2012) 12 *International Criminal Law Review* 665.

[16] Roberto Gargarella, 'Democracy and Rights in Gelman v. Uruguay' (2015) 109 *AJIL Unbound* 115.

[17] Jorge Contesse, 'Contestation and Deference in the Inter-American Human Rights System Subsidiarity in Global Governance' (2016) 79 *Law and Contemporary Problems* 123.

[18] The IAHRS remains at the forefront of international efforts to advance progressive rights interpretations and codification of new human rights standards.

*Table 2.1* *Chronology of adoption of Inter-American Human Rights Instruments*

| Inter-American human rights instruments | Year of adoption | Entry into force | Number of ratifications | Rate of OAS member states acceptance (%) |
|---|---|---|---|---|
| OAS Charter | 1948 | 1951 | 35 | 100 |
| American Declaration on the Rights and Duties of Man | 1948 | 1948 | – | 100 |
| American Convention on Human Rights | 1969 | 1978 | 25 | 71.43 |
| Inter-American Convention on the Prevention and Punishment of Torture | 1985 | 1987 | 18 | 51.43 |
| San Salvador Protocol (ESCR Optional Protocol) | 1988 | 1999 | 18 | 51.43 |
| Optional Protocol on the Abolition of the Death Penalty | 1990 | 1990 | 13 | 37.14 |
| Belem do Para Convention | 1994 | 1995 | 32 | 91.43 |
| Inter-American Convention Against Forced Disappearances | 1994 | 1996 | 15 | 42.86 |
| Inter-American Convention on the Elimination of Discrimination Against Persons with Disabilities | 1999 | 2001 | 19 | 54.29 |
| Inter-American Democratic Charter | 2001 | 2001 | – | 100 |
| Social Charter of the Americas | 2012 | 2012 | – | 100 |
| Inter-American Convention against Racism | 2013 | 2017 | 6 | 17.14 |
| Inter-American Convention Against All Forms of Discrimination | 2013 | 2020 | 2 | 5.71 |

| Inter-American human rights instruments | Year of adoption | Entry into force | Number of ratifications | Rate of OAS member states acceptance (%) |
|---|---|---|---|---|
| Inter-American Convention for the Protection of Older Peoples | 2015 | 2017 | 11 | 31.43 |
| American Declaration on the Rights of Indigenous Peoples | 2016 | 2016 | – | 100 |

Moreover, the widespread domestic constitutionalization of human rights in Latin America (with a markedly lesser incidence in the English-speaking sub-regions of the Americas) constitutes another form of state consent. This process, through which international human rights norms become integrated into national constitutional frameworks, signifies the normative entrenchment of the IAHRS across the region. This highlights not only a thin formal consensus around human rights norms, but also the extent of the formal embedding of the IAHRS in societies across the region, indicating in turn, for some, the constitutionalization of the IAHRS.[19]

## 2.3 Local Stakeholder Participation

The IAHRS remains fundamentally dependent on domestic political processes and stakeholders for the implementation of the system's norms and standards. There are two main aspects of this actor-centric feature of the IAHRS. The first is well documented and concerns the demand-driven developments of the IAHRS propelled by domestic stakeholders. This is reflected and evidenced in the gradually increasing number of petitions submitted to the IACHR by civil

For example, the IACtHR recently broke ground by establishing new standards for corporate liability in environmental damage cases, furthering the development of environmental rights: The Environment and Human Rights (State Obligations in Relation to the Environment in the Context of the Protection and Guarantee of the Rights to Life and to Personal Integrity – Interpretation and Scope of Articles 4(1) and 5(1) of the American Convention on Human Rights), Advisory Opinion OC-23/17, Inter-American Court of Human Rights Series A No 23 (15 November 2017).

[19] Armin von Bogdandy and René Urueña, 'International Transformative Constitutionalism in Latin America' (2020) 114 *American Journal of International Law* 403.

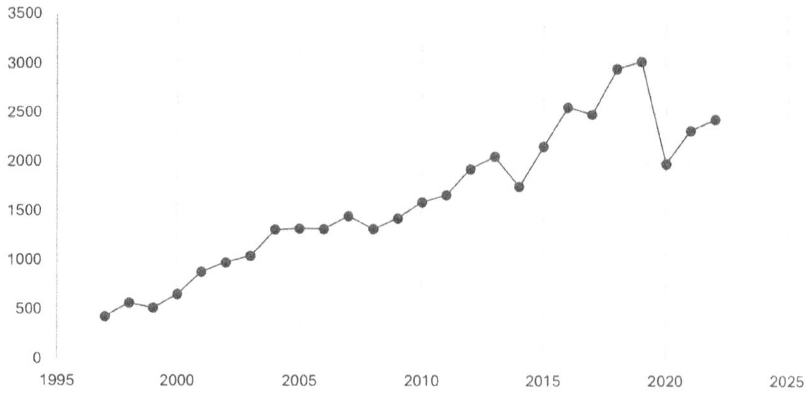


*Figure 2.2* *Annual number of petitions received by the IACHR*

society actors (see Figure 2.2).[20] The IAHRS has demonstrably responded, albeit unevenly, to these local demands across the region, adapting to the evolving needs presented by petitioners and their representatives seeking justice. The IAHRS's evolving victim-centred procedural focus, such as incorporating victim representation in IACtHR proceedings and the incorporation of a substantive victims' rights agenda, further demonstrates this demand-driven development.

The second aspect of this agency-driven account of the IAHRS results from the increasing embedding of the IAHRS in domestic political institutions. In practice, the influence of the IAHRS varies to a significant extent according to both the willingness and the capacity of state authorities to implement human rights locally. State delegation of authority to the IAHRS remains limited and human rights implementation processes rely on state authorities to deliver. This highlights the dynamics of experimental human rights governance: effective compliance with the IAHRS necessitates the formation of domestic coalitions including diverse actors across various branches and levels of government.[21]

20 Petitioners and their representatives who bring their claims and demands before the system are central actors driving the IAHRS's normative and institutional evolution. Par Engstrom and Peter Low, 'Mobilising the Inter-American Human Rights System: Regional Litigation and Domestic Human Rights Impact in Latin America' in Par Engstrom (ed), *The Inter-American Human Rights System: Impact Beyond Compliance* (Palgrave Macmillan 2019).

21 Flávia Piovesan and Julia Cortez Da Cunha Cruz, 'A Multi-Level Process: Compliance with International Human Rights Law in Brazil' in Rainer Grote,

This also allows states and relevant actors a degree of latitude in determining the modalities for implementing and effectuating rights in practice. Put differently, the principle of subsidiarity remains robust in the IAHRS.

This institutional feature of the IAHRS also means that human rights implementation, including compliance with specific rulings and decisions, is dynamic and iterative. The IAHRS is not characterized by a strict enforcement model. Rather than direct enforceability, IAHRS decisions offer general directives that guide state and local actors in the subsequent implementation process. These directives outline the state's human rights obligations in a particular case but generally leave the specifics of implementation to domestic actors. The precise details of how rights will be realized are therefore negotiated during the implementation process, which often involves ongoing negotiations between petitioners, their legal representatives and state and local authorities.[22] Moreover, the implementation of IAHRS orders is not a static process. The process of implementing IAHRS decisions is characterized not only by interaction and dialogue, but also by tension, resistance, and confrontation between different stakeholders.[23] Certainly, this emphasis on dialogue and state discretion does not imply a lack of regulatory intent within the IAHRS. The system clearly endeavours to establish parameters for acceptable state discretion in implementing human rights obligations. Some critics argue that the IAHRS demonstrates an overly prescriptive approach to human rights implementation, exemplified in the Court's continuing rejection of the margin of appreciation doctrine, as well as its regular issuance of detailed and specific reparation policies.[24] These critiques notwithstanding, the successful implementation of the IAHRS's broadly articulated goals relies on contextually situated actors. These actors possess the discretion to adapt the framework norms

Mariela Morales Antoniazzi and Davide Paris (eds), *Research Handbook on Compliance in International Human Rights Law* (Edward Elgar Publishing, Cheltenham, UK and Northampton, MA 2021).

[22] Rene Urueña, 'Compliance as Transformation: The Inter-American System of Human Rights and Its Impact(s)' in Rainer Grote, Mariela Morales Antoniazzi and Davide Paris (eds), *Research Handbook on Compliance in International Human Rights Law* (Edward Elgar Publishing, Cheltenham, UK and Northampton, MA 2021).

[23] This dynamic is particularly pronounced when addressing structural issues that necessitate reforms of domestic legal frameworks, judicial precedents, public policies, and prevailing practices. Piovesan and Cortez Da Cunha Cruz, 'A Multi-Level Process' (n 21).

[24] Contesse, 'Contestation and Deference in the Inter-American Human Rights System Subsidiarity in Global Governance' (n 17).

to the specificities of their contexts, facilitating effective implementation and ensuring the norms remain relevant to diverse local realities.

## 2.4 Institutional Monitoring

The IAHRS has developed institutional mechanisms and procedures to review, report on, and monitor compliance. The Commission has advanced a comprehensive toolset in addition to the processing of individual cases that range from public diplomacy in the form of press releases, public hearings, onsite visits and interim measures to behind-the-scenes negotiations with state officials and individual petitioners (through friendly settlement proceedings). The Court has three main institutional mechanisms at its disposal: contentious jurisdiction designed to resolve complaints submitted by individuals or groups alleging human rights violations by ratifying states of the American Convention;[25] advisory jurisdiction to issue opinions on matters related to the interpretation of the American Convention or other human rights instruments upon request from OAS member states or other authorized bodies; and provisional measures, to prevent irreparable harm to persons or groups.

Undeniably, these are weak accountability mechanisms when exclusively seen from a top-down enforcement perspective. Although Article 65 of the American Convention provides the Court with the mandate to report cases of non-compliance to the OAS General Assembly, these reporting provisions have never been meaningfully used.[26] As a result, in practice there is no clearly mandated political compliance mechanism in the IAHRS, such as that assumed by the Committee of Ministers in the European human rights system. Despite these political constraints, the Court has established innovative institutional approaches to human rights implementation. For example, the Court has developed specific procedures to monitor compliance with its rulings. In response to continuing non-compliance, the Court has started to issue public orders highlighting particularly serious cases of non-compliance.[27] Since

---

[25] Formally, the IACtHR has jurisdiction to adjudicate inter-state disputes as well.

[26] Pablo Saavedra Alessandri, 'The Role of the Inter-American Court of Human Rights in Monitoring Compliance with Judgments' (2020) 12 *Journal of Human Rights Practice* 178.

[27] David C. Baluarte, 'Strategizing for Compliance: The Evolution of a Compliance Phase of Inter-American Court Litigation and the Strategic Imperative for Victims' Representatives' (2011) 27 *American University International Law Review* 263; Michael J. Camilleri and Viviana Krsticevic, 'Making International Law Stick: Reflections on Compliance with Judgments in the Inter-American

initiating this practice, the Court has issued hundreds of compliance orders.[28] The Court also holds supervisory hearings in the countries concerned, allowing a greater number of state officials from different areas of the state administration involved in compliance with the judgment to participate, and not only those who are directly implicated in the case, as occurs when the hearings are carried out in the headquarters of the Court in San José, Costa Rica.[29] Pérez and Sandoval argue that these compliance hearings 'have proven to be particularly important given their ability to promote dialogue with stakeholders, build better understanding of the barriers that need to be addressed to move implementation forward, and their capacity to act as catalyst of key triggers of implementation'.[30] Significantly, the Court has also adopted the practice of conducting on-site visits that serve a dual purpose: to observe firsthand the implementation of court-ordered reparations, and to gather information directly from those affected.[31]

Both the Court and the Commission prioritize fostering domestic impact with their decisions. This is achieved not solely through direct enforcement mechanisms, but rather by efforts aimed at strategically influencing the internal dynamics of states. This approach aims to facilitate a space for constructive dialogue between national authorities and domestic stakeholders. The IACHR, in particular, has developed institutional practices to engage with civil society organizations to advocate for and achieve impact on the ground. From this perspective, compliance monitoring transcends a simple oversight

---

Human Rights System' (2009) *Derecho Internacional y Relaciones Internacionales* 235.

[28] The adoption of these orders is designed to trigger a novel phase of litigation within IAHRS, characterized by debates between states, victim representatives, and the IACHR concerning the adequacy of state-implemented measures aimed at complying with the Court's reparations orders. Baluarte, 'Strategizing for Compliance' (n 27). Moreover, in 2007, the Court also began to hold oral hearings on compliance monitoring. These hearings may either be individual – concerning a specific case – or collective, 'with respect to several cases from the same country that have in common similar forms of reparation the state has not been able to comply with'. Alessandri, 'The Role of the Inter-American Court of Human Rights in Monitoring Compliance with Judgments' (n 26).

[29] It also allows a greater number of victims to participate.

[30] Edward Pérez and Clara Sandoval, 'Compliance Hearings before the Inter-American Court of Human Rights: Unleashing the Dynamics of Implementation' in Rachel Murray and Debra Long (eds), *Research Handbook on Implementation of Human Rights in Practice* (Edward Elgar Publishing, Cheltenham, UK and Northampton, MA 2022) 273.

[31] Alessandri, 'The Role of the Inter-American Court of Human Rights in Monitoring Compliance with Judgments' (n 26).

function; it becomes an integral part of a broader process of human rights transformation within targeted states.[32] Public hearings, for example, offer a valuable mechanism for generating regular feedback to sustain a system of reporting, monitoring, and review. It is precisely this dynamic and iterative process of ongoing implementation and compliance processes that highlights a key feature of experimental human rights governance. The IAHRS's ability to generate continuous feedback loops, facilitated by ongoing implementation processes, regular reporting, and expert review, allows for a dynamic and iterative approach to human rights governance. It fosters the potential for continuous improvement and adaptation of human rights practices.

## 2.5 Dynamic and Iterative Governance

Building on the last point, the IAHRS has developed a dynamic and iterative process of engagement with governments, state authorities, and non-state actors. The normative and institutional evolution of the IAHRS has led to an increased interaction between the IAHRS and domestic political processes and national legal orders. In the process, the IAHRS has become increasingly inserted into domestic policy and legislative debates across the region. This has resulted in a process characterized by increasing interactivity and dynamism, with participation from a progressively broader spectrum of actors. Traditionally, the relationships between the IAHRS and states have been controlled by the executive branch of government, and Ministries of Foreign Affairs in particular. While the influence of these political actors remains important, a growing diversity of actors are now involved in human rights implementation, highlighting the trend towards decentralized enforcement. Moreover, human rights non-governmental organizations (NGOs) leverage the IAHRS as a platform to amplify their advocacy efforts, both domestically and internationally.[33]

These iterative and dynamic dimensions of IAHRS engagement with state and non-state actors allow for periodic reconsideration and possible revision of policy goals. Búrca identifies feedback loops that allow for continuous

---

[32] Bogdandy and Urueña, 'International Transformative Constitutionalism in Latin America' (n 19).

[33] These organizations employ various strategies, including mobilizing public opinion around specific cases, raising awareness through media campaigns, and utilizing domestic litigation processes. Par Engstrom and Peter Low, 'Mobilising the Inter-American Human Rights System: Regional Litigation and Domestic Human Rights Impact in Latin America' in Par Engstrom (ed), *The Inter-American Human Rights System: Impact Beyond Compliance* (Springer International Publishing 2019).

evaluation of both the established policy objectives and implementation methods as a crucial element of experimentalist systems. This iterative approach differentiates experimentalist systems from more static approaches where standards are simply adopted or localized without ongoing assessment and potential refinement.[34] An important aspect of international human rights institutions, such as the IAHRS, is how local experiences are transmitted to the international level. Claims based on lived realities of individuals and groups at the local level are brought to the IAHRS by intermediary actors such as local activists and NGOs, sometimes in collaboration with international solidarity networks. The recommendations, observations, and rulings by the IAHRS based on such claims may then become the starting point for further action at the domestic level, involving domestic advocacy efforts and follow-up measures. These domestic efforts may lead to adjustments and local adaptations ('vernacularization') of human rights standards, policies, and practices.[35] With IAHRS monitoring, review, and further follow-up activities, the policy cycle may then repeat itself.

The IAHRS has been actively developing these iterative relationships through the adoption of innovative institutional practices, in the process adopting the role of an enabler of human rights implementation. For example, since 2001 the Commission has strategically sought to use changes in its rules and practice to leverage the complementary roles of the Commission and the Court to incentivize state compliance with its recommendations. As one astute former IACHR official and participant in this dynamic observes, one key strategy has involved issuing separate reports on admissibility and merits of cases.[36] This has allowed the Commission to use the admissibility stage to encourage states to pursue friendly settlements, offering an alternative to potentially contentious litigation before the Court. Additionally, the Commission has reversed a previous procedural presumption. Traditionally, referral of a case to the Court was considered exceptional. The new rules adopted in 2001 established a presumption in favour of submission, aiming to increase access to the

---

[34] Búrca, 'Human Rights Experimentalism' (n 5).

[35] Mark Goodale and Sally Engle Merry (eds), *The Practice of Human Rights Tracking Law between the Global and the Local* (Cambridge University Press, 2007).

[36] Elizabeth Abi-Mershed, 'The Inter-American Commission on Human Rights and Implementation of Recommendations in Individual Cases' (2020) 12 *Journal of Human Rights Practice* 171. For a compliance-oriented account of the effectiveness of compliance agreements, see: Aníbal Pérez-Liñán, Mariana Brocca, and Isabel Anayanssi Orizaga Inzunza, 'Compliance Agreements: Emergent Flexibility in the Inter-American Human Rights System' (2024) 68 *International Studies Quarterly* sqae032.

Court while simultaneously reminding states of the benefits of compliance with Commission recommendations and avoiding potentially adverse Court rulings.[37]

Similarly, the IACtHR has also sought to play a facilitative role in fostering compliance by mediating agreements through private hearings.[38] In these instances, the Court adopts a more conciliatory approach, akin to a mediator, rather than a strictly adjudicatory one. The agreements reached through this process are typically monitored by the Court and its Secretariat to ensure their implementation. These evolving features of the IAHRS generally align well with an experimentalist approach to human rights enforcement. The system uses relatively flexible intervention standards, allowing for an adaptable approach in addressing human rights violations.[39]

## 3 UNDERSTANDING AND ASSESSING IAHRS IMPACT

Seen from the perspective of experimentalist human rights governance, the transnational dynamics of human rights implementation in the context of the IAHRS offer important insights into how international law and institutions might operate against the odds in politically inhospitable conditions. The IAHRS exerts influence on human rights outcomes from a position of relative institutional weakness. The system has limited political leverage and highly inadequate resources at its disposal, particularly when considered in relation to the scale of the multiple human rights challenges it confronts. It has no consistent backing from powerful states and there are no formal sanction mechanisms underpinning the system's rulings and decisions. The IAHRS is largely disconnected from regional political and economic governance structures. There is no equivalent of European Union accession incentives in the Americas.

---

[37] Abi-Mershed also identifies two key working practices that can foster compliance with human rights decisions. The first involves close supervision of state actions, requiring states to take concrete steps and utilize timelines or action plans to demonstrate progress. The second practice highlighted by Abi-Mershed is the use of negotiated compliance agreements. These agreements involve collaboration between the state and the Commission to identify specific implementation measures. This collaborative approach allows for consideration of the state's specific needs and victim demands. Abi-Mershed, 'The Inter-American Commission on Human Rights and Implementation of Recommendations in Individual Cases' (n 36).

[38] Pérez and Sandoval, 'Compliance Hearings before the Inter-American Court of Human Rights: Unleashing the Dynamics of Implementation' (n 30) 276.

[39] Antkowiak, 'Remedial Approaches to Human Rights Violations' (n 13).

Moreover, the regional context in which the IAHRS operates displays limited normative convergence around values of human rights and democracy.[40] Civil society spaces are restricted in many places and there are both material and political obstacles to the construction of influential epistemic communities that could support the system when most needed.[41]

And yet, the IAHRS matters. The understanding of the potential effects of the IAHRS developed in this chapter is fundamentally actor-centred and highlights the dynamic and interactive character of the system. The emphasis is on the politics of human rights, that is, how both 'pro-' and 'anti-' human rights actors interact, as well as the sociological structures in which these actors operate that shape the salience of human rights, and the ability of the IAHRS to make a difference. Clearly, human rights impact is an inherently complex process, the outcome of multiple forces, and any attempt to assess it is fraught with both conceptual and methodological challenges. This part of the chapter discusses, first, a basic (re-)conceptualization of the notion of human rights impact. It then identifies potential 'causal pathways' of how the IAHRS affects human rights, by developing an actor-oriented model of IAHRS impact. The chapter finally discusses a basic typology of IAHRS impact, with the view to distinguish between different types of impact that the system may have. While a full exploration of IAHRS impact is beyond the scope of this chapter, what follows is a preliminary analytical sketch to provide a framework for further empirical assessment.

### 3.1 (Re-)Conceptualizing IAHRS Impact

The notion of 'compliance' has tended to dominate the literature assessing the effects of international (human rights) law and institutions, including the IAHRS.[42] However, there is a clear conceptual difference between (rule) compliance, that is, the extent to which a specific rule or mandate is obeyed or abided by, and 'impact'. With respect to the IAHRS, specifically, compliance can be conceptualized and assessed through the lens of state implementation of specific obligations. The IACtHR's jurisprudence has proven particularly

---

40 Gillian Kane, Mirta Moragas, and Kiran Stallone, 'Framejacking Rights Discourse to Undermine Latin American Multilateral Human Rights Institutions' in Leigh Payne and others (eds), *The Right against Rights in Latin America* (British Academy 2023).

41 Richard Ashby Wilson, 'Digital Authoritarianism and the Global Assault on Human Rights' (2022) 44 *Human Rights Quarterly* 704; Marie-Christine Doran, 'The Hidden Face of Violence in Latin America: Assessing the Criminalization of Protest in Comparative Perspective' (2017) 44 *Latin American Perspectives* 183.

42 Engstrom, *The Inter-American Human Rights System* (n 6).

amenable to this mode of analysis, as its rulings include specific obligations or mandates for states in each case.

Impact is a broader and fuller notion than compliance. IAHRS impact can be conceptualized as the extent to which the decisions and actions of the IAHRS contribute to the improvement of human rights conditions as assessed by the decrease in the frequency and severity of human rights abuses, and the reduction in the likelihood of the repetition of abuses, coupled with the establishment of effective remedies for victims of violations. Compliance might be necessary for the IAHRS to have an impact, but it is generally not sufficient. Compliance perspectives tend to focus on the direct material effects of IAHRS decisions, particularly the enforcement of specific rulings. However, the IAHRS potentially has a much broader range of effects. This explains why the IAHRS may be seen as ineffective by those who privilege rule compliance, while for others the system might have significant impact as they observe a broader set of potential effects.[43] Put differently, there are notable limitations to the 'fetishiz[ing] [of] compliance as a proxy for real-life impact'.[44]

Indeed, human rights impact is an inherently complex process and the outcome of multiple forces. Human rights impact is rarely linear, but is often manifested as a cascade of effects, where one positive outcome may trigger a series of subsequent improvements. Human rights advancements frequently generate significant feedback effects, including with respect to IAHRS actions. The successful or unsuccessful implementation of the system's rulings and recommendations by states directly influences its legitimacy. In turn, the level of legitimacy and perceived authority accorded to the system impacts states' willingness to implement its rulings and recommendations. For example, compared to responses to decisions issued by the Commission, 'it is quite rare for States to completely fail to comply with Court judgments, and most States advance significantly over time toward implementing these judgments'.[45] Similarly, the IAHRS may be more inclined to adopt a more assertive interpretive approach when it perceives a greater degree of responsiveness to their decisions by states.

The evaluation of human rights impact should also acknowledge the temporal dimension of human rights progress. Sustainable improvements in human rights conditions often require sustained pressure and ongoing engagement over an extended period. Impact also tends to vary according to the issue area and the characteristics of the rights at stake. This variation is contingent upon

---

43 Engstrom, *The Inter-American Human Rights System* (n 6).

44 Bogdandy and Urueña, 'International Transformative Constitutionalism in Latin America' (n 19).

45 Camilleri and Krsticevic, 'Making International Law Stick: Reflections on Compliance with Judgments in the Inter-American Human Rights System' (n 27).

several factors, including the degree of social mobilization that can be galvanized in support of the cause, the level of centralization in the administration of the right with centrally administered rights being more readily observable, as well as whether national security concerns are used to justify non-compliance with the human rights norm concerned.[46] Moreover, the impact of the IAHRS may depend on what the system asks for, and what is politically at stake for the respondent state/government. It is widely recognized that monetary compensation ordered by the Court is generally complied with by states. Similarly, symbolic measures such as public apologies and the publication of court judgments are frequently implemented. Notably, while compliance with court-ordered legal reforms tends also to be relatively robust, the implementation of rehabilitative measures, such as the provision of healthcare and educational benefits, and guarantees of non-repetition through initiatives like the training of public officials, is generally patchier. Unquestionably, the most significant hurdle in ensuring compliance with IACtHR rulings concerns state obligations to investigate and prosecute the perpetrators of the human rights violations in question.[47]

In addition, to understand the impact of the IAHRS, it is important to keep in mind possible areas of non-impact, as well as unintended consequences. The IAHRS clearly sets priorities and gives privileged attention to a selection of human rights violations. Certain categories of human rights issues (e.g. related to socio-economic rights or the climate crisis) may constitute human rights violations but may not be brought before the system or reach an adjudicated outcome at similar levels as other human rights concerns. This raises the question of why some issues are less frequently addressed by the IAHRS, and which areas of governance remain deprioritized in the system's caseload. Furthermore, it is crucial to consider the potential unintended consequences of the IAHRS. These include, for instance, the professionalization and legalization of NGOs, potentially leading these organizations to prioritize legal strategies over broader social advocacy. Additionally, the system's emphasis on adjudication may create winners and losers among rights-holders, potentially neglecting less visible human rights concerns. This is to highlight, simply, the importance of observable behaviour and evaluation of IAHRS impact based

[46] Dia Anagnostou and Alina Mungiu-Pippidi, 'Domestic Implementation of Human Rights Judgments in Europe: Legal Infrastructure and Government Effectiveness Matter' (2014) 25 *European Journal of International Law* 205.

[47] Camilleri and Krsticevic, 'Making International Law Stick: Reflections on Compliance with Judgments in the Inter-American Human Rights System' (n 27). For a discussion of delayed compliance, see: Aníbal Pérez-Liñán, Luis Schenoni and Kelly Morrison, 'Compliance in Time: Lessons from the Inter-American Court of Human Rights' (2023) 25 *International Studies Review* viac067.

on the degree to which its standards and institutional mechanisms ameliorate the human rights problem they are designed to address.

## 3.2 Actor-Oriented Impact

The efficacy of international human rights hinges primarily on the proactive engagement of domestic actors.[48] The domestic implementation of international human rights rulings is a complex and inherently politicized undertaking. This process necessitates the engagement of a diverse range of actors, including the executive, legislative, and judicial branches, as well as civil society organizations. Human rights implementation may take the form of a domestic judicial order rectifying the violation, executive intervention to address the issue, or legislative reform to tackle any identified systemic shortcomings in the domestic human rights framework.[49] Different actors, driven by potentially divergent priorities and preferences, may engage in contestation regarding the scope and nature of implementation.[50] The iterative nature of interaction between domestic actors in the context of the IAHRS shapes the expectations of the actors involved. In essence, iteration not only influences strategic approaches but also transforms the underlying framework itself. As actors interact, they contribute to the evolution of the governing structure, while conversely, being embedded within this structure influences their interests and strategic approaches.[51] The actor-oriented 'impact model' developed in this chapter specifies how the IAHRS affects and shapes political relationships and interactions in relation to three main sets of actors: (i) organized civil society; (ii) domestic judiciaries; and (iii) state authorities and bureaucracies.

---

48 Beth A. Simmons, *Mobilizing for Human Rights: International Law in Domestic Politics* (Cambridge University Press 2009).

49 Rainer Grote, Mariela Morales Antoniazzi and Davide Paris, 'Compliance in International Human Rights Law: Issues, Concept, Methodology' in Rainer Grote, Mariela Morales Antoniazzi and Davide Paris (eds), *Research Handbook on Compliance in International Human Rights Law* (Edward Elgar, Cheltenham, UK and Northampton, MA 2021).

50 Anagnostou and Mungiu-Pippidi, 'Domestic Implementation of Human Rights Judgments in Europe' (n 46).

51 Bogdandy and Urueña, 'International Transformative Constitutionalism in Latin America' (n 19).

### 3.2.1 Civil society

Organized civil society plays a crucial role in the dynamic nature of human rights governance within the IAHRS.[52] Human rights groups serve as a critical bridge between the lived experiences of individuals and the formal mechanisms of the IAHRS. Through advocacy efforts and information sharing, they identify pressing human rights issues in their efforts to make the system responsive to evolving human rights conditions in the region. Civil society actors also actively participate in shaping the responses offered by the IAHRS. By submitting petitions, amicus curiae briefs, and participating in public hearings, they inform the legal reasoning and decision-making processes of the system, shaping its approaches to addressing human rights violations and contributing to the evolution of human rights law in the region. In addition, civil society plays a vital role in pressing for the implementation of orders and judgments rendered by the IAHRS, by monitoring state compliance, advocating for legislative reforms, and seeking to hold governments accountable.

Reflecting its dynamic and experimental nature, the IAHRS has also actively evolved in its engagement with civil society.[53] In 2001, following reforms of the Rules of Procedure for both the Commission and the Court, representatives of petitioners gained the right to participate as a party before the IACtHR. This marked a substantial shift in the IAHRS's approach to civil society engagement, empowering NGOs to play a more active role in litigating human rights cases before the Court. The IAHRS further strengthened victim representation through a subsequent reform in 2010 that elevated the status of victim representatives, making them the principal actors in cases before the IACtHR. The combined effect of these institutional reforms has been transformative for victim representation within the IAHRS, creating a strong expectation that the voices of victims will be heard throughout the litigation process before

[52] Clara Burbano Herrera and Yves Haeck, 'The Historical and Present-Day Role of Non-Governmental Organisations before the Inter-American Human Rights System in Documenting Serious Human Rights Violations and Protecting Human Rights and the Rule of Law Through Ensuring Accountability' (2021) 17 *Utrecht Law Review* 8; Mariela Morales Antoniazzi and Viviana Krsticevic, 'NGOs: A Critical Link to Understanding and Strengthening Compliance of International Decisions' in Rainer Grote, Mariela Morales Antoniazzi and Davide Paris (eds), *Research Handbook on Compliance in International Human Rights Law* (Edward Elgar, Cheltenham, UK and Northampton, MA 2021).

[53] Herrera and Haeck, 'The Historical and Present-Day Role of Non-Governmental Organisations before the Inter-American Human Rights System in Documenting Serious Human Rights Violations and Protecting Human Rights and the Rule of Law Through Ensuring Accountability' (n 52).

the IAHRS.[54] Moreover, at various critical junctures, the system has found allies in regional human rights movements.[55] Civil society actors have also become increasingly involved in appointment procedures of Commissioners and judges; procedures that traditionally have been exclusively governed by state representatives and diplomats at the OAS General Assembly.[56]

It is precisely the dynamic and iterative engagement between organized civil society and the IAHRS that shapes the system's impact. NGOs actively pursue justice at the international level by submitting individual petitions before the IACHR. They act as representatives for victims, often lacking the financial resources or legal expertise to navigate complex legal proceedings, and they function as watchdogs at the national level, monitoring compliance with Court judgments and Commission recommendations. Civil society groups may also act as conduits of information, communicating their findings on human rights situations to the IAHRS, and they leverage their expertise by submitting legal briefs, supporting the IAHRS's deliberations on specific cases. NGOs strategically engage in lobbying efforts with the political organs of the OAS; they actively participate in public hearings, raising awareness about human rights issues; and they strategically utilize media and social media platforms to exert pressure on states.

While the use of the IAHRS by human rights organizations across the region has increased dramatically in recent decades, the capacity of actors to access and to mobilize the IAHRS remains highly unequal. Using the IAHRS requires technical and legal skills, as well as resources.[57] The rise of legalism and judicialization in the IAHRS may create barriers for victims lacking access to legal expertise or resources.[58] The IAHRS is also plagued by delays

---

[54] Baluarte, 'Strategizing for Compliance' (n 27).

[55] For example, sustained civil society mobilisation proved pivotal to counter thinly veiled attempts by some governments to restrain the Commission as part of a recent institutional reform initiative. Kletzel, 'The Inter-American Commission on Human Rights' New Strategic Plan' (n 10).

[56] Laurence Burgorgue-Larsen, 'Between Idealism and Realism: A Few Comparative Reflections and Proposals on the Appointment Process of the Inter-American Commission and Court of Human Rights Members' (2015) 5 *Notre Dame Journal of International & Comparative Law* 1.

[57] The IAHRS has limited resources available to support petitioners in the form of a Victims' Legal Assistance Fund.

[58] Ariel Dulitzky, 'The Inter-American Human Rights System Fifty Years Later: Time for Changes' (2020) *Revue Québécoise de Droit International* 127. Moreover, as highlighted previously, effective participation in the IAHRS often necessitates intermediation by specialized NGOs. While such organizations provide crucial legal expertise, reliance on intermediaries can also create a sense of

in processing cases, with lengthy and costly proceedings often emotionally draining for victims seeking timely redress.

These constraints notwithstanding, organized civil society remains integral in shaping the IAHRS's impact. The effective implementation of IAHRS decisions is demonstrably linked to the active participation of victims and their representatives.[59] The process of litigating before the IAHRS can be personally empowering for victims, allowing them to reclaim agency and assert their rights, as well as politically empowering, providing victims with a platform to advocate for broader human rights reforms. In short, the availability of the IAHRS for human rights groups has the potential to strengthen the domestic position of those groups that engage with the system, particularly when faced with resistance and obstacles at home.

### 3.2.2 Domestic judiciaries

Domestic court systems have come to play increasingly prominent roles as arenas of human rights implementation. The constitutional incorporation of international human rights treaties has made domestic courts key actors in the IAHRS with a potential to activate human rights standards and interpret international norms in light of domestic conditions.[60] As a result, domestic judges have become important political actors that shape the ways in which international human rights are applied domestically. Domestic judiciaries, however, are generally weak political and institutional actors in Latin America, thereby complicating the impact of IAHRS decisions and orders.[61] This is particularly significant because 'national courts are central to compliance with IACtHR remedial orders because a large share of judgments require action

distance between victims and the IAHRS, and pressures to moderate the tone and substance of claims to navigate IAHRS procedures effectively.

59 Abi-Mershed, 'The Inter-American Commission on Human Rights and Implementation of Recommendations in Individual Cases' (n 36).

60 Marcelo Torelly, 'Transnational Legal Process and Fundamental Rights in Latin America: How Does the Inter-American Human Rights System Reshape Domestic Constitutional Rights?' in Pedro Fortes and others (eds), *Law and Policy in Latin America: Transforming Courts, Institutions, and Rights* (Palgrave Macmillan UK 2017); Mariela Morales Antoniazzi and Pablo Saavedra Alessandri, 'Inter-Americanization: Its Legal Bases and Political Impact' in Armin von Bogdandy and others (eds), *Transformative Constitutionalism in Latin America: The Emergence of a New Ius Commune* (Oxford University Press 2017).

61 Cecilia M. Bailliet, 'Measuring Compliance with the Inter-American Court of Human Rights: The Ongoing Challenge of Judicial Independence in Latin America' (2013) 31 *Nordic Journal of Human Rights* 477.

by prosecutors and judges'.[62] Traditionally, a critical impediment to effective human rights enforcement lies in the limited familiarity with international law, particularly international human rights law, exhibited by a significant portion of the judiciary.[63]

Nonetheless, far-reaching legal and jurisprudential shifts have taken place in Latin America in recent decades, shifts in no small part driven by the IAHRS itself. The increasing judicial engagement with the IAHRS can be seen in the context of the steady erosion of the dominance of a formalistic approach to law in the 1990s, the establishment of constitutional courts, the emergence of neo-constitutionalist thought, and the gradual internationalization of the judicial profession in the region. As a result, since the early 2000s Latin American high courts have increasingly started to cite IAHRS jurisprudence in their rulings, reflecting growing regional judicial dialogue.[64] Importantly, the IAHRS itself has played a key role in fostering judicial dialogue. The Court's growing interest in promoting regional legal integration reflects what González Ocantos and Sandholtz refer to as a 'strong pedagogical orientation in the court's citation practices'.[65] Resonating with the dynamic interactions characteristic of experimental human rights governance, transnational judicial dialogue acts as a facilitator for the diffusion of human rights standards. Such dialogues foster dissemination of legal concepts, as well as understandings of the judicial role in human rights protections. They also facilitate routine interactions between

62 Alexandra Huneeus, 'Reforming the State from Afar: Structural Reform Litigation at the Human Rights Courts' (2015) 40 *Yale Journal of International Law* 1.

63 Marcia Nina Bernardes, 'Inter-American Human Rights System as a Transnational Public Sphere: Legal and Political Aspects of the Implementation of International Decisions Implementation at the National Level of the Decisions of the Regional and International Human Rights Systems' (2011) 15 *Sur – International Journal on Human Rights* 131.

64 Ezequiel González-Ocantos and Wayne Sandholtz, 'Constructing a Regional Human Rights Legal Order: The Inter-American Court, National Courts, and Judicial Dialogue, 1988–2014' (2021) 19 *International Journal of Constitutional Law* 1559.

65 In its citation practices, the IACtHR has broadened its focus to include Latin American legal precedents alongside external case law from other international human rights institutions, particularly the European Court of Human Rights. González Ocantos and Sandholtz argue that the IACtHR uses citations 'not just as a way to profit from the persuasive authority of national rulings, or signal deference and horizontality in the construction of regional legal standards, but as an effort to educate courts in the use of Inter-American jurisprudence and thus foster greater integration'. González-Ocantos and Sandholtz, 'Constructing a Regional Human Rights Legal Order' (n 64).

domestic and international judges, thereby increasing the receptiveness within national courts towards international jurisprudence, and the 'perceived utility and persuasive authority of Inter-American precedents'.[66]

Another unique aspect of the IACtHR's relationship with domestic judiciaries is the doctrine of conventionality control, which holds that all state actors must review laws under the American Convention, and not apply laws found to be in violation of it. Through this doctrine, the Court seeks to enlist all state actors in monitoring compliance with the Convention, as interpreted by the Court. Conventionality control has the potential to extend the shadow of the Court far beyond its relatively small docket. Since the emergence of the doctrine, 'there has been a growing understanding of the Court as a true regional constitutional court',[67] indicating, for some, the progressive unravelling of the separation of international law and constitutional law in the region. While some legal scholars have sharply criticized the Court's attempts to extend its authority,[68] on the grounds of both its alleged limited effectiveness and shaky legitimacy, regional jurisprudential interaction and legal dialogues have clearly intensified in recent years.[69]

These developments combine to illustrate the extent to which the regional human rights system in the Americas constitutes an evolving transnational legal order,[70] as part of a broader global human rights system. It is clearly the case that regional human rights systems, including the IAHRS, operate in a fertile environment of interlegality characterized by a plurality of domestic and international legal and judicial systems. This provides ample scope for judicial dialogue and exchange, as evidenced in the IAHRS's evolving human rights jurisprudence. Both the Commission and the Court clearly 'see themselves as integrated into a larger global human rights system',[71] and as active participants in the construction of a growing decentralized institutional framework for the interpretation and application of human rights norms and stand-

---

66 ibid.

67 Jorge Contesse, 'Human Rights as Transnational Law' (2022) 116 *American Journal of International Law* 316.

68 Jorge Contesse, 'Contestation and Deference in the Inter-American Human Rights System Subsidiarity in Global Governance' (2016) *79 Law and Contemporary Problems* 123.

69 Ezequiel González-Ocantos, 'Communicative Entrepreneurs: The Case of the Inter-American Court of Human Rights' Dialogue with National Judges' (2018) 62 *International Studies Quarterly* 737.

70 González-Ocantos and Sandholtz, 'Constructing a Regional Human Rights Legal Order' (n 64).

71 Wayne Sandholtz, 'Human Rights Courts and Global Constitutionalism: Coordination through Judicial Dialogue' (2021) 10 *Global Constitutionalism* 439.

ards.[72] Together with the progressive strengthening of a regional community of human rights practice critically engaging with the IAHRS,[73] these institutional features further sustain the experimentalist character of the regional human rights governance framework.

### 3.2.3 State authorities

Human rights implementation varies with the relative degree of state capacity and government effectiveness.[74] While the allocation of institutional and financial resources is undoubtedly crucial, effective state capacity for human rights implementation requires widespread understanding of and institutional commitment to human rights principles. It also requires specialized expertise within relevant institutions, alongside sustained commitment to applying these human rights principles in practice. With respect to the IAHRS specifically, different state institutions are now engaged with the system, which has led to the 'disaggregation' of the relationship between countries and the IAHRS.[75] The IACHR's friendly settlement procedures, for example, are frequently used to facilitate negotiations between different state institutions and petitioners. Also, due to the IACtHR's creative remedial regime, the Court frequently issues orders that require action from state actors other than the executive.

The IAHRS itself furthers this trend of disaggregation of the state with respect to human rights implementation. Practices developed by the IACtHR to reach 'inside the state' to enable compliance include convening informal dialogues with state representatives or delegations, and engaging domestic institutions and organs strategically positioned to advocate for the domestic human rights implementation, such as National Human Rights Institutions (NHRIs).[76]

---

[72] ibid.

[73] Bogdandy and Urueña, 'International Transformative Constitutionalism in Latin America' (n 19).

[74] Anagnostou and Mungiu-Pippidi, 'Domestic Implementation of Human Rights Judgments in Europe' (n 46); Alejandro Anaya-Muñoz and Amanda Murdie, 'The Will and the Way: How State Capacity and Willingness Jointly Affect Human Rights Improvement' (2021) 23 *Human Rights Review* 127.

[75] This increasingly means that states no longer interact with the IAHRS solely through their respective Ministry of Foreign Affairs, but also through several different institutional channels including Ministries of Justice, *Ministerios Públicos*, as well as sub-national authorities.

[76] Urueña, 'Compliance as Transformation' (n 22). The Court has entered into cooperation agreements with various NRHIs in its efforts to generate assistance in the implementation and supervision of compliance with its rulings. Alessandri, 'The Role of the Inter-American Court of Human Rights in Monitoring Compliance with Judgments' (n 26); Tom Pegram and Nataly Herrera Rodriguez, 'Bridging the Gap: National Human Rights Institutions and the Inter-American Human Rights

Conversely, the IAHRS has also emerged as a platform for state institution agencies with human rights mandates and expertise. The gradual formation of specialized state bureaucracies for human rights can be seen across the region in the rise of 'human rights secretariats and commissions, specialized divisions in Foreign Ministries, ombudsmen, human rights attorneys, public defenders and special prosecutors, among others'.[77] State actors and institutions have the potential to act as 'compliance constituencies' and conduits of domestic implementation linking international human rights norms to domestic political and legal institutions and actors.

The impact of the IAHRS on public policy formulation and implementation is largely a function of its embedment, or institutionalization, in state institutions, and whether the state has effectively organized its institutions in ways that provide effective remedies for human rights violations. The effective implementation of IAHRS rulings and decisions hinges on the existence of robust domestic institutional and legal frameworks, including the establishment of formal mechanisms for integrating international obligations into domestic policy making, as well as specific implementation policies and interagency coordination mechanisms. Interestingly, a more strategic vision of the IAHRS appears to be increasingly recognized within some state bureaucracies across Latin America. State prosecutors' offices in several countries (e.g. Argentina and Brazil) have created dedicated human rights units to actively petition the IACHR. However, only a few Latin American states have formal institutional mechanisms in place to ensure consistent implementation of the IAHRS's decisions and recommendations. The IAHRS provides, nonetheless, an authoritative set of norms and standards to regulate the specific issue-area subject to the reforms, and it can add an additional layer of political pressure, momentum, and urgency to the resolution of human rights problems. The IAHRS also offers a political space for discussion and negotiation between the

System' in Par Engstrom (ed), *The Inter-American Human Rights System: Impact Beyond Compliance* (Springer International Publishing 2019).

[77] Víctor Abramovich, 'From Massive Violations to Structural Patterns: New Approaches and Classic Tensions in the Inter-American Human Rights System' (2009) 6 *Sur. Revista Internacional de Direitos Humanos* 6. Some Latin American states (such as Chile, Colombia, and Brazil) have also created permanent parliamentary bodies to follow up on international human rights decisions. Rainer Grote, 'A Dialogue with the Deaf? The Political Branches as Compliance Partners' in Rainer Grote, Mariela Morales Antoniazzi and Davide Paris (eds), *Research Handbook on Compliance in International Human Rights Law* (Edward Elgar, Cheltenham, UK and Northampton, MA 2021); see generally: Steven L. B. Jensen, Stéphanie Lagoutte and Sébastien Lorion, 'The Domestic Institutionalisation of Human Rights: An Introduction' (2019) 37 *Nordic Journal of Human Rights* 165.

key actors involved in human rights reforms, including different parts of the state. Once more, the dynamic and iterative patterns of interaction between the IAHRS and state authorities beyond government officials traditionally mandated to administer relationships with international institutions (i.e. diplomats) fundamentally shape the system's impact.

## 3.3 Towards a Framework for Assessing IAHRS Impact

Human rights impact is clearly difficult to assess empirically with any reasonable degree of accuracy.[78] There are significant challenges related to the quality of human rights data used to assess the impact of international human rights law and institutions.[79] Some impacts may be more readily measurable than others.[80] A key challenge lies in translating empirical observations of the IAHRS into a comprehensive assessment of its impact. Any empirical assessment of human rights 'impact', therefore, needs to consider several distinct dimensions. Rodríguez-Garavito has developed a helpful analytical framework that distinguishes four types of impact of judicial decisions, which can be amended to develop a typology of IAHRS impact.[81] A first distinction can be made between direct and indirect effects. Direct effects are mandated actions, such as a ruling by the IACtHR, that affect participants in that specific case. Indirect effects, by contrast, are those that were not directly stipulated in the ruling, but that nonetheless derive from the decision. Here the effects are those that relate not only to the parties to the case, but also to other social actors. A second distinction is between material effects and symbolic effects. The former refers to tangible changes in the conduct of actors and institutions that are a result of a specific decision or recommendation, while the latter relates to

---

[78] Richard Carver and Lisa Handley, 'Evaluating National Preventive Mechanisms: A Conceptual Model' (2020) 12 *Journal of Human Rights Practice* 387.

[79] The increased availability of human rights data, improved human rights monitoring, and rising expectations, all potentially skew human rights measurements over time. Ann Marie Clark and Kathryn Sikkink, 'Information Effects and Human Rights Data: Is the Good News about Increased Human Rights Information Bad News for Human Rights Measures?' (2013) 35 *Human Rights Quarterly* 539.

[80] Although empirical observation plays a central role, a critical understanding of human rights requires acknowledging and investigating the hidden realities that may not be immediately apparent. Steffen Jensena and others, 'Torture and Ill-Treatment Under Perceived: Human Rights Documentation and the Poor' (2017) 39 *Human Rights Quarterly* 393.

[81] Cesar Rodriguez-Garavito, 'Beyond the Courtroom: The Impact of Judicial Activism on Socioeconomic Rights in Latin America' (2010) 89 *Texas Law Review* 1669.

*Table 2.2 Direct and indirect effects of the IAHRS*

| - | Direct | Indirect |
|---|---|---|
| Material | • Compliance: implementation of individual IAHRS rulings and decisions<br>• Designing of public policy, as ordered by the IAHRS | • Forming of coalitions<br>• Empowering domestic pro-rights actors<br>• Domestic courts using Inter-American Court jurisprudence in rulings |
| Constitutive | • Defining and perceiving problem as human rights violation<br>• Domestic legislatures debate and develop legislation based on IAHRS standards | • Influencing public opinion about problem's urgency and gravity<br>• Law schools teaching IAHRS legal standards forming future generation lawyers/judges |

changes in ideas, perceptions, and collective social constructs, such as changes in understandings expressed in the media and/or by the public.

These distinctions give rise to Table 2.2, a 2 × 2 table with illustrative examples of direct/indirect effects on the horizontal axis, and material/symbolic effects on the vertical axis.

At the intersection of these two distinctions, four broad types of effects of the IAHRS can be identified. First, there are direct material effects if there are changes in the behaviour directly targeted as a result of a decision or recommendation by the IAHRS. In this respect, evaluating the IAHRS's influence on state behaviour entails gauging the system's effectiveness in influencing the conduct of government authorities and promoting compliance with human rights standards.[82] Another crucial aspect of impact assessment involves analyzing the consequences for victims of human rights violations. This includes examining whether the IAHRS facilitates redress, reparation, and the prevention of future violations. For many, at the centre of any human rights system should be a focus on the individual, including both victims of past human

[82] A common approach to measuring the IACtHR's impact, for example, centres on the degree of state compliance with its rulings. This holds particular significance for general measures, as these judgments often require substantial shifts in government policies and practices. This also allows for an assessment of whether rulings have a tangible impact on state behaviour beyond specific cases. Ultimately, a critical measure of the IAHRS's impact lies in the observed improvements in human rights conditions within member states. This necessitates a broader analysis that goes beyond legal compliance and considers the real-world consequences for those affected.

rights abuses as well as individual constituents who can reap the benefits of improved human rights practices or who suffer the consequences of poor human rights conditions. The IAHRS can generate both wide-ranging and specific material consequences. Examples of narrow effects include the direct prosecution of identified individuals based on IACtHR rulings. Broader effects can be observed in legislative reforms prompted by the IAHRS, such as the adoption of legal norms that combat impunity.

Second, there are indirect material effects, such as the ways in which the IAHRS may prompt the formation of coalitions of activists to push for domestic human rights reforms. One way to assess these effects of the IAHRS is to evaluate the degree to which domestic constituents use the IAHRS, and the rulings and recommendations issued by the Commission and Court to advocate for domestic policy change. A prominent indicator of its impact lies in the increased utilization of IAHRS mechanisms by individuals and rights groups to advocate for stronger domestic human rights protections. An increase in petitions to the IACHR could indicate growing awareness of the IAHRS as a recourse mechanism. This can also be reflected in an observable rise in domestic litigation efforts drawing on IAHRS norms and standards to hold state actors accountable for human rights violations. Another key indicator is the extent to which domestic courts and legal systems incorporate IACtHR jurisprudence into their own rulings. This domestic use of IACtHR precedent reflects the integration of the Court's interpretations into national legal frameworks. This analysis extends to the influence of judgments and recommendations on states beyond those directly involved in a specific case. Such effects, termed 'erga omnes' impacts by Helfer and Voeten, encompass the broader influence of the IAHRS on states' human rights practices.[83]

---

[83] Laurence R. Helfer and Erik Voeten, 'International Courts as Agents of Legal Change: Evidence from LGBT Rights in Europe' (2014) 68 *International Organization* 77. A noteworthy illustration of the erga omnes impact of the IAHRS's case law was Argentina's adoption of legal reforms following the IACtHR's ruling in *Barrios Altos v Peru*, highlighting the potential for IAHRS judgments to influence broader human rights practices even in states not directly involved in a specific case. Par Engstrom and Gabriel Pereira, 'From Amnesty to Accountability: The Ebbs and Flows in the Search for Justice in Argentina' in Leigh A. Payne and Francesca Lessa (eds), *Amnesty in the Age of Human Rights Accountability: Comparative and International Perspectives* (Cambridge University Press 2012). Huneeus also captures such 'erga omnes' aspect of the impact of the IACtHR very well in her analysis of the Court and advances in Indigenous rights in Colombia:

> The Inter-American Court has never issued a judgment against Colombia on Indigenous rights. It has in recent years, however, developed a rich jurisprudence in this area through cases against Nicaragua, Suriname,

Third, there are direct constitutive, or symbolic, effects that involve processes of defining and perceiving policy problems as rights violations. The IAHRS has the potential to shape ideational and normative change through its role in legitimizing human rights claims advanced by individuals and groups. By providing a formal platform for adjudicating human rights violations and issuing binding rulings, the IAHRS bolsters the authority and political leverage of these actors in their advocacy efforts. The IACtHR's case law serves as a crucial reference point, prompting states to re-evaluate their policies in light of human rights obligations and potentially leading to a reframing of specific issues as human rights violations. The system often serves as a vital resource for domestic legislatures, informing legislative debates and the creation of laws designed to uphold the evolving body of human rights jurisprudence. While individual rulings and decisions may not automatically translate into domestic social and political change, they may help in strengthening immediate struggles and long-term prospects for change.

Finally, beyond direct impact, the IAHRS can also generate indirect symbolic effects. The IAHRS's decisions and actions may contribute to a heightened awareness of a human rights problem's urgency and gravity, potentially mobilizing public support for human rights reforms. The system can play a role in shaping public discourse by influencing how human rights issues are framed and understood. This can involve raising awareness of previously neglected issues or prompting a re-evaluation of existing norms. By bringing human rights violations to light and advocating for accountability, the IAHRS can foster a climate of greater public concern. Beyond its impact on public discourse, the IAHRS can also generate symbolic effects that influence the behaviour of social and political actors. These effects can potentially influence various spheres, including legal education, how legislatures deliberate, and how prosecutors conceive of and approach their work.

A comprehensive empirical examination of these diverse types of IAHRS impact certainly falls outside the scope of this chapter. However, future

---

Paraguay and Ecuador, and the CCC [Colombian Constitutional Court] has frequently made reference to these cases and used them to review national legislation and treaties under the constitutional block. The constitutionalization of the [IAHRS] has also meant that the CCC refers to [the system's] jurisprudence even in matters not traditionally considered to be human rights law, such as criminal law, family law, and administrative law. The Supreme Court and the Council of State, Colombia's highest administrative court, also regularly refer to the Inter-American Court's jurisprudence in interpreting questions of national law. (Alexandra Huneeus, 'Constitutional Lawyers and the Inter-American Court's Varied Authority' (2016) 79 *Law and Contemporary Problems* 191.)

research could productively develop these categories of impact through a range of research methodologies to capture the multifaceted potential effects of the IAHRS. This could generate valuable insights into the effectiveness of the IAHRS in advancing the realization of human rights in its region, and potentially beyond.

## 4 CONCLUSION

The normative and institutional evolution of the IAHRS has led to an increased dynamic interaction between the system and domestic political institutions and national legal orders. This process of domestic internalization of IAHRS mechanisms and norms has significantly altered the character of human rights implementation in the region. Throughout, the chapter has emphasized the evolution of features of the IAHRS that correspond to those associated with human rights experimentalism. Framing the IAHRS as an experimental governance framework recognizes the system's inherent dynamism. The system is characterized by continuous evolution through interactions between various stakeholders. Ongoing interaction fosters experimentation, allowing for the iterative development of norms and implementation strategies, and strengthening the capacity to adapt to address emerging human rights challenges in the region. Compared to a purely legalistic framework, the experimental lens goes beyond a focus on formal rules and procedures to capture the system's emphasis on dialogue, negotiation, and adaptation, as well as contestation. Furthermore, the experimental governance approach recognizes the agency of non-state actors within the IAHRS, through litigation, advocacy, and monitoring activities. It offers a detailed explanation of how this interaction can lead to improvements in human rights and social progress. Specifically, the emphasis is on how international efforts and local activism can work together in a back-and-forth way to create positive change for human rights. The experimentalist approach also recognizes that achieving lasting social and fundamental change is a long-term endeavour. Human rights advancements rarely occur rapidly, and sustained efforts are necessary to achieve meaningful progress.

The experimental governance framework does not proscribe a top-down approach, nor does it advance a relativistic and romanticized account of local processes. The experimental governance framework emphasizes dialogue and negotiation within the IAHRS. Unlike some top-down legal regimes, the IAHRS prioritizes collaboration between states and supranational bodies to achieve human rights objectives. This collaborative approach allows for the tailoring of solutions to specific contexts. The system's decisions often set forth broad principles, leaving some latitude for states to determine the most appropriate means of implementation based on their domestic circumstances. This flexibility allows for experimentation and innovation in devising effective human rights implementation strategies. For this approach to function effectively and contribute to compliance with human rights norms, there needs to be a strong presence of contextually situated, locally placed actors. These actors play a vital role in engaging in a dynamic, participatory, and iterative dialogue with the IAHRS, without overlooking the contentious and inherently political character of human rights struggles.

In short, by conceptualizing the IAHRS as an experimental governance framework, we gain a richer and more nuanced understanding of how the system works in practice. This framework captures the dynamic interplay between different actors, the emphasis on dialogue and flexibility, and the ongoing experimentation in devising effective human rights implementation strategies. While recognizing the political contestation that continues to characterize the IAHRS, it offers a valuable lens for analysing the system's strengths, its limitations, and its ongoing evolution in the pursuit of human rights in its region.

# 3. Tools to understand the impact of human rights systems from a comparative perspective

**Sabrina Ragone and Laura Alessandra Nocera**

## AUTHOR NOTE

The chapter has been thought and elaborated jointly by the authors; nevertheless, Sabrina Ragone drafted sections 2, 4, and 5, and Laura Alessandra Nocera drafted sections 1 and 3. Section 6, collecting the conclusion, was written by both.

## 1 INTRODUCTION

In scholarly legal opinions,[1] the term 'impact' is most commonly used to identify the influence and/or the effects of legal norms – and also of courts' decisions – upon different subjects, according to a wide and omni-comprehensive point of view and not only considering whether they are directly recipients of the prescriptive value of such norms. Strictly speaking, it could also be referred to as a cause-and-effect phenomenon, while the 'impact' can be defined as the determination of causality in the world. Through a more focused analysis,[2] it is

[1] On the term 'impact' from a legal perspective, the literature has provided various opinions and considerations, analyzing the function and the implications in different legal contexts. This is not the place to reconstruct the complex scenario behind the use of this term; just take into account: Colin S. Gibson, 'Legal Impact Analysis: The Ideal and The Practicable' (1982) 24 *Journal of the Indian Law Institute* 837.

[2] Such analysis can be conducted by using a retrospective or *ex post facto* investigation (i.e., after the happening of the event) and/or by using a prospective investigation (i.e., before the happening of the event or prognosticating it). Even if the prospective approach is stronger, as it may provide a further advantage in investigating habits and transformation of society, the first approach is the

possible to identify various types of effects, as there are different sources able to generate an impact with a wide range of influence.

Every legal system tends to construe a sphere of influence that has different shapes than the common recipients of destination. This is particularly evident in a legal system aiming to protect fundamental rights. We can generally define those ideal-types of legal system(s) as human rights system(s). In these terms, it acts as a safety net in which individuals can bring complaints against one (or more) of the subjects implicated because of a violation of one (or more) rights as granted in a document recognized as a part of their own legal system. In brief, a system regarding human rights has two important roles: (a) to create a general protection of human rights (i.e., the document/declaration signed and adopted by a certain number of subjects); and (b) to grant effective safety to this protection (i.e., the intervention of judicial bodies in order to improve rights and provide justice to individuals in cases of violation). The second role may be achieved in many different ways, depending also on judgments eventually issued by national courts, legislation passed by national parliaments and promoted by national governments, and decisions made by national authorities. Construing a functioning and safety net also comprehends a common way to judicially treat human rights, recognized by every subject, and destined to create a decisive 'impact' upon every actor of the region, considering both judicial and non-judicial/institutional actors, as well as private actors and societies.

But what is a human rights system? And what are its tasks? To respond to these questions, briefly introducing all the historical steps leading to the construction of common systems for the protection of human rights seems necessary.

After World War II, national governments started to consider the creation of a shared system ruling and preserving fundamental liberties and human rights as a safeguard. One of the main reasons forming the basis of this thought was the desire to redeem themselves, and the will to avoid future situations of human rights violations, as well as the specific intention to provide a system that would ensure reliable protection of human rights and punishment for those who would attempt to violate them.

---

most commonly used as it examines the importance of legal factors from the past situation up to the current one and searches for a practical explanation of present effects. The comparative method offers an effective tool of analysis, for comparing each other how social, economic, and political conditions operate in two or more cases according to a similar legal framework. On the issue: Gibson (n 1) 841–842 and 844.

On 4 November 1950, 13 European countries[3] signed the European Convention on Human Rights (ECHR), an international covenant of regional value, drafted by the Council of Europe to allot judicial protection to fundamental rights in the European area. The document incorporated for the first time in history a permanent judicial mechanism of protection, namely the European Commission on Human Rights (abolished in 1998), and the European Court of Human Rights (ECtHR). In this way, every citizen would be able to appeal to the Court to grant protection of their human rights against an act or a fact potentially undermining them. Such judicial mechanism has a subsidiary role, as it can be accessed after all the remedies and the petitions before national courts and all judicial instruments provided by the country in question are exhausted (Articles 13 and 35, ECHR). In this sense, all the national instruments shall be available to citizens, and appropriate to the case, and shall be characterized by efficiency, accessibility, and a high grade of certainty with chances of success.[4]

The Inter-American human rights system, instead, was established within an organization, formerly the Pan American Union, the purpose of which was to foster cooperation and solidarity among American States. The system was set up in 1890, long before the reflection on the importance of protecting human rights began in Europe after the world wars. It was only in 1948 that the American Declaration of the Rights and Duties of Man was signed by the States, in order to implement human rights in the region. The American Declaration did not have any binding effect on national institutions and did not create a mechanism of protection and promotion. The duty was devolved to the Organization of American States (OAS), an international body of regional value[5] born in 1948 during the 9th International Conference of American

---

[3] The European countries already part of the Council of Europe were: Belgium, Denmark, France, Greece, Ireland, Iceland, Italy, Luxembourg, Norway, Netherlands, United Kingdom, Sweden, and Turkey. The Covenant was enacted three years later, on 3 September 1953.

[4] Janneke Gerards, 'The Prism of Fundamental Rights' (2012) 8 *European Constitutional Law Review* 172, 172–178 and 183–187; Christina Eckes, 'EU Accession to the ECHR: Between Autonomy and Adaptation' (2013) 76 *Modern Law Review* 254, 256–258. See also: Steven Greer, *The European Convention on Human Rights: Achievements, Problems and Prospects* (Cambridge University Press 2006).

[5] The Organization used to define itself as a 'regional agency' within the United Nations. For this reason, it used to affirm that the organs and the institutions of the Organization were the same as those of the United Nations, which have been responsible for ensuring that decisions taken comply with the legal instruments in force, according to the text of the American Convention on Human

States, tasked with maintaining peace and justice in the region, while defending the independence and integrity of the States. In 1959, the members of the OAS decided to draft a Convention for the establishment of the Inter-American Commission on Human Rights (IACHR), as a consultative body in the OAS.[6] While the IACHR's functions were extended in 1965 to includeg individual petitions, the American Convention on Human Rights (ACHR) was adopted in 1969, and entered into force in 1978[7] with the ratification by eight States.[8] The ACHR also regulated the Inter-American Court of Human Rights (IACtHR), a judicial body, whose competence was to decide and solve cases of violations of human rights protection after a petition by a citizen, a State, or an institution.[9] The IACHR and the IACtHR comprised a two-level system of jurisdiction, modelled upon the then similar European system of protection of human rights, but without the character of subsidiarity in domestic legal systems. Even if the starting conditions for, and the historical and political perspectives on the birth of the ACHR are completely different from the ones regarding the draft of the ECHR, American legislators chose to take the European

---

Rights. See also: Thomas Buergenthal, Robert Norris, and Dinah Shelton (eds), *Protecting Human Rights in the Americas: Selected Problems* (N.P. Engel 1982).

[6] Robert K. Goldman, 'History and Action: The Inter-American Human Rights System and the Role of the Inter-American Commission on Human Rights' (2009) 31 *Human Rights Quarterly* 856, 857 ff.

[7] For a clear reconstruction of the facts influencing the draft of the ACHR, and its thematic values, see: Cecilia Medina Quiroga, *The American Convention on Human Rights: Crucial Rights and Their Theory and Practice* (2nd edn, Intersentia 2016); as well as Pablo Santolaya Machetti and María Isabel Wences Simón (eds), *La América de los Derechos* (CEPC 2016); and Christian Steiner and Marie-Christine Fuchs (eds), *Convención Americana sobre Derechos Humanos. Comentario* (2nd edn, Konrad Adenauer Stiftung 2019).

[8] Currently, the States that have ratified the ACHR and accepted the jurisdiction of the IACtHR are: Argentina, Barbados, Bolivia, Brazil, Chile, Colombia, Costa Rica, Dominica, Ecuador, El Salvador, Guatemala, Haiti, Honduras, Jamaica, Mexico, Nicaragua, Panama, Paraguay, Peru, Dominican Republic, Suriname, Trinidad and Tobago, Uruguay, and Venezuela. The States that havenot ratified the ACHR are: Antigua and Barbuda, the Bahamas, Belize, Canada, Guyana, Saint Lucia, Saint Kitts and Nevis, Saint Vincent and the Grenadines, and the United States of America.

[9] Sabrina Ragone, 'The Inter-American Court of Human Rights Turned 40: Achievements and Challenges' (2019) 25 *Revista General de Derecho Público Comparado* 1, 3–6. See also: Sabrina Ragone (ed), 'Encuentros y desencuentros entre el sistema interamericano de derechos humanos y los Estados de la OEA' (2015) 18 *Revista General de Derecho Público Comparado*.

experience as an inspiration to create a system of promoting human rights and a mechanism of their judicial protection within the boundaries of the region.[10]

## 2 THE RATIONALE

This chapter aims to reconstruct the different impacts of the jurisprudence and the activities of the ECtHR and its Inter-American counterpart across the regions of their influence.[11] For this purpose, the methodology recurs to cross-analysis, an established instrument of public comparative law for confronting two different systems, and their dialogue among the courts, the institutions, and the societies of the same region's countries. In fact, both human rights systems, as enforced by the corresponding Courts, have determined a series of effects in the legal context of their region. Indeed, we cannot analyze the issue from a one-dimensional perspective, but rather in a multifunctional dimension by introducing a tripartite reconstruction of the impact of the case law: (a) the 'ordinary impact' (or 'natural impact'), regarding national judges and courts operating in the region; (b) the 'conformative impact', regarding the other national institutions, which, though they are not entitled to judicial powers, are still embedded in public/state authority; and (c) the 'systemic-transformative impact', regarding actors that are not embedded in public organizations, but are part of the society.[12]

---

[10] Ragone, 'The Inter-American Court of Human Rights Turned 40' (n 9) 12 ff.

[11] The European and Inter-American human rights systems also provide a general example to be followed which was certainly adapted by the African Court on Human and Peoples' Rights, a justice system created with the adoption of the African Charter on Human and Peoples' Rights. Because of space and time constraints, but also due to scarce literature and/or secondary sources in comparison to the ECtHR and the IACtHR, the authors decided not to refer explicitly to the African equivalent in their argument. Nevertheless, even if the African Human Rights System has not determined the same impact as its European and the Inter-American counterparts, due to different historical and political contexts, and also a scarce adoption by state members, one cannot ignore the work the African Court attempts to practise, particularly in promoting human rights in a scenario not so much exposed to human rights discourse, in developing instruments of protection, and in mitigating Indigenous interpretations of fundamental rights. On the issue, see also: Rachel Murray, *The African Charter on Human and Peoples' Rights: A Commentary* (Oxford University Press 2011); Charles C. Jalloh, Kamari M. Clarke, and Vincent O. Nmeheille (eds), *The African Court of Justice and Human and Peoples' Rights in Context: Development and Challenges* (Cambridge University Press 2019).

[12] The trichotomy of 'natural impact' (on courts operating in the region), 'conformative impact' (on other institutions), and 'systemic-transformative impact'

In fact, modern international courts are institutions whose systemic function no longer resides just in the settlement of disputes between two or more parties. The core issue stands in the role played by the ECtHR and IACtHR so far, as the influence of the human rights systems – as implemented by the Courts – has been determinant not only in the interaction of different institutional/judicial bodies in the region, but also in shaping societies. Their current roles involve scholars and professionals as well, considering the Courts' actual law-making power, as well as their contribution to the strengthening of normative expectations and to the increase in control and legitimacy of public authority.[13]

Though the actual reconstruction aims to deepen the impacts of international courts in their region, specifically in relation to their decisions, one must bear in mind that the activity of international systems of human rights is not limited to solving judicial conflicts, since the systems also integrate a range of activities, whose nature and analysis are more complex than the mere judicial perspective might provide.[14]

Still, we will focus in this chapter on the judicial aspect of this multifaceted dialogue, in order to underline how the above-mentioned impacts operate comparatively in the two systems. For the sake of uniformity, since we shall analyze the impacts of the Courts upon their regions of influence, no reference will be introduced to reparations, or to remedial measures to the state's judges and/or organs.

Over the decades, the role of international courts has undergone substantial transformation and has, in some instances, differed across states within the region. Such variation reflects diverse historical, political, and social trajectories, as well as the particular features of national political systems and evolving models of statehood.

For instance, Latin America lived through a long period of authoritarian regimes and the denial of democratic institutions, and it is still affected by a

(on different actors and therefore the societies) was first introduced in Sabrina Ragone, 'Las tres vertientes del impacto de la jurisprudencia de la Corte IDH en el continente americano: itinerarios para investigaciones multidisciplinarias' in Pablo Santolaya Machetti and María Isabel Wences Simón (eds), *La América de los Derechos* (CEPC 2016) 435 ff.

13 Sabrina Ragone, 'The Importance of the Relationship between Domestic Institutions and the Inter-American System for the Protection of Human Rights' (2016) 9 *Inter-American and European Human Rights Journal* 456, 459 ff. See also: Armin von Bogdandy and Ingo Venzke, 'On the Functions of International Courts: An Appraisal in Light of Their Burgeoning Public Authority' (2013) 26 *Leiden Journal of International Law* 49 ff.

14 Ragone, 'The Importance of the Relationship between Domestic Institutions and the Inter-American System for the Protection of Human Rights (n 13) 459.

predominant model of 'hyper-presidentialism'. For these reasons, judges have often played a determinant role in supporting transitions to democracy by their request for innovations, protection of human rights, and social reforms. Of course, the context in which the Inter-American Human Rights System[15] operated has also changed since it was set up, and three different periods with three different attitudes of the IACtHR can be envisaged. The first period, also labelled as 'the origins', was characterized by the need to contrast with dictatorships and massive violations of human rights; the second one focused on the 'endorsement of the transitional processes to democracy'; and the third one – still running nowadays – combines old issues and new perspectives in order to integrate new generation rights, such as social exclusion, the rights of Indigenous peoples, or the rights of vulnerable peoples, etc.[16]

On the contrary, the European scenario has traditionally presented differences from the Latin American one, as the European system of human rights arose after a traumatic situation of global conflicts, and within a territory divided into two spheres of influence (liberal and socialist). Since then, Europe has experienced a stable model of democratic arrangements, whose institutions reflected the rule of law and the protection of fundamental rights. Then, the ECHR assumed an important role inside the European Union, as an additional layer of protection. Over time, there has also been a pattern of convergence between the two systems, as will be proved. Finally, the European human rights system also improves the dialogue among Courts, and the implementation of common policies on fundamental rights, attempting to overcome the divergences among the States, even in the current context of rising nationalisms. In these terms, the work of the ECHR and ECtHR plays an ancillary role in the harmonization of politics in the European common space.

---

[15] Felipe González Morales, *Sistema Interamericano de Derechos Humanos* (Tirant lo Blanch 2013) 263 ff.

[16] Ragone, 'The Importance of the Relationship between Democratic Institutions and the Inter-American System for the Protection of Human Rights' (n 13) 460. This division into periods of time is also dealt with by Claudio Grossman, 'The Inter-American System and Its Evolution' (2009) 2 *Inter-American and European Human Rights Journal* 49, 50. See also: Laurence Burgogue-Larsen and Amaya Úbeda de Torres, *The Inter-American Court of Human Rights. Case Law and Commentary* (Oxford 2011). For a general overview of the changing role of the judiciary in the region, see the articles collected in Gretchen Helmke and Julio Ríos-Figueroa (eds), *Courts in Latin America* (Cambridge University Press 2014).

## 3 ORDINARY IMPACT (ON THE COURTS IN THE REGION)

The term 'ordinary impact' (or 'natural impact') in this chapter generally refers to the influence of the decisions made by the Inter-American and/or European Court of Human Rights upon all national judges and courts operating in the same region. It deals with a physiological impact not transcending the system – as the effects stay inside the dialogue among jurisdictional courts – but involving the application of the regional protection to human rights. The critical aspect of this impact lies in the binding and facultative character of a precedent decision bya supranational judge, and also on the social role of domestic judges in developing human rights doctrine by following supranational jurisprudence.

In order to reconstruct how the 'ordinary impact' works, we can consider that ECtHR and/or IACtHR decisions have always played a determinant role not only in protecting human rights according to the Convention(s), but also in reforming the national parameters of protection.

The effectiveness of the European human rights system relies on the proper and timely execution of judgments by the ECtHR at national level. Responsibility for carrying out the Court's judgments lies with the member state concerned.[17] The task of supervising the implementation is carried out by the Committee of Ministers (CM), aided by the Department for the Execution of Judgments, but the duty of maintaining the system's effectiveness also relies on close cooperation betweenthe relevant bodies and authorities at domestic and international level, so that human rights challenges are addressed in a timely way.[18] Even if the ECtHR states that its precedents are not binding, it should not abandon them without a 'good reason' according to legal certainty, predictability, and the principle of equality before law,[19] in an interpretation that maintains its

[17] Karen Alter, 'Explaining National Court Acceptance of European Court Jurisprudence: A Critical Evaluation of Theories of Legal Integration' in Anne-Marie Slaughter, Alec Stone Sweet and Joseph H.H. Weiler (eds), *The European Court and National Courts – Doctrine and Jurisprudence. Legal Change in its Social Context* (Oxford University Press 1998) 227 ff.

[18] Wouter Vandenhole, 'The Execution of Judgments' in Paul Lemmens and Wouter Vandenhole (eds), *Protocol No. 14 and the Reform of the European Court of Human Rights* (Intersentia 2005) 105–121; Marinella Marmo, 'The Execution of Judgments of the European Court of Human Rights – A Political Battle' (2008) 15 *Maastricht Journal of European and Comparative Law* 235.

[19] See *Goodwin v Great Britain* App No. 17488/90 (ECtHR, 11 July 2002). See also: *Mamatkulov and Askarov v Turkey* App nos 46827/99 and 46951/99 (ECtHR 4 February 2005); *Herrmann v Germany* App No. 9300/07 (26 June 2012).

character to be case-by-case.[20] On 1 November 1998, Protocol No. 11 to the Convention entered into force and caused a series of changes in the conventional system: first, the right of all the citizens in member states to have access to the Court with individual petitions and appeals was introduced; then, an obligation for the parties to accept the jurisdiction of the Court over individual applications was introduced.[21] Perhaps, over the last decades – and particularly since Protocol No. 11 entered into force and the number of members in the Council of Europe increased – the ECtHR had been frequently overwhelmed by a lot of individual applications, risking pronouncing repetitive decisions about the same issues; and this was the matter treated in 2005 by Protocol No. 14, which proposed a way to amend the control system of the Convention and to limit the number of identical decisions (and which effectively entered into force in 2010).[22] In response to the need for order, in 2004, the Committee of Ministers had already adopted Resolution No. 3 (Resolution Res(2004)3 of the Committee of the Ministers on judgments revealing an underlying systemic

---

[20] According to Zagrebelsky, the type of reason of the Court is based on the theory of precedents, and when no precedent exists, the Court's interpretation considers every case by separating it from the others and identifying the precedent whose *ratio decidendi* can be useful in solving the case. Vladimiro Zagrebelsky, 'La giurisprudenza casistica della Corte europea dei diritti dell'uomo; fatto e diritto alla luce dei precedenti' (*Dipartimento di Giurisprudenza*, 20 November 2009) www.giurisprudenza.unimib.it.

[21] The same Protocol also eliminated the Commission, an organ that filtered cases inside the Conventional system in order to determine which petitions should be judged by the Court, as analyzed in the first paragraph. See also: Explanatory Report to Protocol No. 11 to the Convention for the Protection of Human Rights and Fundamental Freedoms, restructuring the control machinery established thereby (1994) ETS No. 155.

[22] Steven Greer, 'Protocol 14 and the Future of the European Court of Human Rights' (2005) *Public Law* 83 ff. See also: Explanatory Report to Protocol No. 14 to the Convention for the Protection of Human Rights and Fundamental Freedoms, amending the control system of the Convention (2004) Council of Europe Treaty Series No. 194.

problem),[23] and introduced the so-called 'pilot-judgment' procedure[24] through

---

[23] Committee of Ministers, Declaration of the Committee of Ministers: Ensuring the effectiveness of the implementation of the European Convention on Human Rights at national and European levels, 114th session (12 May 2004). The two previous recommendations, which are also directed at promoting the national implementation of the Convention and of ECtHR judgments, are Recommendation No. R (2000) 2 of the Committee of Ministers on the re-examination or reopening of certain cases at domestic level following judgments of the European Court of Human Rights, 694th meeting of the Ministers' Deputies, 19 January 2000; and Recommendation Rec(2002)13 of the Committee of Ministers on the publication and dissemination in the member states of the text of the European Convention on Human Rights and of the case-law of the European Court of Human Rights, 822nd meeting of the Ministers' Deputies, 18 December 2002 (the latter Recommendation was accompanied by Resolution Res(2002)58 of the Committee of Ministers on the publication and dissemination of the case-law of the European Court of Human Rights, adopted during the same meeting). The prior decision that leads to this statement derived from a Ministerial Conference held in Rome in 2000 about how 'efficiency' and 'effectiveness' of the Court were to be improved. See: Committee of Ministers, Declaration. The European Convention on Human Rights at 50: What Future for the Protection of Human Rights in Europe?, European Ministerial Conference on Human Rights, 3–4 November 2000, 729th meeting (15 November 2000).

[24] The actual introduction of the procedure happened with the entrance into force of Protocol No. 14 to the European Convention on Human Rights in June 2010, and the incorporation in 2011 of Rule 61(6)a into the Rules of Court: 'The Court may initiate a pilot-judgment procedure and adopt a pilot judgment where the facts of an application reveal in the Contracting Party concerned the existence of a structural or systemic problem or other similar dysfunction which has given rise or may give rise to similar applications'. Pilot judgments were proposed by the Court inside the debate that led to the drafting of Protocol No. 14. See also: ECtHR, Position paper of the European Court of Human Rights (12 September 2003) CDDH-GDR(2003)024, paras 43 ff. The entry into force of Protocol No. 14 was followed by Protocols No. 15 and No. 16 to the European Convention on Human Rights. Protocol No. 15 deals with a variety of aspects, such as reducing the number of incoming applications by shortening the deadline for the application and by broadening the scope; it also recalls the principle of subsidiarity, since it places on the member states the duty to secure rights and freedoms as protected by the Convention through the doctrine of the 'margin of appreciation', and judicial supervision by the ECtHR. Protocol No. 16 deals closely with domestic implementation and innovates the advisory function of the Court by allowing national courts to ask for the opinion of the Court on the interpretation and adoption of the dispositions of the Convention. See: Protocol No. 15 amending the Convention for the Protection of Human Rights and Fundamental Freedoms (24 June 2013) Council of Europe Treaty Series No. 213; Protocol No. 16 amending the Convention for the

which, when the Court identifies a repetitive problem in cases to be decided, it shall choose only one case – the 'pilot' one – to examine.[25] The Resolution invites the Court 'to identify [...] what it considers to be an underlying systemic problem and the source of this problem [...], so as to assist states in finding the appropriate solution and the Committee of Ministers in supervising the execution of judgments'.[26] The Court not only may issue a judgment to declare a violation of the Convention but may also 'identify the systemic problem', in order to give 'the Government clear indications of the type of remedial measures needed to resolve it'.[27] By using pilot judgments, the Court can adjourn all the repetitive applications, avoiding the need for time to be spared for the overspreading of similar cases, but it can also indicate only general measures and defer the duty of execution to domestic authorities. The pilot-judgment procedure gives effect to decisions whose nature is traditionally declaratory, and pilot judgments request the necessary support at the national level, as a legal obligation to restore as far as possible the situation existing before the breach.[28] Differently, when the Court decides to adopt a 'quasi-pilot-judgment', meaning a not full procedure, it is only a sort of 'warning' to the respondent state. Under Article 46, quasi-pilot udgments are not merely declaratory, as they identify a method for the Court to address a systemic problem, which can provide general but not imposed measures. The procedure is very similar to the one for the pilot judgment, but quasi-pilot judgments do not discuss the option of adjourning repetitive applications, while their competence exists

---

Protection of Human Rights and Fundamental Freedoms (2 October 2012) Council of Europe Treaty Series No. 214. About the strong impact of Protocol No. 15, see also: Lucius Caflisch and Martina Keller, 'Le Protocole additionnel no. 15 à la Convention européenne des droits de l'homme' in Lucius Caflisch and others (eds), *Liber amicorum Luzius Wildhaber: Human Rights – Strasbourg Views/ Droits de l'homme – Regards de Strasbourg* (Kehl 2007) 91 ff. About the doctrine of 'margin of appreciation' and its functions inside the jurisprudence of the European Court, among others, see: Jeffrey A. Brauch, 'The Margin of Appreciation and the Jurisprudence of the European Court of Human Rights: Threat to the Rule of Law' (2005) 11 *Columbia Journal of European Law* 113 ff; Martin Kuijer, 'The Margin-of-Appreciation Doctrine and the Strengthening of the Principle of Subsidiarity in the Recent Reform Negotiations' (2016) 36 *Human Rights Law Journal* 339.

[25] Markus Fyrnys, 'Expanding Competences by Judicial Lawmaking: The Pilot Judgment Procedure of the European Court of Human Rights' (201) 12 *German Law Journal* 1231.

[26] ECtHR – Press Unit, 'Factsheet – Pilot Judgments' (September 2016) 1.

[27] ibid.

[28] See *Papamichalopoulos and others v Greece* App No. 14556/89 (ECtHR, 31 October 1995) para 34.

only in general and operative measures. For this reason, seldom does the Court pronounce decisions of a hybrid nature between the pilot and the quasi-pilot judgments, which leads to a certain confusion.[29]

Since the cooperation of the state becomes crucial in following the application of the pilot-judgment procedure, this mechanism also reflects the principle of subsidiarity. In other words, the role of the state is at the core of a successful execution of the pilot judgment, while the duty of conformity in interpreting human rights with the ECHR has become the rule for national judges.[30] Pilot and quasi-pilot judgments are derived from the typical 'dynamism' inside the European system of human rights, whose roots are recognized in Article 32 of the Convention, in which the 'competence of the Court extends to all the issues regarding interpretation and application of the Convention and its Protocols',[31] as the Court maintains the duty to decide upon its competence. The Convention is a 'living instrument' also for the Court in interpreting the actual situation and granting rights and liberties.[32] National judges play a special role in the reception of Conventional rights; since the ECHR establishes standards for monitoring operations of national systems of justice (as Articles 5, 6, and 13 impose), judges are particularly exposed to the direct supervision

---

[29] An example is represented by the *Lukenda v Slovenia* decision, a judgment pronounced by the Court on 6 October 2005 (23032/02), only containing general and operative measures without any desire to adjourn repetitive application. The decision may be considered a clear example of a quasi-pilot judgment. Nonetheless, the Court itself recalls this decision in the case *Kuric and others v Slovenia*, of 26 June 2012 (26828/06), defining it as a pilot judgment. Very similar is also the case of *Scordino v Italy* (No. 1), a quasi-pilot judgment pronounced by the Court on 29 March 2006 (36813/97), with many features corresponding to a pilot-judgment.

[30] See also Italian Constitutional Court, decisions No. 348 and 349 (2007), and decision No. 311 (2009). For the reconstruction of the cases and a more detailed presentation of the mechanism elaborated by the Italian Constitutional Court, see also: Lucia Tria, 'La tutela dei diritti fondamentali. Le tecniche di interrelazione normativa indicate dalla Corte costituzionale' (*Corte Costituzionale*, December 2014) www.cortecostituzionale.it. See also Italian Constitutional Court, decision No. 49, 2015. For a reconstruction of the case: Giuseppe Martinico, 'Conflitti interpretativi e concorrenza fra corti nel diritto costituzionale europeo' (2019) 4 *Diritto e Società* 691, 710 and 718 ff.

[31] Lucia Tria, 'Il dialogo tra giudici nazionali, Corte di giustizia e Corte europea dei diritti dell'uomo' (*Giustizia Insieme*, 26 June 2023). www.giustiziainsieme.it.

[32] ibid.

of European case law, while ECtHR judges and domestic judges have been continuously involved in interactions of reciprocity.[33]

Additionally, domestic judges may enrich the parameter of interpretation in order to enlarge the protection of fundamental rights. Even if there is no binding duty for domestic judges to interpret a case in light of the ECtHR jurisprudence, they are obliged to consider it as an international treaty with human rights competence, according to domestic constitutional regulations.[34] In some cases, national judges have begun to consider the ECtHR jurisprudence as a source of law for the national legal system, and to autonomously disapply domestic law when they find it is in conflict with the ECHR's dispositions and values, and/or able to violate the principles behind the Convention and the jurisprudence of the Court: in these situations, national judges become Conventional and European judges, and their decision is substantially equivalent to the ECtHR's decision.[35]

The IACtHR jurisprudence recognizes the fact that national courts are submitted to national law, and to the IACHR, since it was ratified, as judicial power has the duty to exercise the 'control de convencionalidad' (or 'control of conventionality') between national laws and the norms of the ACHR, and to take into account the interpretation by the IACtHR.[36] The doctrine was

[33] Helen Keller and Alec S. Sweet, 'Assessing the Impact of the ECHR on National Legal Systems' in Helen Keller and Alec S. Sweet (eds), *A Europe of Rights: The Impact of the ECHR on National Legal Systems* (Oxford University Press 2008) 687–688. Indeed, in many European states the ECHR was incorporated thanks to the authority of courts. The courts also manage the most important mechanism of reception by identifying the violation of the ECHR found by the ECtHR, to harmonize their jurisprudence with the European one. This authority also includes the power to review the legal validity of governments' acts under Conventional dispositions.

[34] Davide Paris, 'Allies and Counterbalances. Constitutional Courts and the European Court of Human Rights: A Comparative Perspective' (2017) 77 *Heidelberg Journal of International Law* 623 ff.

[35] It depends on how the member states decide to integrate the ECHR into domestic law. An example comes from the UK, where in 1998 the Human Rights Act incorporated the full text of the Convention. This fact transforms domestic judges into conventional judges, with the duty to directly intervene in the hypothetical violations of human rights. In this way, every judge may disapply a law if it contrasts with the intentions of the ECHR, with a 'fast-track' procedure. See also: David Hoffman and John J. Rowe, *Human Rights in the UK. An Introduction to the Human Rights Act 1998* (Pearsons 2003).

[36] Victor Bazán, 'El control de convencionalidad como instrumento para proteger derechos esenciales y prevenir la responsabilidad internacional del Estado' (2015) 19 *Anuario Iberoamericano de Justicia Constitucional* 25 ff. For

elaborated by the interpretation about the value of the binding precedent of the IACtHR decisions by the Court itself, which recognized its role of guidance for the interpretation of all the national judges of the State parties.[37] In fact, in accordance with this doctrine, every national judge of countries subject to its jurisdiction can be considered a judge of the Inter-American system in protecting human rights, supporting democratic values, and implementing the standards of the ACHR. The binding character of a precedent decision is a real obligation for national judges of every state in the region, even if the IACtHR pronounces the decision in a case in which another state is involved.[38] Once

---

a reconstruction about the control of conventionality in different international courts, see also: Pablo González-Domínguez, *The Doctrine of Conventionality Control: Between Uniformity and Legal Pluralism in the Inter-American Human Rights System* (Intersentia 2018); María C. Londoño-Lázaro and Nicolás Carrillo-Santarelli, 'The Control of Conventionality: Developments in the Case Law of the Inter-American Court of Human Rights and Its Potential Expanding Effects in International Human Rights Law' (2019) 22 *Max Planck Yearbook of United Nations Law* 319; Claudina Orunesu, 'Conventionality Control and International Judicial Supremacy: Some Reflections on the Inter-American System of Human Rights' (2020) 40 *Revus* 45; Yota Negishi, *Conventionality Control of Domestic Law: Constitutionalised International Adjudication and Internationalised Constitutional Adjudication* (Nomos Verlagsgesellschaft 2022).

[37] About the doctrine of the control of conventionality and the binding value of a judicial precedent case for all the national judges of the Inter-American region, see the judgments: *Almonacid Arellano and Others v Chile* (Decision) IACtHR Series C No. 154 (26 September 2006); *Trabajadores Cesados del Congreso (Aguado Alfaro and Others) v Peru* (Decision) IACtHR Series C No. 158 (24 November 2006); *Heliodoro Portugal v Panama* (Decision) IACtHR Series C No. 186 (12 August 2008); *Cabrera García y Montiel Flores v México* (Decision) IACtHR Series C No. 220 (26 November 2010); *Gelmán v Uruguay* (Decision) IACtHR Series C No. 221 (24 February 2011).

[38] Particularly, in the case of *Almonacid Arellano and Others v Chile*, the IACtHR affirmed that

> cuando un Estado ha ratificado un tratado internacional como la Convención Americana, [...] como parte del aparato del Estado, también están sometidos a ella, lo que les obliga a velar porque los efectos de las disposiciones de la Convención no se vean memadas por la aplicación de leyes contrarias a su objeto y fin, y que desde un inicio carecen de efectos jurídicos. En otras palabras, el Poder Judicial debe ejercer una especie de 'control de convencionalidad' entre las normas jurídicas internas que aplican en los casos concretos y la Convención Americana sobre Derechos Humanos. En esta tarea, el Poder Judicial debe tener en cuenta no solamente el tratado, sino también la interpretación que el mismo ha hecho la Corte Interamericana, intérprete última de la Convención Americana.

the state ratified the ACHR as an international treaty with the purpose to protect human rights, it became a part of the national legal system, obliging every organ of the state's administration to apply it.[39] Thus, while the ACHR is a yardstick for the implementation of human rights culture, national judges do not find any obstacles in directly implementing the IACtHR's decisions. From this perspective, the interaction between domestic judges and the Inter-American human rights system becomes necessary, and implies not only a vertical impact (from the upper grade – the Inter-American one – to the lower grade – the one of the domestic judges[40]), but also a horizontal and continuous dialogue between national and international levels (since the IACtHR often looks at domestic trends in jurisprudence in order to solve some cases[41]), and among national courts (in different states), with the specific purpose to overcome distance and recognize a common culture in protection of rights.[42]

---

39 Sometimes constitutional texts contain some clauses referring to international treaties, which may be useful in the incorporation of the ACHR. Other times, constitutional and supreme courts may read some cases with an interpretation on human rights as part of the so-called 'bloc de constitutionalité'. This term refers to the parameter of interpretation in order to define the constitutionality of some legal norms which have a fundamental value in the protection of human rights. Laura A. Nocera, 'Contradicciones constitucionales: el Tribunal Constitucional Plurinacional Boliviano y la reelección de Morales. ¿Una práctica de abusivismo constitucional?' (2019) 23 *Anuario Iberoamericano de Justicia Constitucional* 499. See also: Louis Favoreu and Francisco Rubio Llorente, *El bloque de constitucionalidad* (Cuadernos Civitas 1989).

40 There is a top-down influence when domestic constitutional or supreme courts pronounce in favour of the recognition of the binding precedent of the IACtHR, and national judges must be obliged to interpret cases considering Inter-American jurisprudence. An example is the decision of the Sala Constitucional de la Corte Suprema de Justicia de Costa Rica, No. 12703 of 2014. There is a bottom-up influence when the IACtHR directly refers to a constitutional court in order to solve the case. An example is the decision of the IACtHR in the 2014 case *Personas Dominicanas y Haitianas Expulsadas v República Dominicana*.

41 Many scholars talk about a 'dialectic review' for defining this sort of reciprocity between the two levels of judiciaries, the Inter-American one and the domestic one, because of the fact that their relationships are characterized by a mirroring influence and control. Ragone, 'Las tres vertientes del impacto de la jurisprudencia de la Corte IDH en el continente americano: itinerarios para investigaciones multidisciplinarias' (n 12) 441; Ragone, 'The Importance of the Relationship between Domestic Institutions and the Inter-American System for the Protection of Human Rights' (n 13) 463. See also: Diego García Sayán, 'The Inter-American Court and Constitutionalism in Latin America' (2011) 89 *Texas Law Review* 1835 ff.

42 It refers to the concept of judicial dialogue, also defined as a mutual review among judges. Robert B. Ahdieh, 'Between Dialogue and Decree: International Review of National Courts' (2004) 79 *New York University Law Review* 2032.

## 4 CONFORMATIVE IMPACT (ON NON-JUDICIAL INSTITUTIONS)

International courts do also establish a relationship with other actors in the states within the region of influence, provided that all the institutions of every state are involved in the protection and in the implementation of their jurisprudence. The term 'conformative impact' defines the influence of both the ECtHR and the IACtHR upon non-judicial state institutions, particularly considering the interaction with parliaments and legislative bodies, as the principal role in the regulation of human rights nationally is allotted to national parliaments – independently of the specific models of state and forms of government. Domestic legislatures shall pass the corresponding legislation when existing law is not compatible with international standards of protection.[43] Every member state that has signed an agreement should model its legal framework to implement and integrate the international standards of protection of human rights, either by drafting constitutional amendments or by adopting legislative (and/or executive) instruments for this purpose.

The impact of the ECHR derives from a complex social process, called 'reception', a sort of cross-national phenomenon that aims to introduce the dispositions of the Convention – and also all the elements possibly connected to them, such as judicial decisions and interpretation – into domestic law and legal practice.[44] The reception process passes through the judiciary and through all the other institutional levels, also by using ECtHR jurisprudence. The European Court protects the fundamental rights guaranteed by the Convention in different ways, because it functions as a sort of High Cassation Court during the procedure before it, as an international observatory of human rights violations, and as a supreme actor of interpretation of constitutional rights in a community of rights across all the State parties, as established by Articles 8–11 and 14 ECHR.[45] Even if the Convention does not contain a specific clause on the duty to take measures to give effect to conventional rights, non-judicial *ex post* mechanisms of coordination are always adopted by the State parties as an ordinary consequence after a decision pronounced by the

[43] Ragone, 'The Importance of the Relationship between Domestic Institutions and the Inter-American System for the Protection of Human Rights' (n 13) 464. See also: Par Engstrom (ed), *The Inter-American Human Rights System: Impact Beyond Compliance* (Palgrave Macmillan 2019).

[44] Keller and Sweet, 'Assessing the Impact of the ECHR on National Legal Systems' (n 33) 677–678.

[45] ibid 695. See also: Luzius Wildhaber, 'A Constitutional Future for the European Court of Human Rights' (2000) 23 *Human Rights Law Journal* 161.

Court, to respond to the specific violation of human rights and to avoid similar conditions in the future.[46]

Several states have also adopted major legislative reforms in order to deal with failures of a systemic nature identified by the Court.[47] Within these dynamics, national constitutional courts act as mediators and conductors for implementing legislation in conformity with conventional rights and the European Court's jurisprudence, and then, as central actors in the processes of domestic law-making. In fact, although violations of conventional rights are usually caused by domestic legislation, the ECtHR is not entitled to strike down domestic laws.[48] Therefore, constitutional courts have to enter into a sort of 'partnership' with the European Court in striking down national legislation that could be incompatible with the Convention.

Constitutional courts' review, besides checking the constitutionality of domestic laws, can also insert in domestic orders the international standards and their authentic interpretation provided by the corresponding courts.[49] They

---

46 Examples derive from the fast-track procedure already analyzed with respect to the UK's case. Another peculiar case could be seen in the innovative mechanism of reception built in Ukraine. See also: Samantha Besson, 'The Reception Process in Ireland and in the UK' in Helen Keller and Alec S. Sweet (eds), *A Europe of Rights: The Impact of the ECHR on National Legal Systems* (Oxford Academic Press 2008) 31; Angelika Nussberger, 'The Reception Process in Russia and Ukraine' in Helen Keller and Alec S. Sweet (eds), *A Europe of Rights: The Impact of the ECHR on National Legal Systems* (Oxford Academic Press 2008) 603.

47 An example comes from Italy, where parliament adopted an important reform with the purpose of improving the protection of fundamental rights and implementing the Court's ruling after the law *Azzolini* (n.12, January 9th, 2006). On the argument, see: Mercedes Candela Soriano, 'The Reception Process in Spain and in Italy' in Helen Keller and Alec S. Sweet (eds), *A Europe of Rights: The Impact of the ECHR on National Legal Systems* (Oxford Academic Press 2008) 393.

48 Wojciech Sadurski, 'Partnering with Strasbourg: Constitutionalisation of the European Court of Human Rights, the Accession of Central and East European States to the Council of Europe, and the Idea of Pilot Judgments' (2009) 9 *Human Rights Law Review* 441; Jan Petrov, 'Unpacking the Partnership: Typology of Constitutional Courts' Roles in Implementation of the European Court of Human Rights' Case Law' (2018) 14 *European Constitutional Law Review* 513. See also: Alec S. Sweet, *Governing with Judges: Constitutional Politics in Europe* (Oxford Academic Press 2000); Allan R. Brewer-Carías (ed), *Constitutional Courts as Positive Legislators* (Cambridge Academic Press 2013) 153–64.

49 An interesting perspective is provided by the case judged by the Italian Constitutional Court, No. 236/2011. See Giuseppe Martinico, 'National Courts and Judicial Disobedience to the ECHR: A Comparative Overview' in Oddný

can remove legislative obstacles to achieve compliance with the ECHR,[50] and/or derogate legislation excluding some matters from judicial review,[51] and/or give instructions about how to interpret the law before Parliament enacts a new legislative measure.[52] In all these cases, constitutional judges urge legislative bodies (and, sometimes, the executives) to adopt and apply promptly new legislative provisions, respecting the ECHR and the ECtHR's conclusions. As some scholars have pointed out, the Court's impact is becoming so strong that it may build a 'participatory model', overcoming the classical forms of state.[53]

Of course, parliaments can adopt legislative acts in accordance with Strasbourg's jurisprudence also without the input from national constitutional courts. For example, ECtHR jurisprudence has contributed to enlarging the parameter of protection of the right to life (Article 2 ECHR), and the right to be free from torture, and inhuman and degrading treatment (Article 3 ECHR), particularly regarding the conditions injails and detention centres,[54] or discriminatory rules against certain groups. The ECtHR redefines the scope and content of the rights granted by the Convention and (indirectly) by domestic legal norms. A significant example is the reinterpretation made by the Court about Articles 8–11 and Article 14 of the Convention. Domestic parliaments have had to draft and/or reform existing legislation in order to incorporate not only these provisions, but also their jurisdictional understanding. The Convention requires the obedience of national legal systems as national

M. Arnardóttir and Antoine Buyse (eds), *Shifting Centres of Gravity in Human Rights Protection* (Routledge 2016) 74; John Ferejohn and Pasquale Pasquino, 'Constitutional Adjudication, Italian Style' in Tom Ginsburg (ed), *Comparative Constitutional Design* (Cambridge Academic Press 2014) 294.

[50] This is to be found in the case of the decision *Frankowicz v Poland* (ECtHR 16 December 2008, App No. 53025/99). Poland was convicted by the ECtHR for a violation of Article 10 ECHR in disciplinary proceedings for medical practices. The Polish Constitutional Tribunal intervened to foster an interpretation consistent with European rules on human rights.

[51] Two examples come from the cases *Luuko v Slovakia* (ECtHR 2 September 1998, App No. 26138/95) and *Kadubedc v Slovakia* (ECtHR 2 September 1998, App No. 27061/95), in which the Slovak Constitutional Court annulled some problematic provisions of national law, preventing the courts from using them.

[52] *Chrúsciński v Poland* App no 22755/04 (ECtHR, 6 November 2007).

[53] The definition was elaborated by John Jackson in 'The Effect of Human Rights on Criminal Evidentiary Processes: Towards Convergence, Divergence or Realignment?' (2005) 68 *Modern Law Review* 737.

[54] Particularly, it refers to the case of Northern Irish prisoners in British detention centres and to the case of discrimination against Kurdish people in Turkey. Keller and S. Sweet, *Assessing the Impact of the ECHR on National Legal System* (n 33) 697–698.

constitutional rights guardians.[55] This assumes a transnational and constitutional character, at the same time penetrating national legislations.[56]

Regarding the Inter-American scenario, Article 1 of the ACHR disposes of a general obligation to the State parties:

> to respect the rights and freedoms recognized herein and to ensure to all persons subject to their jurisdiction the free and full exercise of those rights and freedoms, without any discrimination for reasons of race, colour, sex, language, religion, political or other opinion, national or social origin, economic status, birth, or any other social condition

(Article 1, ACHR), while Article 2 provides a clause to guarantee domestic legal effects in the exercise of rights protected by the Convention. For these reasons, the State parties 'undertake to adopt, in accordance with their constitutional processes and the provisions of this Convention, such legislative or other measures as may be necessary to give effect to those rights or freedoms' (Article 2 ACHR).[57] This clause regulated the duty of conformity of the legal framework to the international protection of human rights, therefore primarily obliging national parliaments to adapt domestic law to the ACHR. Significantly, there is no differentiation between obligations involving ordinary legislation or those requiring a constitutional reform.[58] Both cases have taken place, although the IACtHR is not entitled to formal annulment of the previous domestic legislation. This mechanism implies a declaration of a non-conventionality, according to the doctrine of conventionality implied in the text (and in the interpretation) of the ACHR. The Court's jurisprudence may be possibly catalogued in two different trends, epitomized by the following two

---

[55] Keller and Sweet, 'Assessing the Impact of the ECHR on National Legal System' (n 33) 699.

[56] On the transnational character, see also: Gregory Shaffer, Tom Ginsburg, and Terence C. Halliday (eds), *Constitution-making and Transnational Legal Order* (Cambridge Academic Press 2019).

[57] On this specific clause, see: Karla I. Quintana Osuna, 'Diálogo entre la jurisprudencia interamericana y la legislación interna: El deber de los Estados de adoptar disposiciones de derecho interno para hacer efectivos los derechos humanos' in Armando Flores (ed), *Derecho Procesal Constitucional. 50 años de desarrollo científico: 1956/2006. Estudios en homenaje a Héctor Fix Zamudio* (Instituto de Investigaciones Jurídicas de la UNAM – Instituto Mexicano de Derecho Procesal 2008).

[58] Ragone, 'Las tres vertientes del impacto de la jurisprudencia de la Corte IDH en el continente americano' (n 12) 442.

cases. In the first case, *Claude Reyes and Others v Chile*,[59] concerning the violation of the right to access to public information (*rectius*, the absence of legislation regarding the access to public information), the Court convicted Chile for an open violation of a right guaranteed in the Convention and, also, for not having conformed domestic law to the conventional system,[60] according to the doctrine of conventionality.[61] In this sense, the IACtHR can urge the reform of national legislation, according to the obligation of conformation disposed of in Article 2 of the ACHR. After the decision, Chile immediately adopted a piece of legislation about the right to access to public information[62] (a virtuous case, which does not reflect the overall statistics on execution of judgments).[63]

In the second case, the judgment *'La Última Tentación de Cristo' (Olmedo Bustos and Others) v Chile*,[64] the IACtHR imposed again on the state the duty

---

59 *Claude Reyes and Others v Chile* (Reparations and Costs) IACtHR Series C No. 151 (19 September 2006). See: Elvira B. Poblete, 'El fallo de la Corte Interamericana de Derechos Humanos en el caso 'Claude Reyes and Others v Chile' (Rol de la Corte en el desarrollo progresivo del respeto de los derechos humanos por parte de los Estados Americanos)' (2007) 69 *Revista de Derecho Público* 331 ff; Leiry C. Chávez, 'The Claude-Reyes Case of the Inter-American Court of Human Rights – Strengthening Chilean Democracy?' (2013) 31 *Nordic Journal of Human Rights* 513 ff.

60 The IACtHR concluded its judgment deciding that the state 'debe adoptar, en un plazo razonable, las medidas necesarias para garantizar el derecho de acceso a la información bajo el control del Estado, de acuerdo al deber general de adoptar disposiciones de derecho interno establecido en el artículo 2 de la Convención Americana sobre Derechos Humanos'. The quote is cited in Ragone, 'Las tres vertientes del impacto de la jurisprudencia de la Corte IDH en el continente americano' (n 12) footnote 21.

61 On the control of conventionality, see also: Natalia Torres Zúñiga, *El control de convencionalidad de las normas constitucionales. El impacto de las sentencias de la Corte Interamericana de Derechos Humanos en la teoría del cambio constitucional* (Editorial Académica Española 2015).

62 The corresponding law (Law No. 20,285) was passed in 2008.

63 Other similar examples may be seen in the case *Herrera Ulloa v Costa Rica* (2004), or the case *Radilla Pacheco v Estados Unidos Mexicanos* (2009), in which the state was obliged to adopt legislation in order to reform the Military Justice Code. The cases are briefly treated in Ragone, 'Las tres vertientes del impacto de la jurisprudencia de la Corte IDH en el continente americano' (n 12) footnotes 22 and 23.

64 *La Última Tentación de Cristo (Olmedo Bustos and Others) v Chile (Reparations and Costs)* IACtHR Series C No. 73 (5 February 2001); Ragone, 'The Importance of the Relationship between Domestic Institutions and the Inter-American System for the Protection of Human Rights' (n 13) 465; Ragone, 'Las tres vertientes del impacto de la jurisprudencia de la Corte IDH en el continente

to 'conform' the domestic legal framework to the ACHR, but, this time, the commitment was addressed to the Chilean amending power, as the violation depended on a clause embedded in the constitutional text. The case was related to the prohibition of the exhibition of Martin Scorsese's film, in accordance with a system of censorship established by Article 19 of the Constitution, but in contrast to freedom of expression as granted by the ACHR. For this reason, Inter-American judges recommended Chile to amend the Constitution and/or to adopt *ad hoc* legislation within a strict period of time, in order to allow for the exhibition of films (and other forms of art) without any censorship, consistently with conventional rights.[65] The attitude of the Court shows that in convictions the hierarchical value of the domestic norm is irrelevant, therefore affecting also constitutional norms, and in this case imposing a supra-constitutional character to the Convention, similarly to what is doctrinally labelled as 'intermediate yardstick'[66]

In other cases, the IACtHR does not refer to a specific 'conformation' of domestic law as a measure of reparation; it rather offers model-type attitudes that can represent sources of inspiration for states.

Indeed, the 'conformative impact' does not determine an obligation addressed to the legislative branch to adopt consistent legislation or amend the current one, but it carries an implicit order to the executive branch, as the duty of implementation also involves the execution of all the measures of reparations established by the Court. The impact of human rights jurisprudence affects national administrations independently from the nature of the conviction, since they shall implement judgments and reparations and, at the same

---

americano' (n 12) 443. On this case, see also: Felipe González Morales, 'Censura judicial y libertad de expresión: sistema interamericano y derecho chileno' (2006) 43 *Revista del Instituto Interamericano de Derechos Humanos* 239 ff.; Eva Leticia O. Trujillo, 'La libertad de pensamiento y de expresión vista desde la Corte Interamericana de Derechos Humanos' (2011) 53 *Latinoamérica* 133.

[65] The IACtHR disposed that the state 'debe modificar su ordenamiento jurídico interno, en un plazo razonable, con el fin de suprimir la censura previa para permitir la exhibición de la película 'La Última Tentación de Cristo', y debe rendir a la Corte Interamericana de Derechos Humanos, dentro de un plazo de seis meses a partir de la notificación de la presente Sentencia, un informe sobre las medidas tomadas a ese respecto'.

[66] Other similar cases are *Suarez Rosero v Ecuador* (1997), *Bulacio v Argentina* (2003), *Boyce and others v Barbados* (2007), *Ticona Estrada v Bolivia* (2008), *Gomes Lund and others (Guerilha do Araguaia) v Brasil* (2010), *González Medina and Relatives v Dominican Republic* (2012), *Romero Feris v Argentina* (2019), *Baena Ricardo and Others v Panamá* (2021), and two cases *Ríos Avalos and Others v Paraguay* (2021 and 2023).

time, they have the duty to implement the reforms that are required to develop the protection of fundamental rights.[67]

## 5 SYSTEMIC-TRANSFORMATIVE IMPACT (ON DIFFERENT ACTORS AND SOCIETIES)

The last impact we shall consider comprehends a large and heterogeneous category of effects on different actors that are neither judicial nor institutional. In fact, the diffusion of international jurisprudence regarding human rights does not affect national institutions exclusively; it can also affect attitudes and values inside the societies of the State parties. Over time, judicial decisions have often triggered processes of self-reflection and debates in the societies affected. This tendency has been particularly growing snce the creation of international systems of protection of human rights, as political scientists and sociologists have proven.[68]

In order to understand this impact, scholars should analyze a series of details and connections that could possibly intervene in the acceptance of human rights doctrines, also considering their transformative impact in shaping societies. First, a leading element is the diffusion of international courts' decisions (also in a cross-analysis examination), the growing number of studies about international jurisprudence, and the increase in human rights doctrine in all the countries involved. Second, there has been an impact of international jurisprudence on practising lawyers' work, particularly in filing issues and petitions to the courts, but also in the contribution to the establishment of associations and organizations for protecting human rights. Third, every decision by the human rights courts' judges might transform the political agenda and legislative priorities, changing the way citizens perceive the implementation of human rights through judicial decisions and the construction of better protection. Fourth, a fundamental role worth mentioning is played by the diffusion

[67] Ragone, 'The Importance of the Relationship between Domestic Institution and the Inter-American System for the Protection of Human Rights' (n 13) 467–468.

[68] Carlos A. Villagrán Sandoval and Fabia F. Carvalho Veçoso, 'A Human Rights' Tale of Competing Narratives' (2017) 8 *Direito & Práxis Revista* 1603; Laurence Bourgorgue-Larsen and René Urueña, 'International Transformative Constitutionalism in Latin America' (2020) 114 *The American Journal of International Law* 402; Jessika Eichler, 'The Transformative Forces of International Law? Questioning Equality Regimes from a Multi-Level Perspective' (2022) 11 *Global Constitutionalism* 325. See also: Eduardo Ferrer Mac-Gregor et al, 'Dialogue Between Regional Human Rights Courts' (*Corte IDH*, 2020) https://www.corteidh.or.cr/sitios/libros/todos/docs/dialogo-en.pdf.

of NGOs defending and nurturing the human rights dialogue in the regions of influence. As societies have been changing over time, without any fixed rule, every society is strongly impacted when international jurisprudence of human rights re-reads and re-interprets the concept of protection, possibly enlarging the requirements of national institutions for implementing fundamental rights, and – sometimes – for considering new rights.[69]

These interactions directly affect the qualification of the democracy of the State parties and go beyond geographical boundaries. In fact, every case submitted to and decided by one of these two international courts of human rights influences the debates in society, and new legal readings and interpretations which also reach beyond the specific region concerned. Societies and states are always in transition in respect of incorporating democratic values, changing their approach to human rights, which has impact on the development of national institutions and the knowledge of society.[70] This fact often redirects domestic policies and plays an important role in citizens' knowledge and sensitivity, leading to a new perspective of human rights theory.[71]

69 The theme has been dealt with in depth by a few scholars. Among others, the authors particularly referred to the studies conducted by Armin von Bogdandy: 'Ius Constitutionale Commune Latinoamericano. Una aclaración conceptual' in Armin von Bogdandy et al (eds), *Ius Constitutionale Commune en América Latina: Rasgos, Potencialidades y Desafíos* (MPIL 2014) 12 ff.; 'Ius Constitutionale Commune en América Latina: Observations on Transformative Constitutionalism' in Armin von Bogdandy, Eduardo Ferrer Mac-Gregor, and Flavia Piovesan (eds), *Transformative Constitutionalism in Latin America* (Oxford University Press 2017) 3; 'Ius Constitutionale Commune en América Latina: un enfoque regional del constitucionalismo transformador' in Armin von Bogdandy, Mariela M. Antoniazzi and Eduardo Ferrer Mac-Gregor (eds), *Ius Commune Constitutionale en América Latina* (Estado de Querétaro/MPIL 2017) 17. See also: Armin von Bogdandy and Rene Urueña, 'International Transformative Constitutionalism in Latin America' (2020) 114 *American Journal of International Law* 403.

70 On the argument, see also: Shale Horowitz and Albrecht Schnabel, *Human Rights and Societies in Transition: Cause, Consequences, Responses* (United Nations University Press 2004); Melina Girardi Fachin, 'Dialogues and (On) Human Rights' (2022) 6 *Católica Law Review* 41.

71 Ragone, 'Las tres vertientes del impacto de la jurisprudencia de la Corte IDH en el continente americano' (n 12) 446–447.

## 6. DIFFERENCES AND SIMILARITIES BETWEEN THE EUROPEAN COURT AND THE INTER-AMERICAN COURT: A COMPARATIVE CONCLUSION

As analyzed in this chapter, both human rights courts produce a general impact in their region, influencing institutional and social dynamics inside the State parties, and favouring dialogue among national judges. In fact, neither the ECtHR nor the IACtHR proves the initial statement of the multi-dimensional role of international courts in contemporary times. Their decisions affect not only the parties, but also involve other aspects of the legal, political, and social life of the states in their region. Consistently with the idea of the multi-functional nature of international courts,[72] legislative aspirations and the political programmes of a state, as well as the legitimacy of public authority, also rely on decisions by international courts.

Of course, the scope and effects of the impact then apply differently depending on the peculiarities of every national reality analyzed, and with the historical and socio-political character of the regional area under the jurisdiction of the international court, also considering the model of state.

In the European context, the role of the ECtHR is relatively pervasive and has progressively entered into judicial and professional practice. The political landscape is generally characterized by established democracies with a set of specific violations of the Convention. The Latin American context features more fragile democracies that have often undergone long-lasting transitional processes. The level of inequalities, injustice, violations of basic rights, and the presence of autocratic regimes has been at the core of the jurisprudence of the IACtHR for many decades. While national institutions continue to be weak, and political parties cannot consolidate their role vis-à-vis strong presidential systems, the judiciary enjoys a higher inspirational role in society's evolution (also called 'judicial activism').[73]

---

[72] A. Von Bogdandy and Ingo Venzke, 'On the Functions of International Courts: An Appraisal in Light of Their Burgeoning Public Authority' (2012) Amsterdam Law School Research Paper No. 2012–69, 49–72; Armin von Bogdandy and Ingo Venzke, 'The Spell of Precedents: Lawmaking by International Courts and Tribunals' in Cesare P. R. Romano (ed), *The Oxford Handbook of International Adjudication* (Oxford Academic Press 2013) 503.

[73] Ragone, 'Las tres vertientes del impacto de la jurisprudencia de la Corte IDH en el continente americano' (n 12) 436. See also: Laurence Burgogue-Larsen, 'La Corte Interamericana de Derechos Humanos como Tribunal Internacional' in Armin Von Bogdandy et al (eds), *Ius Constitutionale Commune en América*

Contextual and historical differences explain part of the distinct outcomes of the two systems, while the different legal framework (namely the existence of Article 2 ACHR and the absence of a similar clause in the ECHR) does not substantially impact the role played by the corresponding Courts. Certainly, the IACtHR has been more imaginative when providing reparations, trying to take into account the conditions of the affected state, the actual violation perpetrated, and the interests and needs of victims and other actors involved.

Overall, both Courts have had an impact on institutional and non-institutional actors at the domestic level, contributing to the increase in awareness of human rights and also to the spread of a sort of constitutional pluralism.[74] Also, the violations that are now being brought before the Inter-American Court are increasingly similar to those being dealt with by the European Court in terms of the gravity of the violation and the set of affected rights. At the same time, the ECtHR has had to respond to systemic violations, partly through pilot judgments. This bidirectional convergence has improved the dialogue between the two systems, shifting from a unidirectional quotation of European precedents by the IACtHR to mutual influence.[75]

---

*Latina: Rasgos, Potencialidades y Desafíos* (Instituto de Investigaciones Juridicas 2014) 421 ff.

[74] Giorgio Repetto, 'Exercises of constitutional pluralism. The transformations of fundamental rights' protection in Europe between scope of application of the Charter and dual preliminarity' (2022) 2 *Diritto Pubblico* 775. See also: Neil Walker, 'The Idea of Constitutional Pluralism' (2002) 65 *Modern Law Review* 317; Cormac S. Mac Amhlaigh, *New Constitutional Horizons. Towards a Pluralist Constitutional Theory* (Oxford Academic Press 2022); Matej Avbelj and Jan Komárek (eds), *Constitutional Pluralism in the European Union and Beyond* (Oxford Academic Press 2012).

[75] Luis López Guerra and Alejandro Saiz Arnaiz (eds), *Los Sistemas Interamericano y Europeo de Protección de los Derechos Humanos. Una Introducción desde la Perspectiva del Diálogo entre Tribunales* (Palestra 2015).

# 4. Impact through aesthetics: narrative, perception, and justice in the Inter-American Court of Human Rights

**René Urueña and Stephania Yate Cortes**

## 1 INTRODUCTION

A constant source of concern and scepticism regarding the work of the Inter-American System of Human Rights (IAHRS, or 'the System') is its impact. While one body of literature argues that the System is a toothless tiger, adopting orders with little expectation of state compliance,[1] another perspective emphasizes the need to go 'beyond compliance' and consider the broader societal impact of its orders.[2] This latter approach moves beyond traditional compliance metrics to examine the System's wider influence – including policy changes, institutional transformation, and the adoption of Inter-American standards in domestic law, among other direct and indirect effects.[3]

In this debate, scholars have explored the incentives and causal mechanisms that drive compliance with the System's orders and explain its broader impact. Regarding compliance, one of us has examined the varying levels of adherence

[1] See the literature references in: Armin von Bogdandy and René Urueña, 'Inducing Compliance as a Transformative Process: The Bright Side of a Dismal Record' in Armin von Bogdandy and others (eds), *The Impact of the Inter-American System of Human Rights: Transformations on the Ground* (Oxford University Press 2024) 17–34.

[2] See: René Urueña and Viviana Krsticevic, 'Transformative Impact of the Inter-American Human Rights System: A Methodology to Think Beyond Compliance' in Armin von Bogdandy and others (eds), *The Impact of the Inter-American System of Human Rights: Transformations on the Ground* (Oxford University Press 2024) 584–602.

[3] Bogdandy and Urueña, 'Inducing Compliance as a Transformative Process: The Bright Side of a Dismal Record' (n 1).

to Inter-American orders in Colombia,[4] while the Notre Dame Reparations Design and Compliance Lab has produced valuable insights into the conditions that facilitate compliance. These conditions include the specificity of Inter-American Court of Human Rights (IACtHR) orders,[5] stakeholder engagement in compliance monitoring[6] and the role of time in protracted compliance processes.[7] Conversely, other scholars have analyzed the pathways through which the System influences human rights realities in Latin America, even when formal compliance is absent. These studies examine the role of domestic litigation in amplifying the System's reach,[8] the impact of Inter-American precautionary measures on persons deprived of liberty,[9] and the effect of Inter-American rulings on domestic institutions.[10] Additionally, a robust body of work has explored the System's influence on substantive human rights issues, including economic, social, cultural, and environmental rights; migration; freedom of expression; and the fight against impunity.[11]

---

[4] René Urueña, Beatriz Sanchez and Sergio Anzola, *Después Del Fallo: El Cumplimiento de Las Decisiones Del Sistema Interamericano de Derechos Humanos. Una Propuesta de Metodología* (Uniandes/Documentos Justicia Global 2015).

[5] Aníbal Pérez-Liñán et al, 'Specificity in the Inter-American Court of Human Rights' (2024) 16 *Journal of Human Rights Practice* 754.

[6] Aníbal Pérez-Liñán and Angie K. García Atehortúa, 'Oversight Hearings, Stakeholder Engagement, and Compliance in the Inter-American Court of Human Rights' (2024) 78 *International Organization* 293–320.

[7] Aníbal Pérez-Liñán, Luis Schenoni and Kelly Morrison, 'Compliance in Time: Lessons from the Inter-American Court of Human Rights' (2023) 25 *International Studies Review* 1.

[8] Par Engstrom and Peter Low, 'Mobilising the Inter-American System of Human Rights: Regional Litigation and Domestic Human Rights Impact in Latin America' in Par Engstrom (ed), *The Inter-American System of Human Rights: Impact Beyond Compliance* (Springer International Publishing 2019) 23–58.

[9] Clara Burbano Herrera and Yves Haeck, 'The Impact of Precautionary Measures on Persons Deprived of Liberty in the Americas' in Par Engstrom (ed), *The Inter-American System of Human Rights: Impact Beyond Compliance* (Springer International Publishing 2019) 89–113.

[10] Oscar Parra-Vera, 'Institutional Empowerment and Progressive Policy Reforms: The Impact of the Inter-American System of Human Rights on Intra-State Conflicts' in Par Engstrom (ed), *The Inter-American System of Human Rights: Impact Beyond Compliance* (Springer International Publishing 2019) 143–166.

[11] See the studies in: Armin von Bogdandy et al (eds), *The Impact of the Inter-American System of Human Rights: Transformations on the Ground* (Oxford University Press 2024).

This chapter contributes to this debate by conceptualizing impact as a continuously evolving description of reality, performed by the Latin American human rights community – a group of actors that interact based on the Inter-American Convention on Human Rights to promote their agendas and to fulfil what they regard as their mandates.[12] These actors participate in the co-construction and contestation of human rights meaning through shared legal practices and interpretive frameworks. While narratives are shaped across multiple sites of practice, this chapter focuses on the Inter-American Court of Human Rights due to its distinctive role in producing legal narratives.[13] The Court's rulings carry particular weight due to its transnational mandate, its authority to validate or reject legal framings, and its success in establishing influential jurisprudential frameworks.[14] This perspective shifts the focus from compliance to narrative construction, emphasizing that impact manifests through narratives – structured cognitive categories that shape how human rights realities are interpreted. By introducing aesthetics into this discussion, we describe how images of reality are created and transformed within these narratives,[15] establishing a shared experiential framework that determines what is visible, sayable, and thinkable within the human rights community.

Engaging with aesthetics provides new analytical tools for understanding the interaction between the IAHRS and its various stakeholders. Recent discussions on aesthetics and international law highlight the intrinsic connection between aesthetics and politics, demonstrating how aesthetics influence the formalization of experience and meaning.[16] Drawing from Jacques Rancière's

---

[12] On this matter, see: René Urueña and Armin von Bogdandy, 'International Transformative Constitutionalism in Latin America' (2020) 114 *American Journal of International Law* 414.

[13] Although the Court plays a prominent role in framing human rights narratives, its interpretations are not beyond contestation. The influence of a particular legal framework does not imply interpretive consensus, as multiple actors within the human rights community continue to engage, negotiate, and challenge dominant understandings. For an in-depth analysis of this dynamic, see: Gwendolyn Leachman, 'Legal Framing' in Austin Sarat (ed), *Studies in Law, Politics, and Society* (Emerald 2013) 25–59.

[14] On this matter, see: Rene Urueña and Stephania Yate Cortes, 'Creating the Narrative of Human Rights Impact in Latin America' in Par Engstrom (ed), *The Impact of the Inter-American Human Rights System* (Oxford University Press 2024) 206.

[15] ibid 119–214.

[16] Robert Knox and Christine Schwöbel, 'Aesthetics of International Justice' in Robert Knox and Christine Schwöbel (eds), *Aesthetics and Counter-Aesthetics of International Justice* (Counterpress 2024) 1–13.

notion of aesthetics, we recognize that every community is organized around a 'sensible delimitation' of what is considered common to it.[17]

To advance this argument, this chapter first explores the significance of aesthetics within the Latin American human rights community. It then examines how aesthetics shape the perception of reality by triggering cognitive processes that consolidate shared understandings. We illustrate this dynamic through an analysis of three Inter-American Court cases: *Villagrán-Morales et al. v Guatemala*[18] ('*Street Children*'), *Miguel Castro Castro Prison v Peru*,[19] and *Villamizar Durán et al. v Colombia*.[20] The final section presents our conclusions.

## 2 AESTHETICS AND NARRATIVES

The IACtHR engages in a continuous process of constructing narratives that are reiterated, contested, and eventually incorporated into the canon of human rights discourse. These narratives function as dominant interpretative frameworks within the human rights community of practice,[21] shaping legal reasoning and influencing the broader discourse on justice. In each case, the IACtHR structures its rulings through cognitive categories[22] that interpret facts, diagnose underlying causes, and propose remedies.[23] This process is inherently narrative-based: rather than presenting an exhaustive procedural account, the Court strategically selects and organizes information to construct a coherent

---

17 Jacques Rancière, 'The Distribution of the Sensible: Politics and Aesthetics' in Gabriel Rockhill (ed), *The Politics of Aesthetics, The Distribution of the Sensible* (Continuum 2011).

18 *Case of the 'Street Children' (Villagran-Morales et al) v Guatemala* (Merits) IACtHR Series C No 63 (19 November 1999).

19 *Miguel Castro Castro Prison v Peru* (Merits, Reparations and Costs) IACtHR Series C No 155 (25 November 2006).

20 *Villamizar Durán et al v Colombia* (Merits, Reparations and Costs) IACtHR Series C No 364 (20 November 2018).

21 A community of practice is a group of actors that interact based on the Inter-American Convention on Human Rights to promote their agendas and to fulfil what they regard as their mandates. On this matter, see: René Urueña and Armin von Bogdandy, 'International Transformative Constitutionalism in Latin America' (2020) 114 *American Journal of International Law* 414.

22 On how this set of concepts works as cognitive categories, see: René Urueña, 'International Law as Expert Knowledge: Exploring the Changing Role of International Lawyers in National Contexts' in André Nollkaemper et al. (eds), *International Law as a Profession* (Cambridge University Press 2017) 389–411.

23 On how narratives of impact are created, see: Urueña and Yate Cortes, 'Creating the Narrative of Human Rights Impact in Latin America' (n 14).

and persuasive argument.[24] As a result, each ruling does more than resolve an individual case – it advances a broader interpretation of human rights issues, introducing new legal concepts and reinforcing evolving standards.

The narratives produced by the IACtHR are not merely legal arguments; they function as cognitive instruments that structure knowledge and influence perceptions of reality.[25] They bridge the persistent reality of human rights violations in Latin America with the transformative aspirations of constitutionalism. For example, in *González et al. v Mexico* (*Cotton Field*), the Court addressed the disappearance and murder of three young women in 2001, situating these crimes within the systemic problem of gender-based violence in the region.[26] This case was pivotal in exposing structural gender discrimination, as the IACtHR's interpretation redefined isolated acts of violence as part of a broader, systemic pattern. By framing these violations within a wider context of systemic gender-based violence, the Court's ruling established a shared legal and conceptual framework that enabled diverse actors to articulate and address these violations in a more comprehensive manner. Moreover, this decision provided the tools to conceptualize such crimes as structural issues, demanding legal and policy responses that address their root causes.

## 2.1 The Aesthetic Dimension of Legal Narratives

The narratives shaped by the IACtHR do not merely structure legal reasoning; they also shape perceptions of reality, fostering particular ways of seeing and experiencing human rights violations. These narratives possess an aesthetic dimension, as they engage readers not only through legal argumentation but also by immersing them in a specific representation of events. The *sensible perception* of how the IACtHR constructs these realities plays a critical role in unifying the human rights community. Sensory experiences are particularly effective in capturing attention and eliciting emotional responses. However, beyond their immediate impact, they influence processes of individual perception and social interaction, shaping intuitive assessments of the 'rightness' of a particular state of affairs.[27]

---

[24] This narrative dimension of legal reasoning has been widely explored in the field of law and literature. See: Robert Cover, 'Foreword: Nomos and Narrative' (1983) 97 *Harvard Law Review* 4.

[25] Julia Otten, 'Narratives in International Law' (2016) 99 *Critical Quarterly for Legislation and Law* 187–216.

[26] *González y otras (Campo Algodonero) v México* (Preliminary Objection, Merits, Reparations and Costs) IACtHR Series C No 205 (16 November 2009).

[27] Randle C. DeFalco, 'Maintaining Invisibility. Aesthetic Perception and the Recognition of International Crimes' in *Invisible Atrocities: The Aesthetic Biases*

According to Xenakis and Arnellos, aesthetic perceptions contribute to *sense-making* – an internal cognitive process in which an agent evaluates, differentiates, and anticipates interactions with an object or situation, thereby establishing a self-defined normative status that reduces uncertainty and enhances meaning-making.[28] This process of evaluation is not confined to perception alone; rather, it serves a preparatory and anticipatory role in shaping action. Individuals and communities assess the affordances of a given narrative and align their responses with the norms and objectives that structure their understanding and adaptation.[29]

This capacity of aesthetic perceptions to structure knowledge and shape intuitive judgments is particularly relevant when examining how the IACtHR constructs its legal narratives. The Court does not merely present legal arguments; it engages the reader at an emotional and sensory level, fostering a deeper sense of involvement. This engagement can be understood through the concept of *aesthetic illusion*, which refers not to deception or fictionalization, but to the immersive experience that arises when readers imaginatively and affectively relate to a representation of real events. As Wolf explains, aesthetic illusion is a mental state triggered by concrete representational forms – such as texts or performances – that produce a sense of being immersed in a represented world.[30] In the context of the Court's rulings, this means that narratives do not simply recount facts; they guide the reader's perception by shaping the interpretation of those facts, problems, and solutions in accordance with a particular interpretive framework.[31]

Although this concept has traditionally been applied to fiction, its use in legal reasoning does not suggest that what is represented is not real. The IACtHR's narratives are based on judicial processes and factual realities. However, they engage the reader in an internal imaginative experience, incorporating emotions and sensory quasi-perceptions (such as visual imagination).[32] However, it is not purely cognitive but also *embodied and affective*, allowing the narrative to resonate more deeply with both individual and collective understandings of justice. Crucially, this process generates affective responses that are not signs

---

*of International Criminal Justice* (Cambridge University Press 2022) 71.

28 Ioannis Xenakis and Argyris Arnellos, 'Aesthetic Perception and its Minimal Content: A Naturalistic Perspective' (2014) 5 *Frontiers in Psychology* 3.

29 Xenakis and Arnellos, 'Aesthetic Perception and its Minimal Content' (n 28).

30 Werner Wolf, 'Illusion (Aesthetic)' in Peter Hühn et al. (eds), *Handbook of Narratology* (De Gruyter 2014) 270.

31 Werner Wolf, Walter Bernhart and Andreas Mahler, *Immersion and Distance: Aesthetic Illusion in Literature and Other Media* (Brill 2013) 9.

32 Wolf, 'Illusion (Aesthetic)' (n 30) 271.

of distortion or manipulation, but mechanisms through which legal meaning is embodied and made socially intelligible. These emotional and sensory reactions are central to how narratives produce a sense of justice and legitimacy within the community of practice, resonating with what has been described as *affective justice*[33] – a mode of engagement where law acquires meaning through embodied feeling and public sentiment.

## 2.2 Aesthetic Narratives and Human Rights Advocacy

By shaping perception in this way, the Court's narratives do more than strengthen human rights standards – they contribute to the formation of a shared interpretative space within the community of practice, reinforcing common understandings and expectations. Imagining the facts as structured by the IACtHR and linking them to the normative horizon of human rights law allows the community of practice to continuously advance the human rights framework. This connection is further reinforced through aesthetic illusion, which enhances the coherence and meaning of legal narratives, even when they diverge from the contingent realities of specific cases.[34] This divergence stems from the tension between the normative aspirations of the IACtHR and the factual conditions surrounding each case. Within its decisions, the Court establishes a general framework that provides a specific way to understand each case, selectively highlighting aspects of perceived reality to promote a particular problem definition, causal interpretation, moral evaluation, and legal remedy.[35]

Understanding this aesthetic dimension not only reveals the persuasive force of these narratives but also invites a broader discussion on the impact of legal aesthetics in shaping regional and global human rights discourse. As with any interpretative field, dominant aesthetics emerge depending on the context – such as the representations promoted by the Inter-American Court within its community of practice, which can become dominant in relation to other actors. At the same time, counter aesthetics also arise in other spaces, such as national contexts or different international justice forums, where the Court's framing

[33] For a broader discussion of how justice is produced through embodied feelings, affective responses, and social practices, see: Kamari Maxine Clarke, *Affective Justice: The International Criminal Court and the Pan-Africanist Pushback* (Duke University Press 2019).

[34] Wolf, 'Illusion (Aesthetic)' (n 30) 272.

[35] Robert M. Entman, 'Framing: Toward Clarification of a Fractured Paradigm' (1993) 43 *Journal of Communication* 43, 52.

may be seen as a counter-aesthetic.[36] Examining these dynamics allows us to identify the distinctive features of the Inter-American System, its alignment with regional contexts, and its potential to transform traditional approaches to international justice.

From this perspective, Rancière's concept of the *distribution of the sensible* becomes particularly relevant. The IACtHR's narratives not only reflect but actively shape the aesthetic and political boundaries of the human rights community. By mobilizing specific images and sensory experiences, these narratives cultivate a shared perception of justice while simultaneously disrupting existing orders, creating space for contestation.[37] This process resonates with historical struggles for human rights in the region, enabling the reconfiguration of what is visible, sayable, and ultimately conceivable within Latin American human rights discourse.

The visual and sensory representations embedded in IACtHR rulings reinforce collective understandings of justice while also shaping the emotional and political engagement of those who interact with them. The Court's narratives are not merely technical legal documents; they are carefully constructed representations that influence how local realities are perceived, contested, and transformed within the broader human rights discourse. The following section explores these arguments in greater depth by examining three particularly significant dimensions of IACtHR narratives: the portrayal of violence, the depiction of victims, and the visualization of justice itself. By analyzing how the Court constructs these images, we can better understand how it shapes both the identity of the human rights community and the legal frameworks through which human rights violations are understood and addressed.

## 3 REACHING FOR NEW NOTIONS OF JUSTICE

Just as dominant aesthetics shape prevailing notions of justice, alternative aesthetics seek to challenge or redefine them.[38] The way key elements – such as violence, victims, and justice – are visually and narratively constructed can either reinforce established representations or introduce new ones. By reshaping these images, the community of practice can strengthen its collective identity. Moreover, appealing to the sensory and emotional dimensions of justice fosters broader recognition and engagement with human rights issues.

---

36 On the idea of counter-aesthetics, see: Knox and Schwöbel-Patel, 'Counter-Aesthetics of International Justice' (n 16).

37 Rancière, 'The Distribution of the Sensible: Politics and Aesthetics' (n 17) 13.

38 Knox and Schwöbel-Patel, 'Counter-Aesthetics of International Justice' (n 16).

The cognitive processes induced by the sensory experiences triggered by various representational artefacts play a powerful role in shaping the human rights landscape. Consequently, the ultimate impact of the IACtHR is to introduce a vision of how reality should be – one that contrasts the existing conditions with normative goals and frames legal and political action accordingly. This notion of impact goes beyond mere compliance, as it is rooted in the construction of narratives that connect facts, values, and possibilities, shaping collective understandings and expectations. Through this lens, the Court not only guides the State and its institutions but also mobilizes the community of practice around evolving normative horizons.[39]

What kinds of images shape the IACtHR's narratives? This section examines three fundamental representations that consistently emerge in its jurisprudence. The first is the portrayal of violence, which shifts from an 'atrocity aesthetic' to a 'structural aesthetic'. The second is the representation of victims, which moves beyond the traditional notion of an 'ideal victim' to introduce the image of an empowered subject. The third is the conceptualization of justice, transitioning from 'distant justice' to 'embedded justice'.

## 3.1 The Image of Violence

The first of these images is that of violence. There are diverse ways of portraying violence; for instance, Defalco has shown how international criminal law (ICL) has tended to an 'atrocity aesthetic', meaning that it highlights specific harms that produce horror, a way to focus on 'spectacular' acts of physical violence.[40] However, in contrast to this form of representation, there are also 'unspectacular' manifestations of violence related to structural oppression. These may be perpetrated through bureaucratic barriers, discriminatory policies, or socioeconomic conditions that result in severe human rights violations.[41] The IACtHR has increasingly incorporated a 'structural aesthetic' of violence, one that considers the multifactorial causes leading to human rights

[39] For a detailed discussion of this narrative approach to impact, see: Urueña and Yate Cortes, 'Creating the Narrative of Human Rights Impact in Latin America' (n 14).

[40] Randle C. DeFalco, *Invisible Atrocities: The Aesthetic Biases of International Criminal Justice* (Cambridge University Press 2022).

[41] For instance, DeFalco explains that in post-Khmer Rouge Cambodia, the survivors continuously highlighted everyday forms of violence and oppression. However, overly simplistic narrations of atrocity violence tend to predominate. Randle C. DeFalco and Savina Sirik, 'The Fluctuating Visibility of Everyday Violence in Khmer Rouge Era Cambodia' (2022) 31 *Southern California Interdisciplinary Law Journal* 217.

violations, thereby shifting the emphasis from physical harm to the broader structural conditions that sustain systemic injustices.

What is particularly significant is the Court's ability to 'zoom in' and 'zoom out', shifting its focus between the specific facts of a case and the broader structural conditions that underpin them. Because an image or an aesthetic illusion can never fully correspond to reality, framing becomes essential in constructing a legal narrative – one that selectively amplifies certain elements while omitting others. While it is crucial to be mindful of what is excluded, the risk of maintaining a fixed aesthetic of violence is that it limits the ability to recognize and address diverse forms of human rights violations. This, in turn, can create an aesthetic bias that restricts the Court's capacity to adapt to evolving contexts.[42] The choice to zoom in or out directly affects how a case is framed, influencing the identification of root causes and shaping the legal response to different types of human rights violations.

Accordingly, the Court modulates the image of violence depending on the case, recognizing different forms of harm. In some instances, the focus is on the immediate physical damage suffered by the victims; in others, the emphasis is placed on the structural conditions that enable such harm. This shifting perspective is achieved through a zoom-in or zoom-out approach, centring either on the victim's personal experience or on the broader systemic forces affecting multiple individuals.

## 3.2 The Representation of Victims

The image of victims raises an important debate, as it can lead to the construction of an 'ideal victim' stereotype. While various scholars have proposed differing definitions of this concept, it generally relies on three key attributes: vulnerability, dependency, and grotesqueness.[43] An 'ideal' victim is perceived as inherently vulnerable, meaning they do not willingly put themselves at risk but rather suffer harm due to external forces beyond their control. This vulnerability is closely tied to a notion of dependency, where the victim is portrayed as entirely passive, reliant on legal representatives or the Court itself to seek justice. Finally, there is an element of grotesqueness, in which suffering must be visible and recognizable – often through physical signs of harm – reinforcing both the victim's status and the brutality of the perpetrator.

---

[42] Regarding criminal international law, an aesthetic bias means assuming that every crime must conform to the atrocity aesthetic, excluding other types of harm. For more on this argument see: DeFalco, *Invisible Atrocities* (n 40).

[43] Christine Schwöbel-Patel, *Marketing Global Justice: The Political Economy of International Criminal Law* (Cambridge University Press 2021).

The notion of the 'ideal victim' presents several challenges, both in terms of the role imposed on victims and the broader assumptions that sustain it. First, this image confines victims to a position of weakness, where their only recognized agency is their ability to establish their status as victims. This perspective does not account for their ability to organize, mobilize, or seek broader political and social change. As Nils Christie has pointed out, for a victim to fit the 'ideal' mould, they must remain weak and passive enough not to pose a threat to dominant interests.[44] If victims were to challenge power structures or advocate for systemic transformation, their legitimacy as 'ideal victims' could be questioned, and their claims might struggle to gain recognition. This restrictive framework not only influences legal and political narratives but also shapes societal responses to human rights violations.

Moreover, this image impacts the general narrative of cases by simplifying and polarizing subjects into two opposing categories: 'good' and 'evil'.[45] In this framework, certain individuals are seen as unequivocally deserving of rights, while others are perceived solely as human rights violators. However, reality is far more complex. As demonstrated in various case analyses, the IACtHR has recognized narratives that transcend this dichotomy, acknowledging a diverse range of victims and considering the broader political and structural contexts surrounding each case.

Throughout its jurisprudence, the IACtHR actively shapes the image of the victim, challenging or redefining aspects of the 'ideal victim' stereotype depending on the case. This process is not arbitrary but is aimed at ensuring the protection of human rights. As a result, the image of the victim is dynamic rather than static, adapting to the complexities of each case and the broader context in which it unfolds.

### 3.3 A Closer Image of Justice

Finally, the third key element in which the Court has been particularly strategic is in fostering a more accessible image of justice, moving away from the traditional notion of 'distant justice',[46] which is often associated with international or transitional justice. The concept of distant justice refers to practices

44 Nils Christie, 'The Ideal Victim' in Ezzat A. Fattah (ed), *From Crime Policy to Victim Policy* (Palgrave Macmillan UK 1986) 21.

45 Christine Schwöbel-Patel, '"Working It" The Brand of the Ideal Victim' in *Marketing Global Justice: The Political Economy of International Criminal Law* (Cambridge University Press 2021) 127–150.

46 For more about the origin of this concept in terms of transitional justice, see: Paul Gready, 'Reconceptualising Transitional Justice: Embedded and Distanced Justice' (2005) 5 *Conflict, Security & Development* 3–21.

in which courts are geographically, politically, or culturally removed from the communities affected by human rights violations. While geographical distance between an international court and the site of violations can pose challenges, the more pressing concern arises when a court deliberately separates itself – politically, culturally, and philosophically – from the domestic realities of the cases it adjudicates.[47]

The IACtHR has implemented various strategies to bridge this gap, influencing not only its public image but also its approach to cases. One of the most significant initiatives has been holding public hearings and sessions in the countries concerned. As noted by the Executive Secretary of the Court, this approach has been framed as a 'Court with robes and a backpack',[48] portraying an institution that is not confined to a distant courtroom but instead travels to where justice is most urgently needed. This practice allows the Court to engage directly with affected communities, hear diverse perspectives, and make itself more visible and accessible.

Moreover, as Steininger explains, the Court has expanded its engagement through various communication strategies aimed at reaching a broader audience.[49] It has developed accessible and clear materials for individuals without legal expertise, ensuring that its decisions and processes are comprehensible to a wider public. Additionally, through social media, the Court has amplified the voices of individual victims, using their stories to illustrate broader patterns of human rights violations. This victim-centred approach not only raises awareness but also empowers others in similar situations to seek justice, recognizing that many structural challenges transcend national borders.

Together, these strategies illustrate the IACtHR's commitment to fostering a more 'embedded justice' – one that resonates locally, encourages participation, and challenges the perception of international justice as distant or detached. Through this approach, the Court not only strengthens its legitimacy but also actively shapes and leads discussions on how justice can be enacted, reimagined, or contested in different contexts. However, this is not merely a symbolic effort; it has a direct impact on how the Court designs remedies. By engaging more closely with local contexts, the IACtHR has been able to propose reparations that more effectively address the specific realities of victims and affected

---

47 Phil Clark, *Distant Justice: The Impact of the International Criminal Court on African Politics* (Cambridge University Press 2018) 35, https://doi.org/10.1017/9781108576260.

48 Silvia Steininger, 'Creating Loyalty: Communication Practices in the European and Inter-American Human Rights Regimes' (2022) 11 *Global Constitutionalism* 176, https://doi.org/10.1017/S2045381721000241.

49 For further details about this set of practices, see: Steininger, 'Creating Loyalty' (n 48).

communities. This is particularly evident in the case studies that follow, where the Court's proximity to local dynamics is reflected in the way it tailors its remedies to tackle structural human rights violations.

Through its narratives, the IACtHR not only reconfigures representations of violence, victims, and justice but also generates multiple aesthetic perceptions that shape how human rights are understood and advocated for in the region. These evolving representations influence the objectives pursued by the broader community of practice. The following section explores how these changing images play a crucial role in constructing the Court's narrative of impact, focusing on three cases: *Villagrán-Morales et al. v Guatemala ('Street Children')*, *Miguel Castro Castro Prison v Peru*, and *Villamizar Durán et al. v Colombia*.

## 4 DEPLOYING AESTHETIC PERCEPTIONS THROUGH NARRATIVES

One of the most significant ways in which the Inter-American Court constructs aesthetic perceptions is through the narratives embedded in its decisions. These narratives shape key images that structure its reasoning. To explore this dynamic, this section examines three emblematic cases of Inter-American adjudication, selected to illustrate how the Court constructs different images of violence, victims, and justice depending on the specific context of each case.[50] These examples allow us to observe how aesthetic elements influence the portrayal of violence, introduce complexity in the representation of actors, and bring justice closer to the local context.

The first case, *Villagrán-Morales et al. v Guatemala* ('Street Children'), adjudicated by the Court in 1999, condemned Guatemala for the killing of five street children by members of the Guatemalan National Civilian Police. In broad daylight, a pickup truck approached the minors, forced them into the vehicle, and took them away. Their bodies were later discovered bearing signs of physical violence, and forensic reports established that they had been killed by gunshot wounds.

The second case, *Miguel Castro Castro Prison v Peru*, concerns the 1992 'Operative Transfer 1' carried out during President Fujimori's administration. This military operation resulted in the deaths of at least 42 inmates, injuries to 175 others, and the cruel, inhuman, and degrading treatment of 322 additional

[50] These cases were not selected as a representative sample, nor is the analysis intended to support generalizable conclusions. Rather, they serve to illustrate different narrative approaches that invite further exploration should the case sample be expanded.

detainees. The attack specifically targeted suspected members of *Sendero Luminoso* (Shining Path) in the context of the internal armed conflict.

Finally, *Villamizar Durán et al. v Colombia* addresses the extrajudicial executions of civilians by members of the Colombian Armed Forces in three separate incidents linked to the broader pattern of *falsos positivos.* This systematic practice involved executing civilians and later presenting them as guerrilla members killed in combat.

## 4.1 Zooming In or Zooming Out: The Image of Violence

As previously discussed, the Court's narratives create an aesthetic illusion that immerses the reader in a specific representation of violence. However, this image does not fully correspond to reality; rather, it frames the issue by selectively emphasizing particular elements. This framing operates as a descriptive move that zooms in or out to shape an image of violence that aligns with the Court's normative framework. The IACtHR does not depict violence uniformly; instead, it highlights specific facts and contextual conditions depending on the core challenge of each case. In some instances, understanding the broader structural conditions is key, while in others, focusing on the victims' individual experiences provides deeper insight into the human rights violations.

In the *Street Children* case, the Court adopted a zoom-out strategy, framing the violence within a broader structural context. Instead of focusing solely on the specific acts of violence suffered by the children, the Court emphasized how life on the streets subjected minors to extreme vulnerability, making them easy targets for drug abuse, delinquency, and exploitation due to the lack of education and employment opportunities.[51] Furthermore, the Court recognized that most street children had experienced domestic violence, physical and sexual abuse, or severe social and economic deprivation that forced them to flee their homes. By adopting this wider perspective, the Court not only identified the State's failure to guarantee the right to life but also underscored its broader duty to implement protective and assistance measures for children under its jurisdiction.[52]

Nevertheless, the Court's broader perspective did not fully capture the extent of the violence affecting Guatemalan society at the time. While the *Street Children* case provided a wider frame for understanding systemic factors behind human rights violations against children, it still omitted crucial aspects of the broader social and political context. The ruling described social

[51] Ismene Zarifis, 'Guatemala: Children's Rights Case Wins Judgment at IACHR' (2001) 9 *Human Rights Brief* 20.

[52] *Case of the 'Street Children' (Villagran-Morales et al.) v Guatemala* (n 18).

conditions that were part of a larger crisis affecting the entire Guatemalan population, which had suffered thousands of deaths during a prolonged armed conflict. The 1980s and 1990s were marked by a devastating internal war that disrupted Guatemalan society and triggered a severe economic recession.[53] The Guatemalan Truth Commission estimated that approximately 200,000 people were killed during the 36-year conflict, with over 90 per cent of the killings, torture, and other acts of violence perpetrated by state security forces and their allies.[54]

In contrast, in *Miguel Castro Castro Prison v Peru*, the Court acknowledged the broader context of the internal armed conflict but focused primarily on the specific conditions of the victims. The Peruvian government argued that the military operation against the prison was a legitimate security measure within the context of the conflict. However, the Court framed the events differently, emphasizing that the inmates were already under State custody and that their actions were aimed at survival rather than confrontation.[55] This distinction was central to the Court's reasoning, as it excluded the possibility of justifying the use of force based on the broader context of political violence.

The Court established that the inmates of Miguel Castro Castro Prison were victims of human rights violations committed by the State. Since they were deprived of liberty, they were under the State's direct custody, which entailed a duty of protection.[56] While the State has the authority to maintain security and public order, it must do so within the limits of domestic law and human rights standards. In this case, the Court found no justification for the use of force, and even if one had existed, the scale of the operation was deemed disproportionate.[57]

Finally, in *Villamizar Durán et al. v Colombia*, zooming out was essential to understanding the magnitude of the case. By adopting a broader perspective, the Court was able to identify a recurring pattern in the extrajudicial executions it examined. The Court noted five consistent elements across the incidents:

1. They all occurred in areas with ongoing military operations.

---

[53] Susanne Jonas, 'Democratization Through Peace: The Difficult Case of Guatemala' (2000) 42 *Journal of Interamerican Studies and World Affairs* 9–38, https://doi.org/10.2307/166340.

[54] Daniel Rothenberg, *Memory of Silence: The Guatemalan Truth Commission Report* (Palgrave Macmillan 2016) 17, https://doi.org/10.1057/9781137011145.

[55] *Miguel Castro Castro Prison v Peru* (n 19) para 242.

[56] *Miguel Castro Castro Prison v Peru* (n 19) para 221.

[57] *Miguel Castro Castro Prison v Peru* (n 19) paras 240–245.

2. They were preceded by the arbitrary detention or disappearance of the victims.
3. The bodies were found in locations different from where the detentions took place.
4. Evidence was manipulated or concealed after the executions.
5. The deaths were officially reported as combat casualties.[58]

Although the Court adjudicated only three incidents in this case, numerous *falsos positivos* cases remain under investigation at both national and international levels. What was initially portrayed as isolated misconduct by individual soldiers is now being examined as a potential State policy, shaped by internal guidelines from the Ministry of Defence that established economic incentives to increase combat casualties.[59]

The three cases illustrate different narrative strategies, depending on the nature of the violations and the applicable normative framework. The Court either zooms in or zooms out on the image of violence, adjusting its narrative accordingly. Whether it employs a structural image of violence or an atrocity aesthetic depends on the case, ultimately, the objective is to find the most effective way to acknowledge victims' rights.

By strategically shifting perspectives, the IACtHR influences how human rights violations are understood and responded to. Through zooming out, the Court connects individual cases to broader patterns of systemic violence, making structural recommendations aimed at preventing future violations. Conversely, by zooming in, it highlights the direct suffering of victims, emphasizing the State's failure to uphold its immediate obligations. This aesthetic modulation is critical in reinforcing the Court's normative objectives, as it ensures that legal reasoning aligns with both contextual realities and broader human rights frameworks.

Through its aesthetic choices, the IACtHR does not merely interpret human rights violations – it actively shapes how they are perceived, remembered, and addressed. By constructing narratives that blend legal argumentation with compelling imagery, the Court reinforces the legitimacy of human rights norms and expands the reach of its jurisprudence beyond individual cases, influencing both regional and global human rights discourse.

---

[58] IACtHR, 'Informe Anual de La Comisión Intermericana de Derechos Humanos 2006. Capítulo IV. Colombia' (*Corte IDH,* 2006) https://www.cidh.oas.org/annualrep/2006sp/cap4a.2006.sp.htm#_ftnref31.

[59] Ministerio de Defensa Nacional de Colombia, 'Directiva Ministerial 29' (2005).

## 4.2 Acknowledging the Complex Reality Behind the Image of the Victims

Closely linked to the image of violence, the portrayal of victims can either conform to the conventional characteristics of the 'ideal victim' or diverge from them, depending on the descriptive approach that best conveys their experiences and acknowledges their rights. A key aspect of the IACtHR's jurisprudence is its expansion of the category of 'victim' to include individuals whose experiences may not fit the conventional 'ideal victim' stereotype but nonetheless constitute human rights violations.

In the *Street Children* case, public institutions such as the judiciary and police treated the victims as delinquents deserving punishment rather than as children in need of protection. Within the local context, their status as minors was overshadowed by the perception that living on the streets inherently placed them at risk, stripping them of the attributes typically associated with the 'ideal victim'. This perception is reflected in testimonies such as that of Rosa Angélica Vega, who recounted how police officers threatened her and her friends, telling them they were 'good for nothing' and would be 'better off dead'.[60] Despite this prevailing narrative, the Court emphasized that three of the five victims were still minors, challenging dominant perceptions and reinforcing their legal status as children.

As Lemaitre points out, the dissonance between these identities creates an almost fantastical narrative when the Court refers to armed young men with adult voices and aggressive sexuality as children.[61] This decision underscored to both the human rights community and the general public that, regardless of the circumstances that led these youths to criminal activities, they remained children with rights.

In *Miguel Castro Castro Prison v Peru*, the categories of victim and victimizer were not mutually exclusive due to the context of the Peruvian internal conflict. *Operative Transfer 1* resulted in a high number of victims who were allegedly members of the guerrilla group *Sendero Luminoso* and, as such, could also be perceived as perpetrators. This case broadens the notion of victimhood, necessitating a more complex narrative approach.

As members of an armed group, the victims of the operation did not fit the description of the 'ideal victim'. Their vulnerability was questioned, and from a perspective beyond the *case sub judice*, they were also regarded as responsible for other crimes. The tension surrounding the decision became even more

---

[60] *Case of the 'Street Children' (Villagran-Morales et al) v Guatemala* (n 18) para 16.

[61] Julieta Lemaitre Ripoll, *El derecho como conjuro: fetichismo legal, violencia y movimientos sociales* (Siglo del Hombre 2009) 396.

pronounced when the Court ordered the State to commemorate the victims by including their names in the monument *El Ojo que Llora* (*The Eye That Cries*), a significant public acknowledgment of victims of violence in Peru.[62]

*El Ojo que Llora* serves as a collective memorial, symbolizing the vast impact of the conflict while preserving a sense of individual loss and trauma through a performative process of mourning and remembrance.[63] By issuing this order, the Court disrupted the prevailing tendency to frame *victim* and *perpetrator* as binary opposites, influencing both the aesthetics of memorialization and the broader political reality of social reconciliation. Rather than simplifying victimhood, the Court expanded its definition, employing aesthetics to illustrate the diverse experiences of victims through a monument embedded in Lima's urban landscape.

However, this reframing of victimhood was not without controversy. Supporters of former President Fujimori vandalized *El Ojo que Llora* by covering it in bright orange paint – a colour associated with his political movement.[64] This act exemplifies the broader struggle to redefine the discourse of *good* and *evil* in favour of more nuanced normative standards. Notably, by ordering the modification of a piece of art, the IACtHR not only recognized a category of victimhood that challenges the conventional 'ideal victim' image but also ignited a significant political debate, in which human rights discourse confronted and prevailed over dominant local narratives of the Peruvian conflict.

In contrast, in *Villamizar Durán et al. v Colombia*, a clear departure from previous cases emerges. The victims of extrajudicial executions were portrayed as members of armed groups and were officially recorded as having been killed in combat. This shift in their legal identity carried significant consequences, as categorizing them as armed actors altered the applicable legal framework, potentially invoking international humanitarian law and activating the jurisdiction of military courts.

Moreover, authorities strategically employed the ideal victim image to delegitimize the claims, arguing that the victims were not innocent civilians but instead members of armed groups. For example, in the broader context of the *falsos positivos* cases, former President Álvaro Uribe, when questioned about the case of eleven young men who disappeared in Soacha and were later found

---

62 *Miguel Castro Castro Prison v Peru* (n 19) para 254.

63 Robin Adele Greeley and Michael R Orwicz, 'An Aesthetics of the Human: Peru's Ojo que Llora Memorial' (2019) 18 *Visual Communication* 358, https://doi.org/10.1177/1470357219842610.

64 Greeley and Orwicz (n 63) 362.

dead in Ocaña, dismissed the claims of extrajudicial execution.[65] Uribe contended that the young men 'were not going to pick coffee; they went with criminal purposes'. Given the persistent denial of the facts, the Court's ruling was significant in vindicating the victims – not to reinforce a narrative of vulnerability, but to expose the way legal frameworks had been manipulated to justify human rights violations. Furthermore, recognizing the victims was crucial for their families, as it restored their dignity after the government had long denied their status as victims of State violence.[66]

These cases highlight the complexities of victimhood, demonstrating how the image of the victim can be constructed, challenged, or distorted depending on the context. From the criminalization of street children to the shifting narratives in extrajudicial executions, the Court's decisions contest traditional notions of the 'ideal victim' and instead focus on the broader need to acknowledge rights.

## 4.3 Notions of Justice

As previously discussed, the Court's approach to justice appears to reflect a movement away from a traditional, detached notion of distant justice toward a more accessible and locally engaged form of *embedded* justice. While this chapter does not aim to offer a comprehensive historical account, the selected cases illustrate how the Court's narrative strategies and reparations orders can be shaped by its proximity to local realities. Rather than making a claim about linear evolution, the analysis highlights moments where the Court's framing of justice engages structural concerns and interacts with broader social and political contexts. This transformation is evident in the Court's adjudication of individual cases, where its proximity to local realities not only informs its decisions but also shapes the reparations it orders.

In the *Street Children* case, the representation of violence was limited, and as a result, the remedies focused on guaranteeing reparations and ordering further investigations to establish responsibility.[67] As one of the Court's earlier cases, it did not yet incorporate a *structural* approach to justice. Nonetheless, it serves as a clear example of how the framing of images and narratives within

65 IACtHR, 'Informe Anual de La Comisión Intermericana de Derechos Humanos 2008. Capítulo IV. Colombia' (*Corte IDH*, 2008) para 68 http://www.cidh.oas.org/annualrep/2008sp/cap4.Colombia.sp.htm.

66 See: Laurence Burgorgue-Larsen and Amaya Úbeda de Torres, 'War in the Jurisprudence of the Inter-American Court of Human Rights' (2011) 33 *Human Rights Quarterly* 154.

67 *Case of the 'Street Children' (Villagran-Morales et al.) v Guatemala* (n 18) para 59.

a case influences its outcome, shaping the Court's approach and broader interpretation of the facts.

By contrast, in *Miguel Castro Castro Prison v Peru*, the Court's ruling extended beyond individual reparations. It ordered the inclusion of the victims' names in an existing memorial, which sparked a national debate. Additionally, the Court framed the case in such a way that it mandated the State to implement human rights education programmes on applicable international standards regarding the treatment of prisoners, to be integrated into the training of Peruvian security forces.[68] Since the case emphasized the State's responsibility toward those in its custody, a *structural* remedy aimed at preventing future mistreatment of prisoners was deemed necessary. These reparations not only acknowledged the specific experiences of the victims but also sought to address systemic issues within the prison system, offering a more comprehensive and lasting solution.

Similarly, in *Villamizar Durán et al. v Colombia*, the Court's decision not only vindicated the memory of the victims and restored the dignity of their families, but also contributed to the recognition of the rights of other victims not included in the case by ordering further investigations.[69] This case exemplifies how *structural justice* extends beyond isolated rulings, demonstrating how the Inter-American Human Rights System interacts with local actors over time to promote broader societal change.

For example, the Inter-American Commission on Human Rights (IACHR) has played a critical role in monitoring events related to the Colombian armed conflict. Since 2006, the IACHR has reported an increase in extrajudicial executions attributed to State security forces. However, the Colombian government initially denied these allegations, asserting that reported cases were combat deaths and that any alleged violations of international humanitarian law fell under military jurisdiction.[70] More than a decade later, Colombia's Special Jurisdiction for Peace (JEP) opened *Macro Case 003*, establishing that between 2002 and 2008, approximately 6,402 people were unlawfully killed and falsely presented as combat casualties.[71]

In 2021, the IACHR admitted the case *Alix Fabián Vargas Hernández et al v Colombia*, which pertains to this issue.[72] Following this admission, the

---

68 *Miguel Castro Castro Prison v Peru* (n 19) para 157.

69 *Villamizar Durán et al. v Colombia* (n 20) para 82.

70 IACtHR, 'Informe Anual de La Comisión Intermericana de Derechos Humanos 2006. Capítulo IV. Colombia' (n 65) para 24.

71 AUTO No 033 de 2021 (Jurisdicción Especial para la Paz 12 de febrero de 2021).

72 *Alix Fabián Vargas Hernández et al. v Colombia* (Admissibility) IACtHR No 1922-21 (29 November 2021).

IACtHR has continued to monitor *Case 003*, demonstrating respect for domestic institutions and the transitional justice process. This case is particularly significant because political actors in Colombia continue to deny the existence of systematic violations, asserting that 'the good name and prestige of the armed forces cannot be stained by the crimes and administrative faults committed by some of its members'.[73] This situation illustrates how the Inter-American System seeks to implement structural justice – justice that acknowledges and respects national actors and institutions while remaining vigilant against potential injustices.

Through its jurisprudence, the IACtHR's vision of *embedded justice* transcends the mere application of legal norms – it becomes a dynamic, performative construct that actively shapes the Court's remedies. By carefully constructing its narratives, the Court ensures that its reparations are not only legally sound but also socially meaningful, influencing both immediate redress and long-term structural transformation.

In conclusion, the three images – violence, victimhood, and justice – are essential tools through which the IACtHR shapes the narratives of each case. The Court's approach to these images is not rigid; rather, it adapts to the specific circumstances of each case, strategically emphasizing certain aspects to support its normative objectives. While the image of violence establishes the framework for understanding the scope of the violation, the portrayal of the victim influences the application of rights, and the image of justice helps define the remedies and their broader social implications. The interplay between these images reflects the Court's flexibility in constructing narratives that not only address the unique facts of each case but also advance structural justice within diverse contexts.

## 5 CONCLUSION

The ultimate role of the Inter-American Human Rights System is to articulate a vision of how reality should be, not only guiding the State and its institutions but also mobilizing the community of practice around these normative goals. The role of aesthetics in the Court's narratives is crucial in shaping both the perception and impact of human rights discourse. Throughout this chapter, we have examined how the Court constructs and modulates representations of violence, victims, and justice, influencing how these realities are understood and internalized by the community of practice. This aesthetic dimension is not

[73] See: Karl Penhaul, 'Colombian Military Fires 27 Soldiers in Probe of Killings' *CNN* (Bogotá, 2008) https://edition.cnn.com/2008/WORLD/americas/10/29/colombia.firings/index.html.

merely ornamental; rather, it serves as a foundational mechanism for sense-making, aligning individual and collective understandings with the broader normative objectives of the human rights system.

Aesthetic perception functions as an interactive process, engaging members of the community of practice beyond passive reception. The IACtHR does not simply present legal arguments; it crafts compelling narratives that incorporate sensory and emotional engagement to reinforce normative commitments. By structuring cases through carefully constructed narratives and imagery, the Court enables the human rights community to connect with violations in a manner that is not only rational but also affective and experiential. This, in turn, fosters a shared sense of meaning and urgency in addressing such violations.

The Court's portrayal of human rights cases demonstrates the adaptability of its aesthetic strategies. While legal narratives often compete with national-level interpretations of events, the Court's ability to frame cases in ways that resonate with its audience enhances its influence. This adaptability does not indicate an arbitrary construction of reality; rather, it reflects an ongoing negotiation of meaning, ensuring that human rights discourse remains relevant to evolving social and political contexts.

Ultimately, the aesthetic dimension of the IACtHR's narratives plays a fundamental role in consolidating the community of practice. It establishes a common ground where legal reasoning, moral imperatives, and sensory perception intersect, shaping both understanding and action. Recognizing the significance of aesthetics in this process allows for a more comprehensive appreciation of how human rights are not only articulated but also experienced and internalized, thereby reinforcing their transformative potential in the region.

# 5. A theoretical model for measuring the impact of urgent measures aimed at protecting at-risk detainees in Latin America

**Clara Burbano Herrera, Yves Haeck and Alberte Verwohlt Hansen**

## 1 INTRODUCTION

This contribution presents a theoretical model for understanding and measuring the impact of urgent measures (UMs) in the context of deprivation of liberty in Latin America.[1] This model requires the inclusion of the voices of those deprived of their liberty, state authorities and members of international human rights bodies in the analysis. Understanding the context and the environment of a person deprived of liberty is also highly valuable as it provides insights into how impact might manifest differently across society, can inform us about the wider impact of UMs, and could also assist in informing interventions to improve the usefulness of this legal tool.

Specifically, this chapter will situate the analysis of the impact of UMs in the context of Latin America. The decision to tackle the issue from a strictly Latin American perspective reflects an understanding of the unique challenges to the human rights of persons deprived of their liberty posed by various

[1] This chapter was developed by the authors within the framework of the Programme for Studies on Human Rights in Context at Ghent University (Belgium) and funded by the European Research Council (ERC) (Grant Agreement No. 101044852), as part of the ERC Project IMPACTUM, and Research Fund at Ghent University. Views and opinions expressed are, however, those of the authors only and do not necessarily reflect those of the European Union, the European Research Council Executive Agency, nor Ghent University. Neither the European Union nor the granting authority can be held responsible for them.

prison systems[2] and political regimes[3] in this region. Moreover, the solutions, initiatives and concepts designed in Latin America regarding crime and the deprivation of liberty offer profound insights that are valuable for understanding human rights violations in the context of deprivation of liberty from a non-Western and decolonial perspective.[4] In so doing, this contribution builds on previous research by two authors of this contribution, who have already analyzed the compliance rate and impact of UMs for persons deprived of their liberty, by examining the actions implemented by the states in response to UMs for their prison population.[5] Additionally, with regard to the methodology, the previous study employed desk-based research for its analysis of UMs[6] and relied on the information provided by international human rights bodies. This chapter aims to extend the analytical framework, thereby offering a more profound and comprehensive examination of the theoretical and methodological approach. In this regard, this theoretical framework proposes a mixed research approach, combining desk research with a qualitative research methodology to assess impact.

The chapter is divided into two sections. The first section contains six subsections. This short introduction, (1), is followed by a discussion of the meaning of the terms 'deprivation of liberty' and 'urgent measures', (2), which is crucial for the understanding of the remainder of the chapter. Subsequently, an in-depth analysis is provided, building upon previous research on the topic. This involves an extensive examination of five key components that constitute our conceptualization of impact, (3). Thereafter, various levels of analysis are introduced and presented, namely the micro, meso and macro levels of analysis, (4). Next, the theoretical model is positioned within the Latin American context, where we reflect upon various power dynamics and other important considerations when conducting research in Latin America, (5) and (6). The

2 Jennifer Peirce and Gustavo Fondevila, 'Concentrated Violence: The Influence of Criminal Activity and Governance on Prison Violence in Latin America' (2019) 30(1) *International Criminal Justice Review* 99–130.

3 Katherine E. Limoncelli, Jeff Mellow and Chongmin Na, 'Determinants of Intercountry Prison Incarceration Rates and Overcrowding in Latin America and the Caribbean' (2019) 30(1) *International Criminal Justice Review* 10–29.

4 David R. Goyes and Máximo Sozzo, 'Latin American Criminologies: Origins, Trajectories and Pathways' (2023) 6(1) *Justice, Power and Resistance* 2–18.

5 Clara Burbano Herrera and Yves Haeck, 'The Impact of Precautionary Measures on Persons Deprived of Liberty in the Americas' in Par Engstrom (ed), *The Inter-American Human Rights System. Impact Beyond Compliance* (Palgrave Macmillan 2019) 89–113, 97–102.

6 ibid.

second section of the chapter contains two subsections that offer a reflection on how to apply such a model in practice by considering evaluation strategies, research methodologies and ethical considerations pertinent to this theoretical framework, (7), and a description of what the framework looks like in practice, (8). The chapter ends with a conclusion, (9). We wish to underline that methodological practicalities, ethical considerations and risk mitigation strategies should be considered in depth every time the framework is applied, and should be adapted according to the circumstances emerging during the fieldwork. Therefore, the chapter refrains from offering a rigid overview of how to apply the theoretical framework in practice; rather, it highlights several critical aspects to consider when applying the framework in a real-world context.

## 2 CONTEXTUALIZATION OF RESEARCH

Prior to presenting the theoretical framework for measuring the impact of UMs in the context of deprivation of liberty, it is essential to define two key terms that will be used throughout this text, namely 'persons deprived of their liberty' and 'urgent measures'.

### 2.1 Persons Deprived of their Liberty

The UN Human Rights Committee ('the Committee' or 'the HRC') defines persons deprived of liberty as those 'subjected to any form of arrest, detention or imprisonment'[7] who require 'special protection against torture and other ill-treatment'.[8] This includes individuals who are in police custody, in remand detention, in prison, under house arrest, in administrative detention or subject to involuntary hospitalization.[9] According to the Optional Protocol to the Convention against Torture and Other Cruel, Inhuman or Degrading Treatment or Punishment, deprivation of liberty means 'any form of detention or imprisonment or placement of a person in a public or private custodial setting, from which this person is not permitted to leave at will, by order of any

[7] HRC, General Comment No. 20 on Article 7: Prohibition of Torture, or Other Cruel, Inhuman or Degrading Treatment or Punishment (10 March 1992), paras 10–11.

[8] Ingrid Nifosi-Sutton, *The Protection of Vulnerable Groups Under International Human Rights Law* (Taylor & Francis 2017) 88.

[9] HRC, General Comment No. 35 on Article 9: Liberty and Security of Person (16 December 2014), CCPR/C/GC/35, para 5. See also: Subcommittee on Prevention of Torture and Other Cruel, Inhuman or Degrading Treatment or Punishment, General Comment No. 1 on Article 4 of the Optional Protocol (Places of Deprivation of Liberty), 4 July 2024, CAT/OP/GC/1.

judicial, administrative or other public authority'.[10] This means that individuals can be deprived of their liberty in a large variety of settings, including, but not limited to, police stations, detention centres, prisons, and mental health and social care institutions.

In certain instances, deprivation of liberty can be justified, for example, when enforcing criminal laws. However, such deprivation should never be arbitrary or without a sufficient legal basis, and human rights still apply to individuals deprived of their liberty.[11] Nonetheless, the rights of those deprived of liberty are sometimes violated and they are, by definition, a vulnerable group as '[t]hey have been taken out of their normal environment and are no longer allowed to manage their own lives'.[12] Persons deprived of liberty are in a special situation of submission with respect to the state, which is entitled to regulate their rights and obligations.[13] Furthermore, the vulnerability of a person deprived of liberty can be amplified by factors such as sex, age, sexual orientation, state of health, and economic status.[14] Lastly, individuals in prison are often perceived by certain societal groups as deserving of their appalling prison conditions, making this a particularly important group to protect.[15]

Evidently, deprivation of liberty is a broad term. However, in this chapter, we will focus specifically on individuals deprived of their liberty in jails or

---

[10] Optional Protocol to the Convention against Torture and other Cruel, Inhuman or Degrading Treatment or Punishment, Article 4(2), Adopted 18 December 2002. See also United Nations, Rules for the Protection of Juveniles Deprived of their Liberty, 14 December 1990, para 11(b).

[11] *Case of Mota Abarullo et al. v Venezuela*, Judgment (IACtHR) (18 November 2020), para 88; and *Case of Bulacio v Argentina*, Judgment (IACtHR) (18 September 2003); IACHR, Report No. 122/18, Case 11.656. Merits (Publication) *Marta Lucia Alvares Giraldo v Colombia* (2018), para 165; and Inter-American Commission on Human Rights (IACHR), *Report on the Human Rights of Persons Deprived of Liberty in the Americas*, 2011, paras 49, 71, 189.

[12] International Committee of the Red Cross (ICRC), 'Protecting People Deprived of their Liberty. Reports and Documents', (2016) 98(3) *International Review of the Red Cross* 1043–1066, 1043.

[13] See Flavia Piovesan and Sandra Serrano Guzman, 'The Implications of the Principle of Equality and Non-discrimination on the Rights of Persons Deprived of Liberty in the Inter-American System' in Clara Burbano Herrera and Yves Haeck (eds), *Human Rights Behind Bars* (Springer 2022) 36; *Case of Mendoza et al. v Argentina*, Judgment (IACtHR) (14 May 2013), para 152.

[14] ICRC, 'Protecting People Deprived of their Liberty. Reports and Documents' (n 12) 1043.

[15] Burbano Herrera and Haeck, 'The Impact of Precautionary Measures on Persons Deprived of Liberty in the Americas' (n 5) 102.

prisons,[16] which includes both those who have been arrested[17] and those who have already been convicted.[18]

## 2.2 Urgent Measures: Definition, Scope and Types

In international human rights law, 'urgent measures'—also often called 'interim measures', 'provisional measures', 'precautionary measures', 'conservatory measures' or 'immediate measures'—are variously provided for under international human rights treaties, additional protocols to those treaties, and the

16 For the purposes of this research, we follow the terminology used in the UN Body of Principles for the Protection of All Persons under Any Form of Detention or Imprisonment, adopted by the UN General Assembly Resolution 43/173, 9 December 1988.

17 Arrest means the act of apprehending a person for the alleged commission of an offence or by the action of an authority. See UN Body of Principles for the Protection of All Persons under Any Form of Detention or Imprisonment, adopted by the UN General Assembly Resolution 43/173, 9 December 1988, Scope of the Body of Principles.

18 Imprisoned person means any person deprived of personal liberty as a result of conviction for an offence. See UN Body of Principles for the Protection of All Persons under Any Form of Detention or Imprisonment, adopted by the UN General Assembly Resolution 43/173, 9 December 1988, Scope of the Body of Principles.

rules of procedure of the respective human rights bodies.[19] In this chapter, we will refer to them as urgent measures (UMs).[20]

In Latin America, UMs can be issued by the Inter-American Commission on Human Rights (IACHR); the Inter-American Court of Human Rights (IACtHR);[21] the Human Rights Committee (HRC); the Committee on the

---

[19] Five UN treaty bodies and two regional human rights courts explicitly received the power to grant UMs from their respective constituent treaty, namely: the Committee on the Elimination of All Forms of Discrimination against Women (CEDAW Committee) (Art 5 Optional Protocol to CEDAW); the Committee for the Protection of All Persons from Enforced Disappearance (CED Committee) (Art 31(4) CPED); the Committee on the Rights of the Child (CRC Committee) (Art 6(1) Optional Protocol to Convention on the Rights of the Child); the Committee on the Rights of Persons with Disabilities (CRPD Committee) (Art 4 Optional Protocol to Convention on the Rights of Persons with Disabilities); the Committee on Economic, Social and Cultural Rights (CESCR) (Art 5 Optional Protocol to International Covenant on Economic, Social and Cultural Rights); the IACtHR (Art 63(2) American Convention on Human Rights), and the African Court on Human and Peoples' Rights (ACtHPR) (Art 27(2) Protocol to the African Charter on Human and Peoples' Rights on the Establishment of an African Court on Human and Peoples' Rights). These powers are specified further in their respective rules of procedure. The remaining three relevant UN treaty bodies and four relevant regional human rights bodies have incorporated the power to grant urgent measures in their rules of procedure (RoP), namely: the Human Rights Committee (HRC) (Rule 92 HRC RoP); the UN Committee Against Torture (Rule 114 CAT RoP); the Committee on the Elimination of Racial Discrimination (CERD Committee) (Rule 94(3) CERD RoP); the European Court of Human Rights (Rule 39 Rules of the Court); the European Committee of Social Rights (Rule 36 Rules of Procedure); the IACHR (Art 25 IACHR RoP); and the African Commission on Human and Peoples' Rights (ACHPR) (Rule 100 ACHPR RoP). Sometimes additional Guidelines (CESCR, *Guidelines* [2019]; CRC Committee, *Guidelines* [2019]) or a Practice Direction (ECtHR, *Practice Direction* [2003]) provide for further guidance.

[20] Chester Brown, *A Common Law of International Adjudication* (Oxford University Press 2007); Yves Haeck and Clara Burbano Herrera, 'Urgent measures' in Christina Binder, Manfred Nowak, Jane Hofbauer and Philip Janig (eds), *Elgar Encyclopedia of Human Rights* (Elgar 2022); Clara Burbano Herrera and Yves Haeck, 'Provisional measures: Inter-American Court of Human Rights' in Hélène Ruiz Fabri (ed), *Max Planck Encyclopedia of International Procedural Law* (Oxford University Press 2019); Cameron Miles, *Provisional Measures before International Courts and Tribunals* (Cambridge University Press 2017).

[21] The IACtHR may request UMs from states that have ratified the ACHR and accepted its jurisdictional competence. As of 2025, only 23 of the 35 member states of the Organization of American States (OAS) have ratified the ACHR,

Elimination of All Forms of Discrimination against Women (CEDAW Committee); the Committee for the Protection of All Persons from Enforced Disappearance (CED Committee); the Committee on the Rights of the Child (CRC Committee); the Committee on the Rights of Persons with Disabilities (CRPD Committee); the Committee on Economic, Social and Cultural Rights (CESCR); the Committee Against Torture, and the Committee on the Elimination of Racial Discrimination (CERD Committee). These human rights bodies can grant UMs, on their own initiative or on the initiative of a party, based on the rights protected by the human rights treaties or other applicable instruments.[22]

UMs aim to preserve a legal situation and the rights of the parties in a legal dispute in order to ensure the effectivity of the judicial proceedings, which can run their proper course, allowing the monitoring body to adopt a final decision without its decision being frustrated through acts or omissions while assessing the case.[23] However, UMs also aim to protect human rights and prevent their violation. They ensure the practical effectiveness of human rights, so that they are not merely theoretical.[24] In that sense, UMs serve two interrelated purposes: they fulfil both a preventive (or precautionary) and a protective role. In their preventive dimension, UMs are issued with the objective of preventing human rights violations. It is therefore evident that these measures give the state the opportunity to act swiftly in order to rectify situations that may result in irreparable damage to the rights of the individual(s) at risk.[25]

---

and of these, only 20 have accepted the contentious jurisdiction of the IACtHR. The states that have accepted the jurisdictional competence of the IACtHR are: Argentina, Barbados, Bolivia, Brazil, Chile, Colombia, Costa Rica, Ecuador, El Salvador, Guatemala, Haiti, Honduras, Mexico, Nicaragua, Panama, Paraguay, Peru, the Dominican Republic, Suriname and Uruguay. On 26 May 1998, Trinidad and Tobago presented an instrument denouncing the ACHR to the Secretary General of the OAS. Pursuant to Article 78(1) of the ACHR, the denunciation took effect one year later, on 26 May 1999. Venezuela also presented an instrument denouncing the ACHR to the OAS Secretary General on 10 September 2012. The denunciation took effect on 10 September 2013.

22 See above note 19.

23 Brown, *A Common Law of International Adjudication* (n 20) 121; Rüdiger Wolfrum, 'Interim (Provisional) Measures of Protection' in Anne Peters and Rüdiger Wolfrum (eds), *Max Planck Encyclopedias of International Law* (Oxford University Press, 2007), paras 4–7.

24 Clara Burbano Herrera, *Provisional Measures in the Case Law of the Inter-American Court of Human Rights* (Intersentia 2010) 1.

25 Clara Burbano Herrera, Yves Haeck and Alessandra Cuppini, 'Transformative Provisional Measures and Prisons in the Americas: Protecting the Invisibles' in Clara Burbano Herrera and Yves Haeck (eds), *Human Rights Behind Bars: Tracing*

Complying with the UMs potentially offers states the opportunity to avoid international responsibility by addressing situations where human rights violations may have occurred.[26] Furthermore, UMs also play a protective role in preserving the rights in question during the adjudication stage.[27] They have protected a variety of people and groups at risk of irreparable harm, including human rights defenders, political opponents, journalists, trade unionists and persons deprived of their liberty.[28] Indeed, it is people deprived of their liberty who are the focus of the highest number of UM requests by the IACHR and the IACtHR.[29] It is feasible to adopt UMs to protect clearly identified at-risk individuals, as well as groups of individuals,[30] including those who, although

---

*Vulnerability in Prison Populations Across Continents from a Multidisciplinary Perspective* (Springer 2022) 142.

[26] Burbano Herrera and Haeck, 'The Impact of Precautionary Measures on Persons Deprived of Liberty in the Americas' (n 5) 90; Burbano Herrera, Haeck and Cuppini, 'Transformative Provisional Measures and Prisons in the Americas: Protecting the Invisibles' (n 25) 142.

[27] For an in-depth study of urgent measures in the Inter-American human rights system, see Burbano Herrera, *Provisional Measures in the Case Law of the Inter-American Court of Human Rights* (n 24); Antonio Cançado Trindade, 'The Evolution of Provisional Measures Under the Case Law of the Inter-American Court' (2003) 24 *Human Rights Law Journal* 162–168; Edgar Corzo Sosa, *Medidas Provisionales de la Corte Interamericana de Derechos Humanos* (Tirant lo Blanch 2014); Felipe González, 'Urgent Measures in the Inter-American Human Rights System' (2010) 7(13) *Revista SUR* 51–73; Jo M. Pasqualucci, 'Medidas provisionales en la Corte Interamericana de Derechos Humanos: una comparación con la Corte Internacional de Justicia y la Corte Europea de Derechos Humanos' (1994) 19 *Revista IIDH* 47–112; Jo M. Pasqualucci, 'Provisional Measures in the Inter-American Human Rights System: An Innovative Development in International Law' (1993) 26(4) *Vanderbilt Journal of Transnational Law* 803–863; Eva Rieter, *Preventing Irreparable Harm: Provisional Measures in International Human Rights Adjudication* (Intersentia 2010); Loretta Vazquez Ortiz, *Las Medidas Provisionales de la Corte Interamericana de Derechos Humanos* (Porrúa 2010).

[28] Burbano Herrera, *Provisional Measures in the Case Law of the Inter-American Court of Human Rights* (n 24) 68–85; Rieter, *Preventing Irreparable Harm: Provisional Measures In International Human Rights Adjudication* (n 27); Loretta Vazquez Ortiz, *Las Medidas Provisionales de la Corte Interamericana de Derechos Humanos* (n 27) 185–196.

[29] IACHR, n.d. About Precautionary Measures, https://www.oas.org/en/IACHR/jsForm/?File=/en/iachr/decisions/about-precautionary.asp, para 3; Burbano Herrera and Haeck, 'The Impact of Precautionary Measures on Persons Deprived of Liberty in the Americas' (n 5) 90 and 94.

[30] Burbano Herrera, *Provisional Measures in the Case Law of the Inter-American Court of Human Rights* (n 28) 68–79.

not identified by name, can be distinguished by objective criteria, such as all people deprived of liberty who are currently detained in a particular prison or who may enter that prison in the future.[31]

In previous academic work, the term 'transformative provisional measures' was introduced to refer to provisional measures adopted by the IACtHR that aim to protect the rights of a number of people who are collectively at risk, such as all inmates in an overcrowded prison.[32] Transformative provisional measures possess three key characteristics: firstly, they address structural problems (such as prison overcrowding); secondly, they seek to protect multiple individuals in situations of extreme gravity and urgency; and thirdly, they involve orders that must be complied with by more than one state body. The failure of public authorities to implement public policies that respect, guarantee and do not discriminate against traditionally excluded groups in society, such as persons deprived of their liberty, has led to structural problems that require transformative provisional measures.[33]

Behind the prison reality lies a complex institutional framework that creates, facilitates and perpetuates situations of extreme gravity and urgency for persons deprived of their liberty.[34] Within this context, standards and practices lead the basic rights of vulnerable groups, such as those of persons deprived of liberty, to be under constant threat and also rendered invisible. In such a reality, it is not sufficient for a single UM to address a sole authority or to call for a singular public policy change, as the situation is one of extreme gravity on several levels in society.[35] It is therefore evident that, to address these

---

[31] For example, in 2017 and 2018 UMs were adopted by the IACtHR to protect the life and integrity of all persons deprived of liberty at the Instituto Penal Placido de Sa Carvalho, numbering 3,820 detainees. See IACHR, *The Socio-Educational Internment Facility of the Penitentiary Complex of Curado, of the Penitentiary Complex of Pedrinhas and the Instituto Penal Plácido de Sá Carvalho v Brazil*, Provisional Measures (22 November 2018 and 13 February 2017).

[32] See Clara Burbano Herrera and Yves Haeck, 'The Use of Transformative Provisional Measures by the Inter-American Court of Human Rights: Toward a Tangible Impact' in Armin von Bogdandy, Flavia Piovesan, Eduardo Ferrer-MacGregor and Mariela Morales Antoniazzi (eds), *The Impact of the Inter-American Human Rights System. Transformations on the Ground* (Oxford University Press 2024) 153–175.

[33] ibid.

[34] Claudio Nash and Constanza Núñez, 'Sentencias Estructurales Momento de Evaluacion, Sobre los Derechos Sociales', 2015 *Revista de Ciencias Sociales (Volumen Monografico Extraordinario)* 284.

[35] According to Nash and Núñez, there are two types of states: (a) states that do not act for ideological reasons, and where the establishment of fundamental rights has not been sufficient to mobilise domestic political decisions; and (b) states that

complex situations, it is necessary to tackle the legal, political and cultural conditions that allow them to occur.[36] In order to respond effectively to situations of extreme risk and urgency, various authorities at the domestic level are required to engage in coordinated action[37] and collaborative participation.[38]

## 3 BROADENING THE ANALYSIS OF THE IMPACT OF URGENT MEASURES FOR PEOPLE DEPRIVED OF LIBERTY IN LATIN AMERICA

A limited number of scholars have undertaken research on UMs with a particular focus on individuals deprived of their liberty in Latin America.[39] Moreover, there exists a significant gap in the existing literature concerning the understanding of the impact of UMs that extends beyond mere compliance. Previous studies have highlighted the utility of UMs for individuals at risk in Latin America, noting that UMs have predominantly been adopted to protect those incarcerated.[40] It has also been emphasized that individuals in prison constitute a vulnerable population in need of prompt protection of their human rights. The granting of UMs for people in prison has been justified on

---

do not have the capacity to act because they lack territorial control or economic resources, or are captured by interest groups. See Nash and Núñez, 'Sentencias Estructurales Momento de Evaluación, Sobre los Derechos Sociales' (n 34) 267–289. The authors refer to Jonathan Di John, 'Conceptualización de las causas y consecuencias de los Estados fallidos: una reseña crítica de la literatura' (2010) 37 *Revista de Estudios Sociales* 46–86; Joel S. Hellman, Geraint Jones and Daniel Kaufmann, 'Capture al Estado, capture el día. Captura del Estado, corrupción e influencia en la transición' (2001) 21 *Gestión y Análisis de Políticas Públicas* 35–62.

36 See Nash and Núñez, 'Sentencias Estructurales Momento de Evaluación, Sobre los Derechos Sociales' (n 34) 287.

37 See for example *Instituto Penal Placido de Sa Carvalho v Brazil*, Provisional Measures (IACtHR) (22 November 2018) Considering paras 61, 62, 68, 69, 72 and 79.

38 See Burbano Herrera and Haeck, 'The Use of Transformative Provisional Measures by the Inter-American Court of Human Rights; Toward a Tangible Impact' (n 32) 153–175.

39 E.g., Burbano Herrera and Haeck, 'The Impact of Precautionary Measures on Persons Deprived of Liberty in the Americas' (n 5) 89–113. For Africa and the Americas, see Clara Burbano Herrera and Frans Viljoen, 'Danger and Fear in Prison: Protecting the Most Vulnerable Persons in Africa and the Americas by Regional Human Rights Bodies through Interim Measures' (2015) 33(2) *Netherlands Quarterly of Human Rights* 163–193.

40 See above note 29.

the grounds of protecting individuals sentenced to death without a fair trial, those with health issues and lacking access to healthcare, and those living in poor conditions.

In addition, the limitations and complexities of studying UMs should be recognized. However, we would like to suggest various essential considerations when assessing the impact of UMs on at-risk persons deprived of their liberty. Based on our previous findings, this section will serve as the foundation for deepening the analysis and including other aspects necessary for conceptualizing impact. The following observations regarding the impact of UMs will be presented: (1) when considering the actors, the impact of UMs can be direct, indirect and symbolic; (2) when considering implementation, the impact of UMs is closely linked to levels of compliance and non-compliance; (3) when considering evaluation, the impact of UMs can be positive, negative, both or neither; (4) when considering the temporal dimension, the impact of UMs can occur over the short, medium and long term (*an evolving characteristic*); (5) when considering the level of analysis, the impact can be evaluated at the micro level, the meso level and the macro level; and (6) when considering external factors, the impact of UMs can be influenced by power dynamics (for the two latter points see subsections 5 and 6).

## 3.1 When Considering the Actors: The Impact of UMs can be Direct, Indirect and Symbolic

Building on existing conceptualizations of impact and deepening the analysis within the framework of UMs in the prison context, the impact of UMs can be defined as the effects of the request(s) made within the adopted UMs. These effects can be considered in three distinct dimensions, namely: (a) the effects on the beneficiaries (*direct impact*); (b) the effects beyond the beneficiaries (*indirect impact*), which encompasses the impact on relatives of the beneficiaries, people living in their neighbourhoods, other persons deprived of their liberty, prison staff, and national, regional and global institutions;[41] and (c) the effects of producing changes in attitudes, ideas or ideology, or simply in terms of producing new ways of looking at things (*symbolic impact*); the latter can be further subdivided into direct symbolic impact and indirect symbolic impact.

A few examples of the different forms of impact may serve to illustrate how each may manifest in practice. An example of *direct impact* would be the recovery of ill prisoners who have received adequate medical treatment following the UMs, while an example of *indirect impact* would be a decrease

[41] Burbano Herrera and Haeck, 'The Impact of Precautionary Measures on Persons Deprived of Liberty in the Americas' (n 5) 93.

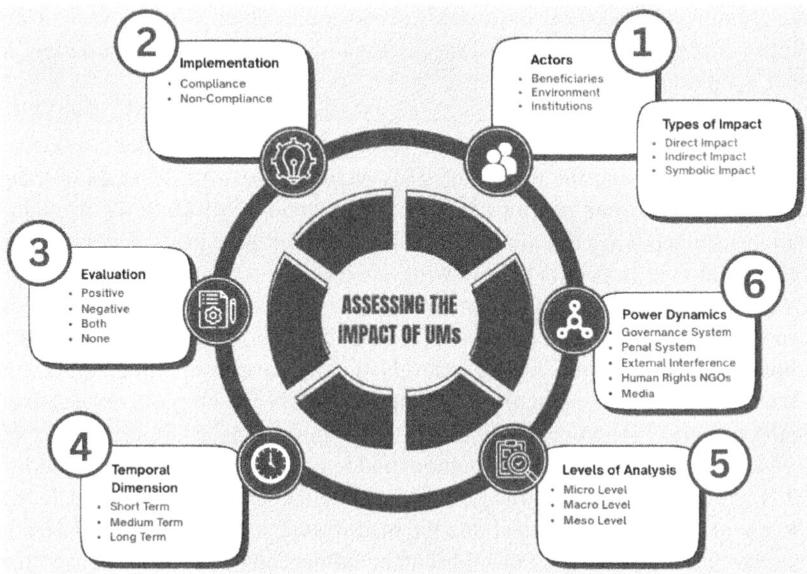


*Figure 5.1* *Theoretical model for measuring impact in the context of deprivation of liberty in Latin America*

in the rate of overcrowding in a prison. As examples of *symbolic impact*, it is conceivable that the detainees who are the foucs of the UMs may begin to regain hope for a brighter future and perceive their incarceration in a different manner (*direct symbolic impact*), or that UMs might alter the public perception of detainees and create public awareness (*indirect symbolic impact*).

## 3.2 When Considering Implementation: The Impact has Close Links with Compliance and Non-Compliance

The term 'compliance' is associated with the actions undertaken by the state in question to abide by the requests made by the international human rights body in the UM decisions or resolutions.[42] As mentioned, we argue that impact is related to the effects of the UMs on the beneficiary and beyond the beneficiary. For instance, amongst others within the Inter-American human rights system (IAHRS), a form of compliance in the area of detention issues relates to the transfer of sick detainees to a specialist hospital. In such cases, the impact may entail the full recovery of the sick detainee (*direct impact*). Other examples of

[42] ibid, 98.

compliance in this context could include suspending an order to implement the death penalty, the hiring of additional prison staff or adapting the detention infrastructure and conditions to those minimally necessary to provide a decent life to the person deprived of their liberty.[43]

On other occasions, states may have failed to undertake any actions following the issuance of an UM. However, it must be emphasized that instances of non-compliance with an UM may also exert an impact, which can result in effects on the beneficiary (*direct impact*) and beyond the beneficiary (*indirect impact*).[44] For instance, the request itself can already have an impact on the beneficiary and/or society; for example, if there is news coverage of the request for an UM.

In order to gain a comprehensive understanding of the full effects of a UM, it is therefore essential to consider both the compliance and non-compliance with the measure. Nevertheless, it is evident that compliance or lack of compliance affects the beneficiary or beneficiaries of a UM directly and most prominently. Moreover, it is important to recognize that establishing whether UMs were the sole cause of a change in the situation of a beneficiary or beyond can be a challenging endeavour. A more detailed examination of this topic will be provided in subsection 5 on power dynamics.

Significant methodological struggles were encountered in our previous research when attempting to assess compliance with UMs, as there was a substantial lack of information, especially related to the limited reporting by

---

43 ibid, 98–99.

44 While compliance is not a prerequisite for UMs to have an impact, it can nevertheless play a role in this regard. According to Engstrom (2019), who looks at the issue from an international human rights perspective, compliance refers to 'the implementation of treaty rules and decisions – rulings, recommendations – handed down by international human rights institutions'. He argues that compliance with judicial rulings does not necessarily have an impact on the people or groups that should benefit from the legal innovation. He also highlights that compliance does not necessarily equate to an impact for the beneficiaries, while also noting that impact can sometimes occur even in the absence of compliance. This can in part be explained because high levels of compliance can be met with ineffective standards and that non-compliance can be effective if it induces changes in behaviour. Thereby, he recognizes that compliance is only a small part of impact, and that solely focusing on compliance would bypass the variety of effects of international human rights. As an example, he states that an individual ruling can have an impact by setting norms and standards in the international community, and that these can be used in future cases and as inspiration. Par Engstrom, 'Introduction: Rethinking the Impact of the Inter-American Human Rights System' in Par Engstrom (ed), *The Inter-American Human Rights System: Impact Beyond Compliance* (Palgrave Macmillan 2019) 4–5.

the international human rights monitoring body on the follow-up of UMs. Additionally, petitioners and states sometimes fail to provide information to the human rights body.[45] The information supplied by, for example, the IACHR and the UN Human Rights Committee is, on many occasions, limited and varies depending on the UMs and the specific period examined.[46] This limits potential further analysis of the compliance with and impact of UMs. While the lack of information poses a barrier to establishing the extent of compliance and impact of UMs, we explained how this information can sometimes be found outside of official IACHR reports, through news coverage of the issue, for example,.[47]

Additionally, there is considerable variation in how states respond to received UMs (see subsection 5 on power dynamics). Factors such as the political affiliation of the president of the state concerned (the executive) or the role of the director of the specific prison may influence the response.[48]

### 3.3 When Considering Evaluation: The Impact of UMs can be Positive, Negative, Both or Neither

The potential impact of the UMs may be either positive (beneficial) or negative (detrimental). As the wording of the definition indicates, a positive impact is defined as the implementation of the UM resulting in a favourable outcome

---

[45] Burbano Herrera and Viljoen, 'Danger and Fear in Prison' (n 39), 163, 171 (notes 44–45), 186, 188, 191; Clara Burbano Herrera and Luna Lanckvrind, 'Assessing the Impact of Interim Measures adopted by the UN Human Rights Committee in Protecting Persons Deprived of Liberty in Latin America' in Clara Burbano Herrea and Yves Haeck (eds), *Human Rights in Latin American Prisons: Towards a More Comprehensive Understanding* (Brill 2025).

[46] Burbano Herrera and Viljoen, 'Danger and Fear in Prison' (n 39) 171 (notes 44–45), 175 (note 75), 188, 191; Burbano Herrera and Lanckvrind, 'Assessing the Impact of Interim Measures adopted by the UN Human Rights Committee in Protecting Persons Deprived of Liberty in Latin America' (n 45).

[47] Burbano Herrera and Haeck, 'The Impact of Precautionary Measures on Persons Deprived of Liberty in the Americas' (n 5) 102.

[48] For instance, in 2004, the then president of Colombia, Álvaro Uribe, explicitly referred to beneficiaries of UMs as actors obstructing justice. In 2003, the then Venezuelan president, Hugo Chávez, stated that even a cabinet minister did not have the protections which were requested by the petitioners of UMs. In 2014, the then president of Ecuador, Rafael Correa, expressed that the IACHR lacked the authority to adopt UMs. See *Case of Peace Community of San Jose de Apartadó Case v Colombia*, Provisional Measures (IACtHR) (17 November 2004) Explanatory Statement 18; and *Case of Liliana Ortega et al. v Venezuela*, Provisional Measures (IACtHR) (21 February 2003).

for the beneficiary (*direct positive impact*) or beyond the beneficiary (*indirect positive impact*).

To illustrate, if a male detainee who is sick, and following the adoption of an UM, receives the medication that he requires (compliance) and subsequently recovers his health, we can speak of a *positive impact*. Nevertheless, it is also possible that the outcome may be negative. For example, if the state, as a result of an UM, employs additional prison officials (*compliance*) with the objective of controlling violence within the prison facility, but these new officials have not received (adequate) training in accordance with human rights standards, they might attempt to control violence through the use of disproportionate force, ultimately exacerbating the problem (*negative impact*). Furthermore, a negative impact can also occur when a state, in response to a request for UMs, not only declines to comply with the request(s) made in the adopted UMs, but in addition decides to denounce the American Convention on Human Rights.[49] In instances where human rights bodies perceive the potential for UMs to result in a negative impact, this may act as a barrier to their future adoption (*indirect impact on the human rights body itself*).

It was previously indicated that the impact may be either positive or negative.[50] However, a dichotomous measurement system of impact would fail to explain any nuance in the outcome of an UM. To elaborate further, it is possible that the outcome of an UM is both negative and positive simultaneously, or that it may vary depending on the perspective from which it is observed. Moreover, it might be a complex combination of positive and negative outcomes and/or thereby fail to fall into those categories at all.

To illustrate, while a stay of execution is inarguably defined as a positive (direct) impact of an UM, the experience of this by the beneficiary might be more nuanced as suspension could trigger a prolonged state of uncertainty,[51] while simultaneously giving hope for the future. As another example shows, relocating detainees because of inhumane prison conditions might be classified as positive from a management perspective, but for the detainees themselves this might have negative implications for the possibilities of visits from their

[49] ibid.

[50] Burbano Herrera and Haeck, 'The Impact of Precautionary Measures on Persons Deprived of Liberty in the Americas' (n 5) 93.

[51] Adeleye discusses how waiting for the death penalty and a date of execution constitutes specific cruel and inhumane treatment as, amongst other things, it creates a prolonged state of uncertainty about one's life. See Nkem Adeleye, 'The Death Row Phenomenon: A Prohibition against Torture, Cruel, Inhuman and Degrading Treatment or Punishment' (2021) 58 *San Diego Law Review* 875–902.

support network.[52] This might result in the impact of the UM being defined differently depending on the perspective of the individual person deprived of liberty, or even of the specific actor(s) involved (e.g., judge, minister of justice or relative).

There are numerous possible ways in which the impacts of UMs could be interpreted and experienced, and as an alternative to a two-sided scale to define the impact, we propose identifying the wide range of impacts an UM can generate. A related issue is the need for an analysis at different levels to capture the full range of different perspectives. This aspect will be addressed later.

## 3.4 When Considering the Temporal Dimension: The Impact can Occur Over the Short, Medium and Long Term

t isIt has been stated that impact may occur over a range of timeframes, including short term, medium term and long term.[53] This is essential to consider in at least two ways. First, this is important to consider as Latin America has a volatile political landscape,[54] meaning that the reaction of the governing system is subject to change. Second, it is relevant because the impact(s) of UMs can look different depending on the point in time at which it is assessed. To elaborate further, there may be certain impacts following the adoption of an UM that are only perceptible over time, which bring an alternative perspective to the impact assessed immediately after the UM was requested. In other words, to create a full image of the impact of an UM, it is necessary to consider its evolution over time. Consequently, the fourth cornerstone of our concept of impact is its evolving characteristic.

It is important to note that this aspect should not be confused with the ongoing evaluation provided by the international human rights body. Indeed, the necessity of the UM in a specific case is subject to ongoing evaluation and can therefore have a short-term, medium-term or long-term duration. In this regard, the decision regarding the lifting or maintenance of the UM is at the discretion of the international human rights body. This determination is made

---

[52] The Prison Reform Trust (2017) describes how being held in an establishment far from family and friends can make it difficult for them to come visit (e.g., Bromley Briefings Prison Factfile (Autumn 2017) 54). If someone is relocated to a prison further away than where they were staying, this could have negative consequences for the possibilities of people in their support network to come and visit them, causing them to describe the impact of the UM as negative.

[53] Burbano Herrera and Haeck, 'The Impact of Precautionary Measures on Persons Deprived of Liberty in the Americas' (n 5) 98–99.

[54] Alejandro Rodriguez, 'Defining Governance in Latin America' (2019) 19(1) *Public Organization Review* 5–19, 17.

on a case-by-case basis, taking into account the specific circumstances of danger in each instance.[55]

# 4 LEVELS OF ANALYSIS

Four key components of the concept of impact of UMs have been identified. These components take into consideration the actors, their links with compliance, the range of impact, and the evolving character. This section will explain the manner in which the concept of impact can operate at different levels of analysis, namely the micro level, the meso level and the macro level.

Previous work discussed the impact of UMs on individuals deprived of their liberty. Furthermore, in that work it was acknowledged that problems within prisons do not solely affect the detainees, but also the staff and visitors. This underscores the notion that UMs can have an impact that extends beyond the individuals (*beneficiaries*) to whom they are directly applied.[56] While previous research does consider the impact of UMs at the level of the beneficiaries (*direct impact*) and beyond the beneficiaries (*indirect impact*), the voices/perspectives of these groups are still missing from the research. It is for this reason that another aim of this framework is to devise a methodology that will enable these perspectives to be included in order to gain a more comprehensive assessment of the impact of UMs. This will be achieved by proposing three levels of analysis, namely the micro level, the meso level and the macro level.

This section serves to give an overview of who is included in the different levels of analysis and how the various types of impact might manifest themselves at these different levels. In addition, different levels of analysis can influence each other. For example, social movements can voice support for people deprived of their liberty (meso level), resulting in the state deciding to implement UMs (macro level) and beneficiaries receiving aid (micro level). Actions at one level can therefore cause change at another.

## 4.1 Micro Level

The micro level relates to the direct beneficiaries of the UMs and thus is connected to the direct impact. Depending on what the UM dictates, beneficiaries

---

[55] Burbano Herrera, *Provisional Measures in the Case Law of the Inter-American Court of Human Rights* (n 24) 169–78; Edgar Corzo Sosa, *Medidas Provisionales de la Corte Interamericana de Derechos Humanos* (n 27) 54–62.

[56] Burbano Herrera and Haeck, 'The Impact of Precautionary Measures on Persons Deprived of Liberty in the Americas' (n 5) 103; Burbano Herrera, Haeck and Cuppini, 'Transformative Provisional Measures and Prisons in the Americas: Protecting the Invisibles' (n 25) 16.

are usually in this instance persons deprived of their liberty. In certain circumstances, the international human rights body may also consider including other individuals as beneficiaries, such as the relatives of beneficiaries of UMs, and employees and officials inside the prison.[57] Therefore, it is essential to conduct a thorough review of each resolution of UMs during the analysis phase, in order to identify who is the beneficiary protected by the UM.

In order to assess the impact of UMs at the micro level, the beneficiaries' experiences with the UM must be included. Critical to including their voices is to ensure that research is conducted *with* the prison population, rather than *on* the prison population. As established, people deprived of their liberty are a particularly vulnerable population, and they are often excluded from conversations about their well-being, resulting in policies being developed on speculations and assumptions about what is best for them.[58] This is particularly problematic as there are many aspects to being deprived of liberty that may not be considered by people who are not in that same situation.

Additionally, when researching the impact of UMs at the micro level it is important to consider the diversity of people deprived of their liberty before making claims about impact. What holds true for one group of people deprived of liberty might not apply to other people deprived of liberty who are experiencing different circumstances. It is thereby essential to apply an intersectional approach, taking into consideration, for instance, gender, sexual orientation, age, race, ethnicity, health, type of sentencing,[59] number of dependents,[60]

---

[57] *Case of Mendoza Prison v Argentina*, Provisional Measures (IACtHR) (30 March 2006), Having seen para 1.

[58] Justin Berk, Josiah D. Rich and Lauren Brinkley-Rubinstein, 'What are the Greatest Health Challenges Facing People Who are Incarcerated? We Need to Ask Them' (2021) 6(10) *The Lancet Public Health* 703–704.

[59] Victoria Lavis, 'Intersectionality and the Prison Crisis: What is it as a Concept and Why Does it Matter Today in Understanding Current Problems in Prison?' in Anastasia Chamberlen, Charlotte Weinberg and Anita Dockley (eds) (2019) 243 *Prison Service Journal*, 'The Prison Crisis – Special Edition' 243; Lucia Bracco Bruce, *Decolonising and De-Patriarchalising Prison: Governance, Social Life and Gendered Subjectivities in a Women's Prison in Peru* (University of Warwick 2010) 26.

[60] Monica Dargis and Arielle Mitchell-Somoza, 'Challenges Associated with Parenting While Incarcerated: A Review' (2021) 18(18) *International Journal of Environmental Research and Public Health* 9927, 2–16.

nationality,[61] level of education, economic status, language, and marital status.[62]

To illustrate the potential impact of UMs at the micro level, the example of a detainee receiving medical support may be considered. In such a case, we might observe changes such as renewed hope for the future, or a sense of being listened to or ignored. In other words, it could be that detainees feel their voice is being heard to a greater or lesser extent; they might feel more or less dependent on the system, or more or less hopeless about their situation. In this case, we could propose that these UMs have the potential to generate a positive or negative symbolic impact at the micro level.

Naturally, these speculations about how impact could look at different levels of analysis are only hypotheses and should not be taken as self-evident. The impact of UMs at these levels needs to be documented, which is what this framework sets out to do.

### 4.2 Meso Level

The meso level refers to individuals who are not included as persons to be protected by the state authorities in the resolution of UMs.[63] The meso level refers to the environment of the persons deprived of their liberty, including their family, their friends, other people in their neighbourhood, and other people in the detention facility (such as their children, other people deprived of liberty, and visitors), that might be affected by implementing UMs. This assumption is made because incarceration can have consequences for the environment of the detainee in various ways.

Firstly, it has been documented that the detention of one individual can result in an overload of care tasks for others,[64] or even the total abandonment

---

[61] Jelmer Brouwer, 'Bordered Penality in the Netherlands: The Experiences of Foreign National Prisoners and Prison Officers in a Crimmigration Prison (2020) 22(5) *Punishment & Society* 703–722.

[62] See Piovesan and Serrano Guzman, 'The Implications of the Principle of Equality and Non-discrimination on the Rights of Persons Deprived of Liberty in the Inter-American System' (n 13) 35–57.

[63] As mentioned in the previous subsection, beneficiaries are typically the individuals deprived of their liberty. However, in certain cases, human rights bodies may also extend beneficiary status to individuals connected to them, such as those in their immediate environment. Therefore, it is crucial to carefully review the resolution of UMs to determine who should be included at each level of analysis.

[64] Astrid Liliana Sánchez-Mejía, Leonardo Rodríguez Cely, Gustavo Fondevila and Juliana Morad Acero, *Mujeres y prisión en Colombia: desafíos para la política criminal desde un enfoque de género* (Pontificia Universidad Javeriana 2018).

of certain tasks.[65] More specifically, if a parent or caretaker is incarcerated, the rights of the child outside are often harmed as their lives can become marked by instability and violence, and they are generally less protected. It has been determined that within Latin America a disproportionate number of individuals in prison come from marginalized communities.[66] Concretely, this can mean that the child of a detainee may also end up in a state institution, is left without anyone to take care of them, is at a higher risk for child labour, and is less likely to follow an education.[67] As women are often the main caregivers of

---

65 Correspondingly, in 2023, the International Network of Women Relatives of Persons Deprived of Liberty (RIMUF) and, in 2024, the Programme for Human Rights in Context and IMPACTUM research group (Ghent University, Belgium) made an oral presentation before the IACHR and the IACtHR, respectively. The presenters described the additional burdens that deprivation of liberty imposes on the relatives of persons deprived of liberty and requested recognition of these relatives as a group in a situation of special vulnerability. RIMUF is a network of associations and organizations of women relatives of persons deprived of their liberty in countries such as Argentina, Brazil, Colombia, Costa Rica, El Salvador, Spain, Mexico and Ecuador. See *Public Hearing on the Request for Advisory Opinion on the Content and Scope of the Right to Care and Its Interrelation with Other Rights*, 14–16 March 2024, San José, Costa Rica. See also: Clara Burbano Herrera et al., *El contenido y el alcance del derecho al cuidado y su interrelación con otros derechos humanos: Contribución en el marco de la solicitud de opinión consultiva por parte de la República de Argentina ante la Corte Interamericana de Derechos Humanos* (Costa Rica 2023). Additionally, see IACHR, *Public Hearing on the Impact of Women Relatives of Persons Deprived of Their Liberty in the Americas*, 12 July 2023; and Paula Casco and Laura Maccarrone – Red Internacional de Mujeres familiares de Personas privadas de La Libertad (RIMUF), *Informe sobre el impacto de la cárcel en las mujeres familiares y las afectaciones a sus derechos humanos* (RIMUF s.d.).

66 Sánchez-Mejía et al., *Mujeres y prisión en Colombia: desafíos para la política criminal desde un enfoque de género* (n 64).

67 Annette Lyth and Cecilia Anicama, *Children Speak about the Impact of Deprivation of Liberty: The Case of Latin America* (Office of the SRSG on Violence against Children/United Nations Publications 2016) 24–26.

children[68] in heterosexual relationships,[69] these consequences are especially noticeable when a mother is incarcerated.[70] Furthermore, as states neglect to take proper care of people in prison, their relatives – mostly women – make up the majority of people who care for those in prison across Latin America. They are often responsible for procuring food, medicines, and other essential needs that states fail to provide.[71]

Secondly, it can create or deepen economic poverty. Detention and incarceration can harm the wider neighbourhood, as it risks destabilizing the social capital and informal social control through the mass incarceration of certain groups. This is especially evident in poor and minority communities with high incarceration rates.[72] Explicitly, it can lead to 'strain and stress associated with the incarceration as well as stigma',[73] financial difficulties for dependents, but also the wider society when eligible workers are removed en masse from the workforce, and can also affect feelings of safety in the neighbourhood.[74] Accordingly, including the voices at the meso level is essential, as it helps gain

---

[68] For instance, a study conducted between 1991 and 2018 reveals that the majority of women deprived of liberty in Colombia share the following profile: they are of productive and reproductive age, self-identify as heterosexual, are single, and have a low socio-economic status. A significant proportion of these women had a monthly family income of less than two legal minimum wages prior to their detention. Furthermore, most of these women (75%) were heads of households, highlighting their responsibility for the economic well-being of their families. Their limited education has contributed to a workforce that is vulnerable in the face of precarious employment opportunities. See Sánchez-Mejía et al., *Mujeres y prisión en Colombia: desafíos para la política criminal desde un enfoque de género* (n 64) 11.

[69] Carlos Gailán, Mónica Rubio, Gerardo Escaroz and Alejandre Florencia, *Review of Care and Support Systems in Latin America and the Caribbean: a Framework for UNICEF Action* (2023).

[70] Lyth and Anicama, *Children Speak about the Impact of Deprivation of Liberty: The Case of Latin America* (n 67) 24.

[71] Isabelle Oliver and Josefina Salomón, *The Invisible Resistance to Latin America's Prison Systems* (WOLA Advocacy for Human Rights in the Americas, 2022) para 6; Corina Giacomello et al., 'Women's Incarceration and the Impact of Drug Policies in Latin America and Mexico', in Clara Burbano Herrea and Yves Haeck (eds), *Human Rights in Latin American Prisons: Towards a More Comprehensive Understanding* (Brill 2025).

[72] Todd R. Clear and Chase L. Montagnet, 'Impact of Incarceration on Community Public Safety and Public Health' (2021) *Public Health behind Bars*, 13–29.

[73] Elizabeth J. Gifford, 'How Incarceration Affects the Health of Communities and Families' (2019) 80(6) *North Carolina Medical Journal* 372.

[74] ibid, 372–375.

insight into the broader indirect impacts of the UMs and could, in turn, help devise measures to avoid harmful effects of deprivation of liberty.

An impact of UMs at this level could, for example, mean that the visiting conditions change, making it easier (or less easy) to visit the person in prison. Relatedly, the impact might be that the family then has more time and resources to dedicate to other activities. As the person is now better taken care of by the system, this frees up the family's time and resources which can instead be invested in activities for their own benefit. It could also mean that the community receives new hope for the future of the detained person. In this case, we would propose that UMs have the potential to generate a positive symbolic impact at the meso level.

### 4.3 Macro Level

It is essential to understand how UMs work from the perspective of the human rights bodies which granted them, as well as the authorities who have to implement the UMs in practice (i.e., prison staff), and to grasp the operational, financial, political and institutional challenges and difficulties related to UMs. The term 'macro level' is used to describe all impacts that can be observed at the institutional level, including those occurring at the national, regional and global levels. This encompasses all the impacts of UMs on international and national authorities' initiatives, including changes in domestic law, references in case law, public discourse from authorities, and reforms in international human rights bodies. The macro level is also connected to the indirect impact.

The impact of UMs at the macro level may include fostering new debates within parliament, as well as reframing the situation of the detainee(s) within public discourse and official documents. Such a shift in perspective could also prompt a change in the authorities' opinion of the incarcerated individuals. Furthermore, it could entail the establishment of effective participatory mechanisms that guarantee the contribution of those who have been traditionally excluded. Alternatively, the state could take other actions, such as reforming laws and policies to prevent further human rights abuses. In this case, we propose that these UMs have the potential to generate a positive impact at the macro level over the long term.

## 5. THE LATIN AMERICAN CONTEXT AND ITS POWER DYNAMICS

There are five crucial and relevant aspects of the *power dynamics* in the region that can influence whether and how UMs in Latin America in the context of deprivation of liberty are able to have an effect. Therefore, these aspects are important to consider from the very start when analyzing the impact of UMs in a particular country. As they are socially fluctuating factors, these aspects are also likely to intersect and influence each other.

Latin America is a vast region, with many differences between its 33 countries. The authors of this chapter therefore by no means wish to treat Latin America as a homogeneous whole, and instead seek to pay attention to the extensive variability between countries in the region. Nevertheless, there are some general considerations to be made when striving to analyze the deprivation of liberty, UMs and their impact in Latin America. This is important to consider at the outset of creating a theoretical framework, as there are some foreseeable obstacles and limitations to conducting research with prison systems in Latin America. Additionally, to understand, and thus to assess the impact of UMs, it is critical to understand the power dynamics in the region. Consequently, a number of factors that could potentially influence the impact of UMs were identified. In this contribution, we have identified these as *power dynamics*, which include a range of elements, namely governance and penal systems, external interference, human rights NGOs and the media, all of which are relevant to the context in which UMs operate.

It is crucial to gain an understanding of these factors, as states have distinctive relationships with their own institutions, and states themselves are responsible for implementing the requested UMs. Furthermore, it is essential to contextualize the research in terms of the legal and socio-political factors present in the geographical location in which the UMs operate. These factors inevitably affect the outcome of the UMs and therefore must be taken into account.

In this regard, the following subsection contextualizes UMs in Latin America, highlighting these five crucial and relevant aspects of power dynamics in the region that influence the extent to which UMs in situations of deprivation of liberty are able to exert an impact. It is therefore important to consider these aspects from the outset when analyzing the impact of UMs in a given state. As has been mentioned, it is likely that these aspects will intersect and influence each other, given that they are socially fluctuating factors.

## 5.1 Governance Systems

The different governance systems[75] in Latin America are a first factor that can influence the outcome of UMs. Rodriguez underlines the variations in governance systems and history within Latin American states, while highlighting

[75] The governance system relates to the regime under which decisions are made, and the degree to which power over a given decision is shared among actors, or across different sectors.

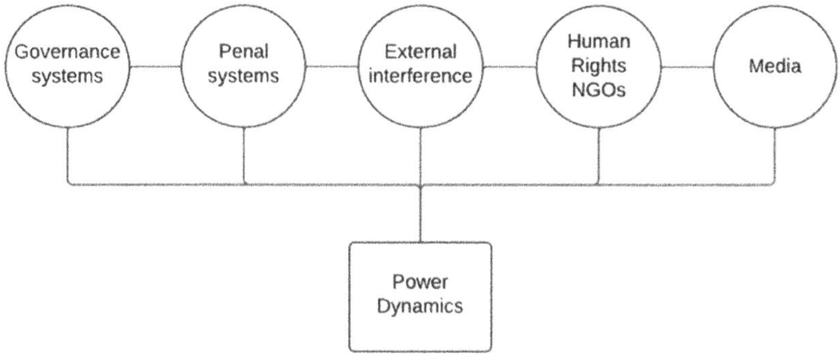


*Figure 5.2* *Illustration of five aspects of power dynamics where UMs operate, essential for contextualizing UMs regarding deprivation of liberty and for understanding their impact*

some general concerns with governing bodies in the region. Latin American states have several historical factors in common, such as the influence of colonialism and authoritarian regimes, which affect their contemporary governance structures.[76]

While democratization, decentralization and citizen participation have spread throughout the region and have had a significant influence, several ongoing issues continue to challenge these efforts. As an example of the various challenges to systems of governance, Rodriguez discusses political instability, different levels of corruption within the ruling institutions, the trust of the population in the government, the strength of the judicial system, and the degree of democracy. As a common factor, he concludes that governments in Latin America seem to be highly hierarchical and lack collaboration between the different sectors of society. In addition, he mentions the socio-economic and political inequalities with which countries in the region continue to struggle.[77]

Relatedly, Villa et al. describe a system of hybrid governance in South America[78] and highlight how violent non-state actors (VNSAs) may provide

[76] Rodriguez, 'Defining Governance in Latin America' (n 54) 5–19.
[77] ibid, 15–17.
[78] Rafael Duarte Villa, Camila de Macedo Braga and Marcos Alan S.V. Ferreira, 'Violent Nonstate Actors and the Emergence of Hybrid Governance in South America' (2021) 56(1) *Latin American Research Review* 36–49.

services where the state fails to.[79] This results in these actors mirroring services that would typically be expected of formal government, such as physical protection and social security. More specifically, this can include provision of public goods, such as security, food, and creating employment, and even controlling the prison system.[80] This means the authority over certain regions is shared between the state and alternative organizations, if not fully led by the latter. In other words, VNSAs create complex governance structures that mix formal state authority with informal local power structures. This hybrid system of governance typically occurs in regions where state institutions are weak or absent, allowing violent non-state actors to exert influence and even legitimacy in the eyes of local populations. In some socially marginalized spaces, VNSAs even gain community support and sometimes fulfil public roles, complicating efforts to fully reestablish state control. Violent non-state actors consequently challenge traditional conceptions of state sovereignty and security as they fill governance voids rather than simply engaging in criminal activities.[81]

Latin America thus presents a uniquely challenging political climate, and being aware of the sometimes turbulent and changing governance systems is essential to understanding the response of states to UMs. Consequently, understanding how UMs are received in different regimes and settings is of interest when assessing the extent of implementation (compliance) and the impact they may have on persons deprived of their liberty.

## 5.2 Penal Systems

The penal systems in the Latin American region are a second decisive factor which may influence the outcome of UMs. Similar to the above, there are some overlapping concerns about the penal systems across Latin America. Understanding the incarceration rate, the political and social stance towards those imprisoned, and the organization of the prisons is essential for discerning how UMs operate within the systems they are supposed to have an impact on. Peirce and Fondevila, for example, begin their work by underlining the considerable variation in the management of Latin American prison

[79] While in their contribution Duarte Villa, Macedo Braga and Ferreira (2021) mention the rising social violence within Latin America, they focus on the situation in the South American region, with a specific focus on Brazil and Colombia. ibid.

[80] ibid, 46.

[81] Duarte Villa, Braga and Ferreira, 'Violent Nonstate Actors and the Emergence of Hybrid Governance in South America' (n 78) 36–49.

systems, including differences in 'political and social context, infrastructure and resources, programmes and services, and internal culture and social interactions'.[82]

While in some countries, prisons are managed at the federal level, in others these facilities are overseen by authorities at the state or even the local level. However, Peirce and Fondevila persist in drawing attention to a range of general problems within the Latin American penal system, including overcrowding, harsh drug laws, the excessive use of pretrial detention, poor or inadequate investigations and judicial proceedings, the lack of separation between individuals sentenced and those awaiting trial, scarce state-provided resources, permeable and unregulated prisons with a low staff-to-inmate ratio, and prisoner-led governance. To illustrate how some of these similar issues manifest differently across situations, they explain that in some countries a fragmented criminal landscape leads to inter-gang rivalries, while in others centralized criminal groups dominate, influencing the prison's power structure more coherently.[83]

The conditions listed previously contribute to an overall high level of violence in Latin American prisons. Again, it should be noted that the circumstances leading to criminal activity and the differing governance systems play a role in shaping the penal system. In other words, criminal organizations, institutional control and governance systems influence the prison system in Latin America, and should be taken into account when trying to analyze the overall situation and/or to bring about change.[84]

Considering these many variables, it thus becomes evident that a comprehensive understanding of the penal system and prison management within the Latin American context is crucial for contextualising the impact of UMs.

## 5.3 External Interference

External interferences may also play a certain role with regard to the outcome of UMs. It is essential to consider colonial, imperial, and other sorts of external interference in the region when attempting to understand its contemporary organizational systems. Goyes and Sozzo analyze the development of criminological theory in Latin America and observe how 'Northern' countries (referring mainly to the United States and Europe) traditionally impose theories and policies which undermine an understanding of the Latin American context of crime from a decolonial perspective and the creation of a model adaptable

82 Peirce and Fondevila, 'Concentrated Violence: The Influence of Criminal Activity and Governance on Prison Violence in Latin America' (n 2) 100.

83 ibid.

84 ibid.

to specific problems in the region.[85] Initially, criminology in Latin America was shaped by colonial legacies, authoritarian regimes and social inequalities, leading to a criminological approach that emphasized structural and social justice issues. Over time, the criminological approach started to diverge from European and North American models, developing a focus on issues specific to Latin America, such as poverty, political violence and the impacts of globalization.[86] An example of the imperativeness of a Latin American perspective is given in the study of Peirce and Fondevila, who found that classical North American and European theories of prison violence failed to explain the prison violence in Latin America, and moreover described how Northern research strategies were not applicable in the Latin American context. More precisely, they found that traditional North American and European theories of prison violence did not fully account for the complex dynamics present in Latin American prisons. They failed to look past individual behaviour, and to take into account inmate socialization, the prison environment, criminal networks, state corruption, and other general socio-economic and political factors.

In addition, Latin American prisons are generally harder for researchers to access than European and North American prisons (because of safety and political/bureaucratic reasons), and the data provided by the prisons or the prison system is not always complete or reliable. This makes some research strategies harder in Latin American prisons.[87] In a complementary manner, Goyes and Sozzo note that Latin American criminologists frequently employ participatory and ethnographic research methods, allowing researchers to work closely with affected communities, providing insights that challenge dominant narratives about crime and justice.[88] Fischer-Hoffman's concept of carceral coloniality, moreover, looks at prisons 'beyond *locales* of punishment but also as institutions that are shaped by and reinforce hierarchies built on superiority/inferiority-reflecting; coloniality/modernity and eurocentrism', as prisons themselves are 'integral institution(s) in the structural practices of global capitalism, masculinist heterosexism, authority, and a Eurocentric white racism that projects Eurocentrism "as epistemological perspective"'.[89] In other words,

---

85 Goyes and Sozzo, 'Latin American Criminologies: Origins, Trajectories and Pathways' (n 4) 1–17.

86 ibid.

87 Peirce and Fondevila, 'Concentrated Violence: The Influence of Criminal Activity and Governance on Prison Violence in Latin America' (n 2).

88 Goyes and Sozzo, 'Latin American Criminologies: Origins, Trajectories and Pathways' (n 4).

89 Cory Fischer-Hoffman, 'Carceral Coloniality in Venezuela: Theorizing beyond the Latin American Penal State', in: S. Darke, C. Garces, L. Duno-Gottberg,

colonial influence runs through the current penal systems and understandings of criminal policy in Latin America.

Consequently, the application of Northern theories will always fall short in grasping and contextualizing Latin American specific issues, thereby impeding the development of effective solutions to these issues. Moreover, from the perspective that prison systems and current understandings of incarceration are inherently colonial and unjust, it is important to ensure that researching UMs in the region will not lead to the (further) legitimization of prison systems and overincarceration in Latin America.[90] In other words, should the results of this research show that UMs are beneficial for the people incarcerated and have positive effects for society, this should not be interpreted as (further) legitimization of the current prison system. Lastly, other influences could manifest themselves in the form of financial foreign aid to Latin America, with the donors expecting them to operate in a certain way.[91] Decolonial perspectives and research methodologies will be elaborated on later in the chapter.

## 5.4 Human Rights NGOs

NGOs can be a relevant factor influencing the outcome of UMs in Latin America. The Latin American region has historically and contemporarily been characterized by the development and presence of strong social movements and human rights NGOs.[92] Rich describes how the social movements in Latin America manage not only to mobilize publicly, but also to influence policies in a similar way to interest groups, without losing their capacity for public pressure tactics.[93] Social movements in Latin America have adapted from rigid

---

and A. Antillano (eds) *Carceral Communities in Latin America. Palgrave Studies in Prisons and Penology* (Palgrave Macmillan), 163.

90 Chris Cunneen, *Decoloniality, Abolitionism, and the Disruption of Penal Power* (Oxford University Press 2023) 19–36.

91 Goyes and Sozzo, 'Latin American Criminologies: Origins, Trajectories and Pathways' (n 4) 1–17; Alejandro Rodriguez, 'Defining Governance in Latin America' (2019) 19 *Public Organization Review* 5–19.

92 Clara Burbano Herrera and Yves Haeck, 'The Historical and Present-Day Role of Non-Governmental Organisations before the Inter-American Human Rights System in Documenting Serious Human Rights Violations and Protecting Human Rights and the Rule of Law through Ensuring Accountability' (2021) 17(2) *Utrecht Law Review* 8–24.

93 Social movements may be considered as broader, grassroots-driven efforts aiming to achieve wide-scale social change, often challenging systemic inequalities or advocating for fundamental rights. In comparison, interest groups tend to focus on more specific, often policy-oriented, goals that represent the interests of a particular group, industry or demographic, rather than seeking broad social

organisational structures to a more flexible approach, enabling them to navigate political, social and economic changes with greater ease. This flexibility demands finding a constant balance between decentralization and uniting a movement. Their increased flexibility also includes the integration of using online platforms to heighten participation and visibility.[94]

Previous research has elucidated the relevant role of human rights NGOs in Latin America in terms of documenting human rights violations and seeking justice at the national and international level for the victims of those violations, even in contexts where the rule of law has been under attack.[95] Human rights NGOs have been very active at the regional level.[96] The role played by them in Latin America reflects the political reality of repressive regimes and present-day fragile democracies struggling to uphold human rights and rule of law standards. The bleak situation was of a continent almost full of non-democratic states, ruled by military dictatorships, such as Argentina (1976–83), Chile (1973–90), Brazil (1964–85) and Uruguay (1973–85), and/or states confronted with internal armed conflicts, such as Guatemala (1960–96), El Salvador (1979–92), Peru (1980–2000) and Colombia (1960–2016). These regimes were repressive and violent towards society, as almost anyone who was perceived as subversive was quickly arrested, imprisoned, tortured, summarily executed or forcibly disappeared.[97] As a reaction to those repressive regimes, human rights NGOs started to be created, especially in Argentina, in contrast with Brazil or Chile.[98] Some NGOs were founded by relatives of the

transformation. Rich (n 94) suggests that contemporary social movements in Latin America sometimes blend strategies typical of interest groups to enhance their influence, while still maintaining the larger vision and grassroots dynamics that characterize true social movements. This blending of strategies underscores the flexibility and innovation of modern activism.

94 Jessica Alexis Jolicoeur Rich, 'Organising Twenty-First-Century Activism: From Structure to Strategy in Latin American Social Movements' (2020) 55(3) *Latin American Research Review* 430–444.

95 Burbano Herrera and Haeck, 'The Historical and Present-Day Role of Non-Governmental Organisations before the Inter-American Human Rights System in Documenting Serious Human Rights Violations and Protecting Human Rights and the Rule of Law through Ensuring Accountability' (n 92) 8–24.

96 ibid.

97 ibid. See also *Amnesty International Report 1975–76* (1976) 85–116.

98 Alison Brysk, *The Politics of Human Rights in Argentina: Protest, Change, and Democratization* (Stanford University Press 1994); Patrick W Kelly, *Sovereign Emergencies. Latin America and the Making of Global Human Rights Politics* (Cambridge University Press 2018) 215; Héctor Leis, *El movimiento por los derechos humanos y la politica argentina* (Centro Editor de América Latina 1989) 17–19; Burbano Herrera and Haeck, 'The Historical and Present-Day Role

victims of human rights violations[99] and were mostly comprised of nationals of the affected country.[100] That was the case, for example, of the Argentine NGO La Asociación de las Abuelas de La Plaza de Mayo (Association of the Grandmothers of the May Square) created in 1977. The NGO is composed of Argentinian grandmothers whose children were imprisoned or disappeared and whose grandchildren were illegally adopted during the military dictatorship between 1976 and 1983.[101]

Human rights NGOs found the IACHR to be the only platform available to denounce and document the human rights violations which were occurring at the national level.[102] Indeed, they have brought several cases before

---

of Non-Governmental Organisations before the Inter-American Human Rights System in Documenting Serious Human Rights Violations and Protecting Human Rights and the Rule of Law Through Ensuring Accountability' (n 92) 13.

99 This was, for example, the case for CELS, which has been established by the lawyer Emilio Mignone, together with three like-minded lawyers and four women belonging to the Madres de la Plaza de Mayo, all of whom had lost family members (Mignone had lost his daughter) after the coup in Argentina. Burbano Herrera and Haeck, 'The Historical and Present-Day Role of Non-Governmental Organisations before the Inter-American Human Rights System in Documenting Serious Human Rights Violations and Protecting Human Rights and the Rule of Law Through Ensuring Accountability' (n 92) 13.

100 On national and international human rights NGOs: Henry Steiner, *Diverse Partners, Non-Governmental Organizations in the Human Rights Movement, Report of a Retreat of Human Rights Activists* (Harvard Law School Human Rights Program and Human Rights Internet 1999) 4–9; Burbano Herrera and Haeck, 'The Historical and Present-Day Role of Non-Governmental Organisations before the Inter-American Human Rights System in Documenting Serious Human Rights Violations and Protecting Human Rights and the Rule of Law Through Ensuring Accountability' (n 92) 8–24, 13.

101 The NGO brought cases before the Argentinian courts, thereby exhausting domestic remedies, in order to find the children. The NGO is mentioned in the Annual Report of the Commission of 1980. See Burbano Herrera and Haeck, 'The Historical and Present-Day Role of Non-Governmental Organisations before the Inter-American Human Rights System in Documenting Serious Human Rights Violations and Protecting Human Rights and the Rule of Law Through Ensuring Accountability' (n 92) 13.

102 See David Padilla, 'The Inter-American Commission on Human Rights of the Organization of American States: A Case Study' (1993) *American University Journal of International Law & Policy* 95; Monica Pinto, 'NGOs and the Inter-American Court of Human Rights', in Tullio Treves et al. (eds), *Civil Society, International Courts and Compliance Bodies* (Asser Press 2005) 49; Enzamaria Tramontana, 'La Participacion de las ONG en el Sistema Interamericano de Proteccion de los Derechos Humanos: Avances, Desafios y Perspectivas' in Armin

the Inter-American human rights system. Their work must be understood within the context of the specific political and legal-normative framework on the continent.[103] Furthermore, the legal-normative context, i.e., the American Convention on Human Rights and the interpretation provided by the IACHR and the IACtHR to its provisions, has also granted NGOs significant space to engage through various methods, such as by requesting and following up on UMs.[104] Considering the pivotal role played by social movements and human rights NGOs in shaping Latin American public policy,[105] their influence on power dynamics within the region must be carefully considered.

## 5.5 Media

Finally, the media may also influence the outcome of UMs. We use the term 'media' here to refer to the broader public discourse and the manner in which international and national media outlets portray persons deprived of their liberty, prisons, the prison system, UMs, the international human rights bodies that grant UMs, and the authorities who have to implement them. As mentioned, places where people are deprived of liberty and associated with criminal activity are often viewed negatively. The way these individuals are discussed in the media, including the language used to describe them, the stories put forward, and the contextualization of what occurred, naturally plays a role in how people not deprived of liberty perceive them. To clarify, by broader discourse, we include media at the (inter)national and regional levels, personal blogs and influencers, university courses, local councils, and any other means capable of reaching a large audience and potentially influencing the conceptualization of people deprived of their liberty. Should UMs be discussed within the broader public discourse, it is of interest for us to observe how this might alter the perception of UMs and deprivation of liberty more generally.

---

von Bogdandy, Eduardo Ferrer-MacGregor and Mariela Morales Antoniazzi (eds), *La Justicia Constitucional y su Internacionalizacion* (Instituto de Investigaciones Juridicas 2010) 536; Burbano Herrera and Haeck, 'The Historical and Present-Day Role of Non-Governmental Organisations before the Inter-American Human Rights System in Documenting Serious Human Rights Violations and Protecting Human Rights and the Rule of Law Through Ensuring Accountability' (n 92) 13.

103 Burbano Herrera and Haeck, 'The Historical and Present-Day Role of Non-Governmental Organisations before the Inter-American Human Rights System in Documenting Serious Human Rights Violations and Protecting Human Rights and the Rule of Law through Ensuring Accountability' (n 92).

104 ibid.

105 Rich, 'Organizing Twenty-First-Century Activism: From Structure to Strategy in Latin American Social Movements' (n 94).

## 6 THEORETICAL FRAMEWORK

As shown in Figure 5.2, a theoretical framework is presented for assessing the impact of UMs in the context of deprivation of liberty in Latin America. This is a unique framework for measuring impact, applicable to the aims of the research project 'IMPACTUM' and may benefit other scholars who are interested in understanding UMs beyond compliance in the context of prisons in Latin America.[106] However, it was not the goal to create a generalizable framework, as this is never favourable for understanding specific situations nor for considering a range of standpoints.

In order to achieve a thorough analysis of impact, it is essential to examine in depth the concrete situation of risk, the broader context of the case (i.e., the legal system) and the power dynamics. This contribution does not advocate for an *objective analysis*. It is instead suggested that researchers should *attempt to be objective*, and constantly reflect (and explain) on why they are doing something, and to try to understand their own perspective. Social research is often case-dependent with so many variables. Therefore, it is suggested that the diversity of results be embraced.

As previously stated, a number of factors may influence any potential impact that UMs might have. For example, it is relevant to ascertain the circumstances that gave rise to the specific danger, the measures requested by the international human rights body, the actions taken by the state, and the extent to which the beneficiary's situation has been altered following the implementation of the aforementioned measures. It is similarly pertinent to ascertain whether external factors have played a role in influencing the outcome.[107] For instance, an analysis of the potential influence of the media or social activism in specific contexts would be a valuable contribution to the field. Furthermore, the political system of the state concerned may play a significant role in determining the manner in which UMs are implemented and understood.[108] In the context of incarceration, an assessment of the impact of such actions may also require a more comprehensive examination of a number of additional factors,

[106] IMPACTUM is a research project led by Prof Clara Burbano Herrera and funded by the European Research Council (ERC). It analyzes the impact of urgent (precautionary or provisional) measures adopted by international human rights bodies to protect at-risk detainees in six Latin American countries, namely Colombia, Ecuador, El Salvador, Guatemala, Nicaragua and Peru. More information is available at www.humanrightsincontext.be/copy-of-research (accessed 20 July 2025).

[107] ibid, 98.

[108] Burbano Herrera and Haeck, 'The Impact of Precautionary Measures on Persons Deprived of Liberty in the Americas' (n 5) 101.

including the prevalence of overcrowding within the detention facilities and the resources allocated to the prison system as well as any observed changes in the short, medium and long term to the mental and/or physical health of the beneficiaries. Therefore, conducting desk-based research and interviews are both crucial elements of the research process.

## 7. ASSESSING IMPACT: PRACTICAL FRAMEWORK 'REALIST EVALUATION MODEL'

For the purpose of assessing the impact of UMs as outlined in the previously introduced theoretical framework, a practical framework is proposed based on the *realist evaluation model*. A realist evaluation model is useful when there is limited prior knowledge of the topic, which is the case in this study. The main benefit of a realist evaluation model is that it takes into account 'social and behavioural mechanisms that underlie the interventions they assess'.[109] Moreover, a realist evaluation aims to answer the question of how an intervention or policy works, rather than simply looking at whether an intervention or policy works. This means that realist evaluations answer questions such as under which circumstances and for which population this intervention works.[110]

In the interest of our evaluation, this question would be: in what circumstances and for which populations does this UM/do these UMs have an impact (and to what extent) and what does this impact look like? Such questions are crucial when aiming to include several perspectives at different levels of analysis, and especially for making sure that the diverse experiences of people at the micro and meso level are included equally with those of the people operating the systems at the macro level. Moreover, by studying the mechanisms-context configurations of interventions that appear to be ineffective, we can gain valuable insights into the conditions that are necessary for mechanisms to work.[111]

Decolonial scholars have critiqued evaluation methods for adopting Western standards in evaluating outcomes based on Western theory, knowledge and practices. As an example, based on neoliberal values, Western evaluations tend to include economic growth as a measure and equate it with positive development. Adopting a decolonial perspective means not only undoing certain assumptions and practices, but also adopting positive actions that allow for alternative knowledge, the inclusion of local people from where one wishes

---

109 Leontien M. van der Knaap, Frans L. Leeuw, Stefan Bogaerts and Laura T. J. Nijssen, 'Combining Campbell Standards and the Realist Evaluation Approach: The Best of Two Worlds?' (2008) 29(1) *American Journal of Evaluation* 50.

110 ibid.

111 ibid, 55.

to conduct research, and focusing on what benefits their needs and priorities rather than certain systems or the researcher's idea.[112] The next subsection on research methodologies will elaborate on how to adopt decolonial perspectives.

As mentioned, to understand prison systems in Latin America, a decolonial perspective is not only valuable but critical, considering the continent's colonial history. Bracco describes how brutal colonial systems and theories of punishment were not only imposed during colonial times but continued to be used afterwards.[113] Right up to today we see perspectives of crime and justice imposed on Latin America, for example through the export of European criminological theories,[114] and the 'war on drugs' which lays disproportionate responsibility on Latin America in the global drug trade and has therefore justified the import of zero tolerance policies and excessive violence in the region.[115] This also affects how we analyze prison systems in the region, as they are often measured against Northern standards which are seen as an objective, and we therefore fail to situate Latin American prisons within their own context. In other words, this approach often looks at prisons in Latin America through their deficiencies defined by a Northern prison model, instead of examining them on their own terms. This negates, for example, the negotiations of power that occur between prison staff and incarcerated individuals. In these negotiations, detainees do not remain passive or submissive,[116] which is much more prevalent in Latin American prisons than Northern models which impose more control and can contribute to the dehumanization of Latin American incarcerated people.[117] Relevant is Cunneen's critique of the way Western perspectives on crime and justice view prisons as evident, by stressing that Northern research focuses on how to improve systems of policing, rather than asking how to make society better, and without considering the people affected by the systems.[118]

---

112 Ayabulela Dlakavu, Jabulani Mathebula and Samukelisiwe Mkhize, 'Decolonising and Indigenising Evaluation Practice in Africa: Roadmap for Mainstreaming the Made in Africa Evaluation Approach' (2022) 10(1) *African Evaluation Journal* a620.

113 Bracco, *Decolonising and De-Patriarchalising Prison: Governance, Social Life and Gendered Subjectivities in a Women's Prison in Peru* (n 59).

114 Goyes and Sozzo, 'Latin American Criminologies: Origins, Trajectories and Pathways' (n 4).

115 Bracco, *Decolonising and De-Patriarchalising Prison: Governance, Social Life and Gendered Subjectivities in a Women's Prison in Peru* (n 59).

116 ibid, 189.

117 ibid.

118 Chris Cunneen, *Decoloniality, Abolitionism, and the Disruption of Penal Power* (Oxford University Press 2023) 19–36.

Lastly, a benefit of realist evaluations is their external validity, which refers to 'the extent to which findings from an evaluation can be applied to other situations'.[119] As a realist evaluation creates an understanding of how and when an intervention works, it becomes easier to apply similar interventions in similar situations.[120] However, Shahjahan and Wagner regard the idea of a universally applicable theory as colonial thinking that presumes one truth or one way of doing that could justify the implementation of the same measures everywhere. They state that this would ignore the vast social and cultural differences in the world, so researchers should pay attention to avoid overgeneralization. They also discuss the *Śūnyatā* perspective, which rejects the idea of being able to measure direct causality from social interventions, as we live in a socially complex world where everything inevitably has an influence on everything else, and which rejects the ability to objectively quantify everything.[121]

Shahjahan's and Wagner's contribution focuses on scholarly impact, and they specifically state that 'from this perspective, the mainstream Western conceptualisation of impact is overly casual and simplistic, as it is grounded in a belief that a scholar's impact can be directly connected to a series of causes'.[122] Therefore, maintaining a wide understanding of what impact is or can be is crucial from this perspective. Moreover, the Western notion of being able to find a causal link between an intervention and a result, which can be attributed to a single intervention, becomes less important from this perspective. Rather, it becomes important to consider the intervention in relation to social interactions. It is important to look at how UMs interact in a complex social landscape and to analyze a wide conceptualization of impact.

In conclusion, following the critique of decolonial scholars on Western evaluation standards, it is therefore beneficial to aim at documenting the full range of impacts that UMs can potentially bring about, and not limit ourselves to rigid definitions of what constitutes impact. Accordingly, the broader definition of impact is also favourable, as it helps to capture the numerous possible impacts of UMs. Therefore, the realist evaluation model is optimal, as it aims to look at the specific situation wherein a measure has been granted and takes into consideration underlying assumptions. The next section will further elaborate on the workings of a realist evaluation model and how research methodologies can be adopted and applied to our specific situation.

---

119 Van der Knaap et al., 'Combining Campbell Standards and the Realist Evaluation Approach: The Best of Two Worlds?' (n 109) 50.

120 ibid, 48–57.

121 Riyad Shahjahan and Anne E. Wagner, 'Unpacking Ontological Security: A Decolonial Reading of Scholarly Impact' (2018) 51(8) *Educational Philosophy and Theory* 779–791.

122 ibid, 788.

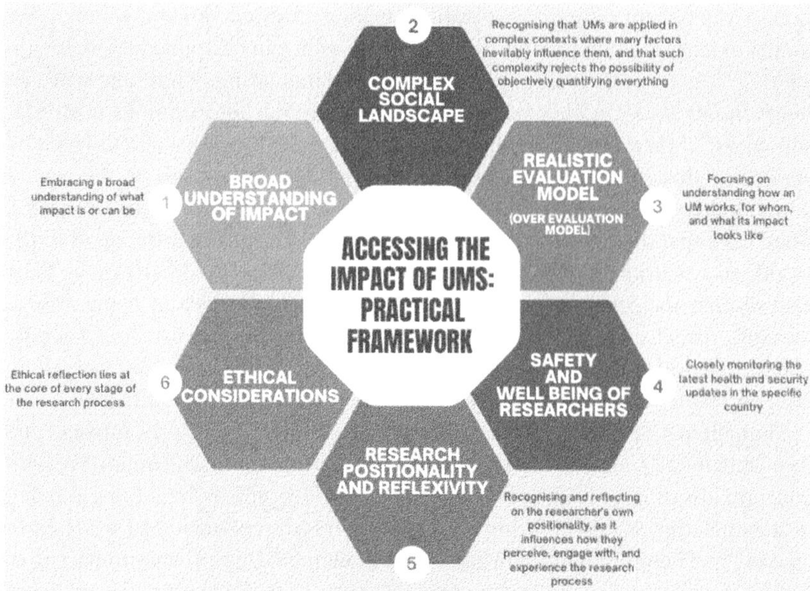


*Figure 5.3* *Practical framework for measuring impact in the context of deprivation of liberty in Latin America*

## 7.1 The Context-Mechanism-Outcome Model: A Realist Evaluation

The context-mechanism-outcome (CMO) model is an approach used to conduct a realist evaluation. This model considers three factors: mechanisms, context and outcome.

The *mechanisms* 'are underlying entities, processes, or structures which operate in particular contexts to generate outcomes of interest'.[123] In other words, 'mechanisms are the engines behind behaviour'[124] that address the question of why or why not an intervention has a certain outcome. In addition, the theories and assumptions regarding why an intervention is or is not working are often not explicitly stated, and often result in misunderstandings about the precise nature of the mechanisms behind an intervention. Astbury and

[123] Brad Astbury and Frans L. Leeuw, 'Unpacking Black Boxes: Mechanisms and Theory Building in Evaluation' (2010) 31(3) *American Journal of Evaluation* 368.

[124] Van der Knaap, et al., 'Combining Campbell Standards and the Realist Evaluation Approach: The Best of Two Worlds?' (n 109) 50.

Leeuw refer to the example of Weiss, who states that sexual education about contraception can lead to fewer pregnancies.[125] In this case, the mechanism behind the decline in pregnancies is not the counselling, but could potentially be the knowledge and confidence gained from the counselling which results in people making different decisions. Mechanisms require someone to look deeper into underlying reasons why and how something might cause a certain effect. Mechanisms and underlying assumptions are crucial for understanding and creating useful policies, as policymakers might implement novel programmes, but if the mechanisms and underlying assumptions are the same, every new programme might end up with a similar result.[126] Consequently, if the goal is to defend the claims related to the impact of the UMs, to find improvements, and/or to fully understand the impact of an UM, understanding the mechanisms behind the functioning of the UMs and the assumptions on which they were built is highly beneficial.

As the mechanisms are often implicit, there are several ways to trace them back, such as through path analysis,[127] observations of the programme in action, and formal (argumentation) analyses of programmes and policy documents.[128] However, uncovering the mechanisms behind an intervention can be time-consuming work. Hence, in cases where time and resources are lacking, where it is not of interest to fully understand an intervention, and/or where

---

125 Astbury and Leeuw, 'Unpacking Black Boxes: Mechanisms and Theory Building in Evaluation' (n 123) 363–1. They refer to Carol H. Weiss, 'Theory-Based Evaluation: Past, Present, and Future' (1997) 76 *New Directions for Evaluation*.

126 ibid, 363–381.

127 Path analysis is a form of multiple regression statistical analysis used to evaluate causal models by examining the relationships between a dependent variable and two or more independent variables. It allows the researcher to estimate both the magnitude and the significance of causal relationships between variables. Path analysis forces the researcher to specify the relationships between all independent variables. The result is a model that shows the causal mechanisms by which independent variables have both direct and indirect effects on a dependent variable. Path analysis was developed by geneticist Sewall Wright in 1918. Today, researchers can perform path analysis using statistical programs such as SPSS and STATA. The method is also known as causal modelling, analysis of covariance structures, and latent variable models. See Ashley Crossman, 'Understanding Path Analysis: A Brief Introduction' (27 March 2019), www.thoughtco.com/path-analysis-3026444.

128 See Sewall Wright, 'Correlation and Causation' (1921) 20 *Journal of Agricultural Research* 557–5; Sewall Wright, 'The Theory of Path Coefficients: A Reply to Niles's Criticism' (1923) 8(3) *Genetics* 239–255.

uncovering the information about the assumptions is too hard,[129] it can be a first step to look at whether the UMs are able to live up to their goals, and to understand their impact at the different levels by using a simplified methodology based on those parts which seem to fit. Considering the substantial lack of information and analysis about UMs, this would be an important first step towards gaining knowledge on the topic without immediately exhausting all the resources on a complicated endeavour.

The CMO model further assumes that the mechanisms that enable an intervention to have the desired effect or not depend on the *context* wherein the intervention takes place.[130] Following this, it is important to look not only at 'who does the programme work for' in relation to the research population, but also with regard to the programme stakeholders.[131] For example, in this context, do the UMs serve the views/interests of politicians or the interests of individuals in prison? As extensively argued earlier, the political context and the politics within which an initiative is implemented are important, as these are essential to comprehend what the political regime in power wants, what it really was trying to achieve with its actions, and whether it will cooperate with the evaluation.

Finally, the *outcome* simply refers to the observed outcomes of an intervention. These may be intended or unintended,[132] and should take into consideration the original aims of an intervention.

To illustrate with a current example, policymakers might reason that being hard on crime and adopting deterrence towards drugs will lead to fewer people being involved with drugs (selling, buying, etc). This might be based on an underlying assumption that people get involved in the drug trade on a voluntary basis and that harsh punishments will deter them from continuing. However, such policies do not, in reality, deter people from selling or using drugs.[133] The

---

129 Astbury and Leeuw, 'Unpacking Black Boxes: Mechanisms and Theory Building in Evaluation' (n 123) 363–1.

130 Van der Knaap et al., 'Combining Campbell Standards and the Realist Evaluation Approach: The Best of Two Worlds?' (n 109) 48–57.

131 ibid.

132 ibid.

133 A recent study in the UK looking at global drug policies confirms that the threat of receiving a punishment for using drugs, or having received a punishment for taking drugs, did not lower the number of people using drugs. Likewise, removing the penalties for drug usage did not lead to more people using drugs. Neither is there a significant difference in the number of people using drugs in countries with harsh drug policies in comparison with countries with more lenient policies. Lastly, the study found that the main concern of people who did not use drugs was not the fear of receiving a punishment, but rather health concerns. See Transform,

implicit mechanisms explaining why these policies are not working could be that many people do not enter the drug trade voluntarily, but because of other reasons, such as economic hardship.[134] In addition, many people do not take drugs randomly, and genetic predisposition plays a large role in drug addiction.[135] Any further policies aiming to control the drug trade based on the premise that people partake voluntarily and fear punishment will probably continue to show similar results, as the mechanisms would be ignored and the policies would continue to be based on invalid assumptions. This takes place in a context, in several Latin American states, of political volatility, economic insecurity and gang violence, which all influence drug policies and provide reasons to start dealing drugs. Should the context change, and another neighbouring state offer better economic circumstances, political stability or support for people with a drug addiction, people who can do so might seek a life elsewhere, and the deterrence policy might show a decrease in drug sales/people using drugs.

## 7.2 Research Methodologies

In order to analyze the impact of UMs, it is essential that the study applies the relevant methodology. The research should employ a qualitative research approach, using empirical case studies, desk research and field research to identify the main variables of interest and the possible dynamics and causal relationships between them.[136] As there are no existing academic studies on the impact of UMs, the research should be exploratory and explanatory in nature. The case study approach allows for a detailed description of the context and the use of multiple sources.[137] This research strategy is particularly

---

'Criminalisation Does Not Deter People from Taking Drugs' (Transform 2023), https://transformdrugs.org/blog/criminalisation-does-not-deter-people-from-taking-drugs.

[134] Prichard's and Payne's research takes place in juvenile detention in Australia. They uncover several reasons for why teenagers sell drugs. One of the main reasons was needing/wanting money. See Jeremy Prichard and Jason Payne, *Alcohol, Drugs and Crime: A Study of Juveniles in Detention* (Australian Institute of Criminology 2005).

[135] Alexander S. Hatoum et al., 'Multivariate Genome-Wide Association Meta-Analysis of over 1 Million Subjects Identifies Loci Underlying Multiple Substance Use Disorders' (2023) 1(3) *Nature Mental Health* 210–223.

[136] Rhona Smith and Lorna Smith, 'Qualitative methods', in Lee McConnell and Rhona Smith (eds), *Research Methods in Human Rights* (Routledge 2018) 70–93.

[137] Colin Robson, *Real World Research. A Resource for Social Scientists and Practitioner Researchers* (Blackwell 1993); Rob Van Wynsberghe and Samia

important when the boundaries between the phenomenon and the context are not clearly delineated.[138] This approach is especially appropriate where one of the project's methodological aims is to gain insight into how the various actors involved in the implementation of UMs interpret them and the process of their enforcement in their specific context. The objective is to explore, describe, understand and explain the diverse impacts of UMs on detainees' cases and the factors that influence these impacts. Qualitative studies should adopt an interpretative, naturalistic approach and should be applicable to real-world scenarios, without manipulation or control. It is imperative that the researchers employ rigorous data-coding techniques and facilitate the incorporation of new insights that may shape their interpretation of how UMs have been implemented and understood in diverse and unanticipated ways.

The information should be analyzed inductively (exploring open-ended questions, with no hypothesis to test). Furthermore, the interpretation of results should consider the meanings that people attach to the implementation of UMs within their social worlds.[139] This approach is particularly well suited to a research project which involves the evaluation of ongoing processes, and which seeks to address the contextual conditions.[140] Consequently, the qualitative approach will permit the researcher to gain an in-depth contextual understanding of how UMs are applied and understood by diverse actors at the international, regional and domestic levels (process) and what happens in reality (outcome).

An overview of a set of key considerations to inform research on prison populations will be presented in this subsection. However, as mentioned, it is important to adapt adequate research methodologies to specific projects, and for the scope of this contribution, it is impossible and unnecessary to provide a detailed examination of how best to conduct interviews. Rather, the contribution will focus on some general considerations.

### 7.2.1 Desk research

Desk research makes it possible to collect data on, *inter alia*, the UMs granted by international human rights bodies, the actions taken by the state concerned, the specific characteristics and context of the state in question, and the research

---

Khan, 'Redefining Case Study' (2007) *International Journal of Qualitative Methods* 89–94.

138 Robert Yin, *Case Study Research: Design and Methods* (Sage 2014).

139 Michael Patton, *Qualitative Research and Evaluation Methods* (Sage 2002); Dawn Snape and Liz Spencer, 'The Foundations of Qualitative Research' in Jane Ritchie and Jane Lewis (eds), *Qualitative Research Practice: A Guide for Social Science Students and Researchers* (Sage 2003).

140 Yin, *Case Study Research: Design and Methods* (n 138).

population and its environment. At the same time, it allows the researcher to gain an in-depth understanding of the context of deprivation of liberty and the functioning of human rights systems. During this process, researchers can collect and analyze a large variety of documents containing information on the UMs compiled by state organs, representatives of the beneficiary or beneficiaries, NGOs, the media, experts, scholars and the international human rights bodies.[141] Desk-based research could include, among others, a review of: (1) national reports and official documentation on the UMs requested; information about the detainee population (profile); type of crime; conditions of overcrowding; data about pre-trial detention; the national budget; and the resources allocated to detention centres; (2) domestic laws, regulations and policies; (3) legal doctrine and criminology/political science literature; and (4) media coverage in newspapers.

Desk research should also include an examination of all the UMs adopted by the international human rights bodies, from the year that each issued its first UM until a predetermined timeframe that is adapted to the situation and the available time. The respective starting years for the analysis will be as follows: 1970 for the IACHR, 1979 for the IACtHR, 1986 for the HRC and 1993 for the CAT. This information will facilitate a better understanding of the evolution of case law and the diversity of UMs submitted at the international level. Information related to the case law of UMs is (partly) accessible online and can be complemented by archival research in the respective international human rights bodies. Lastly, a discourse analysis would be advantageous if the researcher decides to analyze how UMs have an effect on the language used in national media and official documents when discussing deprivation of liberty, and/or how people describe people in prison in general.[142]

### 7.2.2 Interviews

Rodriguez-Garavito describes how qualitative methodologies are most beneficial for uncovering indirect and symbolic impacts.[143] We argue, however, that these methodologies are also valuable for revealing direct impacts at the micro level of analysis, especially in the context of deprivation of liberty. Such impacts may not be immediately evident to the researcher through mere observation or adequately covered by available and/or trustworthy resources.

---

[141] Sandra van Tiel, *Research Methods in Public Administration and Public Management: An Introduction* (Routledge 2014).

[142] James Paul Gee, *An Introduction to Discourse Analysis: Theory and Method* (Routledge 2014).

[143] Cesar Rodriguez-Garavito, 'Beyond the Courtroom: The Impact of Judicial Activism on Socioeconomic Rights in Latin America' (2010) 89 *Texas Law Review* 1669.

Hence, qualitative methodologies that allow for communication are also key to understanding potential direct impact at the micro level, in addition to the other types of impact at the meso level and macro level. Conducting interviews is beneficial for a number of reasons. Among others, it facilitates direct conversation with the research population, which enables the co-construction of knowledge, and is useful for clarifying ambiguous questions.[144]

Moreover, in-person interviews allow the researcher to gain insights and impressions of additional aspects, such as the physical situation of the interviewee (for example, the state of the prison when interviewing a person deprived of liberty, the odour of the cell, or the workload of the authority or authorities responsible for implementing the UM), as well as non-verbal expressions of the researched population, leading to a more comprehensive perspective.[145] Additionally, the research can easily be adapted to emerging findings in the field that might not previously have been considered. As securing an interview with the research participants may already be challenging, it would be advantageous to include questions related to all types of impact in a focused interview. However, to avoid asking questions limited to the researcher's perspective, there should also be room for new interpretations, which can be achieved through including (semi-)open questions.[146] Lastly, the process of drafting questions may reveal some prejudices of which the researcher was previously unaware.[147] Therefore, being open to change during the process is critical.

Interviews should be conducted with a diverse range of participants to gain a more comprehensive understanding of the phenomenon of UMs.[148] Once a respondent has been identified, a snowball sampling technique could be employed to identify key participants at the national level, including state authorities, detainees, representatives, members of NGOs, healthcare professionals, journalists and scholars. At the international level, interviews could be undertaken with judges, commissioners, members and staff of the secretariat

---

[144] Jennifer Rowley, 'Conducting Research Interviews' (2012) 35(3–4) *Management Research Review* 260–71.

[145] See 'Interview of Mr Jorge Errandonea, Senior Staff Attorney, Inter-American Court of Human Rights', in *The Inter-American Court of Human Rights (Podcast)*, Clara Burbano Herrera (IMPACTUM and Human Rights in Context Research Group, Ghent University), Season 2, Episode 17, 2025.

[146] Wendy Hollway and Tony Jefferson, 'Eliciting Narrative through the In-Depth Interview' (1997) 3(1) *Qualitative Inquiry* 53–70.

[147] Vivitha Thambinathan and Elizabeth Anne Kinsella, 'Decolonizing Methodologies in Qualitative Research: Creating Spaces for Transformative Praxis' (2021) 20(2) *International Journal of Qualitative Methods*.

[148] Yin, *Case Study Research: Design and Methods* (n 138).

of each of the respective international human rights bodies. In this kind of research, it is crucial that the researchers are supported by key local and international actors, who may be consulted, for example, regarding the selection of respondents. Finding participants who are deprived of their liberty, along with individuals in their environment, who may be located in challenging political regimes, can be a difficult process. It is realistic to expect that it might take a significant amount of time to find participants, and it is therefore helpful to keep an open mind about different ways to gather data. This could possibly include the use of online interviews.

Less time-consuming alternatives to conducting interviews include organizing focus groups, which allow for more people to be interviewed simultaneously,[149] or using questionnaires which include several open questions.[150] Focus groups can have both advantages and disadvantages: they require space to be conducted, and one might not receive the same answers as in one-on-one interviews. This is not necessarily negative, as it may be that hearing other people share their stories might encourage some to be more open.[151] Handing out questionnaires might allow the researcher to reach more participants and provides the participants with the opportunity to fill in the questions at their own time.[152] However, questionnaires exclude people who are illiterate[153] and, in the prison context, respondents would need the privacy to complete them. Furthermore, other qualitative research methods can be explored as alternatives to conducting interviews, which might ease the process of respondents talking about their experiences and/or uncover emotions that cannot be expressed through words, such as art-based methodologies. This should again be examined in relation to the specific context, but one such approach could be collage making.[154]

Lastly, any complications in identifying (former) individuals deprived of their liberty to participate in an interview can also be a finding in itself. It raises questions about why it is difficult in that particular situation to find participants and this should certainly be included in the analysis. Moreover,

---

[149] Anita Gibbs, 'Social Research Update 19: Focus Groups' (University of Surrey 1997), https://sru.soc.surrey.ac.uk/SRU19.html.

[150] Keath A. Meadows, 'So You Want to Do Research? 5: Questionnaire Design' (2003) 8(12) *British Journal of Community Nursing* 562–570.

[151] Gibbs, 'Social Research Update 19: Focus Groups' (n 149).

[152] Rowley, 'Conducting Research Interviews' (n 144).

[153] Joost Kappelhof, 'Survey Research and the Quality of Survey Data among Ethnic Minorities' in Paul P. Biemer et al. (eds), *Total Survey Error in Practice* (Wiley 2017) 235–252.

[154] Paula Gerstenblatt, 'Collage Portraits as a Method of Analysis in Qualitative Research' (2013) 12(1) *International Journal of Qualitative Methods* 294–309.

people who were unable to participate, such as those in poor health, deserve to be included in the analysis as well.

Conducting interviews with people at the macro level, who work in international human rights bodies, domestic human rights institutions, and within state authorities, poses different challenges. It is reasonable to assume that they will have a busy schedule, making it potentially more challenging for them to find time to participate in an interview. Equally, the difficult or sensitive political situation can make conducting interviews nearly, or even wholly, impossible. Pereira conducted research with medical professionals who were often willing to participate but had little time. As a solution, she remained flexible over when and how to conduct the interviews. This meant that sometimes the interviews would be cut short and held on the phone.[155] While face-to-face interviews have the added benefit of creating a connection with the participant and examining other factors, online interviews offer more flexibility, which might be valuable in these circumstances.

## 7.3 Researcher Positionality and Reflexivity

Researcher positionality and reflexivity are crucial when conducting research with individuals in vulnerable situations.[156]

Researcher positionality refers to the identity and 'position' of the researcher in relation to the research being conducted. When conducting research with people deprived of liberty, one key difference between the researcher and the research population is the freedom that the researcher possesses at the time of the study. Other reflections on the position of the researcher might include aspects such as gender, socio-economic status, ethnicity and cultural background. It is essential to recognize the researcher's position, as it influences how researchers perceive and experience their research.[157] Having similarities, for instance, in terms of background or gender, may be beneficial for establishing a connection with the research population. However, caution should be exercised when making generalizations about shared experiences with the

155 Hannah Pereira, *The Professional Identity of Doctors who Provide Abortions: A Sociological Investigation* (University of Kent 2021).

156 Rhona M. Shaw, Julie Howe, Jonathan Beazer and Toni Carr, 'Ethics and Positionality in Qualitative Research with Vulnerable and Marginal Groups' (2019) 20(3) *Qualitative Research* 17; Thambinathan and Kinsella, 'Decolonizing Methodologies in Qualitative Research: Creating Spaces for Transformative Praxis' (n 147).

157 Andrew Gary Darwin Holmes, 'Researcher Positionality – A Consideration of its Influence and Place in Qualitative Research – A New Researcher Guide' (2020) 8(4) *Shanlax International Journal of Education* 1–10.

research population. Such assumptions could lead to the research population assuming that the researcher understands their experiences, which in turn may hinder the development of more in-depth discussions on certain topics.[158]

Reflexivity refers to the process of reflecting on how the research is carried out and influenced by the researcher's position and experiences, particularly in terms of, for example, methodologies and analysis, and how certain conclusions were reached.[159] Thambinathan and Kinsella call for critical reflexivity, which goes beyond recognizing certain privileges one might enjoy in comparison to the research population, and extends to examining 'epistemological assumptions', 'situatedness with respect to the research' and 'power dynamics in research'.[160] This is crucial to continuously resist colonial methodologies and ways of thinking.

Moreover, conducting research on socially sensitive topics, such as deprivation of liberty, can be hard for researchers, as they might struggle between establishing a connection with the research participants and maintaining a certain distance. Researchers have a responsibility towards their participants, and witnessing certain struggles that they might experience is very likely to affect the researchers.[161] As a way of analyzing researchers' own positionality, documenting how their opinions change throughout their research, performing critical reflexivity, and making room for their feelings, an autoethnography could be beneficial, should there be time. An autoethnography is useful because it allows researchers to situate their experiences during their research.[162] Alternatively, journalling can offer room for reflection, and having a support network comprising people conducting similar research, but also outside the field, can be beneficial in navigating the research.[163]

---

158 Shaw, Howe, Beazer and Carr, 'Ethics and Positionality in Qualitative Research with Vulnerable and Marginal Groups' (n 156).

159 Caitlin Wilson, Gillian Janes and Julia Williams, 'Identity, Positionality and Reflexivity: Relevance and Application to Research Paramedics' (2022) 7(2) *British Paramedic Journal* 43–49.

160 Thambinathan and Kinsella, 'Decolonizing Methodologies in Qualitative Research: Creating Spaces for Transformative Praxis' (n 147) 2.

161 Alison Liebling, 'Being a Criminologist: Investigation as a Lifestyle and Living' in Mary Bosworth and Carolyn Hoyle (eds), *What is Criminology?* (Oxford 2011).

162 Tony E. Adams, Carolyn Ellis and Stacy Holman Jones, 'Autoethnography' in *The International Encyclopedia of Communication Research Methods* (Wiley 2017).

163 Shaw, Howe, Beazer and Carr, 'Ethics and Positionality in Qualitative Research with Vulnerable and Marginal Groups' (n 156).

## 7.4 Ethical Considerations

It is recommended that researchers seek ethical guidance from an ethics committee or ethics advisor throughout the course of their study. All necessary ethical approvals should be secured, and informed consent templates should be made available, before the study begins.[164] The selection of participants should be guided by privacy and safety considerations, and in cases where interviewee safety cannot be guaranteed, alternative participants or methods should be identified. The research focus, on UMs involving at-risk detainees, implies that personal information is likely to be uncovered during the research. Consequently, extra precautions in relation to ethical standards are therefore required, and a robust ethical framework should be developed and maintained throughout the research.[165] Furthermore, researchers are required to obtain prior and informed consent from all interviewees and to adhere to protocols related to personal data management and storage. Besides the general ethical considerations of data protection, there are some other considerations to be made when conducting research with people in prison from a decolonial perspective. Firstly, it is important to properly manage the expectations of the participants, as they might expect the researcher to be able to do something about their situation, or that the research may lead to immediate results.[166] Secondly, considering the sensitive nature of the topic, consent should not only be sought before starting the data collection but should continue to be sought throughout all stages of the research. For example, should the participants struggle during the interviews, the researcher can remind them that they can stop or take a break at any time should they wish, thereby continuing to gain consent during the data collection.

Both Liebling and Thambinathan and Kinsella discuss the responsibilities that researchers have towards their participants.[167] Thambinathan and Kinsella underline that the well-being of the people they work with should come first, and not the outcome of the research.[168] This is in line with the principle of doing research with people and not on people, refraining from seeing the par-

---

[164] George Ulrich, 'Research Ethics for Human Rights Researchers' in Bård A. Andreassen, Hans-Otto Sano and Siobhán McInerney-Lankford (eds), *Research Methods in Human Rights: A Handbook* (Elgar 2018).

[165] Smith and Smith, 'Qualitative methods' (n 136).

[166] Liebling, 'Being a Criminologist: Investigation as a Lifestyle and Living' (n 161).

[167] ibid; Thambinathan and Kinsella, 'Decolonizing Methodologies in Qualitative Research: Creating Spaces for Transformative Praxis' (n 147).

[168] Thambinathan and Kinsella, 'Decolonizing Methodologies in Qualitative Research: Creating Spaces for Transformative Praxis' (n 147).

ticipants as objects to fulfil one's research goals. It is thereby also misplaced for researchers to think of themselves as on a noble quest to give voice to oppressed people, 'since it wrongfully implies that communities are unable to achieve on their own what researchers are able to provide'.[169] In relation to the history of Western research, this is crucial, as research has previously served to legitimize systems of oppression and appropriated the wisdom of the research participants as its own.[170] Finally, Thambinathan and Kinsella also state that adopting anti-colonial methods is a way of living, and that it is something that researchers should consider in all areas in order to reflect solidarity with oppressed people.[171] Likewise, Liebling discusses how conducting social research and standing up for people's rights becomes an integral part of the researcher's identity, which continues beyond their job. This process might cause discomfort when confronted with prejudices previously unrecognized. However, this should not stop one from remaining committed to learning and improving.[172]

## 7.5 Safety and Well-being of the Researchers: Health Crisis and Other Factors

A further essential aspect to be considered is the safety and well-being of the researchers. It is imperative to remain flexible and introduce the necessary changes to ensure that the highest-quality research can be carried out despite the constraints imposed by, for instance, a health or political crisis. No field research activity should be undertaken if the researchers have not yet received appropriate vaccinations for the research location or if the public health or political context is not sufficiently secure. To guarantee the safety of the research team, it is imperative that the research leader or principal investigator closely monitor the latest health and security updates from the World Health Organization and local embassies or consular posts, and convene regular meetings with key local stakeholders to assess the evolving health and safety situation in the specific country.

In instances where safety cannot be guaranteed, alternative methods of conducting the research should be identified (e.g., online interviews, meetings and/or webinars). Field research activities should be submitted to the appropriate safety board and the research leader for review and approval before the commencement of any activities. In the event that field research activities with

---

169 ibid, 5.

170 ibid.

171 ibid.

172 Liebling, 'Being a Criminologist: Investigation as a Lifestyle and Living' (n 161).

persons deprived of their liberty, or other participants such as their relatives or prison staff, have to be postponed or cancelled, alternative methodologies can always be employed. For instance, additional interviews can be conducted with individuals with experience of working with UMs and (inter)national NGOs. In instances where contact with detainees is not permitted, their representatives should be interviewed.

# 8 THE THEORETICAL FRAMEWORK FOR ASSESSING IMPACT: WHAT IT LOOKS LIKE IN PRACTICE

This chapter presents a comprehensive conceptualization of impact and its components. It is challenging for a single researcher to provide a full and detailed analysis of all aspects of the conceptualization of impact, given the time, political, and financial constraints which may influence the shape of the study.

Consequently, the researcher must first make some decisions about what to focus on, such as the state(s) where their research will be conducted and the prison population(s) involved. Subsequently, it is important to understand the mechanisms, assumptions and context of the UMs for the chosen frame of analysis (if it has indeed been decided that the research aims to explore how the UMs work). If deemed manageable and necessary, the mechanisms behind, and the context surrounding, the implementation of the UMs should be investigated through desk research. Additionally, it is beneficial to include the goal(s) of the UM being analyzed. Overall, this helps to establish how the UMs are intended to work and how it is hoped that would have an impact, facilitating a subsequent examination of how the UMs have worked in practice. Moreover, it helps to uncover underlying assumptions as to why they do or do not work, and to expose for whom they are really supposed to work.

Secondly, the data should be gathered. A combination of desk-based research and interviews has been proposed as a feasible methodology to gather data on all the different types of impact. However, as mentioned, other methodologies may be useful for the specific context of the research.

Thirdly, the data must be analyzed. The outcomes can be segregated by the diverse typologies of impact. In this stage, the researcher should consider the various ways in which the UMs had an impact at the diverse levels: on the research population, people close to them, the state authorities and the international human rights bodies themselves. As research is scarce on this topic, the mechanisms and assumptions behind the UMs can be uncovered both during the data collection phase and afterwards during the analysis. This helps create a deeper understanding of how the UMs work in a socially complex world and what this impact looks like.

Lastly, as mentioned above, the impact of UMs can change over time. Therefore, it is necessary to repeat the process at different time intervals. As there might be considerable financial and time constraints on repeating this type of research, the cases can also be monitored through media analysis, content analysis, or online interviews, for example, instead of by renewed face-to-face interviews.

:In sum, there are four components of UM impact assessment: (1) understanding the mechanisms and the context; (2) gathering the data; (3) analyzing and reporting the data; and (4) repeating the research at a later stage. Moreover, much is left to the discretion of the researcher, such as the analysis to determine the actual impact, and the feasibility of different strategies and methodologies. It is important to substantiate any decisions made during the process with valid arguments, and to be aware of why one is making such decisions. For this purpose, in this context, decolonial scholars and perspectives are indispensable, and an autoethnography can help bring clarity to decisions that sometimes might seem self-evident when not reflected upon. It is of the utmost importance that additional precautions be taken with regard to ethical standards, and that a robust ethical framework be established and maintained throughout the research process. Furthermore, the safety and well-being of the researchers must be considered at all times.

## 9 CONCLUSION

In the context of UMs granted to protect persons deprived of their liberty, we define impact as the effects of the request of the UMs on the beneficiary and beyond. Measuring impact is a difficult task, as it is a fluctuating result of analysis that depends on the specifics of the situation in question. Taking this into consideration, and based on the realization that researchers are undoubtedly incapable of foreseeing all the possible features of impact, this chapter has aimed to present a theoretical framework of impact that is broad and flexible, while indicating some key factors that are useful for the analysis. By considering a broad definition of impact, the contribution also wishes to stay open-minded and flexible to any inputs discovered by the researchers during the data analysis. In other words, it is important to keep an open mind during the fieldwork about what the meaning of impact is, and not see this as a final answer.

This contribution has also considered how impact might look different from different perspectives throughout society and accordingly proposes a multilayered framework that considers the (in)direct and symbolic impact, as well as the micro level, meso level, and macro level of analysis. The possibility that impact may occur over a range of timeframes, including short, medium and long periods, is also recognized, and that impact may look different depending on the point in time at which it is assessed. The chapter has situated the research in Latin America, which presents a number of significant challenges, notably regarding how to contextualize the research adequately and refrain from applying or taking for granted Western notions of crime and imprisonment. We have subsequently considered and are suggesting applying decolonial methodologies throughout the whole research procedure. Subsequently, we also wish to emphasize once more that this research does not seek to contribute to the legitimization of the prison system in Latin America, which has led to the violation of a whole range of human rights. Nor does this research aim to contribute to the dehumanization of individuals in prison in general. In other words, should this research indicate overall quite positive impacts of UMs, this should not be interpreted as a legitimization of the current systems and their operation in many countries.

We recognize the barriers and complexities involved in assessing the impact of UMs. Nevertheless, we have sought to propose a somewhat idealistic approach to analyzing this important legal instrument, which aims to protect the basic human rights of at-risk detainees and prevent these rights from being infringed. While not all aspects may be feasible in practice, it remains crucial to reflect on the best way to conduct such ambitious research to safeguard the humanity and the personhood of the research participants in the best way possible. Starting from an idealistic framework, with high standards, is essential to ensure the upholding of quality ethical standards.

# PART II

# Applying the impact model to specific cases and/or countries studies

# 6. Impact of the Inter-American jurisprudence on the fight against impunity in Colombia: the case of the Special Jurisdiction for Peace

**Oscar Parra Vera and Mónica Trespalacios Leal**

## 1 INTRODUCTION

Based on international treaties, the international human rights systems and national and international criminal tribunals have emphatically underscored the states' obligation to investigate, try, and punish those responsible for gross violations of human rights and for international crimes, in order to prevent further breaches in the future[1] and satisfy the victims' rights to justice, truth, and reparation.[2] This objective has been extremely hard to achieve in Colombia, where the armed conflict has left over nine million victims of all sorts of crimes,[3] including gross violations of human rights and grave breaches of international humanitarian law. In recent years, several strategies have been made to reduce impunity in the country, in which we can trace the profound influence of the Inter-American system of human rights (IAHRS). In this chapter we will explore the impact of the IAHRS in the main transitional tribunal recently created to fight against impunity in Colombia, the Special Jurisdiction for Peace (JEP, for its acronym in Spanish), and the way in which the Inter-American jurisprudence influenced its design and implementation.

[1] Kathryn Sikkink, *The Justice Cascade* (W.W. Norton & Company 2011) 28.

[2] Diane Orentlicher, 'Updated Set of Principles for the Protection and Promotion of Human Rights through Action to Combat Impunity' E/CN.4/2005/102/Add.1 (18 February 2005).

[3] Government of Colombia, 'National Information Network for Care and Reparation of Victims' (*Unidad para las Víctimas*, 22 July 2023), https://www.unidadvictimas.gov.co/es/registro-unico-de-victimas-ruv/37394.

There is a wide and growing literature on the debates surrounding the impact of the judgments of the Inter-American Court of Human Rights (IACtHR) and the Inter-American Commission on Human Rights (IACHR), where different categories have been developed, such as instrumental, structural, and symbolic effectiveness, among others. This chapter contributes to that literature by performing a specific analysis of the innovative strategy in transitional justice created in Colombia after the Peace Agreement, to appraise it as a sort of impact of the IAHRS, especially from the dialogues between tribunals on the best way to protect victims' rights from systematic violence. This leads us to develop a broad vision of 'impact', in light of the symbolic, structural, instrumental, and jurisprudential components that we can trace in different moments of this transitional tribunal.[4]

The chapter is divided into two sections. The first section will present the concept of impact and the categories described by some scholars, in particular Par Engstrom. The second section will describe, as a form of impact, how the JEP has appropriated and implemented the standards of justice and the fight against impunity developed by the IAHRS. To do so, the section will briefly describe the institution, to later develop the following three aspects that exemplify the impact of the IAHRS jurisprudence: (i) the prohibition against providing full amnesties and judicial pardons in cases of gross violations of human rights; (ii) the macro-criminal investigation as a development of the logical lines of investigation; and (iii) the robust participation of victims within the JEP, which has paved the way to restorative moments within judicial procedures.

The chapter employs a methodology of normative and jurisprudential analysis, the latter applied in two sets of decisions. In terms of design, we analyze the rulings of the Constitutional Court of Colombia (CCC) which played a key role in the JEP's regulatory frame by providing a concrete form to a mandate broadly developed by the IACtHR: the obligation to investigate, prosecute, and punish (IPP) those responsible of gross human rights violations. We emphasize the Court's understanding of the core of such obligation in the context of the Colombian armed conflict, characterized by massive human rights violations and structural impunity. Regarding the implementation of the JEP, we analyze the normative framework, along with the indictments issued by the Chamber for Acknowledgment of Truth and Responsibility (SRVR) in the more advanced cases in terms of procedure: Case No. 1 on kidnappings committed by the FARC-EP (Revolutionary Armed Forces of Colombia – People's

[4] To address the question, we will employ a broad theoretical approach of *impact*, mainly developed by Par Engstrom (see n 22), also considering his recent claim to go further in technical discussions to broaden the human rights salience in the convulsive context of Latin America (see n 22).

Army); and Case No. 3 on murders and forced disappearances committed by the Army. These decisions allow us to assess how the standards of macro-criminal investigation, set indirectly by the IAHRS and interpreted by the CCC, were materialized in the JEP. Next, we present the normative framework for victims' participation. In connection with this, we analyze the restorative justice approach adopted in the JEP and the potential to generate transforming narratives and conditions for peacebuilding.

This first analysis, which can be complemented with subsequent judicial decisions, aims to contribute to the literature on the impact of the IAHRS by analyzing some results of the 'dialogue' between human rights tribunals and constitutional and criminal courts on how best to protect victims of serious human rights violations in transitional contexts. Certainly, the IAHRS has played a major role in the design and implementation of public policies to promote justice in the region;[5] however, the states and the internal tribunals are the ones who lead the implementation, so the dialogue between them enriches and grounds the discussions. We focus on the Colombian case as it has the potential to provide valuable elements for situations characterized by generalized violence, committed by complex armed actors, that led to a massive victimization of civilians.

## 2 THEORETICAL APPROACH: IMPACT BEYOND COMPLIANCE

This chapter adopts two theoretical decisions for analyzing the JEP's design and implementation in the light of the IAHRS jurisprudence. Firstly, we will focus on the *impact* rather than *compliance* and *effectiveness* of the IAHRS decisions, and secondly, we adopt a constructivist approach to analyze such impact of Inter-American decisions, as we will explain later.

According to the specialized literature on the topic, the rates of compliance measure the degree of implementation of the orders issued in a judicial decision.[6] In a previous article, we have analyzed the low rates of compliance with the orders to investigate, prosecute, and punish those responsible for serious

[5] Oscar Parra Vera and Mónica Trespalacios Leal, 'Desafíos para el cumplimiento de la obligación de investigar, juzgar y sancionar emitida por la Corte Interamericana de Derechos Humanos en casos colombianos' (2019) *Anuario de Derecho Constitucional Latinoamericano* 609.

[6] Par Engstrom, 'Introduction: Rethinking the Impact of the Inter-American Human Rights System' in Par Engstrom (ed), *The Inter-American Human Rights System: Impact Beyond Compliance* (Palgrave Macmillan 2019) 4.

human rights violations issued by the IACtHR against Colombia[7] to draft a diagnosis useful for public policy design. On this occasion, we would like to delve into an impact approach that allows us to provide a comprehensive perspective and address additional effects that go beyond the subjects and specific decisions.

Furthermore, in the present case where the measures adopted by Colombia to reduce impunity are analyzed, it is justified to abandon the compliance approach, since the result would provide a limited response that does not account for all the efforts taken in the field. Indeed, Colombia has only complied with one judgment[8] over 30 cases before the IACtHR,[9] which could be interpreted as a poor outcome. On the contrary, despite the long road still ahead to reduce impunity and the low rates of compliance, we will show why the country has made significant progress in criminal justice and why the IAHRS has had positive and demonstrable effects on that outcome.[10]

Regarding the impact of judicial decisions, there are two perspectives to address it: (i) the neorealist perspective, which focuses on 'direct and palpable effects'[11] and (ii) the constructivist perspective, which also takes into consideration 'indirect transformations in social relations or when they alter social actors' perceptions and legitimize the litigants' worldview',[12] and which we consider to be the most appropriate perspective for this analysis.

Additionally, based on empirical studies of the IAHRS, Engstrom has described three typologies of impact of the IAHRS: (i) institutional development of the IAHRS, (ii) influence on domestic political and judicial actors and institutions;[13] and (iii) the influence of IAHRS rulings, recommendations,

---

[7] Parra Vera and Trespalacios Leal, 'Desafíos para el cumplimiento de la obligación de investigar, juzgar y sancionar emitida por la Corte Interamericana de Derechos Humanos en casos colombianos' (n 5).

[8] In this count we only include those cases where the IACtHR declared a violation of Articles 8 and 25 of the ACHR and ordered the state to investigate, try, and prosecute those responsible for the violations of human rights.

[9] *Escué Zapata v Colombia* (Monitoring Compliance with Judgment) Order of the Inter-American Court of Human Rights (22 November 2016).

[10] Damián A. González-Salzberg, 'The effectiveness of the Inter-American Human Rights System: a study of the American states' compliance with the judgments of the Inter-American Court of Human Rights' (2010) 16 *International Law: Revista Colombiana de Derecho Internacional* 115.

[11] César Rodriguez-Garavito, 'Beyond the Courtroom: The Impact of Judicial Activism on Socioeconomic Rights in Latin America' (2011) 89 *Texas Law Review* 1669.

[12] ibid.

[13] Which explores how the Inter-American Commission's human rights standards, and the Inter-American Court's jurisprudence are shaping domestic

and human rights standards in domestic institutions, policies, and judicial debates,[14] while other authors have characterized different types of impacts as unblocking, deliberative, creative, public policy, coordinating, and social.[15]

We will build on the notion of impact described by Engstrom (2019) for it explores prolonged and complex processes to show 'how the IAHRS influences the politics and struggles of actors and institutions seeking to advance the realization of human rights and those who resist their efforts',[16] which allows us to consider a wide range of effects caused by judicial decisions, such as direct effects, indirect effects, dialogue with internal institutions, and symbolic effects, which are crucial when analyzing the JEP.

## 3 IMPACT OF THE IAHRS IN THE FIGHT AGAINST IMPUNITY IN COLOMBIA

Engstrom describes how the IAHRS performs 'a crucial function in the development of an increasingly expansive set of human rights standards' followed by the 'increasing insertion into domestic policy, and legislative and judicial debates beyond responses to rulings in individual cases'.[17] In this section, we will briefly present the main influence of the IAHRS in Colombian transitional justice, which has been the extensive jurisprudence on the obligation to investigate, prosecute, and punish those responsible for serious human rights violations. We will describe the main mandates and consequences arising from this obligation that have shaped much of the design and implementation of the JEP.

State parties to the American Convention on Human Rights (ACHR) must fight against impunity, which is understood as the lack of investigation, prosecution, and sanction of those responsible for human rights violations.[18] Since

---

constitutional debates, litigation strategies, judicial thinking, and practice.

[14] Also considering that 'the IAHRS provides opportunities for domestic and transnational human rights actors to bring pressure for change in their domestic political and legal systems'. Engstrom, 'Introduction: Rethinking the Impact of the Inter-American Human Rights System' (n 6) 7.

[15] See: Oscar Parra Vera, 'Institutional Empowerment and Progressive Policy Reforms: The Impact of the Inter-American Human Rights System on Intra-state Conflicts' in Par Engstrom (ed), *The Inter-American Human Rights System: Impact Beyond Compliance* (Palgrave Macmillan 2019) 143.

[16] Engstrom, 'Introduction: Rethinking the Impact of the Inter-American Human Rights System' (n 6) 6.

[17] Engstrom, 'Introduction: Rethinking the Impact of the Inter-American Human Rights System' (n 6).

[18] *Velásquez Rodríguez v Honduras* (Judgment) IACtHR Series C No. 4 (29 July 1988); *Case of the Mapiripán Massacre v Colombia* (Reparations and Costs) IACtHR Series C No. 134 (15 September 2005) para 237.

its first judgment, the IACtHR derived this positive obligation from the duty to protect human rights, access to justice, and the effective remedy of Articles 1.1, 8.1, and 25.1 ACHR.[19] Therefore, whenever violations occur, states must conduct impartial and serious investigations *ex officio* to determine the truth, allowing the 'persecution, arrest, and eventual punishment of the perpetrators of the incident'.[20]

On the contrary, when public authorities fail to investigate with due diligence, the IACtHR declares a breach of the ACHR and international liability, and consequently, the reparations include the order for the state to deploy all necessary actions to prosecute the crimes.[21] Some scholars have attributed such jurisprudence to the fact that the IAHRS exercises its jurisdiction in a region characterized by widespread impunity,[22] while others have pointed out some consequences of this mandate, relevant for this analysis: (i) the Court encourages states to prosecute human rights violators in domestic courts, even after the ruling, and (ii) during the supervision of the rulings, the IACtHR exercises a quasi-criminal jurisdiction to oversee the criminal proceedings against perpetrators.[23]

The IACtHR has stated that criminal investigations must be 'serious, impartial and effective, not undertaken as a mere formality doomed in advance to be useless',[24] conducted within a reasonable time,[25] and where the procedural guarantees of the ACHR must be respected. However, this is a *means*

---

19 Ana María Idárraga Martínez and Juana Acosta López, 'Alcance del deber de investigar, juzgar y sancionar en transiciones de conflicto armado a una paz negociada: convergencias entre el Sistema Interamericano de Derechos Humanos y la Corte Penal Internacional' (2020) 45 *Revista Derecho del Estado* 55.

20 *Arrom Suhurt and Others v Paraguay* (Merits) IACtHR Series C No. 377 (13 May 2019) para 142; *Alvarado Espinoza and Others v Mexico* (Merits, Reparations and Costs) IACtHR Series C No. 370 (28 November 2018) para 215; *Velásquez Rodríguez v Honduras* (Judgment) IACtHR Series C No. 4 (29 July 1988) para 177.

21 Alexandra Huneeus, 'International Criminal Law by Other Means: The Quasi-Criminal Jurisdictions of Human Rights' (2013) 107 *American Journal of International Law* 1.

22 Par Engstrom, 'Between Hope and Despair: Progress and Resilience in the Inter-American Human Rights System' (2019) 113 AJIL Unbound 370.

23 Huneeus, 'International Criminal Law by Other Means: the Quasi-Criminal Jurisdictions of Human Rights' (n 21).

24 *Ituango Massacres v Colombia* (Preliminary Objections, Merits, Reparations and Costs) IACtHR Series C No. 148 (1 July 2006).

25 *La Rochela Massacre v Colombia* (Merit and Reparations) IACtHR Series C No. 221 (11 May 2007).

*obligation*[26] where no specific results are compulsory but the judicial authorities are required to act with due diligence and use every available means to clarify the case and punish those responsible.

Certainly, the Court has made a distinction between human rights violations that could be considered isolated and those that are inserted in a context of systematicity, massiveness, political violence, and armed conflict. Concerning the latter, specific rulings have stated the need to adjust the investigations when dealing with cases of massive and systematic violations of human rights and transitional justice systems, considering that 'the duty of due diligence takes on a special and stricter nature'.[27] In those cases, 'all necessary measures must be taken to make visible the systematic patterns that allowed the commission of serious human rights violations'.[28] Therefore, states should not only prosecute the immediate perpetrators[29] but should strive to disarticulate the structures

---

26 *Velásquez Rodríguez v Honduras* (Judgment) IACtHR Series C No. 4 (29 July 1988) para 177; *Godínez Cruz v Honduras* (Merits) IACtHR Series C No. 3 (20 January 1989) para 88; *Villagrán Morales and Others ('Street Children') v Guatemala* (Reparations and Costs) IACtHR Series C No. 77 (26 May 2001) para 226; *Durand and Ugarte v Peru* (Merits) IACtHR Series C No. 89 (16 August 2000) para 123; *Bámaca Velásquez v Guatemala* (Merits) IACtHR Series C No. 70 (25 November 2000) para 212; *Serrano Cruz sisters v El Salvador* (Preliminary Objections) IACtHR Series C No. 118 (23 November 2004) para 61; *Vereda La Esperanza v Colombia* (Preliminary Objections, Merits, Reparations) IACtHR Series C No. 341 (31 August 2017) para 185; *Maidanik and Others v Uruguay* (Merits and Reparations) IACtHR Series C No. 444 (15 November 2021) para 139.

27 Juana I. Acosta and Lina Álvarez, 'Las líneas lógicas de investigación: Una contribución del Sistema Interamericano De Derechos Humanos al juzgamiento de los crímenes de Sistema en marcos de justicia transicional' (2011) 18 *International Law: Revista Colombiana De Derecho Internacional* 57. Besides, the IACtHR stated that 'this obligation of due diligence takes on particular intensity and importance in view of the gravity of the crimes committed and the nature of the rights violated', in the *Case of La Rochela Massacre v Colombia* (Merit and Reparations) IACtHR Series C No. 221 (11 May 2007) para 156.

28 *La Rochela Massacre v Colombia* (Merit and Reparations) IACtHR Series C No. 221 (11 May 2007) para 156.

29 'It is not enough to know the material circumstances of a crime; it is essential that the investigations analyze the knowledge of the power structures that permitted, designed and executed the crimes intellectually and materially, as well as the persons or groups that were interested in or benefited from the crime'. *Manuel Cepeda Vargas v Colombia* (Preliminary Objections, Merits, Reparations) IACtHR Series C No. 213 (26 May 2010); see also Acosta and Álvarez, 'Las líneas lógicas de investigación' (n 27).

behind the crimes, as well as the causes, beneficiaries, and consequences,[30] unveiling the criminal patterns,[31] and, accordingly, judicial bodies must contemplate hypotheses that explain the complexity of criminal phenomena and must adopt coherent logical lines of criminal investigation.[32]

On the other hand, numerous rulings issued by the IACtHR have protected the rights of victims and their relatives to be heard in the criminal proceedings involving human rights violations, based on Article 8.1 ACHR.[33] The Court stated that victims should not be mere spectators of the criminal proceedings carried out to investigate gross violations of human rights.[34] On the contrary, victims must be active participants, and should have opportunities to participate and be heard throughout the process,[35] even to introduce new evidence. In

---

[30] 'In complex cases, the obligation to investigate entails the duty to direct the efforts of the state apparatus to unravel the structures that allowed these violations, their causes, their beneficiaries and their consequences, and not only to uncover, prosecute and, where appropriate, punish the immediate perpetrators'. *Manuel Cepeda Vargas v Colombia* (Preliminary Objections, Merits, Reparations) IACtHR Series C No. 213 (26 May 2010) para 118; see also *Isaza Uribe and Others v Colombia* (Merits, Reparations and Costs) IACtHR Series C No. 363 (20 November 2018) para 153.

[31] *La Rochela Massacre v Colombia* (Merit and Reparations) IACtHR Series C No. 221 (11 May 2007) para 156; *Tiu Tojín v Guatemala* (Merits and Reparations) IACtHR Series C No. 190 (26 November 2008) para 77; *Ibsen Cárdenas and Ibsen Peña v Bolivia* (Merits and Reparations) IACtHR Series C No. 217 (1 September 2010) para 166; *Afro-Descendant Communities Displaced from the Cacarica River Basin (Operation Génesis) v Colombia* (Preliminary Objections, Merits, Reparations) IACtHR Series C No. 270 (20 November 2013) para 372.

[32] In this regard, the IACtHR pointed out that 'certain lines of investigation, when they elude the analysis of the systematic patterns in which certain types of human rights violations are framed, can generate ineffectiveness in the investigations'. *González and Others ('Cotton Field') v Mexico* (Preliminary Objection, Merits, Reparations and Costs) IACtHR Series C No. 205 (16 November 2009).

[33] 'In accordance with the right recognized in Article 8(1) of the American Convention, in relation to Article 1(1) thereof, this Court has established that the states have the obligation to guarantee that, at all stages of the respective proceedings, the victims may make statements, receive information, provide evidence, formulate allegations and, in short, assert their interests'. *Radilla Pacheco v México* (Preliminary Objections, Merits, Reparations) IACtHR Series C No. 209 (23 November 2009).

[34] *Villagrán Morales and Others ('Street Children') v Guatemala* (Merits) IACtHR Series C No. 63 (19 November 1999).

[35] *Case of the Mapiripan Massacre v Colombia* (Preliminary Objections, Merits, Reparations) IACtHR Series C No. 134 (15 September 2005) 219.

the same way, in *Barrios Altos v Perú*,[36] the IACtHR developed the victims' right to have their interests effectively represented during the trial to pursue truth, justice, and reparations. Such jurisprudence has been a constant reference for the CCC, as we will develop.

Having described the obligation to investigate, prosecute, and punish, we will argue why it became the main yardstick by which the JEP is measured, with some nuances determined by the CCC.

## 3.1 Supranational Constraints on Peace: The JEP as a Response to Inter-American Limits on Amnesty

One of the impacts analyzed by Engstrom is the policy-creating impact, whereby the Inter-American jurisprudence adds 'pressure on governments to adopt policies, implement legislative changes, and reform institutions that advance the realization of rights – even in the absence of a formal ruling requiring them to do so'.[37] Certainly, such pressure describes how the IAHRS ended up influencing the JEP's design during the negotiations held in Havana. Hence, we will briefly present the context in which the Tribunal arose and began its work, along with its structure, which responds to the system of incentives designed to guarantee the victims' rights.

Unlike the peace agreements signed by the Colombian government in the 1980s, in which broad amnesties were granted to former combatants, the scenario during the Havana negotiations imposed strong restrictions on the government delegation in justice concessions.[38] By that time, Colombia was part of numerous human rights treaties and had more than twenty rulings by the IACtHR declaring international liability for human rights violations and 19 orders to prosecute the perpetrators, many of which were committed within the armed conflict or were related to it.

As mentioned earlier, the IAHRS jurisprudence on the obligation to investigate, prosecute, and punish was key to understanding the government constraints in the peace negotiations, by considering that the IACtHR ends up restricting the possibility of delivering full amnesties or judicial pardons in

---

36 IACtHR. *Case of Barrios Altos vs. Peru*, Judgment of 14 of March 2001.

37 Par Engstrom, 'Mobilising the Inter-American Human Rights System: Regional Litigation and Domestic Human Rights Impact in Latin America' in Par Engstrom (ed), *The Inter-American Human Rights System: Impact Beyond Compliance* (Palgrave Macmillan 2019) 51.

38 Camilo Sánchez and Uprimny Yepes, 'The Challenges of Negotiated Transitions in the Era of International Criminal Law' in Sánchez León and others (eds), *Beyond the Binary: Securing Peace and Promoting Justice after Conflict* (Dejusticia 2019) 33–7.

cases of gross human rights violations.[39] Although there are recent criticisms regarding the applicability of this jurisprudence in the context of armed conflicts where transitional justice strategies are implemented,[40] the truth is that these standards were an important limitation at the time of the negotiations and, to date, have remained relatively static in the IACtHR.[41] This is an impact of the Inter-American standards on the contemporary agendas associated with the construction of peace and transitions from authoritarian regimes to democracies.[42]

With the previous benchmarks in mind, the government insisted on the prosecution of former combatants to provide a legal shield to the Peace Agreement, both internally and before the IACtHR.[43] On the other hand, due to historical and political reasons, the FARC-EP guerrilla rejected the 'Peace and Justice'

---

39 Javier Dondé Matute, 'El concepto de impunidad: leyes de amnistía y otras formas estudiadas por la Corte Interamericana de Derechos Humanos' in Kai Ambos, Gisela Elsner and Ezequiel Malarino (eds), *Sistema interamericano de protección de los derechos humanos y derecho penal internacional* (Konrad Adenauer Stiftung 2010) 263–294.

40 Andrés Cervantes Valarezo, 'El impacto Sistema Interamericano de Derechos Humanos en la justicia transicional, ¿existe un lugar legítimo para el perdón?' (Doctoral Thesis, Universitat Pompeu Fabra 2020). Valarezo recalls that such a mandate does not constitute an absolute duty of the states; it is also problematic to conceptualize justice as a victim's human right to punishment, and there are other procedural guarantees in the ACHR that cannot be neglected with regard to perpetrators.

41 ibid 357.

42 Courtney Hillebrecht, Alexandra Huneeus and Sandra Borda, 'The Judicialization of Peace' (2018) 59 *Harvard International Law Journal* 279. Hillebrecht, Huneeus and Borda argue about the effects 'under the shadow' of the ICC and the IACtHR on peace negotiations in Colombia. They focus on effects that are not generated from a formal case opened before these courts, but by previous decisions or the threat of future litigation due to consolidated jurisprudential standards that end up impacting the peace negotiations, which were the most predominant for the Havana negotiations. The so-called 'shadow effects' are generated by 'the threat of future litigation as well as the imprint of prior litigation that has already shaped institutional processes and normative understandings mean that courts exert power over domestic decision-making even without issuing a judgment'.

43 Indeed, 'the Santos government concluded – after an exhaustive review of the country's existing legal standards and international precedents – that the only option to guarantee long-term legal security for FARC combatants who lay down their arms and members of the security forces was to address directly at the negotiating table the issue of accountability before a specialized tribunal for crimes committed in the conflict'. Andrés Bermúdez Liévano (ed), *Los debates de la Habana:*

(P&J) transitional system that was still operating in Colombia, mainly for paramilitary leaders, and the judgment conducted by the ordinary justice, making those options a red line for the negotiators.[44]

This is how the necessity arose to create a transitional justice body that could, on the one hand, reasonably meet the international human rights standards and, on the other hand, provide incentives or guarantees to former combatants. However, further changes were required to create such a tribunal, including constitutional reforms, intense legislative debates to issue the operating laws, and the formal review of the CCC on different milestones of the JEP's normative framework towards fulfilling those standards.

Firstly, the Colombian Constitution had to be changed, so that it would be possible to introduce case 'selection' in the prosecution of crimes that would fall under the JEP's competence. The normative framework of the JEP begins with the Legal Framework for Peace, a constitutional reform that took place in 2012 to provide a legal basis for the agreements. Mainly, this reform allowed for the first time the selection and prioritization of cases in Colombia, which allows criminal action to be concentrated on those most responsible for international crimes.[45] The reform was analyzed by the CCC in Ruling C-579 of 2013 to verify that Congress had not exceeded its power of reform by substituting the Constitution. In this way, the legislative act was analyzed in relation to the constitutional postulates, and, through the constitutional block, the Court made a careful review of the Inter-American jurisprudence on the obligation to investigate, prosecute, and punish concerning due diligence and victims' rights. In 2013, the Court finally declared that the reform was constitutional and established one of the main guidelines for the transitional justice model, which we will later develop: the viability of implementing selection and prioritization criteria to prosecute those most responsible for international crimes, since it 'contributes effectively to unravelling criminal macro-structures and revealing patterns of massive human rights violations, ultimately ensuring non-repetition'.[46]

After five years of intense negotiations in Havana, the government and the FARC-EP guerrilla group signed a Final Peace Agreement in 2016 to end more than fifty years of internal armed conflict and trace the route to building stable and lasting peace. Point number five regarding victims was certainly the

---

*una mirada desde adentro* (Institute for Integrated Transitions 2018) 213. Own translation.

[44] Bermúdez Liévano, *Los debates de la Habana: una mirada desde adentro* (n 42) 233.

[45] Bermúdez Liévano, *Los debates de la Habana: una mirada desde adentro* (n 42) 235.

[46] Decision No. C-579 (2013) Constitutional Court of Colombia.

most difficult to negotiate and required a specialized commission to unlock the debate on justice and accountability for crimes committed during the armed conflict. The result was the creation of a system composed of two extrajudicial mechanisms, called the Truth Commission and the Unit for the Search for Persons Reported Missing, and a judicial component, the JEP.

After the rejection of the original agreement in the plebiscite,[47] which was followed by an intense process of renegotiation and political endorsement to allow its implementation, the Congress approved the new text and issued Legislative Act No. 01 of 2017, to formally introduce the transitional institutions into the Constitution, and Legislative Act No. 02 of 2017, to secure the obligation of public authorities to comply with the agreements, along with crucial laws as to the JEP's operation, such as the procedural law and the statutory law.

When analyzing the norms of the Peace Agreement, the CCC acknowledged that it was impossible for the JEP to investigate every crime and every perpetrator. Therefore, it focused the duty to investigate on those most responsible for international crimes,[48] making the core of the obligation to investigate, prosecute, and punish applicable for the JEP. Therefore, the JEP aims to investigate, prosecute, and punish those most responsible forgross human rights violations committed during the conflict to fulfil the victims' rights to truth, justice, reparation, and non-repetition.[49]

The JEP was designed to focus on trying those most responsible for the most serious crimes, promoting their acknowledgment of truth and responsibility through sanctions and procedures, while generating alternative solutions for the remaining perpetrators, which vary between conditional amnesties, substitution of the criminal sanction and other judicial pardons. These purposes are reflected in the complex organisational structure that makes up the JEP.

---

47 For an in-depth reflection on the plebiscite see: Gabriel I. Gómez, 'Political conflicts over the JEP: a sociolegal perspective' in Kai Ambos and Stefan Peters (eds), *Transitional Justice in Colombia: The Special Jurisdiction for Peace* (Nomos 2022) 63–84. See also: Gwen Burnyeat, *The Face of Peace: Government Pedagogy amid Disinformation in Colombia* (The University of Chicago Press 2022).

48 Judgment C-370 (2006) Constitutional Court of Colombia; Judgment C-579 (2013) Constitutional Court of Colombia; Judgment C-674 (2017) Constitutional Court of Colombia; Judgment C-007 (2018) Constitutional Court of Colombia.

49 Office of the High Commissioner for Peace of Colombia, 'Final Agreement to End the Armed Conflict and Build a Stable and Lasting Peace' (24 November 2016); Government of Colombia 'Agreement regarding the Victims of the Conflict: Comprehensive System for Truth, Justice, Reparations and Non-Recurrence' (2016) 132–203. See also: Legislative Act No. 01 of 2017.

The JEP functions as a system of incentives, where those who acknowledge the truth and fulfil the victims' rights receive special non-custodial sanctions, while others, who do not, face an adversarial process in which they may eventually receive prison terms of up to 20 years.

The JEP is composed of chambers that operate as parallel opening doors which issue first instance decisions and, according to the circumstances, transfer the cases to the different sections of the Tribunal. The Chamber for Amnesties decides on conditional liberty and conditional amnesty requests mainly from the FARC-EP, while the Chamber for Definition of Legal Situations resolves submission requests, requests on conditional freedoms, and judicial pardons for former Army members, civilians, and state agents other than the security forces. Meanwhile, the SRVR is the main gateway for initiating criminal investigations, as we will describe later.

In a broad sense, the SRVR receives reports from judicial entities and victims' organisations, analyzes them, and applies the selection and prioritization criteria to formally open macro-cases to initiate the procedure with recognition.[50] The SRVR analyzes the reports in greater depth, and transfers them to the participants to initiate the call for voluntary testimonies. It also carries out additional investigative work, such as carrying out judicial inspections, transferring files from other jurisdictions, and receiving testimonies. Subsequently, the victims present their observations to the voluntary testimonies and the SRVR compares all of the information gathered to determine the patterns of macro-criminality and to identify those most responsible in the Decision of Determination of Facts and Conduct (ADHC for its acronym in Spanish), where they are also convened to acknowledge responsibility.

The JEP includes the special sanctions, which may consist of restorative mechanisms rather than prison sentences. When truth is not acknowledged, the case is sent to the Investigation and Prosecution Unit, so that this body investigates and eventually presents its accusation before the judicial Section for Absence of Acknowledgment of Truth and Responsibility. Before this Section, the adversarial process takes place and custodial sanctions may be imposed, depending on the moment at which responsibility is accepted.[51]

Having described the generalities of the JEP, we will show how it has been deeply influenced by the jurisprudence of the IAHRS, which is reflected in the regulatory framework and the execution of judicial functions.

---

[50] Described in title one, chapter one of Law 1922 of 2018.

[51] For further details on the JEP's procedure and the structure see: Diego Tarapués Sandino, 'Special Jurisdiction for Peace and Sui Generis Transitional Justice' in Kai Ambos and Stefan Peters (eds), *Transitional Justice in Colombia: The Special Jurisdiction for Peace* (Nomos 2022) 63–84.

## 3.2 Supranational Constraints on Peace: the JEP as a Response to Inter-American Limits on Amnesty

Another type of impact described by Engstrom focuses on understanding 'how regional human rights standards and the Inter-American Court's jurisprudence are shaping domestic constitutional debates, litigation strategies, judicial thinking and practice'.[52] In this subsection we will trace the influence of several IAHRS decisions that have stressed the need to implement logical lines of investigation in cases of gross human rights violations in the Colombian 'Peace and Justice' process which, years later, became crucial for the JEP.

Law 1592 of 2012 and the subsequent norms[53] reformed the P&J Law to introduce the analysis of systemic criminality and its structures, the investigation of macro-criminal patterns, and the need to prosecute those most responsible.[54] Certainly, those first attempts to overcome the case-by-case logic in criminal investigation that led to de facto impunity in the past rapidly became new directions in transitional justice in Colombia and later permeated the regulation of the JEP, from the constitutional norms to the internal operating rules.[55]

Since Legislative Act No. 01 of 2012, the CCC determined one of the most important paths for the JEP to reasonably meet the international obligation to investigate, prosecute, and punish, which consisted of the investigation of macro-criminality patterns. Although there are different definitions and components of the concept,[56] instead of the specificities in an individual and

---

52 Par Engstrom, 'Reconceptualising the Impact of the Inter-American Human Rights System' (2017) 8 Rev Direito e Práxis 1250, 2160.

53 For instance, the Guideline No. 01 of 2012 of the General Attorney's Office that later developed the prioritization criteria and was further modified by the Guideline No. 2 of 2015.

54 Law 1592 of 2012, Article 15 on clarification of the truth states that: 'Within the procedure established by this law, public servants shall make the necessary arrangements to ensure the clarification of the truth about the pattern of macro-criminality in the actions of organized armed groups operating outside the law and to unveil the contexts, causes and motives'. Own translation.

55 In this regard, it is worth mentioning that during the first years of the JEP, the judges had to deal with considerable regulatory gaps and complex situations that constantly challenged the few existing norms they had. In this scenario of normative and operational uncertainty, the main and closest references for the JEP were the CCC and the IAHRS when determining the standards under which it should deliver justice.

56 See: Juan Pablo Cardona Chávez, 'Priorización, contextos y patrones de macrocriminalidad: estrategia de investigación en el marco de la justicia transicional en Colombia' (2020) 52 *Revista Pensamiento Jurídico* 223.

isolated case, there is a mandate to identify criminal organisations' policies, practices, and modus operandi, understanding the context in which they operated. The Court pointed out that

> the approach of Legislative Act 01 of 2012 is not aimed at establishing impunity for certain crimes, but at changing the 'case by case' investigation strategy, which hinders the guarantee of the right to justice of the victims of massive human rights violations, *for the structuring of macro-processes in which there is massive participation of all victims and which are not structured by chance, but by virtue of investigations based on contexts and the analysis of organized criminal structures.* (emphasis added)[57]

Later on, the CCC explicitly connected the macro-processes with the mandate to identify and determine criminal patterns when analyzing the JEP's statutory law, 'grouping individual cases according to criminal patterns, constructed by crossing different variables (time, geography, quality of the victim, etc.), and thus concentrating investigative efforts on certain suspects or criminal organisations'.[58]

Therefore, the JEPs' constitutional and legal mandate to investigate the most serious and representative crimes and prosecute those most responsible became a benchmark for its judicial activity and laid the groundwork for macro-criminal investigation in the SRVR.[59] Such emphasis allowed the configuration of 11 macro-cases in the SRVR,[60] in which multiple acts committed

---

57 Ruling C 579 (2013) Constitutional Court of Colombia.

58 Ruling C-674 (2017) Constitutional Court of Colombia.

59 Indeed, Law 1922 of 2018, Article 11 states the following objectives of the investigation of crimes under the JEP jurisdiction: '1. Determine the geographic, economic, social, political, and cultural circumstances in which the crimes under the jurisdiction of the JEP took place. 2. When appropriate, describe the structure and functioning of the criminal organization, its support networks, the characteristics of the attack, and the macro-criminal patterns. 3. Unveil the criminal plan. 4. Associate cases and situations. 5. Identify those responsible. 6. Establish the most serious and representative crimes. 7. Identify the victims and the conditions that cause them differentiated affectations.' Law 1922 of 2018. Own translation.

60 Case No. 1 on kidnapping and other serious deprivation of liberty committed by the FARC; Case No. 2 on the territorial situation of Tumaco, Ricaurte and Barbacoas municipalities (Nariño); Case No. 3 on extrajudicial executions and enforced disappearance committed by state agents; Case No. 4 on the territorial situation of the Urabá Region; Case No. 5 on the territorial situation of the Northern Cauca and Southern Cauca Valley; Case No. 6 on the victimization of Patriotic Union (UP) members; Case No. 7 on recruitment of children; Case No. 8 on crimes committed by members of the armed forces and other state agents, in association with paramilitary groups or civilian third parties; Case No. 9 of

by thousands of perpetrators are investigated while thousands of victims are recognized and have participated.

The investigations made it possible to convene thousands of FARC-EP and Army perpetrators who revealed new information on human rights violations, other violations previously unknown, and key actors that were part of criminal alliances and who sometimes provided information to locate the remains of persons reported missing.[61]

We can trace the macro-criminality approach in the first eight indictments issued by the SRVR. However, we will focus on six corresponding to Case No. 1 on kidnappings and Case No. 3 on murders and forced disappearances presented as casualties committed by the Army, as these are the most advanced in the procedure. The first Case covers more than 21,000 events, 7,000 perpetrators and more than 3,000 victims participating; while Case No. 3 covers an estimated 6,402 events, 3,000 perpetrators and more than 3,000 victims participating.

The SRVR has identified and reconstructed patterns with capacity to illustrate a myriad of crimes which share common elements, which were not committed by chance, and which show the behaviour of criminal organizations that attack particluar people, using specific means of violence, acting under different motivations.[62]

In an unprecedented decision, the SRVR issued the first Decision of Determination of Facts and Conduct against the FARC-EP leaders and described in considerable detail the policies, modalities, purposes, and consequences for the victims and their families of the kidnapping carried out by

---

crimes against ethnic peoples and territories; Case No. 10 of crimes committed by FARC-EP during the armed conflict; and Case No. 11 on crimes of sexual violence, reproductive violence and other crimes committed because of prejudice, hatred or discrimination based on gender, sex, gender identity, and sexual orientation. For further information on the cases opened see: https://www.jep.gov.co/Paginas/casos.aspx.

[61] The emblematic case of the recovery of mortal remains thanks to the information provided to the JEP is the sub-case of Dabeiba, Antioquia, within Case No. 3. The contributions provided by the participants allowed 71 forensic findings of corpses that were hidden in the cemetery of Dabeiba, and five dignified handovers of bodies to the families of reported missing persons. See: https://www.jep.gov.co/Sala-de-Prensa/Paginas/La-JEP-retoma-exhumaciones-en-Dabeiba.aspx.

[62] Ruling No. 19 of 2021 defined the concept of a pattern of macro-criminality as 'the non-accidental repetition of a similar criminal conduct in terms of its purposes, mode of commission, and characteristics of the victims', which was also adopted in the subsequent orders in Case No. 3.

the guerrillas.[63] Although this criminal phenomenon had important visibility during the armed conflict, the formalities of the criminal process did not allow giving a voice to the surviving or indirect victims, to directly relate the suffering they endured, nor the levels of cruelty reached by the FARC-EP and its leaders, who extended this practice in much of the national territory to finance their organization, to exercise control over the territory and its population, and to seek political power over the national government.

Several documents issued by the FARC-EP secretariat setting out the policy of financing the organization through kidnapping, later complemented by the policy of kidnapping people to force the exchange of imprisoned guerrillas, allowed for a 'top-down' investigation. Along with the explicit policies issued by the FARC-EP leaders, the SRVR determined the pattern of deprivation of liberty due to territorial and social control, the generalized pattern of ill-treatment of victims in captivity, and some cases of forced displacement and sexual violence.[64] In this decision, the SRVR charged eight members of the FARC-EP secretariat (top leaders of the organisation) with war crimes and crimes against humanity for the commission of more than 21,300 kidnappings carried out by all factions of the guerrillas. More than 3,000 victims participated before the SRVR from the opening of the case until the issuance of the order, which incorporated unpublished testimonies to reconstruct their suffering.

In contrast, Case No. 3 investigated a criminal phenomenon widely denied in the armed conflict narrative, for it called into question the truthfulness and legitimacy of the security forces. Although there were extrajudicial executions falsely presented as combat casualties along the whole country, with more than 6,402 fatal victims,[65] there was a general denial about the very existence of the phenomenon within the Army and in public opinion. This particularity of the case led to the implementation of a 'bottom-up' investigation strategy that started with the direct perpetrators of the crimes, which would allow the reconstruction of macro-criminality patterns to continue with the subsequent prosecution of those most responsible at higher levels.

The way to address a national phenomenon of massive proportions was the prioritization of critical territories using a mix of quantitative criteria, such as the number of victims, with qualitative criteria, such as the capacity to illustrate the criminal phenomenon. Thus, the SRVR internally prioritized six critical

63 Ruling No. 19 of 2021 (26 January 2021) Chamber for the Acknowledgment of Truth.

64 Ruling No. 19 of 2021 (26 January 2021) Chamber for the Acknowledgment of Truth.

65 Ruling No. 33 of 2021 (12 February 2021) Chamber for the Acknowledgment of Truth.

territories to begin the investigation[66] and recently opened the national phase to analyze the highest responsibilities within the military chain of command.[67]

Up to October 2023, there have been four judicial ADHC in Case No. 3, and 59 persons identified as most responsible, charged for international crimes[68] and convened to acknowledge truth in public hearings, with victims' participation.

After having cross-checked hundreds of voluntary testimonies with countless judicial files and military documents, the SRVR issued four decisions in Case No. 3 which illustrate the macro-criminal approach. These decisions cover the same criminal phenomenon in four regions, with different military units and conflict dynamics. One decision is issued at the battalion level,[69] two decisions combine battalions with mobile brigades,[70] and one, the largest, covers a territorial brigade of the National Army.[71] All identify a significant number of extrajudicial executions falsely presented as combat casualties, ranging from 47 cases in Dabeiba to 295 in Casanare, which were grouped together to establish criminality patterns.

In this way, the Chamber was able to identify common patterns in different territories, such as the commission of crimes to satisfy the demand for military results or casualties in combat, others committed as part of a counter-insurgency strategy, and the pattern of deception with promises of work or sums of money to transfer victims who would later be killed without any kind of military confrontation. In Dabeiba, the Chamber found a distinctive pattern which consisted of murders and subsequent forced disappearances of people from cemeteries to prevent their identification at all costs. This exercise revealed the true functioning of the structures that committed the crimes and led to the

---

66 Ruling No. 33 of 2021 (12 February 2021) Chamber for the Acknowledgment of Truth.

67 Ruling OPV No. 305 of 2023 (14 July 2023) Chamber for the Acknowledgment of Truth.

68 Corporación Excelencia en la Justicia, 'Observa JEP: Progress of the special jurisdiction for peace' (2022) https://drive.google.com/file/d/1b_59htKLhYRCbY7BQqINbGImtiENXqTF/view.

69 Ruling No. 128 of 2021 of the Caribbean Coast, Chamber for Acknowledgment of Truth.

70 Ruling No. 125 of 2021 of the 15th Mobile Brigade and the 'General Francisco de Paula Santander' Infantry Battalion with jurisdiction in the Catatumbo Region, 'Norte de Santander', Chamber for Acknowledgment of Truth; Ruling No. 1 of 2022 of Dabeiba, Chamber for Acknowledgment of Truth.

71 Ruling No. 55 of 2021 of the 16th Brigade of the Army in the Casanare Department, Chamber for Acknowledgment of Truth.

identification of 56 top perpetrators and three key participants, who were all charged with war crimes and crimes against humanity.

So far, the rigorous and forceful nature of the investigations has allowed most of the accused, including a Major General of the Army, to acknowledge their responsibility before the surviving victims, overcoming the systematic denial of these cases, and restoring the victims' reputations.

The previous decisions show that the SRVR avoided the 'case by case' logic and has made genuine efforts to reduce impunity by adopting a macro-criminal approach in the prioritized cases, no matter the different prosecution strategies that have been employed.[72] This has been materialized in the collection and analysis of large amounts of information from different sources on the serious violations of human rights, the characterization of the armed groups that carried them out, the unveiling of their chains of command, and the constant concern to identify those most responsible for the crimes, approaching the standards indicated by the IACtHR.[73] At different levels and scales, the SRVR has charged international crimes to those most responsible in four cases[74] and has continued to carry out investigations in the remaining seven.

### 3.3 Impact of the IAHRS Standards on the Design of Mechanisms for Robust Victims' Rights and Their Participation in the JEP

Among the different notions of impact, we want to focus on those that allow us to analyze the design of policies and programmes based on standards and practices from the IAHRS. Considering the standards of victims' participation developed by the IACtHR, we will briefly describe the CCC statements applicable for the JEP and how they have been implemented in the Chamber for Acknowledgment of Truth and Responsibility. We will then outline the

---

72 As mentioned previously, Case No. 3 opted for a 'bottom-up' investigation, while Case No. 1 adopted a 'top-down' approach.

73 'Due diligence in the proceedings for the facts of this case required that they be conducted taking into account the complexity of the facts, the context in which they occurred and the patterns that explain their commission [...] all necessary measures must be adopted to make visible the systematic patterns that allowed the commission of serious human rights violations.' See also: *La Rochela Massacre v Colombia* (Merit and Reparations) IACtHR Series C No. 221 (11 May 2007); *Radilla Pacheco v México* (Preliminary Objections, Merits, Reparations) IACtHR Series C No. 209 (23 November 2009).

74 Case 1: Chamber for Acknowledgment of truth. Ruling No. 19 of 2021. 26th January 2021 and Ruling No. 1 of 2023, 4th July 2023. Case No. 2: Ruling No. 03 of 2023, Case No. 3: Ruling No. 125 of 2021, Ruling No. 128 of 2021, Ruling No. 55 of 2021 and Ruling No. 1 of 2022. Case No. 5: Ruling No. 01 of 2023.

infrastructure and services provided to reduce the obstacles that victims face in accessing justice, which has enabled massive participation and paved the way to implement restorative justice mechanisms. Finally, we will show in broad strokes the attempts of the JEP to generate scenarios for victims' dignification and restorative justice, which constitute the main innovation of the model regarding the prosecution of serious human rights violations.

Based on human rights treaties and mainly on Inter-American jurisprudence, the CCC has stated in numerous rulings that victims' rights are the foundation and essential purpose of the JEP[75] and has determined specific stages in the procedure to materialize the effectiveness of such participation.[76] For instance, the CCC has ruled on the conditionality regime for judicial pardons, on the various means to prove victim status, on collective representation, and has reiterated the rules on publicity and the possibility of appeals against prioritization decisions.

Consequently, all the governing principles, procedural laws, and substantive laws of the JEP develop the victims' participation and centrality.[77] Victims' participation must be present in all proceedings, even in those conceived to provide judicial pardons and conditional amnesties, and precisely the conditions for accessing these benefits consist in the satisfaction of the victims' rights.[78] However, the legal provisions were not limited to the enunciation of rights but were accompanied by an institutional framework and resources to reduce the obstacles which victims face when seeking justice.

Undoubtedly, the participation of victims in criminal proceedings in Colombia faces numerous obstacles, which were contemplated in the JEP's

---

75 Judgment C-080 (2018) Colombian Constitutional Court. 'This Court has also highlighted the special importance of the Inter-American system and the jurisprudence of the Inter-American Court of Human Rights regarding the rights of victims of serious human rights violations to justice, truth, reparation and non-repetition.'

76 Ruling C-579 (2013) Colombian Constitutional Court.

77 Law 1957 of 2019, Article 13 on the victims' centrality principle; Law 1922 of 2018, first Title on gratuity in the JEP: 'free access for victims will be guaranteed'; Law 1957 of 2019, Article 11 on victims' effective participation; Law 1957 of 2019, Article 14: 'The rules of procedure of the JEP shall provide for the effective participation of victims in the proceedings of this jurisdiction [...] and at least with the rights given by the quality of special intervener according to national and international standards on procedural, substantive, evidential guarantees, access to an effective judicial remedy and other applicable rights'; Law 1957 of 2019, Article 15 on victims' rights; Law 1957 of 2019, Article 16 on special rights of victims of sexual violence.

78 Law 1957 of 2019, Article 49 on the contribution to the fulfilment of victims' rights.

design. After enduring human rights violations, surviving victims must face long and painful judicial processes to vindicate their rights. In addition to the damages, which are often irreparable, victims must incur significant expenses to participate in criminal proceedings, travel to hearings, hire lawyers and face constant psychosocial risks, not to mention the risks to their safety or the threats they receive during the process.[79] Aware of these risks and the adverse experience of victims in the P&J process,[80] the JEP regulations developed different services.

The JEP's Registrar, through the department for victim assistance (DAV, for its acronym in Spanish) and the victims' advice and legal representation system (SAAD Victims, for its acronym in Spanish), provides free services for victims ranging from preparation for participation,[81] to autonomous and free judicial representation to defend their interests through lawyers hired by the Registrar.

Likewise, the JEP provides psychosocial support and preparation for victims throughout the process, not to shape their impressions or speeches during the hearings but by explaining the nature of each judicial stage, performing emotional containment, and handling tensions that may arise from dialogue scenarios between perpetrators and victims.[82] Finally, and under certain circumstances, the Registrar provides resources to facilitate the participation of victims in the hearings, reducing some of the obstacles they face to attend. This has had a positive impact on the participation of victims before the SRVR, as shown in Table 6.1.

Once recognized, victims and their representatives become active participants before the SRVR: they have access to the macro-case files, they can submit questions or requirements to be resolved during the voluntary hearings or directly participate, provide evidence, and file appeals.[83] When a person 'is

---

[79] Centro Nacional de Memoria Histórica, 'La lucha de las víctimas por la justicia' (2022) https://centrodememoriahistorica.gov.co/micrositios/derechoJusticia/lucha-victimas-justicia.html

[80] Andreas Forer, 'La participación de las víctimas en el marco de un proceso de justicia transicional – el caso colombiano en la Ley de Justicia y Paz' in Claudia López Díaz (ed), *Participación de las víctimas en la Ley de Justicia y Paz y la Corte Penal Internacional* (Deutsche Gesellschaft Für Internationale Zusammenarbeit 2011) 31–52.

[81] Including assistance for reports' presentation.

[82] Oscar Parra Vera, 'The Special Jurisdiction for Peace and Restorative Justice: First Steps' in Kai Ambos and Stefan Peters (eds), *Transitional Justice in Colombia, The Special Jurisdiction for Peace* (Nomos 2022) 135–160.

[83] Special Jurisdiction for Peace, 'Victims' Participation Handbook' (JEP, 2020) https://www.jep.gov.co/Infografas/participacion/manualparticipacion.pdf.

*Table 6.1 Recognized victims in macro-cases*

| Case | | Individual victims | Collective victims | Estimated individuals comprising the collective victims |
|---|---|---|---|---|
| 1 | Kidnapping and other serious deprivation of liberty committed by the FARC | 3,422 | No data reported | No data reported |
| 2 | Territorial situation of Tumaco, Ricaurte and Barbacoas municipalities (Nariño) | 48 | 11 | 105,241 |
| 3 | Extrajudicial executions and enforced disappearances committed by state agents | 2,723 | No data reported | No data reported |
| 4 | Territorial situation of the Urabá Region | 137 | 111 | 46,709 |
| 5 | Territorial situation of the Northern Cauca and Southern Cauca Valley | 68 | 129 | More than 180.000 victims |
| 6 | Victimization of Patriotic Union Members (UP) | 297 | 4 | No data reported |
| 7 | Recruitment of children | 635 | 3,130 | 3,765 |

*Note:* Special Jurisdiction for Peace. Cases of the JEP. Retrieved from: https://www.jep.gov.co/Paginas/casos.aspx. Given the discrepancy between the figures reported in Case No. 3, we prefer to use the data from the most recent prioritization ruling, i.e., Chamber for Acknowledgment of truth. 14 July, 2023. Ruling OPV No. 305 of 2023.
*Source:* Cases of the JEP, 14 October 2023. Case No. 3: Ruling OPV No. 305 of 2023.

recognized as a victim, they can provide observations, not just on their individual case, but also on the macro-case more generally',[84] and later, they can participate in the formulation of restorative projects.

As shown in Table 6.2, victims' legal advice and representation has grown each year, which can be interpreted not only as increased case coverage but

[84] Parra Vera, 'The Special Jurisdiction for Peace and Restorative Justice' (n 81) 135–160.

*Table 6.2 Annual services provided by the SAAD Victims*

| | 2018 | 2019 | 2020 | 2021 | 2022 |
|---|---|---|---|---|---|
| Legal advice provided to victims | 168 | 107 | 3263 | 3318 | 1594 |
| Number of individual victims represented | 16 | 1390 | 1735 | No data reported | 2058 |
| Number of collective victims represented | – | 100 | 247 | 21 | 13 |

*Note:* Available at: https://www.jep.gov.co/SiteAssets/Paginas/Transparencia/Balance2019-Proyeccion-2020-JEP/SUB-SE_Reporte_Estadistico_SAADVic.pdf; https://www.jep.gov.co/SiteAssets/Paginas/Transparencia/Balance2019-Proyeccion-2020-JEP/SUB-SE_Reporte_Estadistico_SAADVic.pdf; https://www.jep.gov.co/Planeacion1/Informes%20de%20gestión/2020/20210121%20SE_Dpto_SAADVic.pdf?csf=1&e=W4mT0d; https://www.jep.gov.co/Planeacion1/Informes%20de%20gestión/2021/20211231_DSAADV.pdf; and https://www.jep.gov.co/Planeacion1/Informes%20de%20gestión/2022/Visor%20ENE-DIC%202022%20SAAD%20V.pdf.
*Source:* Management reports (2018–2022), victims' legal advice and representation system.

also as a sign of victims' confidence in the system. Furthermore, the institutional design of both the DAV and the SAAD Victims within the Registrar created a direct contact between victims and the JEP, which has no precedent in Colombia.

While there is still a long way to go to meet all the needs of the victims, the portfolio of services provided by the Registrar has allowed massive participation in the judicial procedures and materialized the approach of restorative justice, as we will develop later.

Regarding restorative justice, it is worth mentioning that the IACtHR does not have an established position on the topic. Nevertheless, a closer look at the integral reparation objectives and specifically 'satisfaction measures' reveals a conception of the damage suffered that goes beyond the economic sphere, which also suggests a concern for immaterial damages, collective memory, and victims' dignity. In fact, in the reparations ordered by the Court, it is common to find measures such as the publication of rulings in mass media, public apologies by state agents, the commemoration of people or events, and other types of measures aimed at victims' dignification (e.g., scholarship programmes in the name of the mortal victims, commemorative plaques, among others).[85]

[85] Juana I. Acosta López and Diana Bravo Rubio, 'El cumplimiento de los fines de reparación integral de las medidas ordenadas por la Corte Interamericana de

Such measures 'seek to repair non-pecuniary damages, which do not have pecuniary scope, and must have public scope and repercussion'.[86] They have points of coincidence with the principles of restorative justice, insofar as they conceive the damage as a complex process that goes beyond the pecuniary detriment, promote narratives in a public sphere that lead to reflection on what happened, and share a concern for the victims' reparation and dignification.

Within the CCC, the discussion on restorative justice began with special sanctions, but was not limited to them, as the JEP model adopts this paradigm which radiates victims' participation and judicial procedures. The Court analyzed the restorative justice postulates of focusing on the damages suffered, victims' reparation, and generating conditions for reconciliation through dialogue between victims, perpetrators, and communities. Those postulates are in accordance with constitutional principles, and the Court concluded that this may be a better instrument to achieve peace and reconciliation, restore damages, and empower victims, compared to the traditional punishments of ordinary justice, which are eminently retributive. Additionally, the CCC stated that restorative justice 'can be an appropriate complement in transitional situations, both for the design of transitional justice mechanisms and for the implementation'.[87] In this way, the CCC endorsed the restorative justice model and the special sanctions under conditions which ensured their compliance.[88]

Parra (2022) analyzed in detail the main debates around the implementation of restorative justice in the SRVR, its potential and limitations, considering the inherent risks of massiveness, re-victimization in the early stages of the process, and false expectations as towhat the JEP can do.[89] However, the observation hearings, designed as the first public moment for the victims to speak, proved to be indispensable for reconstructing comprehensive narratives of the armed conflict. With previous psychosocial support provided by the JEP, victims were able to reveal unknown facts, expose the impacts caused, and sometimes make direct requests to the perpetrators.

A year later, four hearings on acknowledgment of truth took place in Case No. 3[90] with profound restorative impacts that are worth mentioning, both

---

Derechos Humanos: énfasis en la experiencia colombiana' (2008) 13 *Int. Law: Rev Colomb. Derecho Int. Bogotá* 323.

86 *García Asto and Ramírez Rojas v Perú* (Preliminary Objections, Merits, Reparations) IACtHR Series C No. 137 (25 November 2005) para 276.

87 Ruling C-080 (2018) Constitutional Court of Colombia.

88 Article 13 of the Legislative Act No. 01 of 2017.

89 Parra Vera, 'The Special Jurisdiction for Peace and Restorative Justice' (n 81) 135–160.

90 The hearings took place on 26–27 April 2023 in 'Norte de Santander', on 27–28 June 2023 in Dabeiba, on 18–19 July 2023 in Valledupar, and on 18–20

for the parties involved in the proceedings and for society in general. All these hearings took place directly in the territories where the victimization occurred, which is novel in a country as centralized as Colombia. The judges of the JEP approached the victims, reducing barriers to access to justice which they would have traditionally faced.

During the public hearings, the perpetrators acknowledge the truth while facing the victims, their representatives, and the judges. Statements are expected from them, comprising three dimensions which are mainly determined in the ADHC: factual, legal, and harm caused to the victims. For their part, the victims and their representatives express their views on these acknowledgments, along with further demands or requests. All of this happens on a public stage which is broadcast live, challenging society as a whole and generating significant impacts on the narrative of the conflict.

The main challenges and recommendations previously identified in Parra (2022) were present at this stage too, and became even more pronounced. Prior psychosocial preparation was crucial, consisting of: (i) victims' encounters, where they relate to each other and reflect on the truth obtained so far and their demands; (ii) perpetrators' encounters to reflect on their statements before the SRVR, the narratives around the crimes, the damage caused. and the demands of truth from the victims; and, finally, (iii) private encounters between victims and perpetrators which were accompanied by mediators and psychosocial professionals.

The hearings were particularly emotional, since there was a legitimate concern to treat all participants with dignity and humanity, avoiding justifying speeches and revictimizing expressions. Victims had the opportunity to express their pain, frustrations, and familiar tragedies before the judges and the audience, while the SRVR constantly sent the message that it was a safe space for them. None of the participants were stripped of their dignity and, sometimes for the first time, they recognized the dignity of the counterpart.

The dignification of the mortal victims was of considerable importance in Case No. 3, due to the deliberate intention of the perpetrators to portray them as guerrillas, criminals, or extortionists. The forcefulness of the public acknowledgments of the military, especially the highest ranks, had wide media coverage and produced broad discussions in a society that had for a long time denied these facts. Dignification acts were expressed in different ways, such as the recognition of each of the victims as civilians who did not belong to any armed group or criminal organization, public apologies, and the offering of medals to the victims as a symbol of forgiveness.

September 2023 in Casanare.

Certainly, the massiveness of victimizing events and, consequently, time management posed significant challenges during the Casanare and Dabeiba hearings. There were some contentious moments that did not, however, denaturalize the restorative nature of the proceedings. After all, encounters between victims of gross violations of human rights and perpetrators were possible, victims' dignification was at the centre, and a different narrative on false positives is taking place.

# 4 CONCLUSIONS

It is still premature to appraise the JEP's results in light of the obligation to investigate, prosecute, and punish, and the interactions that will exist in the future with the IACtHR when the first sanctions are imposed. In the same way, it is possible to anticipate that there will be further discussions on the need to update the content of the obligation to investigate, prosecute, and punish to contexts of transitional justice in which the aim is to overcome an armed conflict, along with more dialogues between domestic courts and the IAHRS on this matter.

However, the different types of impacts described by Engstrom allow us to appreciate the influence of the IAHRS on the design and implementation of the JEP, which is the most important public policy of transitional justice in Colombia in recent years, based on its consolidated jurisprudence on the obligation to investigate, prosecute, and punish. Undoubtedly, this jurisprudence made the negotiators seek the maximum possible justice, while the CCC conditioned all benefits on the satisfaction of the victims' rights. The Inter-American standards also laid the groundwork for putting victims at the centre of the proceedings, which translated into the creation of an infrastructure and a range of services which have enabled massive participation in the JEP.

Finally, the judgments of the CCC may shed light on a viable formula for adjusting the standards of the obligation to investigate, prosecute, and punish to the massiveness and complexity of the victimizations inherent in an armed conflict, which in turn are aligned with the logical lines of investigation developed by the IAHRS. For its part, the SRVR materialized the logical lines of investigation in concrete methodologies, which made it possible to unveil patterns of macro-criminality and the indictment of those persons who, due to their leadership or participation, created and deployed those patterns.

# 7. Behind the scenes of impact in the *Yanomami* case (1980–85): civil society and bureaucratic politics in the Inter-American Commission on Human Rights

**Bruno Boti Bernardi and João Roriz**

## 1. INTRODUCTION

During the Brazilian military dictatorship, from 1964 to 1985, the state officialized a policy of forced integration and assimilation towards Indigenous peoples, culminating in large numbers of deaths, and episodes of genocide.[1] The pressure from religious missions, the expansion of the agricultural and mining fronts, and the developmentalist infrastructure projects denied Indigenous peoples their lands and the preservation of their worldviews and ways of life. In addition, these peoples were exposed to armed violence, epidemics, environmental contamination, expropriation of natural resources, processes of forced displacement, and numerous other factors of disintegration and ethnic-cultural extermination.

As part of the myth that Brazil was supposedly a racial democracy built upon a single pacific national communion, Indigenous peoples were portrayed

[1] According to official figures produced by the Brazilian National Truth Commission (BNTC), there are records of at least 8,350 Indigenous persons killed during this period as a direct result of the actions and omissions of state forces and policies. In many cases, various Indigenous peoples were left on the brink of total annihilation, and the actual toll of deaths will be exponentially greater than the estimations, since only a small fraction of the affected Indigenous communities – 10 ethnic groups out of a total of 305 – was analyzed in the works of the BNTC. Brazilian National Truth Commission, *Relatório da Comissão Nacional da Verdade* (2014), vol 2, 205; Rubens Valente, *Os fuzis e as flechas: história de sangue e resistência indígena na ditadura* (Companhia das Letras 2017).

both as obstacles to the progression of capitalism and as potential threats to national security by the prevailing doctrines of the internal enemy and unbridled economic developmentalism. Despite the fact that, since the late 1960s, manifold allegations and accusations of genocide had been circulating in foreign public spaces against Brazil,[2] the first formal international case concerning Brazilian Indigenous peoples was opened only in 1980 by the Inter-American Commission on Human Rights (IACHR).[3] This case resulted in a recommendation in 1985, exactly when the dictatorship ended, without any express reference to genocide. The recommendation addressed the territorial deprivation and a long list of human rights abuses against the Yanomami people in the Brazilian northern regions of Amazonas and Roraima, near the Venezuelan border.[4] It endorsed the creation of a demarcated Indigenous territory, the Yanomami Park, as requested by the petitioners.

At that time, the 1983 Martínez Cobo Study was still defining the concept of Indigenous peoples at the United Nations, while the International Labour Organization (ILO) was criticized for its assimilationist 1957 Convention No. 107. In such a scenario, transnational pressure from a network of civil society organizations supporting the Yanomami stimulated a hitherto hesitant IACHR to speak about their land rights. The IACHR recommendation contributed at last to the demarcation of the Yanomami lands in 1992, yielding a concrete and measurable impact.[5] In this sense, the IACHR integrated a more extensive transnational campaign in favour of the Yanomami, known for sensibilizing foreign governments and global public opinion, as well as for its actions

---

[2] Paulo Cesar Gomes and Carlos Benitez-Trinidad, 'A questão indígena durante a ditadura militar brasileira e a opinião pública estrangeira em perspectiva transnacional' (2022) 14 *Revista Tempo e Argumento* 1.

[3] The Inter-American Commission on Human Rights is an international body of the Organization of American States (OAS). In tandem with the Inter-American Court of Human Rights, it comprehends the American hemisphere's regional human rights protection system. As Brazil only joined the American Convention on Human Rights in 1992, accepting the Court's competence even later, in 1998, the cases against the country during the military regime were processed only by the Commission, which made reference exclusively to the 1948 American Declaration of the Rights and Duties of Man (ADRDM) when analyzing human rights violations supposedly perpetrated or neglected by state agents. The Commission's reports and decisions have a recommendatory status for the states and are not binding.

[4] Among the many allegations, petitioners claimed violations had occurred against the Yanomami's rights related to life, freedom, security, personal integrity, equality before the law, religious freedom, health, well-being, and property.

[5] IACHR Resolution No. 12/85, *Coulter and Others v. Brazil – Yanomami* case, Case No. 7615 (5 March 1985).

in other international organizations and UN forums like the Human Rights Commission.

Given the long and traditional silence regarding the rights of Indigenous peoples that prevailed in international human rights regimes,[6] the recommendation was both a turning point and a precedent for the subsequent decisions and jurisprudential advances of the Inter-American system from the 2000s onwards. Thus, since the *Yanomami* case, the IACHR has issued other recommendations impacting the recognition and strengthening of land and other rights for Indigenous peoples in the Americas.[7] What are the factors explaining such an important institutional shift in the IACHR?

To answer this question, in this chapter we adopt the perspective of historical institutionalism[8] as our theoretical framework. Then we analyze the interactions between the Brazilian government, the IACHR, and the organizations petitioning for the Yanomami during the proceedings of the case from 1980 until 1985. We reconstruct these actors' interests and strategies to consider the reach and repercussions of their actions, highlighting the positions assumed by: (i) the Brazilian state and its human rights foreign policy; (ii) the IACHR and its institutional politics as an international human rights bureaucracy; and (iii) the various denouncing non-state actors and their transnational human rights politics.

By shedding light on the intersections of these analytical dimensions (state, IACHR, and civil society), the chapter reveals that, when dealing with human rights decisions, impact analysis is only complete when one looks at the decision-making micro-dynamics within the human rights bodies (HRBs). Since such an argument implies that the main frameworks available in Political Science and International Relations for impact analysis need to be expanded,[9]

---

[6] Karen Engle, *El desarrollo indígena, una promesa esquiva: derechos, cultura, estrategia* (Siglo del Hombre Editores; Universidad de los Andes 2018).

[7] Luis Rodríguez-Piñeiro Royo, 'El sistema interamericano de derechos humanos y los pueblos indígenas' in Mikel Berraondo (ed), *Pueblos indígenas y derechos humanos* (Universidad de Deusto 2006) 153–206; James S. Anaya, *International Human Rights and Indigenous Peoples* (Aspen Publishers 2009); James L. Cavallaro, Claret Vargas, Clara Sandoval, and others, 'Indigenous and Tribal Peoples' Rights and the Inter-American System' in James L. Cavallaro and others (eds), *Doctrine, Practice and Advocacy in the Inter-American Human Rights System* (Oxford University Press 2019) 637–685.

[8] James Mahoney and Kathleen Thelen, 'A Theory of Gradual Institutional Change' in James Mahoney and Kathleen Thelen (eds), *Explaining Institutional Change: Ambiguity, Agency and Power* (Cambridge University Press 2010) 1–37.

[9] Beth A. Simmons, *Mobilizing for Human Rights: International Law in Domestic Politics* (Cambridge University Press 2009); Thomas Risse, Stephen

we must understand in the first place what impact analysis means and its main indicators in order to stress our contribution more clearly.

Traditionally, the analysis of compliance with HRBs in specific cases assesses whether states and their corresponding organs have upheld or disregarded the resolutive aspects of international human rights decisions, employing a checklist-style approach in relation to the implementation of individual rulings and recommendations. On the other hand, impact analysis – as the type of analysis developed in this chapter – covers a broader scope, assessing the extensive consequences of international decisions in other processes that go beyond both designated institutional actors and specific recommendations and resolutive points.

Impact analysis involves exploring additional spheres, dynamics, and stakeholders, not limited solely to the state apparatus but extending into society as well, and even beyond the individual cases under question. These stakeholders, even if not explicitly mentioned in the human rights bodies' decisions, may still engage politically and legally with the relevant human rights concerns at stake, possibly spilling over the concrete international recommendations and orders' effects in unanticipated and not formally requested ways.

Therefore, impact analysis 'adopts a broader understanding (…) to include indirect effects [beyond rule compliance] such as ideational change and empowerment of local actors'.[10] In this sense, it is possible for significant impacts to arise, even in situations characterized by limited compliance, when substantial behavioural change unforeseen – but triggered – by the formal international decisions may occur while many resolutive points of lesser importance remain under non-compliance. Conversely, the reverse situation is also plausible, when high compliance may be the result either of 'low, readily met and ineffective standards'[11] or of window-dressing policies designed just to appease HRBs while producing minimal reverberations in real terms of impact.

In terms of indicators of impact, following Simmons' framework (2009)[12], international human rights decisions will cause discernible impact when triggering: (i) shifts in national political agendas – with either the approval of new legislation, procedures, and public policies by elected officials at the executive

C. Ropp, and Kathryn Sikkink, *The Persistent Power of Human Rights: From Commitment to Compliance* (Cambridge University Press 2013).

[10] Par Engstrom (ed), *The Inter-American Human Rights System: Impact Beyond Compliance* (Palgrave Macmillan 2019) 5.

[11] Kal Raustiala and Anne-Marie Slaughter, 'Law, International Relations and Compliance' in Walter Carlsnaes, Thomas Risse and Beth Simmons (eds), *Handbook of International Relations* (SAGE 2002) 539.

[12] Simmons, *Mobilizing Human Rights: International Law in Domestic Politics* (n 9).

and legislative branches of government – or simply with positive discursive changes and a higher priority level ascribed within the public opinion to the human rights issues pointed out by HRBs; (ii) either litigation for new rights – or for new interpretations of existing rights – in national courts or changes in legal understandings and jurisprudential aspects by the judicial system in response to the human rights bodies' decisions (when provoked or *ex officio*); or (iii) new incentives, persuasive ideas about rights, and potential rewards for social movements struggling to sustain and spread waves of resistance and collective action, therefore spurring and stimulating new cycles of civil society mobilization and activism.

However, following the existing literature, for the materialization of such indicators of impact, the political and institutional factors of the respective states are crucial. According to the spiral model,[13] five variables pertaining to the countries' domestic political realm are decisive, acting as favourable or unfavourable filtering scope conditions for international pressures: type of political regime (democratic or authoritarian); level of state sovereignty and authority (consolidated or limited statehood); process of policy implementation needed for behavioural and practical changes (centralized or decentralized implementation); and the two-sided levels of material and social vulnerability in response to human rights demands (how much the target nation's political leaders, concerned about reputation damage and financial consequences, genuinely engage with received criticisms and human rights discourse).

In sum, the more susceptible countries are, both materially and socially, and the more firmly established their democracies, statehood power, and levels of centralization during the implementation of novel policies, the more pronounced the levels of willingness and capability of governments and judicial systems in relation to human rights. Consequently, this would significantly heighten the probability of human rights bodies' impact, fuelling the indicators provided by Simmons.

The main point of our chapter is that such perspectives on impact are not enough. Besides looking at how impact unfolds in the countries targeted by human rights bodies' decisions[14] and at the levels of impact of human rights bodies' decisions both on the domestic setting of specific states and local civil societies, and also on legal and jurisprudential aspects more broadly,[15] we must additionally consider the very conditions that enabled the elaboration of such decisions by HRBs.

---

13 Risse, Ropp and Sikkink, *The Persistent Power of Human Rights: From Commitment to Compliance* (n 9).

14 ibid.

15 Simmons, *Mobilizing Human Rights: International Law in Domestic Politics* (n 9).

Therefore, we must delve into the political and legal interactions taking place within the international HRBs themselves, opening the 'black box' on what happens when such bodies receive human rights complaints against states. Before studying possible local effects either generated or driven by HRBs' decisions in countries, with the concurring mediation process of domestic conditions, it is necessary to first understand the HRBs' bureaucratic politics and links to civil society groups, as such dynamics help explain the specific decisions made.

In other words, our approach does not see impact analysis as only a question of matching up HRBs' final decisions, on the one hand, and the domestic filtering scope conditions posed by states' political and institutional configurations, on the other hand, with the final listing of impact indicators. We argue it is necessary to take a step back and look at the politics taking place also within the bureaucratic realm of HRBs in order to understand how and why HRBs act the way they do. In the first place, we must ask: what types of political conditions (involving state and civil society actors) and internal institutional features of HRBs are necessary for bodies such as the IACHR to advance progressive agendas on human rights that will later spur impact in multiple contexts and different settings of scope conditions in specific countries?

Using the *Yanomami* case as an example, we argue that at least two dimensions are pivotal for an enlarged understanding of impact: the role of civil society – and how it manages to channel and convey demands from local victims towards HRBs – and the internal bureaucratic politics within these organizations, involving the correlation of forces among its members, the external political conditions faced by the body, and their institutional properties and strength.

Concerning the role of civil society, non-state actors must be able to tackle the incisive pressures and interferences of states – like Brazil did in the *Yanomami* case – with the follow-up of the complaints by the HRBs, through active and persistent political-legal advocacy, rooted in credible and verifiable information from the field. In addition, such political and legal work of intermediating the demands of historically marginalized and oppressed groups like the Yanomami towards the HRBs needs to maintain and respect to some considerable extent the original radicalism of the victims' demands, even though going through the filtering and moderating requirements imposed by the language of international law.[16]

[16] In the politics of technical knowledge, the experts responsible for navigating through bureaucratic codes and procedures impose specific framings upon the demands made by victims and social movements. In this sense, human rights groups may either uphold or dilute, within their formal and legal claims, the inherent level of antagonism embedded in stakeholders' original grievances.

The political and legal advocacy of civil society cannot be diverted or dissolved by juridical technicalities, repetitive concessions, or excessive moderation in case proceedings, even when such strategies might seem to increase the odds of success in litigation, at the cost of sacrificing the original spirit of the demands. In the *Yanomami* case, when framing Indigenous demands into the human rights language, the litigating organizations kept their original claims over the territory. Faced by an international regime that did not contain any legal provision in that regard, moderation – (albeit it was not considered) – could have been a more rational and attractive path to ensure a somewhat unprecedented legal victory.

Finally, looking at the internal dimension of international human rights bureaucracies, one needs to consider HRBs' internal and external political conditions. In other words, in each historical setting under analysis, we must evaluate and map the international political context to assess the existence or not of extra-institutional veto powers to the work of HRBs – like powerful states – and also examine the institutional properties and cleavages among decision-making members.

In the *Yanomami* case, the IACHR faced a historical and political context that decisively affected its work and the impact of its recommendation. The 1980s inherited from the 1970s two fundamental processes for the IACHR's work: (i) the institutional strengthening of the IACHR, after the Carter administration (1977–81) and the Commission's high-profile critiques against the Chilean and Argentinian dictatorships, which took place between 1976 and 1980;[17] and (ii) the emergence and consolidation of the first transnational pro-Indigenous civil society networks.[18]

Regarding the first process, when the Commission received the *Yanomami* case, its bureaucratic structure was undergoing an institutional strengthening

[17] Tom Farer, 'The Rise of the Inter-American Human Rights Regime: No Longer a Unicorn, Not Yet an Ox' (1997) 19 *Human Rights Quarterly* 510; Klaas Dykmann, *Human Rights Policy of the Organization of American States in Latin America: Philanthropic Endeavors or the Exploitation of an Ideal*? (Markus Wiener Publishers 2008); Robert K. Goldman, 'History and Action: The Inter-American Rights System and the Role of the Inter-American Commission on Human Rights' (2009) 31 *Human Rights Quarterly* 856.

[18] Engle, *El desarrollo indígena, una promesa esquiva: derechos, cultura, estrategia* (n 6); Jochen Kemner, 'Fourth World Activism in the First World' (2014) 12 *Journal of Modern European History* 262; Ronald Niezen, *The Origins of Indigenism: Human Rights and the Politics of Identity* (University of California Press 2003).

process in parallel with the reduction of veto points to its work.[19] A more progressive group of commissioners, provoked by civil society, was then able to instrumentalize the IACHR's institutional discretion for the application of norms that would extend the existing human rights protections to Indigenous peoples, even though the normative and legal instruments did not mention them expressly.

Meanwhile, as regards the second process, the civil society networks had also accumulated institutional resources and repertoires. The preceding years had witnessed the unparalleled mobilization of new indigenist social actors, who harnessed in unprecedented ways the international human rights language.[20] These two processes finally intertwined, working together to influence the political struggle for Yanomami land rights taking place in the IACHR.

In this sense, the *Yanomami* case reveals a changing institutional scenario characterized by conversion[21] – that is, the action of institutional innovators interested in exploring the ambiguities of pre-existing norms and rules to broaden the scope of the IACHR's original institutional mission. In this specific case, it implied encompassing Indigenous peoples with novel and unexplored legal interpretations, and increasing the impact of IACHR's norms in contexts of Indigenous rights violations. Such institutional conversion was decisive for the later impact of the Commission's and Court's decisions stemming from such precedents in a series of other cases (e.g., the emblematic *Awas Tingni v Nicaragua*[22] and *Saramaka v Suriname*[23] cases), contributing to greater-scope normative discussions on Indigenous peoples and their land rights in the world.

---

19 At the beginning of the 1980s, the resistance against a more active posture of the IACHR had weakened in the OAS, and also within the very internal structure of the Commission, among its members, many of whom had traditionally been more inclined toward defending the sovereignty of states. Finally, the United States prioritized the anti-communist agenda and was not interested in blocking the work of the Commission in Indigenous matters and other issues during the Reagan administration. Farer, 'The Rise of the Inter-American Human Rights Regime' (n 16); Dykmann, *Human Rights Policy of the Organization of American States in Latin America* (n 16); Goldman, 'History and Action' (n 16).

20 Niezen, *The Origins of Indigenism: Human Rights and the Politics of Identity* (n 17); James S. Anaya, *Indigenous Peoples in International Law* (Oxford University Press 2000) 45–47.

21 Mahoney and Thelen, 'A Theory of Gradual Institutional Change' (n 8).

22 Inter-American Court of Human Rights, *Case of the Mayagna (Sumo) Awas Tingni community v. Nicaragua*, Judgment of August 31, 2001 (Merits, Reparations and Costs), Series C No. 79.

23 *Inter-American Court of Human Rights, Case of the Saramaka People v. Suriname, Judgment of November 28, 2007 (Preliminary Objections, Merits, Costs, and Reparations), Series C No 172.*

Explaining this case not only helps to understand its dynamics and the IACHR's normative development regarding Indigenous rights, but it also contributes to mapping the different variables and conditions that may incline HRBs to embark on processes of institutional conversion for other areas and issues, leaning towards more progressive and inclusive decisions and potentially increasing the reach and quality of their norms.

Our methodology for analyzing the *Yanomami* case made use of primary sources from the diplomatic archives of the Brazilian Ministry of Foreign Affairs (*Ministério das Relações Exteriores*, MRE), located in Brasília. Although these files represent the state's perspectives, they contain copies of documents sent by the petitioners and reveal backstage political movements of the commissioners, transcending a merely state-centric top-down approach. Such data are absent in the IACHR's protocolar annual reports publicly available regarding this and other cases. These elements from the primary sources are useful in allowing the reconstruction of interaction contexts and the mapping of these actors, their ideas, and strategies, therefore complementing the characterization of how they used the IACHR's institutional arena and its rules.

The *Yanomami* proceedings were chosen for this case study for two main reasons. First, parallel to the case of the Miskitu people in Nicaragua, processed at the same time by the IACHR,[24] the *Yanomami* case had enormous historical and normative relevance both for the demarcation of Yanomami lands in Brazil, in 1992, and for similar cases brought later to the IACHR.[25] Thus, joining this research with pre-existing empirical findings regarding the *Miskitu* case amplifies our understanding of this key moment for the IACHR in the 1980s, when it came to integrate the struggle for Indigenous land rights. Second, the *Yanomami* case is exemplary and revealing for broader discussions on the analyses of the impact of HRBs' norms and decisions.

---

[24] Engle, *El desarrollo indígena, una promesa esquiva: derechos, cultura, estrategia* (n 6) 245–246; Anaya, *International Human Rights and Indigenous Peoples* (n 6); Anaya, *Indigenous Peoples in International Law* (n 19) 168–70.

[25] In the *Miskitu* case in Nicaragua, confronted with the Sandinista administration's programme of land reform that did not account for Indigenous property in several lands, in addition to numerous episodes of violence committed against Indigenous persons and communities, the IACHR ruled in favour of ethnic groups' right to special cultural protections, which included, although in a limited way, the right to their ancestral and communal lands. Engle, *El desarrollo indígena, una promesa esquiva: derechos, cultura, estrategia* (n 6) 245–246. According to Anaya, 'the commission recommended measures to secure Indigenous land rights and to develop a new institutional order that would better accommodate to the distinctive cultural attributes and traditional forms of organization of the Indigenous groups'. Anaya, *Indigenous Peoples in International Law* (n 19) 169.

In particular, the disclosure of secret Brazilian archives and their privileged information, extremely hard to find in other contemporary cases, allows the opening of the IACHR's black box by looking at the bureaucracy from the inside. Official documents reveal how progressive commissioners joined forces with continuously mobilized and well-prepared petitioners – which were supported by a broader network of other indigenist groups allied to the Yanomami cause – to advance novel legal interpretations within the IACHR, prompting a crucial institutional conversion.

In short, the case shows the overall required political conditions and necessary societal links for bodies such as the IACHR to fulfil and advance their mandates, eliciting progressive understandings without ceding to pressures and temptations of strategic deference or neglect vis-à-vis the states. Before considering the odds of norms' impact in countries, one must bear in mind this background analysis on the process of how HRBs' decisions were initially made, since that accounts in large part for decisions' contents and potential reach.

The chapter is divided into seven sections. After this Introduction, section 2 presents debates on historical institutionalism, the theoretical reference of the study. Section 3 presents the elementary aspects of the *Yanomami* case. The following sections treat each of the analyzed actors in turn: NGOs and petitioners (section 4), the Brazilian state (section 5), and the Inter-American Commission on Human Rights (section 6). We present some final remarks at the end.

## 2 ANALYTICAL FRAMING: THE CHANGES IN THE IACHR AS A CASE OF INSTITUTIONAL CONVERSION

The most recent studies in historical institutionalism, a subfield of Political Science, seek to understand the questions 'How do institutions change?' and 'What is the relationship between institutional change and political outcomes?'[26] In an attempt to delve into the analytical challenge of understanding such dynamics, Mahoney and Thelen state:

> the characteristics of both the political context and the institution in question together drive the type of institutional change we can expect. Political context and institutional form have these effects because they shape the type of dominant

[26] Jacob S. Hacker, Paul Pierson and Kathleen Thelen, 'Drift and Conversion: Hidden Faces of Institutional Change' in J. Mahoney and Kathleen Thelen (eds), *Advances in Comparative-historical Analysis* (Cambridge University Press 2015) 180–208, 182.

> change agent that is likely to emerge and flourish in any specific institutional context, and the kinds of strategies this agent is likely to pursue to effect change.[27]

According to the authors, 'differences in veto possibilities [characteristics of the political context] and the extent of discretion in institutional enforcement and interpretation [characteristics of the institution] are associated with different modes of institutional change'.[28] Each of these modalities is fostered by specific types of institutional actors with distinct profiles and interests, resulting in four possible patterns of change: by displacement, by layering, by institutional drift, or by conversion. In other words, depending on the extent of veto power wielded by defenders of the *status quo* and on the margin for autonomous institutional action, some paths for change are more likely, while others are blocked.

The most radical and drastic changes correspond to contexts with weak veto points and players, on the one hand, and low levels of institutional discretion, on the other. In these cases, agents interested in driving change may simply act as insurgents: given the reduced reach and reverberation of pro-*status quo* forces, averse to change, the existing rules may be abandoned in favour of new ones, with more discretionary space. As a result, the old institution is completely replaced (displacement).

Institutions with low levels of discretion in the application or interpretation of rules, when inserted in political contexts beset by actors defending the *status quo* with significant veto powers, cause the agents of change to behave as subversives. Instead of radically redirecting and creating alternative institutions, the chosen path is systematically introducing small alterations, amendments, and additives in layers (layering), superposing them on the former rules and institutions, which are fixed and protected.

Displacement and layering both involve institutions with low degrees of discretion. To have a chance of succeeding in these institutions, the strategies of the agents of change need to attain some level of alteration of over-strict formal rules according to the possibilities regarding the presence and strength of veto points. However, these two patterns of change are not generally applicable to

---

[27] Mahoney and Thelen, 'A Theory of Gradual Institutional Change' (n 8) 15.

[28] Mahoney and Thelen, 'A Theory of Gradual Institutional Change' (n 8) 18. According to the authors, 'veto possibilities are high where there exist actors who have access to institutional or extrainstitutional means of blocking change. These actors may have access to veto capabilities regarding both changes in the (formal or informal) rules themselves and changes in the rules' enactment in practice'. ibid, 19. The institutional discretion in applying and interpreting rules and norms refers to 'differences in the extent to which institutions are open to contending interpretations and variations in their enforcement'. ibid, 20.

the situation of HRBs, whose external norms, formal rules, and procedures are more stable and rigid, on the one hand, and more malleable in terms of application and interpretation, on the other.

Therefore, given their institutional characteristics, HRBs are more prone to changes that do not require shifting either their internal rules or their treaty-like sources of rights and legal reasoning, as foreseen in the two other forms of institutional change described in historical institutionalism (drift and conversion). The main issue to be evaluated on which type of institutional change among these two will prevail is the substantive presence (or not) of veto points regarding the bodies' actions.

In the first possible scenario, that of strong veto points and high institutional discretionary levels in the application or interpretation of rules, the most favoured actors of change will be the symbionts. These are actors who, when facing powerful intra- and/or extra-institutional pressures in favour of the *status quo*, instrumentalize the institution's rules according to their own interests, promoting a 'context discontinuity'.[29] In this case, these agents refuse to apply the institutional rules in new and more updated ways in order to keep up with changes and new challenges posed by the external naturally evolving political and contextual conditions. As a result, the ensuing institutional changes will emerge as failures, negligence, and institutional drift, with the progressive withdrawal from the original institutional mission and the inability to deal with new challenges, benefitting the powerful veto-wielding actors.

When the other possibility is confirmed, merging weak veto powers with the same multiple institutional opportunities for the interpretation and application of rules, conditions are created for the agents interested in changes within the institutions to act as opportunists. Without powerful intra- and extra-institutional actors in favour of the *status quo*, the rules continue to be the same and are formally supported, as in the drift mode. Nonetheless, it becomes possible to interpret and implement such formally unaltered rules in different and potentially innovative ways in practice, exploring their ambiguities and producing effects not anticipated by their original creators, therefore generating an 'actor discontinuity'.[30] In other words, opportunists 'do not need to pursue insurrectionary strategies [for radical changes]' or tactics aiming at institutional evolution through the creation of new rules by layering, 'since gaps between rules and enactment are [already] available for them to exploit' much more easily.[31]

[29] Hacker, Pierson and Thelen, 'Drift and Conversion: Hidden Faces of Institutional Change' (n 23).
[30] ibid.
[31] Mahoney and Thelen, 'A Theory of Gradual Institutional Change' (n 8) 29.

In our case study concerning the IACHR, in operational terms, the veto possibilities corresponded to intra- and extra-institutional actors who were in favour of the *status quo* that prevailed until 1980, that is, the Commission's relative silence regarding Indigenous peoples, which implied a contrary position to the extension of the IACHR's rules to protect them. Besides, the discretion both in the application and institutional interpretation was related to the IACHR's margin of manoeuvre to use the existing norms in innovative ways to reach Indigenous peoples – and the willingness, or lack of it, among its individual members to explore such a path.

Assessing the factors that affected the IACHR during the *Yanomami* case enables an analysis of the interaction between structural factors (political and institutional) and the level of agency, that is, of the choices and strategies of specific actors like the commissioners, the Brazilian government, and the petitioners. Thus, in a context in which the IACHR was caught between pro-*status quo* pressure from the Brazilian government and societal claims for radical changes in terms of Indigenous land demarcation from the petitioners, one can understand how most members of the IACHR finally leaned toward important changes in the body's position regarding Indigenous peoples' rights. Indeed, they decided to explore the Commission's institutional discretion, redirecting its pre-existing rules and international norms to new purposes.

To delineate the explaining variables of the case study, we separate the characteristics of the political context (veto points and veto players) and the institutional properties of the IACHR (discretion in interpretation and application), pointing out the following factors:

(1) *the weakening of extra-institutional veto points related to the IACHR's actions:* the leverage of the Commission's actions was amplified by the ascending priority level attributed to human rights matters and Indigenous issues in the international agenda, especially after the US Carter administration and the emergence of a new transnational Indigenous – and indigenist – movement in the 1970s;[32]

(2) *the difficulties faced by the Brazilian government of ignoring the case and exerting veto power:* Brazil's vulnerability and its level of engagement towards the critiques spurred by the Yanomami situation demonstrated that the state cared about the negative repercussions of the case, a condition that created windows of opportunity for the IACHR's incidence (as we will see in the case analysis);

(3) *the lack of interest from the United States regarding Brazilian issues and cases discussed by the IACHR and OAS, an additional factor weakening*

---

[32] Engle, *El desarrollo indígena, una promesa esquiva: derechos, cultura, estrategia* (n 6); Kemner, 'Fourth World Activism in the First World' (n 17); Niezen, *The Origins of Indigenism: Human Rights and the Politics of Identity* (n 17).

*veto possibilities:* from 1981 onwards, the US focus on anti-communist policies in Central America[33] created more spaces for questioning and criticism against Brazil,[34] which further weakened the veto points to the Indigenous rights' agenda;

(4) *civil society's legal framings and pressures stimulating the IACHR's use of institutional discretion:* the expressive transnational mobilization of anthropological and litigation associations in the *Yanomami* case, combined with the support of indigenist organizations and networks, offered new juridical-legal reasoning and justifications to buttress and legitimate the IACHR's actions, contributing to actor discontinuity and its innovations (as we will demonstrate later on);

(5) *progressive commissioners and the IACHR's bureaucratic strengthening as propelling forces for using institutional discretion:* in the context of shrinking veto actors, the IACHR's composition[35] and level of structural

---

[33] Farer, 'The Rise of the Inter-American Human Rights Regime' (n 16) 541; Dykmann, *Human Rights Policy of the Organization of American States in Latin America* (n 16) 311–422.

[34] Given Brazil's geostrategic relevance for the US anti-communist foreign policy, a 'gentlemen's agreement' in OAS not to criticize Brazil because of human rights violations prevailed at least until the mid-1970s. *Human Rights Policy of the Organization of American States in Latin America* (n 16) 150, 160–161, and 217; Bruno Boti Bernardi, 'Silence, Hindrances and Omissions: The Inter-American Commission on Human Rights and the Brazilian Military Dictatorship' (2018) 22 *The International Journal of Human Rights* 1123, 1133. In the 1980s, Reagan's counter-insurgent and anti-communist offensive actions were centred in Central America, largely ignoring human rights and Brazil. In relation to its position – and diminished interest – towards the IACHR, the US revealed a reluctant, apathetic, and indifferent position. Farer, 'The Rise of the Inter-American Human Rights Regime' (n 16) 542; Dykmann, *Human Rights Policy of the Organization of American States in Latin America* (n 16) 311–422. Such changes in the US foreign policy meant Brazil had no longer the assured hegemonic shield of its ally for diverting human rights criticisms.

[35] The progressive pair of commissioners behind the distinguished role of the IACHR between 1976 and 1980 was formed by Andrés Aguilar and Tom Farer, who remained on the Commission and followed almost all the processing of the *Yanomami* case until 1985. According to Dykmann, the two often managed to attract the support of Commissioner Marco Gerardo Monroy Cabra to their causes and also had trust in Commissioner César Sepúlveda's commitment to human rights. Dykmann, *Human Rights Policy of the Organization of American States in Latin America* (n 16) 87–93. In this sense, it can be said that this group of commissioners was opposed to other pro-government commissioners, notably Francisco Bertrand Galindo and Carlos A. Dunshee de Abranches (replaced in 1983 by Gilda Russomano, who had the same political inclination).

> autonomy[36] opened spaces for institutional innovators or, in Mahoney and Thelen's (2010) terms, opportunists – more progressive commissioners interested in exploring new paths for the IACHR's actions.

To sum up, according to Mahoney and Thelen's (2010)[37] theoretical framework, at least in the Indigenous issue, these political and institutional factors provoked the strengthening of the IACHR and its discretionary powers, and also prompted the weakening of actors opposed to the human rights agenda, who had acted thus far, in the 1970s, as veto powers against the progress and advancement of previous Brazilian cases.[38]

## 3 THE *YANOMAMI* CASE

We now turn to the analysis on the proceedings and main landmarks of the *Yanomami* case in the Inter-American human rights system. The complaint arrived at the Commission at the end of 1980. It was first considered in the 53rd session of the IACHR, in 1981, and its conclusion was deliberated in 1985, during the 64th session. The case sparked great concern in the Brazilian government and within the Commission, mobilizing a dynamic transnational advocacy network that included foreign anthropologists, international non-governmental organisations (NGOs), and pro-Indigenous groups rooted in Brazil but also beyond its borders.[39] In the six years of the IACHR proceedings, the exchange of information between petitioners, the IACHR, and Brazil,

---

[36] Until 1976, there were only two attorneys besides the executive secretary working in the IACHR Secretariat, and the rest of the staff were clearly not acquainted with human rights issues. The IACHR's offices were third class, permeated by a feeling of sleepiness, paralysis, and depression. Dykmann, *Human Rights Policy of the Organization of American States in Latin America* (n 16) 94–95. With the rise of the Carter administration, from 1977 onwards, in addition to the decisive political support for the IACHR, US financial contributions to the body increased substantially, which allowed: change to larger facilities; hiring several attorneys and new employees; carrying out numerous activities and trips, such as on-site visits; establishment of a documentation centre and library; and the purchase of a computerized data system. Dykmann, *Human Rights Policy of the Organization of American States in Latin America* (n 16) 723.

[37] Mahoney and Thelen, 'A Theory of Gradual Institutional Change' (n 8).

[38] Bernardi, 'Silence, Hindrances and Omissions: The Inter-American Commission on Human Rights and the Brazilian Military Dictatorship' (n 31).

[39] Brazilian Ministry of Foreign Affairs – IACHR, 'Denúncia contra Brasil 18 de dezembro', Washington D.C. (18 December 1980) Delbrasupa para Exteriores, Confidential.

as well as between the Ministry of Foreign Affairs and other Brazilian governmental agencies, was intense and coupled with lots of diplomatic movements.

In the IACHR, besides Edmundo Vargas Carreño, the Commission's executive secretary, the commissioners mostly active in handling the case during its proceedings were the case rapporteurs Tom Farer and Cesar Sepúlveda, along with Carlos A. Dunshee de Abranches and his successor, Gilda Maciel Corrêa Meyer Russomano. Defenders of and collaborators with the Brazilian dictatorship, both Abranches and Russomano were Brazilian professors of International Law at the State University of Rio de Janeiro (Universidade Estadual do Rio de Janeiro, UERJ) and the Law College in Pelotas, respectively.[40]

The petition was lodged by anthropology associations and NGOs – the American Anthropological Association from Washington, the Anthropology Resource Centre (ARC) from Boston, Survival International (London and US sections), and the Indian Law Research Centre (ILRC) from Washington. Although not formally included among the petitioners, the Commission for the Creation of the Yanomami Park (*Comissão pela Criação do Parque Yanomami*, CCPY), a Brazilian NGO led by photographer and activist Cláudia Andujar, also played an important role throughout the proceedings, participating in the transnational advocacy campaign and providing updated field information on the developments regarding the Yanomami. The complaint was presented on behalf of over 10,000 Yanomami who, according to the estimates, lived in the states of Amazonas and Roraima.

Abundant allegations of violations of the American Declaration of the Rights and Duties of Man (ADRDM, or the American Declaration) perpetrated against the Yanomami were listed in the document. It claimed that individuals and groups – particularly gold prospectors, local farmers, road construction workers, and other outsiders – acting in collusion with governmental agents were violating the Indigenous peoples' rights to have their juridical personality and civil rights recognized, and also those guarantees related to life, freedom,

[40] Abranches served as a commissioner for nearly twenty years (1964–83), while Russomano served from 1984 until 1991. Since the adoption of the IACHR statute of 1979, commissioners serve four-year terms and may be re-elected once, but during the 1960s and 1970s these rules did not exist, which explains Abranches' long tenure from 1964 until his death in 1983. Commissioners like Abranches and Russomano were also allowed to act on cases, decisions, and investigations regarding their countries of origin, a regulation that would be eliminated only in 1985. Dykmann, *Human Rights Policy of the Organization of American States in Latin America* (n 16) 77.

security, personal integrity, equality before the law, religious freedom, health, well-being, and property.[41]

The complaint mentioned the 'huge land invasion, social disintegration, dissemination of diseases, deaths, and destruction', with 'FUNAI not taking any measures to prevent the destruction of the Yanomami communities'.[42] It pointed to the government's unwillingness to demarcate the Yanomami lands and its posture of ignoring twelve demarcation proposals elaborated by pro-Indigenous anthropologists and missionaries between 1968 and 1979. Finally, the petitioners required an on-site investigation and a resolution urging the creation of the Yanomami Park.[43]

In July 1981, the IACHR met with the petitioners, who reinforced the request for a visit from the Commission and an on-site investigation. In 1982, after the Brazilian dictatorship's pressures against American commissioner Tom Farer, then in charge of the case, the Mexican commissioner César Sepúlveda was appointed as the new rapporteur for the petition. In the same year, activists visited the IACHR a second time, restating the urgency of the land demarcation. In 1983, with the death of Abranches, the Brazilian commissioner who had been a vocal defender of Brazil's dictatorship within the Commission since 1964, another Brazilian citizen, Gilda Russomano, took his place in the IACHR and continued to pass privileged information to the Brazilian dictatorship, articulating delays in the case. The petitioners sent more information to the IACHR in the following year.

The case was concluded at last in 1985, when Brazil was undergoing the last stages of its re-democratization process. The Sarney administration (1985–90), Brazil's first non-military government since 1964, sent new information

---

41 Since Brazil had not ratified the American Convention on Human Rights, whose entry into force had happened in 1978, the cases against the country were based on the 1948 American Declaration. Brazilian Ministry of Foreign Affairs – IACHR, 'Denúncia contra Brasil 18 de dezembro', Washington D.C. (18 December 1980) Delbrasupa para Exteriores, Confidential.

42 FUNAI (*Fundação Nacional do Índio*) is the National Indian Foundation, a Brazilian state body created in 1967 to handle the official indigenist policy towards the promotion and protection of Indigenous peoples' rights. Since its inception, and especially during the military dictatorship, FUNAI has been involved in multiple cases of rights abuses. The lack of resources and personnel has also compromised its activities throughout the decades.

43 The Yanomami Park was finally demarcated in 1992 by the Collor administration (1990–92). Brazilian Ministry of Foreign Affairs – IACHR, 'Denúncia contra Brasil 18 de dezembro', Washington D.C. (18 December 1980) Delbrasupa para Exteriores, Confidential.

to the IACHR in August of that year, and the IACHR recommended in its 64th session the demarcation of the Yanomami Park.[44]

## 4 THE PETITIONER ORGANISATIONS AND THEIR STRATEGIES

The actions of NGOs, anthropological associations, and the transnational campaign around the CCPY's agenda were decisive in the *Yanomami* case. The petitioners quickly contested the Brazilian government's first answer against their claims, received in 1981.[45] Throughout the proceedings, the documents supporting their arguments demonstrated impressive consistency and refuted each and every argument of the Brazilian state, demonstrating: a deep anthropological understanding of the Yanomami situation; updated information on the violations that were taking place in the territory; and a complete comprehension of the juridical and political issues concerning Indigenous peoples.

Among several points, the documents questioned the Brazilian judicial system and showed how the dictatorship's tutelage regime enforced upon Indigenous peoples restricted their rights and promoted official policies of forced integration and assimilation. They also pointed out the inefficacy of FUNAI's surveillance work: the deadlines for land demarcations were continually disrespected and the limits of Indigenous lands were constantly changed to benefit private interests. The construction of the BR-210 (Northern Perimeter) highway and the economic pressures in favour of mining and gold prospecting had resulted in the spread of diseases and addictions, amidst ecological imbalance and exploitation of Indigenous labour. FUNAI was both unable and unwilling to protect the territories from invasions by non-Indigenous squatters, farmers, and wildcat miners.[46]

The petitioners would continue to pressure the IACHR after sending this documentation and later reports with additional data. In October 1982, Cláudia Andujar, CCPY's coordinator, and Curtis G. Berkey, ILRC's attorney, participated in an audience on the case during the IACHR's 58th session, reinforcing their direct advocacy engagement with members of the Commission and its specialized personnel. Such tactics are essential for the proceedings'

---

44 IACHR Resolution No. 12/85, *Coulter and Others v Brazil – Yanomami* case (n 5).

45 Adopting a nationalist and paternalistic tone, Brazilian authorities had denied reports of invasions by wildcat miners. They argued that Brazilian legislation granted adequate protection to Indigenous peoples. FUNAI, 'Official Letter No. 22/Press' (25 March 1981) FUNAI to Mário David Andreazza.

46 Brazilian Ministry of Foreign Affairs – OAS, 'Caso Nr. 7615', Washington D.C. (28 July 1981f) Delbrasupa para Exteriores, Confidential.

progression in any petition inasmuch as they help both to raise the awareness of the commissioners and to call attention to the case within the IACHR's busy agenda, characterized by a heavy caseload .

In an ILRC document issued in November 1982, the petitioners highlighted that the Yanomami situation was unusual, since it represented '10,000 Yanomami persons whose rights had been violated as individuals and as a group'.[47] The document had robust juridical argumentation, which was essential in stimulating the IACHR to use its institutional discretion in favour of the Yanomami. The complainants recognized that the case was probably unprecedented and extremely challenging in terms of Indigenous collective rights related to the American Declaration , especially regarding the collective property of land.

Despite the American Declaration's individualized focus on human rights and its lack of direct and explicit normative mentions of Indigenous peoples' rights, factors that could either block or moderate the IACHR's actions in the *Yanomami* case, the ILRC presented a clear juridical route for the commissioners. The NGO argued that the IACHR could perfectly interpret and accommodate the American Declaration and its private property liberal framings and bias in order to ensure 'the Yanomami's right as a group to regulate and possess land and [...] [the] rights of Yanomami individuals to maintain their properties under their own system of land possession'.[48] Besides reiterating all the other violated rights, the NGO reinforced that the IACHR had the means to issue a resolution and that the case outcome depended essentially on the land demarcation of the Yanomami Park.

The incisive and systematic action of the petitioners and their allies impacted the case proceedings. The CCPY and the formal petitioners, especially the ILRC and the ARC, diligently contested the dictatorship's documents, presented sophisticated legal arguments, regularly sent updated information on the Yanomami situation, and participated in the Commission's sessions. Their actions as a solid transnational network differ from the situation encountered by Brazilian petitioners in other cases. Lacking such organized legal support in the United States, as well as evidentiary data and resources, complainants

47 Brazilian Ministry of Foreign Affairs – OAS – IACHR, 'Caso Nr. 7615. Índios Yanomami', Washington D.C. (24 November 1982d) Delbrasupa para Exteriores, Confidential.

48 Brazilian Ministry of Foreign Affairs – OAS – IACHR, Caso Nr. 7615. Índios Yanomami, Washington D.C. (24 November 1982d) Delbrasupa para Exteriores, Confidential.

in other cases from the 1970s faced difficulties in accessing and developing advocacy strategies in the IACHR.[49]

In reaction to such high-level transnational campaigning, after replying to the documents sent by petitioners in the first years of the case, the Brazilian dictatorship decided not to send more information to the IACHR from 1983 onwards, 'as such correspondence could even come to provide opportunities for new group initiatives, either national or foreign'.[50] Thus, at a certain point, the dictatorship retreated to a silent position in the face of the network's permanent activism.

In early 1984, the petitioners sent new information to the IACHR. The document provided updates on new actions carried out against the Indigenous Yanomami people since the previous communication. As will be discussed in the following section, by that time, Brazil had adopted a strategy of purposeful silence. The government had learned that each new reply would be followed by diligent responses on the part of petitioners. As a result, trying to avoid such an influx of constant information that would push the case even further into the spotlight, Brazil stopped answering the petitioners, despite the IACHR's requests.

## 5 THE BRAZILIAN DICTATORSHIP AND ITS DEFENCE STRATEGIES

In response to the petitioners' accusations, aimed at the elaboration of replies to the IACHR, the Figueiredo administration (1979–85), Brazil's last military government, reacted with an intense interplay of federal state organs like the MRE, the Ministry of the Interior, and FUNAI, along with the permanent gathering of privileged information stemming from relevant allies such as the IACHR's executive secretary and the Brazilian commissioners. Brazil's diplomatic strategies comprehended the following elements: (i) a diversionist formal defence entrenched in information provided by FUNAI; (ii) a limited and reluctant cooperation with the IACHR, with dissimulating concessions; and (iii) a series of processual manoeuvres coordinatedwith Brazilian commissioners Abranches and Russomano, as well as with executive secretary Vargas Carreño, to postpone and eventually file the case. Despite such an intricate web of multiple strategies, due to the prominent advocacy transnational campaign

[49] Bernardi, 'Silence, Hindrances and Omissions: The Inter-American Commission on Human Rights and the Brazilian Military Dictatorship' (n 31); James Naylon Green, *Apesar de vocês: oposição à ditadura brasileira nos Estados Unidos, 1964–1985* (Companhia das Letras 2009).

[50] Brazilian Ministry of Foreign Affairs – OAS – IACHR, 'Caso Nr. 7615. Índios Yanomami', Brazil (29 April 1983c) Exteriores para Delbrasupa, Confidential.

launched in favour of the Yanomami and also as a result of the stance assumed by more progressive commissioners, Brazil was unable to amass sufficient influence to veto the case, as it had been able to do with several claims the IACHR processed in the 1970s regarding the country.[51]

## Formal Defence

Responsible for the defence's specific arguments, presented to the IACHR by the Ministry of Foreign Affairs, FUNAI sought to respond to each and every accusation against the state. The tone of the responses – 'the Yanomami is, first of all, a Brazilian' – was nationalist and paternalist, reiterating the Indigenous peoples' status as somewhat incapable in juridical terms.[52] FUNAI denied the data provided by the petitioners on the thousands of non-Indigenous wildcat miners who were constantly invading Yanomami lands, focusing instead on praising Brazil's supposedly advanced juridical and institutional framework, which, according to the dictatorship, served the best interests of the Yanomami. The indigenist state organ also mentioned that the works on the BR-210 highway had been paralyzed since 1974, highlighting that the Yanomami land demarcation process had already reached its final phase. Despite the apparently protective tone, the Brazilian government explicitly reinforced the references both to the 'historical process of internalization' and to the official and forced politics of driving Indigenous peoples 'to their integration in the national collectivity'.[53]

## Limited Cooperation and Dissimulating Concessions

In order to convey an image of cooperation that could conceal its diversionist intentions, for a while, the Brazilian government informed the IACHR about the window-dressing public policies adopted during the proceedings of the case regarding the Yanomami. Decrees were issued as an attempt to 'largely

---

[51] Bernardi, 'Silence, Hindrances and Omissions: The Inter-American Commission on Human Rights and the Brazilian Military Dictatorship' (n 31).

[52] Before the 1988 Brazilian Constitution, the 1916 Civil Code and the 1973 Indian Statute stipulated that Indigenous persons were relatively incapable before the juridical system and had to be tutored and represented by the Indian Protection Service and, afterwards, by FUNAI.

[53] Brazilian Ministry of Foreign Affairs – IACHR, 'Caso Nr. 7615. Índios Yanomami. Informações adicionais. 53 Sessão. 8 janeiro, 1981', Brazil (8 January 1981a) Exteriores para Missão OEA, Confidential.

desinflate the very accusation formulated before the Commission',[54] such as Administrative Measure/GM/n.025, which encompassed the interdiction of the Yanomami Indigenous area, supposedly a step towards the effective demarcation. Given the dictatorship's concern with its image and reputation, such measures were merely a calculated effort to fend off the criticism, a dissimulating tactical concession that did not prevent new violations – and was thus criticized by the claimants.

After a year and a half without any updated information sent to the IACHR, at the end of 1984, the Ministry of Foreign Affairs alleged that FUNAI had decisively advanced toward the delimitation of the Yanomami Park, planning health and educational projects for the Indigenous people. In the meantime, petitioners denounced the damages caused by wildcat mining and the worsening human rights violations, contesting the state's version with data from local civil society organizations.

## Articulation for Postponing and Filing the Case

The dictatorship's collaboration with the IACHR's executive secretary, Vargas Carreño, affected the case proceedings. Such linkage kept the military regime informed and influenced the decision-making process, allowing Brazil to design and calculate its silencing and dissimulating strategies to postpone the case. For instance, in mid-1983, the executive secretary reported that 'facing the existence of priority issues (among which the report on Suriname), it did not seem likely that case Nr. 7615 [that is, the *Yanomami* case] would come to be included in the agenda'. Thus, given its interest in postponing the decision, the Brazilian government decided not to send additional information to the IACHR.[55]

With inside information concerning the agenda of the IACHR's meetings and sessions, the dictatorship's diplomacy could plan its following steps and assess the political atmosphere within the institution. In other petitions against Brazil, Vargas Carreño had assured Brazilian representatives that procedures would be taken to close the cases. As executive secretary, he could use not only provisions of the IACHR regulations but also the access and trust he had with the commissioners to defend the closures. However, in the *Yanomami* case, continuous transnational pressure from petitioners and the relevance of the

---

[54] Brazilian Ministry of Foreign Affairs – OAS – IACHR, 'Caso Nr. 7615. Informações adicionais', Washington D.C. (26 March 1982b) Delbrasupa para Exteriores, Confidential.

[55] Brazilian Ministry of Foreign Affairs – OAS – IACHR, 'Caso Nr. 7615. Índios Yanomami', Washington D.C. (19 September 1983d) Delbrasupa para Exteriores, Confidential.

issue in the Commission's agenda limited Vargas Carreño's actions. Even so, his meetings with Brazilian diplomats were a constant source of information and cooperation.

In addition, considering that, until 1985, an institutional loophole in the IACHR's internal regulation allowed commissioners to act on cases and investigations regarding their countries of origin, the Brazilian commissioners in the IACHR played a crucial role in the state's strategy to deal with the cases against the country throughout the entire authoritarian period. Abranches had served on the Commission since 1964, and his actions in the *Yanomami* case demonstrated his intense cooperation with Brasília up until his death in 1983. His reports depicted the IACHR's political environment and the behind-the-scenes negotiations among commissioners, pointing out which IACHR members were more sympathetic to Brazil and which were more concerned with allegations of human rights abuses in the country. He forwarded to the Brazilian government, in advance and through informal channels, a large number of confidential documents the petitioners produced, granting Brazil more time for political articulations and formal defence preparations. Abranches also orchestrated support for Brazil among the Commission's members and was able to reduce the time and number of participants in the petitioners' first audience with the Commission in June 1981. His intervention was so relevant that he occasionally assisted the dictatorship's response directly.

After Abranches' passing, Brazil promptly assigned Gilda Russomano as his replacement. Russomano kept her predecessor's practices of informal conversations with Brazilian diplomats and channelling of inside information. She also continued suggesting defence strategies and reporting both on the proceedings and progress of the cases against the country. According to Brazilian diplomats, Russomano softened the draft resolution's language on the *Yanomami* case, managing to postpone the IACHR's final decision.[56]

## 6 INDIGENOUS PEOPLES' RIGHTS AND THE IACHR

In the IACHR, Tom Farer was a leadership and progressive commissioner who helped the Commission to become the 'Hemispheric Grand Jury' from 1976 to 1983.[57] His designation as the *Yanomami* case rapporteur was met with profound dissatisfaction by Brazilian diplomacy during the Commission's 53rd session, given his publicly notorious progressive positions and criticism against the dictatorship. As a consequence, in the 55th session, early 1982,

---

[56] Brazilian Ministry of Foreign Affairs – OAS – IACHR, 'Caso Yanomami', Washington D.C. (3 October 1984d) Delbrasupa para Exteriores, Confidential.

[57] Farer, 'The Rise of the Inter-American Human Rights Regime' (n 16).

Vargas Carreño anticipated to the Brazilian representative that the Mexican commissioner César Sepúlveda would take Farer's place.

Sepúlveda was a renowned jurist and diplomat and had Farer's confidence as a true human rights defender,[58] even though he was also well known for his attachment to the principles of national sovereignty and non-intervention. About his position, Abranches considered that 'as a Mexican citizen, [Sepúlveda] could not leave out a concern with possible repercussions, in his own country', of issues related to 'ethnic minorities',[59] given the relevance of Indigenous matters in Mexico.

However, the stance assumed by Sepúlveda on the case would prove that Abranches had made a mistake. The *Yanomami* and *Miskitu* cases, both processed in the same period by the Commission in relation to Brazil and Nicaragua, coalesced as a turning point of change in the IACHR's posture regarding Indigenous peoples. In March 1981, Abranches warned Alarico Silveira, the Brazilian representative in the OAS, 'that, in the present session [the 52nd], the debate on the human rights of Indigenous populations would be highlighted', thus indicating that the issue had been fully integrated into the Commission's agenda. The commissioner evaluated that Tom Farer, then the IACHR's president, was greatly interested in the theme, which had a few antecedents in the IACHR. Among these were: the IACHR's decision, in 1971, to compile all cases related to Indigenous peoples under the supervision of commissioner Gabino Fraga and the later approval of a recommendation to indigenist state agents on the 1972 IACHR annual report;[60] the positions about Paraguayan Indigenous communities; and the activities carried out regarding older cases related to Indigenous questions by the former American commissioner Robert Woodward.[61]

---

[58] Dykmann, *Human Rights Policy of the Organization of American States in Latin America* (n 16) 91.

[59] Brazilian Ministry of Foreign Affairs – OAS – IACHR, 'Caso Nr. 7615. Índios Yanomami', Washington D.C. (28 June 1982c) Delbrasupa para Exteriores, Confidential.

[60] In 1971, in response to the United Nations Economic and Social Council resolution 1589 (L) ('The problem of Indigenous populations'), commissioner Gabino Fraga was designated to compile all IACHR petitions regarding violations of Indigenous peoples' rights. The purpose was to prepare a report with conclusions and recommendations regarding the eradication of any kind of discrimination against Indigenous peoples. In 1972, a resolution proposed by commissioner Justino Aréchaga was finally approved on that matter (doc. 38-29), urging states to pay attention to the training of indigenist officials, sanctioning those directly involved in cases of discrimination and abuses (CIDH, 1973).

[61] Brazilian Ministry of Foreign Affairs – OAS – IACHR, 'Caso Nr. 7615. Índios Yanomami', Washington D.C. (4 March 1981b) Delbrasupa para Exteriores,

Why was the IACHR dedicating its attention to cases related to Indigenous peoples? The international pro-Indigenous movement had emerged and gained traction in the 1970s.[62] Although this transnational network did not always frame its demands within the human rights vocabulary (given the lack of normative mentions to Indigenous peoples in its main documents), the increasing visibility of Indigenous struggles' called the attention of international organizations, including the Commission.

Another important change was the arrival of Ronald Reagan at the White House and the revitalization of a Cold War confrontational rhetoric. Carter's non-re-election was a hard blow, with global consequences for those actors seeking to maintain human rights at the top of the international political agenda.[63] The Commission, which would face renewed financial difficulties, lost its place as a crucial body for US foreign policy and was largely absent in the debates that would take place during the 1980s on the conflicts occurring in Central America. Besides that, Chilean and Argentinian dictatorships had toughened their positions regarding the Commission by that time.[64] Thus, the IACHR started to seek new issues and framings to make its work visible once again. When the Indigenous debate became prominent in the 1980s, these cases seemed like a window of opportunity for the institution to maintain its relevance and drive new legal discussions.[65] With an increasing and burgeoning number of new and important human rights NGOs, the IACHR had to prove its lasting importance before the public domain.[66]

---

Confidential.

62 Engle, *El desarrollo indígena, una promesa esquiva: derechos, cultura, estrategia* (n 6) 97–132; Kemner, 'Fourth World Activism in the First World' (n 17); Niezen, *The Origins of Indigenism: Human Rights and the Politics of Identity* (n 17) 40–42.

63 Farer, 'The Rise of the Inter-American Human Rights Regime' (n 16) 541–542; Goldman, 'History and Action' (n 16) 872.

64 Farer, 'The Rise of the Inter-American Human Rights Regime' (n 16) 531 and 539–42.

65 The Brazilian representative before the OAS, Alarico Silveira, pondered: 'on the IACHR's tendency to turn to certain issues that have not been thoroughly discussed so far, but that may connect to the general problematics of human rights, as a compensation for its current state of relative weakening' (Brazilian Ministry of Foreign Affairs – OAS – IACHR, 'Caso Nr. 7615. Índios Yanomami', Washington (4 March 1981) Delbrasupa para Exteriores, Confidential).

66 According to Farer, with new NGOs like Americas Watch disputing the public attention on human rights matters with budgets larger than the Commission's, the IACHR ceased to be 'a riveting star giving solo performances', and 'found itself just a bit adrift on a stage crowded with more deft and arresting actors'. Farer, 'The Rise of the Inter-American Human Rights Regime' (n 16) 542.

In the 1970s, faced with cases about Guahíbo Indigenous communities from Colombia and the Aché-Guayaki Indigenous people in Paraguay, the IACHR deliberately eluded the discussion on land rights conflicts and culture, as it decided to employ an individualist interpretation of civil and political rights to frame and refer to Indigenous peoples' situations. At that time, the IACHR avoided debating the destruction of Indigenous cultures as a direct consequence of the non-assurance of land rights, which revealed how its lack of a proper historical and anthropological understanding biased its work and blocked the realization that land rights were, and still continue to be up to now, a prerequisite for the survival of many aspects of Indigenous cultures.[67]

Such a prevailing perspective was significantly changed in the *Yanomami* and *Miskitu* cases. In these two turning-point cases, although Indigenous self-determination and issues of political autonomy were not considered, the IACHR's final resolutions stimulated states to ensure demarcation and respect for ancestral lands to preserve their Indigenous peoples' rights to culture and special protections as ethnic minorities.[68]

In both cases, the IACHR shied away from acknowledging that Indigenous peoples do possess collective property rights entitlements to their lands. As a result, change was still incipient. However, it was also extremely novel in terms of legal interpretations, considering the assimilationist perspective that prevailed in international human rights law regarding Indigenous peoples.[69]

In later decades, the two precedents on the Yanomami and Miskitu paved the way for the IACHR and the Inter-American Court of Human Rights to recognize Indigenous peoples' rights in other cases.[70] In order to preserve the Indigenous peoples' cultures, the IACHR and the Court decided from the early 2000s onwards that the transcending connections these peoples have with their territories must be guaranteed through collective land property rights, the only effective way to assure the reproduction of their ways of life, knowledge, and existence.

---

67 Shelton H. Davis, *Land Rights and Indigenous Peoples: The Role of the Inter-American Commission on Human Rights* (Cultural Survival Inc. 1988) 63.

68 Engle, *El desarrollo indígena, una promesa esquiva: derechos, cultura, estrategia* (n 6) 244–248; Rodríguez-Piñeiro Royo, 'El sistema interamericano de derechos humanos y los pueblos indígenas' (n 7).

69 The main example was ILO's Convention No. 107, dating from 1957, the only international treaty that focused exclusively on Indigenous peoples. It had a stigmatizing and colonial bias marked by a strategy of economic integrationism, stipulating clear limits to the right to traditional lands. Engle, *El desarrollo indígena, una promesa esquiva: derechos, cultura, estrategia* (n 6) 76–79.

70 Anaya, *International Human Rights and Indigenous Peoples* (n 7).

## 7 FINAL REMARKS

Unlike other IACHR cases against the Brazilian military dictatorship,[71] the *Yanomami* case benefitted from a set of key aspects that influenced the petition's outcome. In the first place, civil society's complainants were extremely motivated and technically very well prepared. They were able to use their transnational links, along with their US-based members and facilities, to intervene systematically before the IACHR, therefore leveraging their direct political and legal advocacy with commissioners and IACHR personnel. In addition, they had not only updated and gathered reliable evidence and information on violations that were taking place on the Indigenous territory, but also a solid legal argumentation that never strayed from the radical Indigenous claims for the Yanomami Park's demarcation.

Second, regarding the IACHR, it went through an institutional change that could be considered a conversion. Facing a political context without explicit blockages and with a significant level of institutional discretion, it began to interpret and implement its rules and norms in new and different ways using the data and legal formulations proposed by civil society. Thus, it advanced to the Indigenous problem, which it was neither entitled nor authorized to do by any explicit legal provision, clearly seeking to increase its relevance, prestige, fields of expertise, and jurisprudential and normative docket case.

By the time of the *Yanomami* case's arrival at the Commission, the Carter administration had already fomented a decisive IACHR institutional strengthening which took place along with an expressive change in the commissioners' membership, characterized by the entrance of more progressive institutional innovators. In parallel, the political context of the early 1980s had fewer veto points to expanding rights agendas and initiatives in comparison with the anti-communist repression framework of the 1970s. Institutionally more consolidated, on the one hand – especially after the American Convention on Human Rights' entry into force – and, on the other hand, having the transnational support and pressure from civil society gathered around the *Yanomami* case, the IACHR had more political space, legal tools, and reasonings to expansively explore the ambiguity of its norms, beginning to encompass the Indigenous issue with new positions.

As in the 1970s, the IACHR kept its autonomy to create its own understandings and promote concrete applications of the norms pertaining to the Inter-American human rights regime. However, in the 1970s, political and sovereignty-inclined pressures stemming from Brazil, the US, and OAS internal

---

[71] Bernardi, 'Silence, Hindrances and Omissions: The Inter-American Commission on Human Rights and the Brazilian Military Dictatorship' (n 31).

bodies caused the IACHR to drift from a more activist approach, blocking and vetoing its eventual efforts of normative experimentation. In the 1980s, such a scenario gave space both to civil society's voices and to commissioners prone to pressure states for meeting higher human rights standards, even if in a totally unprecedented field lacking clear-cut legal provision.

The IACHR's final recommendation in favour of the demarcation of Indigenous peoples' lands and all its later impact related not only to the concrete case, but also in regard to the future jurisprudence of the Inter-American system, depended decisively on three factors: (i) the role of civil society; (ii) the IACHR's internal politics and its institutional repertoire; and (iii) the lack of relevant extra- and intra-institutional veto-wielding actors capable of blocking the IACHR's new agenda.

In general, the case demonstrates that HRBs may undergo institutionally relevant changes even if their formal rules remain the same. In other words, the HRBs' scope and focus may expand, even to encompass new rights and new subjects of rights, despite norms remaining strictly the same. As our study demonstrates, the IACHR opened its agenda to include the debate on the rights of Indigenous peoples as a result of the *Yanomami* case and did not depend on the entry into force of new treaties or formal rules in order to do so.

A few lessons can be drawn from the application of the theoretical model, both for future analyses and for actors who seek to foster institutional conversion and increase the potential impact of HRBs' decisions.

First, changes of institutional conversion like the IACHR's in the *Yanomami* case only happen when the HRB involved has sufficient discretionary space to explore ambiguities in the application of their rules. Second, certain types of interactions between social, state, and inter-governmental actors are crucial in enabling institutional conversion. More specifically, the following factors are necessary: (i) pressure from specialised pro-human rights civil society actors, who must be able to invest time and resources into the legal cause; (ii) renewals of HRB members, with progressive actors' formal entry; and (iii) international political changes both decreasing political resistance to the HRB's intended changes and leaning favourably towards the human rights agenda's position – which, even if occupying a secondary place in political terms, must not openly get into conflict with the priorities of great powers or relevant states with key interests at stake in the issue at hand.

Therefore, in order to point out, confirm, and even anticipate institutional conversion, a few questions are relevant: (i) in terms of both the HRB's bureaucratic features and the correlation of forces among its members, are there enough spaces and resources for institutional innovative actions and strategies; (ii) regarding the possible alliances between the HRB and civil society, do the networks of the transnational activists who advocate for shifts and expansions of the HRB's actions have significant potential reverberation?; and, finally, (iii) on the position ascribed to human rights agendas in the international and regional contexts at a certain historical setting, are the extra- and intra-HRB's veto possibilities effectively weak or insufficient to the point of allowing conversion-like institutional changes and the consequent later impact on HRB decisions?

In this sense, pro-human rights drivers of change may be triggered by the actions of any of the following actors: states, HRBs, or civil society. However, such changes will more likely amass strength and chances of success in tandem. For human rights advances to take place, the agenda cannot be blocked by a coalition of powerful states; also, both civil society's political-legal advocacy and favourable institutional conditions as well as political willingness within HRBs are required.

Nonetheless, when compared with the HRB's internal politics and civil society's mobilization, the opening of the human rights inter-state agenda and its resulting reduction of veto points, albeit only partially observed, are more important. Profound pressure from civil society coupled with a favourable HRB composition prone to conversion will not be able to fully support human rights progress without some inter-state porosity, or in the presence of overt antagonism from governments. In these cases, blockages and veto points from states will persist against the HRB's institutional advances and innovations.

In other words, formal changes in the HRB's external and internal rules are not preconditions for them to expand: the range of protected rights; their reach in terms of groups and subjects under their coverage; and the potential impact of their decisions. However, for such processes to happen, specific dynamics involving the HRB's relations with governments and civil society actors must also be observed. Future research must aim to improve our understanding of the strategies, interactions, and circumstances behind such changes.

# 8. Towards the consolidation of the *Ius Constitutionale Commune* in Latin American LGBTIQ+ rights: the transformative impact of Advisory Opinion OC-24/17

**Mariela Morales Antoniazzi and Carolina Bejarano Martínez**

## 1 INTRODUCTION[1]

This chapter adopts a regional approach to transformative constitutionalism, arguing that the emergence of a *Ius Constitutionale Commune* (ICCAL) in Latin America is reflected in a set of common standards. This development has advanced international law and expanded our understanding of its impact.[2] The regional convergence of these standards is driven by three key factors: (a) international and Inter-American treaties and their incorporation into national constitutions; (b) the transformative jurisprudence of the Inter-American Court of Human Rights (IACtHR) and the broad mandate of the

[1] The authors would like to express their sincere gratitude to Alina Ripplinger, Eleanor Benz, Alejandro Gómez López, Mareike Ronellenfitsch, Hannah Dora, Denise Zöller, Friedrich Berg, and Sandro Gorski Silva for their invaluable research assistance and collaboration in the development of this chapter. A special thanks to Flávia Piovesan for her always generous support and unwavering disposition to work in collaborative networks, which greatly enriched the ICCAL community.

[2] Paradigmatic, among many others: Kathryn Sikkink, 'Latin America's Protagonist Role in Human Rights' (2015) 12 SUR 207. A more current and comprehensive view in: Alejandro Chehtman, Alexandra Huneeus, and Sergio Puig, 'Introduction to Latin American International Law' in Alejandro Chehtman, Alexandra Huneeus, and Sergio Puig (eds) *Latin American International Law in the Twenty-First Century* (Oxford University Press 2025).

Inter-American Commission on Human Rights (IACHR); and (c) the legal practices of states and the active engagement of a Latin American community, including judges, policymakers, social movements, academia, national human rights institutions, and civil society.

The IAHRS's common standards have profoundly influenced the region, shifting the focus from state compliance with judicial rulings to a broader understanding of human rights impact.[3] As scholars note, analyzing 'impact' rather than mere 'compliance' provides deeper insights into human rights dynamics.[4] This includes advancements in human rights protection within the IAHRS, state adherence to Inter-American standards, and their strategic use by civil society.[5]

---

3 Rene Urueña, 'Compliance as Transformation: The Inter-American System of Human Rights and its Impact(s)' in Rainer Grote, Mariela Morales Antoniazzi, and Davide Paris (eds), *Research Handbook on Compliance in International Human Rights Law* (Edward Elgar Publishing Limited 2021) 225–247, 225.

4 On the notion of transformative impact we have been collaborating in the ICCAL network since 2015, pointing out the paradigm shift from measuring compliance (a necessary but insufficient notion) to mapping impact: Armin von Bogdandy, Mariela Morales Antoniazzi, and Manuel Góngora Mera (eds), *Ius Commune en migración y constitucionalismo transformador en Colombia: Un enfoque de derechos para la movilidad humana* (Instituto de Estudios Constitucionales 2022); Mariela Morales Antoniazzi, 'The Inter-American System's Transformative Mandate as a Response to the Pandemic in Light of the Democratic Test' (2021) 19 *International Journal of Constitutional Law* 1229.

5 Par Engstrom, 'The Impact of the Inter-American Human Rights System beyond Latin America' in Armin von Bogdandy and others (eds), *The Impact of the Inter-American Human Rights System: Transformations on the Ground* (Oxford University Press 2024) 100–121; Viviana Krsticevic and René Urueña, 'Transformative Impact of the Inter-American Human Rights System: A Methodology to Think beyond Compliance' in Armin von Bogdandy and others (eds), *The Iimpact of the Inter-American Human Rights System: Transformations on the Ground* (Oxford University Press 2024) 583–602; Chris Esdaile and others, 'The Impact beyond Compliance of the Case of Azul Rojas Marin' in Armin von Bogdandy and others (eds), *The Impact of the Inter-American Human Rights System: Transformations on the Ground* (Oxford University Press 2024) 303–325; Clara Burbano Herrera and Yves Haeck, 'The Use of Transformative Provisional Measures by the Inter-American Court of Human Rights: Toward a Tangible Impact' in Armin von Bogdandy and others (eds), *The Impact of the Inter-American Human Rights System: Transformations on the Ground* (Oxford University Press 2024) 153–175; Ezequiel Gonzalez-Ocantos and Wayne Sandholtz, 'Constructing a Regional Human Rights Legal Order: The Inter-American Court, National Courts, and Judicial Dialogue, 1988–2014' (2021) 19 *International Journal of Constitutional Law* 1559.

Latin America's distinctive historical, social, and political context makes it especially fertile ground for studying transformative impact.[6] In today's global landscape, the role of the IAHRS offers valuable lessons not only for the region but worldwide.[7] Ortiz Ocaña and Pérez-Liñán conceptualize impact as the intended or unintended effects on practices, structures, and social outcomes resulting from international bodies' actions.[8] They identify three key components: (a) an international body taking action through binding or non-binding instruments, such as the IACtHR's interpretation of the American Convention on Human Rights (ACHR); (b) a sequence of effects, including actions by civil society and state institutions to align with IAHRS standards; and (c) potential transformations in socio-legal practices, institutions, or society.[9]

Building on this conceptualization, the chapter first presents ICCAL as a framework for analyzing impact, emphasizing the IAHRS's responsiveness to human rights, democracy, and the rule of law. It highlights the circulation, appropriation, and use of Inter-American standards within Latin America's human rights community.

Second, it examines regional LGBTIQ+ rights standards through Advisory Opinion No 24 of the IACtHR. Rather than focusing on a case decision, this chapter demonstrates how an advisory opinion can influence practices,

---

6 Mariela Morales Antoniazzi, Flávia Piovesan, and Júlia Cortez da Cunha Cruz, 'Inter-American System of Human Rights: Sociopolitical, Institutional, and Cultural Dimensions of its Transformative Impact' in Armin von Bogdandy and others (eds), *The Impact of the Inter-American Human Rights System: Transformations on the Ground* (Oxford University Press 2024) 49–75.

7 Pablo Saavedra Alessandri, 'La defensa pública interamericana y su trabajo en casos ante la corte IDH. Ampliando y fortaleciendo el horizonte del acceso a la justicia interamericana a través de los y las DPI: Breves reflexiones' in Pablo Saavedra Alessandri and Sebastián Van Den Dooren (eds), *Impacto de la jurisprudencia de la corte interamericana de derechos humanos desde la perspectiva de la defensa pública* (Instituto de Estudios Constitucionales del Estado de Querétaro 2023) 315–320, 320; Ramos Vázquez and Eréndira Nohemí, *La doctrina del control de convencionalidad* (Editorial Porrúa 2021) 96–98; Sergio García Ramírez, 'Prólogo. Sobre el control de convencionalidad y el derecho común interamericano' in Ramos Vázquez and Eréndira Nohemí (eds), *La doctrina del control de convencionalidad* (Editorial Porrúa 2021) IX–XI.

8 Mayra Ortiz Ocaña and Aníbal Pérez-Liñán, 'Transformative Impact: A Framework for Analysis' in Armin von Bogdandy and others (eds), *The Impact of the Inter-American Human Rights System: Transformations on the Ground* (Oxford University Press 2024) 17698.

9 Ortiz Ocaña and Pérez-Liñán, 'Transformative Impact: A Framework for Analysis' (n 8).

structures, and social outcomes within and beyond the Inter-American system.[10] The term 'LGBTIQ+ human rights protection constellation' describes the broad legal interactions surrounding Advisory Opinion OC-24/17.

Third, this chapter explores how the *ius commune* has influenced LGBTIQ+ rights in Brazil, Mexico, and Colombia, illustrating its impact on judicial rulings, national policies, and civil society initiatives, including LGBTIQ+ movements and academic discourse. The ongoing construction of a human rights community of practice is evident in these countries' engagement with the LGBTIQ+ human rights constellation.

Finally, the conclusion identifies trends in how regional standards shape both theoretical understandings and the practical implementation of human rights protections across Latin America, emphasizing their transformative impact.

## 2 ICCAL AS A REGIONAL APPROACH TO TRANSFORMATIVE CONSTITUTIONALISM TO UNDERSTAND IMPACT

The *Ius Constitutionale Commune* in Latin America is a regional approach to transformative constitutionalism rooted in the principle of human dignity. It builds upon transformative constitutionalism by integrating Latin American legal traditions and human rights frameworks.[11] Initially conceptualized by Karl Klare in the context of South African law,[12] transformative constitutionalism has been adapted in Latin America to address structural challenges such as violence, exclusion, and weak institutions.[13]

---

10 Jorge Ernesto Roa, *La función consultiva de la Corte Interamericana de Derechos Humanos* (1st Edition, Universidad Externado de Colombia, Instituto de Estudios Constitucionales 2015) 96; Eleanor Benz, *The Advisory Function of the Inter-American Court of Human Rights* (Nomos 2024).

11 Manuel José Cepeda Espinoza, *La Constitución de 1991: viviente y transformadora* (Universidad de los Andes 2022).

12 Karl E. Klare, 'Legal Culture and Transformative Constitutionalism' (1998) 14 *South African Journal on Human Rights* 146, 146; von Bogdandy and Urueña, 'Inducing Compliance as a Transformative Process' in Armin von Bogdandy and others (eds), *The Impact of the Inter-American Human Rights System: Transformations on the Ground* (Oxford University Press 2024) 17–33.

13 von Bogdandy and Urueña, 'Inducing Compliance as a Transformative Process' (n 12) 19; Manuel José Cepeda Espinosa and David E. Landau, *Colombian Constitutional Law: Leading Cases* (Oxford University Press 2017); Manuel José Cepeda Espinosa, *La Constitución de 1991: viviente y transformadora* (Ediciones Uniandes 2022).

Latin American constitutionalism, spanning over two centuries, emphasizes the role of law in advancing democracy and human rights.[14] It aligns with Nonet and Selznick's concept of *responsive law*, which posits that legal systems should address social needs while maintaining autonomy from politics.[15] The IACtHR exemplifies this approach, interpreting the ACHR to drive regional transformation.[16] The Court's role as a constitutional tribunal[17] is evident in its authority to invalidate national laws that contradict the Convention, reinforcing transformative constitutionalism.[18]

ICCAL focuses on the vocation of transformative constitutionalism. In a region with severe structural deficiencies and weak institutions, the Latin American path to transformative constitutionalism strives to advance the principles set out in national constitutions and international treaties since the second half of the twentieth century,[19] along with regional integration initia-

---

14 Diego Valadés, *Visión panorámica del constitucionalismo en el siglo XX* (Cuadernos de la Coordinación de Humanidades Universidad Nacional Autónoma de México 2016); Roberto Gargarella, *Latin American Constitutionalism, 1810–2010: The Engine Room of the Constitution* (Oxford University Press 2013).

15 Philippe Nonet and Philip Selznick, *Law and Society in Transition: Toward Responsive Law* (Harper & Row 1978).

16 In this study, we adopt Armin von Bogdandy's concept of the transformative mandate of the IACtHR. See further: Armin von Bogdandy, 'El mandato transformador del sistema interamericano d e derechos humanos: Legalidad y legitimidad de un proceso jurisgenerativo extraordinario' (2019) 9 *Revista del centro de estudios constitucionales* 113.

17 See: Antônio Augusto Cançado Trindade, *International Law for Humankind: Towards a New Jus Gentium. Third Revised Edition* (BRILL 2020); Cecilia Medina Quiroga, 'The Court and Its Circumstances' in Cecilia Medina Quiroga, *The American Convention on Human Rights: Crucial Rights and Their Theory and Practice* (Intersentia 2016) 1–62.

18 Paz González, and others, *La Constitución Convencionalizada: A 40 Años de La Vigencia Del Pacto de San José* (Tirant lo Blanch 2022); María Sofía Sagüés, 'Diálogo jurisprudencial y control de convencionalidad a la luz de la experiencia en el caso argentino' in Miriam Henrïquez Viña and Mariela Morales Antoniazzi (eds), *El Control de Convencionalidad: Un balance comparado a 10 años de Almonacid Arellano vs. Chile* (DER Ediciones 2017) 281–370; Christina Binder, 'The Prohibition of Amnesties by the Inter-American Court of Human Rights' (2011) 12 *German Law Journal* 1203; Laurence Burgorgue Larsen, 'Conventionality Control: Inter-American Court of Human Rights (IACtHR)' (*Max Planck Encyclopedias of International Law*, December 2018) https://opil.ouplaw.com/display/10.1093/law-mpeipro/e3634.013.3634/law-mpeipro-e3634 (accessed 18 September 2024).

19 Armin von Bogdandy, 'Ius Constitutionale Commune na América Latina. Uma Reflexao sobre um Constitucionalismo Transformador' in Armin

tives.[20] This course of action promotes progress, justice, and societal development, with a specific focus on vulnerable groups. It seeks to address persistent challenges, such as high levels of inequality, poverty, unacceptable living conditions, and social exclusion, from a legal perspective.[21]

Domestic constitutional courts frequently reference Inter-American law, consolidating human rights standards across various legal domains – what we term *constellations of protection*. These constellations encompass Indigenous rights, socio-economic and environmental rights, and migrant protections. Since 2004, academic discourse has reinforced this framework, with ICCAL engaging a wide range of actors, including IAHRS judges, domestic courts, legal professionals, activists, policymakers, and social movements.[22] This network forms a *community of practice*, collectively shaping human rights protections in the region.[23]

Empirical research further illustrates ICCAL's impact. For example, the Tandem Team studied how ethnic communities in Colombia use international law in local and national legal processes through a blend of legal ethnography,[24]

---

von Bogdandy, Mariela Morales-Antoniazzi and Flavia Piovesan (eds), *Ius Constitutionale Commune Na America-Latina. Volumen I. Marco Conceptual* (Jurua 2016) 11–51; Rodrigo Uprimny, 'Las transformaciones constitucionales recientes en América Latina: tendencias y desafíos' in César Rodríguez Garavito (ed), *El derecho en América Latina. Un mapa para el pensamiento jurídico del siglo XXI* (Siglo Veintiuno Editores 2011) 109–137, 109.

[20] Mariela Morales Antoniazzi, *Protección supranacional de la democracia en Suramérica. Un estudio sobre el acervo del Ius Constitutionale Commune* (Universidad Nacional Autónoma de México, Instituto de Investigaciones Jurídicas 2015) 2392.

[21] Carlos Rodríguez Castelán, Hugo Ñopo and others, 'Nine Key Facts about Poverty and Inequality in Latin America and the Caribbean' (*World Bank Blog*, 2 July 2024) https://blogs.worldbank.org/en/opendata/key-facts-about-poverty-and-inequality-in-latin-america (accessed 18 September 2024).

[22] Mariela Morales Antoniazzi and Viviana Krsticevic, 'NGOs: A Critical Link to Understanding and Strengthening Compliance of International Decisions' in Rainer Grote, Mariela Morales Antoniazzi and Davide Paris (eds), *Research Handbook on Compliance in International Human Rights Law* (Edward Elgar Publishing Limited 2021) 485–508.

[23] Armin von Bogdandy and René Urueña, 'International Transformative Constitutionalism in Latin America' (2020) 114 *American Journal of International Law* 403.

[24] The Tandem team employed research methodologies from the social sciences to trace the uses and transformations of international law amidst complex social interactions. These methodologies have also been utilized by other scholars. For more on the anthropology of international law, see: Nancy Yañez, 'The

legal geography, and transformative constitutionalism. Their case studies in Cartagena[25] and Buenaventura[26] show that these communities actively shape judicial decisions and employ innovative legal strategies to protect their rights. ICCAL provides a platform for legal discourse on human rights, democracy, and the rule of law in Latin America. Its multilevel interaction allows domestic courts to interpret constitutions in light of IAHRS standards while contributing to a shared legal framework. Three core principles define ICCAL's legal integration: the *open state* principle enshrined in national constitutions,[27] the *block of constitutionality* (which integrates domestic constitutions with Inter-American law),[28] and the doctrine of *control de convencionalidad*.[29] While general critiques of the limits of human rights,[30] as well as specific criticisms of ICCAL, exist,[31] this approach emphasizes the constitutional and conventional foundations that make it possible to speak of a *ius commune* in the region.

---

Juridification of Indigenous Claims in Latin America: Obstacles and Challenges' in Collin Casagrande and others (eds), *Law and Diversity: European and Latin American Experiences From a Legal Historical Perspective. Vol. 1: Fundamental Questions* (Max Planck Institute for Legal History and Legal Theory 2023); Mark Goodale, *Reinventing Human Rights* (1st edition, Stanford University Press 2022); Luis Eslava, *Local Space, Global Life: The Everyday Operation of International Law and Development* (1st edition, Cambridge University Press 2015); Sally Engle Merry, 'Transnational Human Rights and Local Activism: Mapping the Middle' (2006) 108 *American Anthropologist* 38; Anna Lowenhaupt Tsing, *Friction: An Ethnography of Global Connection* (Princeton University Press 2005).

[25] Carolina Bejarano Martínez, 'Gente de Mar: Expansión urbana, luchas étnico-territoriales y jurisdicciones contingentes en Cartagena de Indias' (Doctoral Thesis, Universidad de los Andes 2024) 26571.

[26] Joaquín Antonio Garzón Vargas, 'Luchas negras en Buenaventura y el gobierno del futuro. alter-logísticas, derecho y economía global' (Doctoral Thesis, Universidad de los Andes 2024).

[27] Mariela Morales Antoniazzi, *El Estado Abierto como Objetivo del Ius Constitutionale Commune. Aproximación desde el Impacto de la Corte Interamericana de Derechos Humanos* (MPIL 2014).

[28] See: Manuel Góngora-Mera, *Inter-American Judicial Constitutionalism* (IIDH 2011).

[29] Sergio García Ramírez, 'Sobre el control de convencionalidad' (2016) 21 *Pensamiento Constitucional* 173.

[30] Samuel Moyn, *Not Enough: Human Rights in an Unequal World* (Harvard University Press 2018).

[31] Juan Camilo Herrera, 'The idea of a common law in Latin America in light of its critiques' (2021) 19 *International Journal of Constitutional Law* 1385.

These foundations open national law to international law, moving beyond a rigid understanding of sovereignty and the supremacy of domestic constitutions over international law. They also offer a new legal language to address the region's structural challenges, which can be practically and theoretically understood from the lenses of impact beyond compliance.[32] Finally, the conceptual framework offered by ICCAL allows for an understanding of the interplay of diverse actors in the formation and permanent transformation of Inter-American human rights law.

On the 65th anniversary of the IACHR and the 45th anniversary of the IACtHR, significant concerns and challenges have emerged. These include addressing dynamic issues from a human rights perspective, such as climate change,[33] increasing threats to democracies,[34] and the broader global political landscape regarding security and peace.[35] Taking these challenges into account, this chapter understands international law in general, and Inter-American law in particular, as a toolset to achieve both local and global common goals and address international crises.[36]

---

[32] Krsticevic and Urueña, 'Transformative Impact of the Inter-American Human Rights System' (n 5).

[33] The request for three advisory opinions on this issue is a sign of the relevance of climate change in this sphere. See: Daniel Bodansky, 'Advisory Opinions on Climate Change: Some Preliminary Questions' (2023) 32 *Review of European, Comparative and International Environmental Law* 185–92; Melissa Stewart, 'Climate Change Advisory Opinion Requests: Risk and Reward' (*Lawfare*, 2023) https://www.lawfaremedia.org/article/climate-change-advisory-opinion-requests-risk-and-reward.

[34] The most comprehensive global democracy index is produced every year by the V-Dem Institute. For the 2024 report, see: V-Dem Institute, 'Democracy Report 2024: Democracy Winning and Losing at the Ballot' (2024) https://www.v-dem.net/documents/43/v-dem_dr2024_lowres.pdf; Fathali M. Moghaddam, *Threat to Democracy: The Appeal of Authoritarianism in an Age of Uncertainty* (American Psychological Association 2019); Mariana Llanos and Leiv Marsteintredet, *Latin America in Times of Turbulence: Presidentialism Under Stress* (Taylor & Francis 2023).

[35] See: Anne Peters, 'The Russian Invasion of Ukraine: An Anti-Constitutional Moment in International Law?' (2024) 86 Ruch Prawniczy, *Ekonomiczny i Socjologiczny* 5; Adam Taylor, 'Why the Israel–Gaza War Represents a Broader Crisis for Global Justice: Luis Moreno Ocampo, Former Prosecutor of the International Criminal Court, Says Both Sides May Have Committed War Crimes, but There's Little Appetite for Justice', *The Washington Post* (Washington, D.C., 2023).

[36] Anne Peters, Raphael Schäfer and Hendrik Simon, '(Writing) International Legal Histories – Continuation of Politics by Other Means? An Interview with

Inter-American innovative law-making offers interpretative tools to address some contemporary challenges. Several decades ago, the American Declaration of the Rights and Duties of Man, adopted approximately eight months before the Universal Declaration, was recognized as the first human rights instrument. Its innovation lay in affirming that 'the essential rights of man are not derived from the fact that he is a national of a certain state but are based upon attributes of his human personality'.[37]

Alongside the American Declaration, the normative, jurisprudential, and discursive developments that have emerged over the past decades have progressively shaped a common framework for respecting, protecting, and guaranteeing human rights. This process has not been linear and remains subject to ongoing threats,[38] framed by the understanding of an emerging democratic society in a context marked by the legacies of dictatorship, civil war, and persistent structural inequalities in Latin America.[39] Despite these challenges, the progressive configuration of human rights obligations continues to evolve within the region, even in very contested legal constellations like LGBTIQ+ rights, as shown in the following sections.

---

Anne Peters and Raphael Schäfer' (*Völkerrechtsblog*, 2021) https://voelkerrechtsblog.org/writing-international-legal-histories-continuation-of-politics-by-other-means/.

[37] American Declaration of the Rights and Duties of Man, OAS Res XXX adopted by the Ninth International Conference of American States (1948) reprinted in Basic Documents Pertaining to Human Rights in the Inter-American System OEA/Ser L V/II.82 Doc 6 Rev 1 at 17 (1992).

[38] Ximena Soley and Silvia Steininger, *Parting Ways or Lashing Back? Withdrawals, Backlash and the Inter-American Court of Human Rights* (Social Science Electronic Publishing 2018).

[39] These challenges are visible in both the Court and the Commission's annual reports: IACtHR, '2023 Annual Report' (*Corte IDH*, 2024) https://www.corteidh.or.cr/docs/informe2023/ingles.pdf; IACHR, '2023 Annual Report' (*OAS*, 2024) https://www.oas.org/en/IACHR/reports/IA.asp?Year=2023. See also: Flávia Piovesan, 'Ius Constitutionale Commune Em Direitos Humanos E Constitucionalismo Regional Transformador: O Impacto do Sistema Interamericano' in Armin von Bogdandy and others (eds), *Ius Constitutionale Commune Na America-Latina. Volumen I. Marco Conceptual* (Jurua 2016) 75–95; Flávia Piovesan, 'Direitos Humanos E Dialogo Jurisdicional no Contexto Latino-Americano' in Armin von Bogdandy and others (eds), *Direitos Humanos, Democracia E Integração Jurídica: Emergência De Um Novo Direito Público* (Elsevier 2013) 388–409.

## 3 THE INTER-AMERICAN STANDARDS AND THEIR IMPACT: ADVISORY OPINION OC-24/17 ON LGBTIQ+ RIGHTS

From a Latin American perspective, one particularly relevant case for applying the concept of impact through the lens of transformative constitutionalism is Advisory Opinion OC-24/17, which protects LGBTIQ+ rights. This case gains significance when considering the IACHR's agenda and the rulings of the IACtHR. We chose to analyze this advisory opinion as a remarkable example of the impact Inter-American decisions have on different legal spheres and for a variety of actors, including national judicial authorities and civil society organizations.[40]

For instance, the IACtHR has referenced its Advisory Opinion 24/17 on 32 occasions in various resolutions, including 21 times in the argumentation of rulings in contentious cases, 10 times in the resolution of other advisory opinions, and once in the issuance of provisional measures.[41] The impact of the Advisory Opinion 24/17 has been demonstrated to extend beyond the Inter-American system, having influenced other regional systems of protection of human rights, including the European and the United Nations systems. For instance, the European Court of Human Rights (ECtHR) cited the advisory opinion in the case of *Fedotova and Others v Russia*,[42] where Russia was found liable for violating Article 8 of the European Convention on Human Rights (protection of private and family life) because it failed to justify the absence of any legal recognition of same-sex relationships. With regard to the Universal Human Rights System, the United Nations has cited Advisory Opinion 24/17 in 17 documents,[43] thereby identifying the advisory opinion as a relevant source of international law.

---

[40] Esdaile and others, 'The Impact beyond Compliance of the Case of Azul Rojas Marin' (n 5) 320.

[41] Data obtained from the IACtHR Jurisprudence website: IACtHR, 'Jurisprudencia de la Corte IDH' (*Corte IDH*, 2024) https://jurisprudencia.corteidh.or.cr/es/vid/883977259/cited_by/jurisdiction:EA+aplica_ley:883977259/*/by_score/p2.

[42] *Fedotova and Others v Russia* App nos 40792/10, 30538/14 and 43439/14 (ECtHR, 17 January 2023) paras 63–4.

[43] See: *V.W.G. and E.H. v Albania* (2023) UN Doc CCPR/C/138/D/3031/2017; United NAtions General Assambly (UNGA), 'Report of the Independent Expert on protection against violence and discrimination based on sexual orientation and gender identity' (12 July 2018) UN Doc A/73/152; Convention on the Elimination of All Forms of Discrimination against Women (CEDAW), 'Concluding observations on the eighth periodic report of Costa Rica' (2 March 2023) UN Doc

This example highlights the dimensions and reach of an advisory opinion as one of the instruments contributing to the creation of a *ius commune*, and, in turn, illustrates the concept of transformative impact at the level of the IACHR itself, as well as the impact on national jurisdictions, and other normative

CEDAW/C/CRI/CO/8; Center for Civil and Political Rights (CCPR), 'Summary record of the 4128th meeting' (29 July 2024) UN Doc CCPR/C/SR.4128; Human Rights Council, 'Gender-based violence and discrimination in the name of religion or belief: Report of the Special Rapporteur on freedom of religion or belief' (24 August 2020) UN Doc A/HRC/43/48; Human Rights Council. 'National report submitted pursuant to Human Rights Council resolutions 5/1 and 16/21 – Costa Rica' (29 August 2024) UN Doc A/HRC/WG.6/47/CRI/1; UNGA, 'Freedom of religion or belief and freedom from violence and discrimination based on sexual orientation and gender identity' in 'Report of the Independent Expert on protection against violence and discrimination based on sexual orientation and gender identity, Victor Madrigal-Borloz' (24 January 2024) UN Doc A/HRC/53/37; UNGA, 'The law of inclusion' in 'Report of the Independent Expert on protection against violence and discrimination based on sexual orientation and gender identity, Victor Madrigal-Borloz' (3 June 2021) UN Doc A/HRC/47/27; Committee on Economic, Social and Cultural Rights, 'Concluding observations on the third periodic report of Panama' (31 March 2023) UN Doc E/C.12/PAN/CO/3; Human Rights Committee, 'Concluding observations on the fourth periodic report of Panama' (12 April 2023) UN Doc CCPR/C/PAN/CO/4; CEDAW, 'Eighth periodic report submitted by Costa Rica under article 18 of the Convention, due in 2021' (4 October 2021) UN Doc CEDAW/C/CRI/8; Human Rights Council 'Summary of stakeholders' submissions on Peru' in 'Report of the Office of the United Nations High Commissioner for Human Rights' (27 October 2022) UN Doc A/HRC/WG.6/42/PER/3; Human Rights Council, 'Note by the Secretariat, Report of the Independent Expert on protection against violence and discrimination based on sexual orientation and gender identity' (11 May 2018) UN Doc A/HRC/38/43; International Law Commission, 'Crimes against humanity' in 'Comments and observations received from Governments, international organizations and others' (21 January 2019) UN Doc A/CN.4/726; International Law Commission, 'Chapter IV Crimes against humanity' in 'Draft report of the International Law Commission on the work of its seventy-first session' (19 June 2019) UN Doc A/CN.4/L.928/ADD.1; International Law Commission, 'Fourth report on crimes against humanity' (18 February 2019) UN Doc A/CN.4/725; International Law Commission, 'Report of the International Law Commission Seventy-first session (29 April to 7 June and 8 July to 9 August 2019) UN Doc A/74/10. Data obtained from the United Nations Official Document System: https://documents.un.org.

regimes, such as the United Nations[44] or the ECtHR.[45] While mapping the impact of the advisory opinion on national jurisdictions, we also highlight socio-legal practices that serve as drivers of the transformative impact of the LGBTIQ+ *ius commune* in the region.

Advisory Opinion OC-24/17 has garnered significant attention in recent years. On one hand, several constitutional courts have issued rulings that recognize the relevance of advisory opinions. We challenge the idea that implementing advisory opinions within the domestic legal frameworks of Inter-American states is more difficult or less feasible compared to the implementation of rulings in contentious cases by the IACtHR.[46] Instead, using the example of the LGBTIQ+ rights constellation, we demonstrate that legal actors, including high courts, actively adhere to human rights standards established in Advisory Opinions. For instance, in Argentina, Colombia, and Ecuador, the highest courts have acknowledged the legal authority of IACtHR advisory opinions, deeming them essential for the interpretation and application of international human rights treaties.[47] Moreover, legal scholarship has increasingly focused on advisory opinions and their significance.[48]

To explore the impact of OC-24/17, this analysis will focus on three central axes. First, it will provide the context that justifies giving visibility to the human rights situation of the LGBTIQ+ community in the region. Second, it will systematically examine the contributions of the standards established by the IACtHR. Finally, it will outline the multidimensional routes of impact generated by Advisory Opinion OC-24/17.

---

44 See: OHCHR, 'Sexual orientation and gender identity: UN expert hails historic legal opinion issued in the Americas' (Media Centre, 2018) https://www.ohchr.org/en/press-releases/2018/01/sexual-orientation-and-gender-identity-un-expert-hails-historic-legal.

45 *Transgender Europe and ILGA-Europe v the Czech Republic* App No. 117/2015 (European Committee of Social Rights, 15 May 2018).

46 Roa, *La función consultiva de la Corte Interamericana de Derechos Humanos* (n 10) 121.

47 José Roberto Castro, 'El valor jurídico de las opiniones consultivas de la Corte Interamericana de Derechos Humanos' (2024) 5 *Iustitia et Pulchritudo* 17, 24.

48 Benz, *The Advisory Function of the Inter-American Court of Human Rights* (n 10); Alvaro Paul Díaz, 'Rechazo de Solicitudes de Opinión Consultiva Por Parte de La Corte Interamericana de Derechos Humanos' (2023) 8 *Revista Chilena de Derecho y Ciencia Política* 119; Roa, *La función consultiva de la Corte Interamericana de Derechos Humanos* (n 10).

### 3.1 The Socio-Legal Context of the LGBTIQ+ Community in Latin America

The global Pride movement continues to gain momentum, drawing millions of participants worldwide to advocate for LGBTIQ+ rights.[49] However, this progress is uneven, as many countries still impose harsh restrictions, with penalties ranging from imprisonment to death for exercising these rights.[50] In Latin America, while some states visibly advance the legal protection of the LGBTIQ+ community, others have enacted policies that further marginalize this population.

Despite the broader global challenges, Latin America has seen notable legal advancements in the recognition of LGBTIQ+ rights.[51] Several countries have decriminalized same-sex relationships and legalized same-sex marriage.[52] Argentina, in particular, has led the way with its ground-breaking 2012 Gender Identity Law, which allows individuals to change their gender on official documents without requiring surgery or psychiatric evaluation.[53] Uruguay and Costa Rica have also made significant strides, legalizing same-sex marriage and recognizing adoption rights for same-sex couples.[54] However, resistance remains strong in other countries like Paraguay, where constitutional prohibitions against same-sex unions are firmly in place.[55]

---

49 Justin Trudeau, 'Providing LGBTQI+ people with a safe home in Canada' (*Canada*, 8 June 2023) https://www.pm.gc.ca/en/news/news-releases/2023/06/08/providing-lgbtqi-people-safe-home-canada; Associated Press, 'Joe Biden marks Pride month with high-profile support of LGBTQ+ community', *The Guardian* (Washington D.C., 8 June 2023) https://www.theguardian.com/us-news/2023/jun/08/joe-biden-pride-month-support-lgbtq-community.

50 See Human Dignity Trust, 'Map of Jurisdictions that Criminalise LGBT People' (Human Dignity Trust, 2025) https://www.humandignitytrust.org/lgbt-the-law/map-of-criminalisation/.

51 Gabriela Farrell, 'The State of LGBTQ+ Rights in Latin America' (Wilson Center, 25 June 2021)https://www.wilsoncenter.org/blog-post/state-lgbtq-rights-latin-america-0.

52 Maximiliano Campana and Juan Marco Vaggione, 'Courts and Same-Sex Marriage in Latin America' (*Oxford Research Encyclopedia of Politics*, 22 January 2021) https://oxfordre.com/politics/view/10.1093/acrefore/9780190228637.001.0001/acrefore-9780190228637-e-1189 (accessed 17 September 2024).

53 Inés Arístegui, and others, 'Impact of the Gender Identity Law in Argentinean Transgender Women' (2017) 18 *International Journal of Transgenderism* 446.

54 ILGA World Database, 'Legal Frameworks: Same-Sex Marriage and Civil Unions' (ILGA, 2025) https://database.ilga.org/same-sex-marriage-civil-unions.

55 ILGA World Database, 'Country: Paraguay' (ILGA, 2025) https://database.ilga.org/paraguay-lgbti.

Yet, despite these legal gains, social realities in Latin America paint a more troubling picture.[56] Discrimination, violence, and exclusion remain daily challenges for many LGBTIQ+ individuals,[57] particularly in conservative religious contexts. This is especially pronounced in countries like Honduras, where fundamentalist beliefs amplify systemic discrimination. The region is one of the most dangerous in the world for LGBTIQ+ individuals, with over 3,500 murders of LGBTIQ+ people between 2014 and 2020, 80% of which were trans-related homicides. In 2023 alone, 235 LGBTIQ+ individuals were killed, further underscoring the severity of this violence.[58]

There is also significant regional disparity in the recognition and protection of LGBTIQ+ rights. Countries such as Argentina, Brazil, Colombia, and Uruguay have legalized both same-sex marriage and joint adoption for same-sex couples. However, over ten other nations in the region still deny legal protection for these rights, with countries like El Salvador, Guatemala, Honduras, and Panama banning same-sex adoption outright. Mexico's legal system has further complicated this issue, with disparities between federal recognition of equal marriage and varying state-level restrictions impacting adoption processes. This gap between legal progress and social acceptance remains one of the largest challenges for LGBTIQ+ rights in Latin America. This ongoing exclusion highlights the need for deeper societal transformation to bridge the gap between legal recognition and everyday reality for LGBTIQ+ individuals.

### 3.2 The LGBTIQ+ *Ius Commune* in the Decisions of the Inter-American Court of Human Rights

Facing the challenging socio-legal context for the LGBTIQ+ community, the IACtHR has successfully established standards to reduce structural discrimination, stigmatization, and various forms of violence directed against the LGBTIQ+ population, which infringe upon their rights. These standards, as reflected in the Court's rulings and advisory opinions, are informed by other international and regional legal instruments and jurisprudence. In this subsection, we explore the developments of LGBTIQ+ rights by the IACtHR as

---

56 Statista Research Department, 'Countries with the highest number of murders of trans and gender-diverse people in Latin America from October 2022 to September 2023' (Statista, 5 July 2024) https://www.statista.com/statistics/944650/number-trans-murders-latin-america-country/.

57 Indyra Mendoza, 'For me, being a Human Rights Defender is rewarding, but it is also an act of courage' (2020) 17 SUR 30, 2020 35.

58 Statista Research Department, 'Countries with the highest number of murders of trans and gender-diverse people in Latin America from October 2022 to September 2023' (n 56).

well as by the IACHR. To do so, we first describe the content and impact of the LGBTIQ+ rulings of the Court before the publication of the Advisory Opinion OC-24/17. Then we explain in detail the content of the Advisory Opinion. Following this, we will explain how the Advisory Opinion impacted the IACtHR's own jurisprudence.

Over time, the IACtHR has addressed several human rights guarantees of the ACHR in relation to LGBTIQ+ rights. These cases have often involved, for instance, the protection of the right to privacy (Article 11 ACHR), as in *Flor Freire v Ecuador,*[59] or the right to a family (Article 17 ACHR), as in *Atala Riffo and Daughters v Chile*[60] and *Duque v Colombia*,[61] all of which are linked to the legal obligation of non-discrimination (Article 1 ACHR). In the latter, the Court also recognized that same-sex couples in Colombia are entitled to equal social benefits.

The landmark case of *Atala Riffo and Daughters v Chile* was the first case related to LGBTIQ+ rights brought before the Court. In this ground-breaking ruling, the Court determined that sexual orientation and gender identity are protected categories under the Convention. As a result, any regulation, action, or practice deemed discriminatory based on sexual orientation is prohibited. Therefore, no domestic law, decision, or practice, whether by state authorities or individuals, may limit or restrict the rights of any person on the basis of sexual orientation (para. 91).[62] In its decision, the Court explicitly referenced the standards previously set by the ECtHR in Strasbourg.[63]

Following these initial LGBTIQ+ individual cases, the Court issued Advisory Opinion OC-24/17, which was requested by Costa Rica in 2016 and marked a pivotal moment for LGBTIQ+ rights in the region.[64] In this opinion, the Court reaffirmed its previous rulings in *Atala Riffo and Daughters v Chile, Duque v Colombia*, and *Freire v Ecuador*, confirming that sexual orientation

---

59 *Flor Freire v Ecuador* (Preliminary Objections, Merits, Reparations and Costs) IACtHR Series C No 315 (31 August 2016).

60 *Atala Riffo and Daughters v Chile* (Reparations and Costs) IACtHR Series C No 239 (24 February 2012).

61 *Duque v Colombia* (Judgment) IACtHR Series C No 310 (26 February 2016).

62 *Atala Riffo and Daughters vChile* (Reparations and Costs) IACtHR Series C No239 (24 February 2012), para. 91.

63 The Court explicitly cited the European Convention (para. 87) and the ECtHR *Case of Tyrer v United Kingdom* (para 83), among other citations.

64 Benz, *The Advisory Function of the Inter-American Court of Human Rights* (n 10); Luis Antonio Bolaños Bolaños and Luis Guillermo Chinchilla Mora, *Para entender el fallo OC-24/17 de la Corte Interamericana de Derechos Humanos, y su efecto sobre los procedimientos registrales y civiles en Costa Rica* (Instituto de Formación y Estudios en Democracia 2020).

and gender identity are protected under the ACHR. Additionally, the Court expanded its interpretation of identity rights, stating for the first time that the right to identity includes not only a person's name but also the recognition that sex, sexual orientation, and gender are fundamental aspects of one's personality.[65] The Court emphasized that the expression of individuality is 'part of the constructed identity that results from each person's free and autonomous decision'[66] and is not solely determined by genitalia.

In general, Advisory Opinion OC-24/17 emphasizes the fundamental principles of equality and non-discrimination for LGBTIQ+ individuals.[67] It asserts that any form of discrimination, including that based on sexual orientation and gender identity, violates the inherent dignity of individuals and is prohibited under international law.[68] States are obligated to prevent both direct and indirect discrimination as protected by the American Convention on Human Rights.[69] The ACHR mandates that rights must be guaranteed without discrimination (Article 1.1) and ensures equal treatment under the law (Article 24).[70] Discriminatory practices based on sexual orientation, gender identity, or gender expression are impermissible, and national laws must protect these rights without restrictions.[71]

The IACtHR also held that the right to change and correct public identity documents is protected under the ACHR. Individuals have the right to access a fair and straightforward procedure for changing their gender identity, and states must ensure access to existing legal mechanisms, including the right to marriage on equal terms as those for the rest of society, to protect the rights of families formed by same-sex couples without discrimination compared to heterosexual couples.[72] In reaching this decision, the Court also relied on international standards set by bodies such as the United Nations and the ECtHR.[73]

---

65 *Gender Identity, and Equality and Non-Discrimination of Same-sex Couples*, Advisory Opinion 24/17, IACtHR Series A No 24 (15 November 2017) para 104.

66 Nicolás Carrillo-Santarelli, 'Gender Identity, and Equality and Non-discrimination of Same Sex Couples' (2018) 112 *American Journal of International Law* 479–485.

67 *Gender Identity, and Equality and Non-Discrimination of Same-sex Couples* (n 65) para 61.

68 ibid.

69 ibid.

70 ibid para 64.

71 ibid.

72 ibid para 104.

73 ibid para 77.

This Advisory Opinion signalled the beginning of a new phase in Inter-American jurisprudence on LGBTIQ+ rights, broadening the IACtHR interpretive approach to the human rights of sexual and gender minorities. Although only four rulings have been issued since the Advisory Opinion, the complexity of these cases and the relatively short period in which they were decided suggest the emergence of a new body of case law that assigns state responsibility.[74] As we will demonstrate in subsection 3.3, this new body of case law has shaped legal interpretations within domestic legal systems, extending beyond the compliance of the specific states involved in the contentious cases. This underscores the broader impact of Inter-American LGBTIQ+ jurisprudence and the gradual regional consolidation of an LGBTIQ+ *ius commune*.

Given the context of violence against the LGBTIQ+ population in the region, the scope of the Court's rulings has expanded to address issues such as sexual violence as a form of torture, and the murders of LGBTIQ+ individuals. In *Azul Rojas Marín v Peru*,[75] the Court ruled that the petitioner's detention was arbitrary, as it was based solely on the petitioner's sexual orientation and gender expression. The Court recognized that the violence suffered by the victim (rape) constituted torture and a hate crime. This ruling highlighted the systemic violence faced by LGBTIQ+ individuals in Peru, driven by deep-rooted social prejudices.[76] Additionally, the Court criticized the failure to conduct a proper investigation and the use of discriminatory stereotypes during the legal process.[77]

The Court also made efforts to respect the victim's gender identity throughout the proceedings.[78] The *Azul Rojas Marín* case represents a landmark for transgender rights, particularly in its innovative approach to recognizing torture based on sexual orientation discrimination – the first time a supranational body has ruled in such a case on the grounds of sexual orientation. This case has impacted not only the individual petitioner but also the LGBTIQ+ community and the community around Azul. As Sandoval and others note, 'in the case of *Azul*, the IACtHR ordered important reparation measures, including

---

[74] Augustín Pelayo and Bernarda Betín, 'La Protección de las Personas LGBTIQ en la Jurisprudencia Interamericana' (2024) 78 *Revista IIDH/Instituto Interamericano de Derechos Humanos* 162 ff.

[75] *Azul Rojas Marín and Others v Peru* (Preliminary Objections, Merits, Reparations and Costs) IACtHR Series C No 402 (12 March 2020).

[76] ibid para 46.

[77] ibid para 164.

[78] ibid para 52.

key guarantees of nonrepetition, as well as comprehensive reparations for both individual and community harms'.[79]

The first case involving a transgender person to reach the IACtHR was *Vicky Hernández v Honduras*.[80] The petitioner, a transgender woman, human rights defender, and sex worker, was murdered. The IACtHR found that the state had violated her right to life and physical integrity (Articles 4 and 5 ACHR) and applied the Inter-American Convention on the Prevention, Punishment, and Eradication of Violence against Women (the Convention of Belém do Pará) to trans women for the first time. The Court addressed the autonomous right to gender identity, recognizing violations in various stages, including the motive for Hernández's murder, which was based on her gender identity, the biased investigation, and the state's inability to recognize her gender identity in official documents.[81]

In 2022, the Inter-American Court ruled on the case of *Sandra Pavez Pavez*,[82] a teacher who was prohibited from teaching Catholic religion in a Chilean public school because of her sexual orientation. Pavez Pavez, a lesbian, was pressured to 'end her homosexual life' and was required to undergo psychiatric treatment as a condition for continuing her role.[83] The Court found that Pavez Pavez was subjected to discrimination and that the revocation of her teaching licence was an excessive restriction that violated her rights to personal liberty and privacy.

This case provided an opportunity to further the IACtHR interpretation of the right to privacy for LGBTIQ+ individuals, which had been previously addressed in the case of *Rojas Marín v Peru*. In the *Pavez Pavez* case, the IACtHR also innovatively analyzed discrimination in connection with economic, social, and cultural rights (ECSR). It applied the doctrine of direct and autonomous justiciability of ESCR and ruled that there was a violation of the right to job security and the right to work (Article 26 ACHR) due to the discrimination Pavez Pavez faced, which prevented her from continuing her job as a religion teacher because of her sexual orientation. Additionally, the Court addressed the state's responsibility for actions committed by non-state actors, affirming that states must ensure human rights protection in individual

79 Esdaile and others, 'The Impact beyond Compliance of the Case of Azul Rojas Marin' (n 5) 320.

80 *Vicky Hernández and Others v Honduras* (Merits, Reparations and Costs) IACtHR Series C No 422 (26 March 2021).

81 Pelayo and Betín, 'La Protección de las Personas LGBTIQ en la Jurisprudencia Interamericana' (n 74) 170 ff.

82 *Pavez Pavez v Chile* (Merits, Reparations and Costs) IACtHR Series C No 449 (4 February 2022).

83 ibid para 23.

interactions. In doing so, the Court invoked the doctrine of extended state responsibility, as developed in its previous Advisory Opinion OC-17.[84]

The Court reaffirmed that discrimination against LGBTIQ+ individuals occurs in both public and private spheres in the case of *Olivera Fuentes v Peru*.[85] The Court revisited the issue of state obligations concerning private sector activities, emphasizing that businesses must respect human rights and that states must prevent, investigate, punish, and remedy violations by private entities, ensuring effective access to remedies.[86] The IACtHR established concrete standards for both states and private businesses concerning their duty to uphold equality and non-discrimination.[87] It stressed that states must regulate, monitor, and oversee private actors, while businesses must implement policies to respect human rights, including those of LGBTIQ+ individuals, exercise due diligence to prevent negative impacts, and provide effective grievance mechanisms.[88]

In this case, the IACtHR found that Peru violated several articles of the ACHR, including the right to equal access to justice for Olivera Fuentes.[89] The Court underscored that the American Convention mandates equal treatment for LGBTIQ+ individuals in public displays of affection, rejecting homophobic and discriminatory justifications for restricting such expressions.

Advisory Opinion OC-24/17 has had a significant influence not only on the Court's own case law but also on subsequent advisory opinions, for example, in Advisory Opinion OC-27/21 on the right to freedom of association, collective bargaining, and the right to strike, with a gender perspective, from 2021.[90] While the primary request concerned women's gender perspective on labour rights, the Court briefly noted that a gender perspective also applies to other vulnerable groups, including LGBTIQ+ individuals. The Court reiterated that sexual orientation and gender identity are protected under the ACHR. This

---

84 *The Environment and Human Rights*, Advisory Opinion OC-23/17, IACtHR Series A No 23 (15 November 2017). The Court used this argument for the first time in Advisory Opinion OC-23/17. Later on, in the same year as *Pavez Pavez v Chile*, the Court used the argument again in the *Case of Members and Militants of the Patriotic Union v Colombia* (2022).

85 *Olivera Fuentes v Peru* (Preliminary Objections, Merits, Reparations and Costs) IACtHR Series C No 484 (4 February 2023).

86 ibid para 95 ff.

87 ibid.

88 ibid para 103 ff.

89 ibid para 129.

90 *Right to Freedom of Association, Right to Collective Bargaining and Right to Strike, and their relation to other rights, with a gender perspective*, Advisory Opinion OC-27/21, IACtHR Series A No 27 (5 May 2021).

expanded gender sensitivity has major significance for addressing LGBTIQ+ discrimination in the workplace, a persistent issue in Latin America.

The Court further applied the principles of Advisory Opinion OC-24/17 in its Advisory Opinion OC-29/22, where it adopted a differentiated approach for certain groups of individuals deprived of liberty. In this opinion, the Court addressed the need for special measures for specific groups, including LGBTIQ+ persons.[91] Concerning their placement in prison, the Court emphasized that decisions regarding LGBTIQ+ individuals must respect their gender identity and specific risks, avoiding isolation or inferior treatment. The Court held that states must ensure that transgender individuals in detention receive necessary medical care, including access to hormonal and surgical treatments. Moreover, LGBTIQ+ detainees must have the right to intimate visits without arbitrary or discriminatory restrictions, with the same guarantees of safety, hygiene, and privacy afforded to other detainees.

These cases, and particularly Advisory Opinion OC-24/17, illustrate how the IACtHR has concretized common standards of protection for LGBTIQ+ individuals as set out in the American Convention, emphasizing equality and non-discrimination as central principles. Unlike the ECtHR, the IACtHR has not focused as heavily on finding a regional consensus among member states but has instead followed its transformative mandate to establish what the conventional standard should be.[92] In line with this transformative approach, the Court's jurisprudence has had a tangible impact on the legal protection of LGBTIQ+ rights in the region.

On another institutional site of recognition, LGBTIQ+ rights protection has also been an important topic for the IACHR. Both the Commission and the Court built their interpretation of LGBTIQ+ rights on a concept that originated within the United Nations. This international organization has largely protected the right to live free from discrimination based on sexual orientation or gender identity. They emphasize that international human rights law guarantees equality and non-discrimination for all, regardless of sex, sexual orientation, gender identity, or any other status.[93] The IACHR interprets 'other

---

91 *Differentiated approaches with respect to certain groups of persons deprived of liberty*, Advisory Opinion OC-29/22, IACtHR Series A No 29 (30 May 2022).

92 Urueña, 'Compliance as Transformation' (n 3) 246.

93 UNGA, 'Statement on human rights, sexual orientation and gender identity' (22 December 2008) UN Doc A/63/635; Human Rights Council, 'Report of the High Commissioner for Human Rights on discrimination and violence against individuals based on their sexual orientation and gender identity' (4 May 2015) UN Doc A/HRC/29/23; United Nations Human Rights Office of the High Commissioner (OHCHR), 'Born Free and Equal: Sexual Orientation and Gender Identity in International Human Rights Law' (United Nations 2012); Committee

status' to include body diversity, often related to intersex individuals. Thus, under international human rights law, discrimination based on sexual orientation, gender identity, and body diversity is prohibited. This means that denying rights to individuals based on their status as lesbian, gay, bisexual, transgender, or intersex (LGBTI) is as unlawful as discrimination based on skin colour, race, sex, religion, or any other status.[94]

The IACHR reached this conclusion in its 2018 *Report on the Recognition of the Rights of LGBTI Persons*, closely following the Inter-American Court's Advisory Opinion OC-24/17. The report examines the situation of LGBTI individuals within the Inter-American system, highlighting progress made in recognizing their rights and identifying the challenges that remain in ensuring the full respect and protection of these rights.

The IACHR has interpreted the ACHR to include sexual orientation and gender identity as protected categories under Article 1.1 of the Convention. The Commission has consistently reaffirmed that non-discrimination is a cornerstone of democratic systems and a fundamental element of the human rights framework established by the Organization of American States (OAS). Non-discrimination, equality before the law, the right to life, and personal integrity are essential principles of both regional and universal human rights systems, and these are particularly important for protecting the rights of LGBTIQ+ individuals in the Americas.[95] Additionally, the IACHR has summarized the standards related to equality and non-discrimination, aligning them with those expressed in the Court's Advisory Opinion OC-24/17. These standards overlap in areas such as the protection and empowerment of LGBTIQ+ persons with respect to their identity and their right to democratic and political participation.[96]

The Commission further underscores that international law extends the prohibition of discrimination to include economic, social, and cultural rights, such as social security, health, and labour rights, all of which are recognized under

on Economic, Social and Cultural Rights (CESCR) 'General Comment No 20: Non-discrimination and economic, social and cultural rights' (2 July 2009) UN Doc E/C.12GC/20, para 32.

[94] IACHR, 'Recognition of the Rights of LGBTI Persons' (7 December 2018) OEA/Ser.L/V/II.170, para 37.

[95] ibid para 29; IACHR, 'The Situation of People of African Descent in the Americas' (5 December 2011) para 1; citing IACHR, '1999 Annual Report: Chapter VI, Considerations Regarding the Compatibility of Affirmative Action Measures Designed to Promote the Political Participation of Women with the Principles of Equality and Non-discrimination'.

[96] IACHR, 'Recognition of the Rights of LGBTI Persons' (n 94) para 36.

the ESCR framework derived from the OAS Charter.[97] Furthermore, the Inter-American Convention Against All Forms of Discrimination and Intolerance, adopted in 2013 and endorsed by the OAS General Assembly, mandates that member states enact legislation explicitly prohibiting discrimination and intolerance. This legislation should cover all sectors, including employment, professional organizations, education, training, housing, health, social protection, economic activity, and public services.[98]

Additionally, the Commission's 2015 report on violence against LGBTIQ+ persons in the Americas highlighted that LGBTIQ+ individuals, or those perceived as such, face various forms of violence and discrimination based on their sexual orientation, gender identity or expression, or non-normative body characteristics. This discrimination constitutes a clear violation of their human rights, as recognized by Inter-American and international human rights standards.[99]

## 3.3 The Impact of Advisory Opinion OC-24/17: Local Uses and the Inter-Americanization of LGBTIQ+ Rights

As Pablo Saavedra signals, the advisory opinion has had a broad influence beyond the interpretation of the court itself, in the sense that it 'became a mechanism to assist the States in effectively guaranteeing the protection of the rights of LGBTIQ+ persons and a tool to promote changes where situations of discrimination still exist'.[100] In this subsection, we map local uses of the Advisory Opinion OC-24/17 both by institutional actors as well as by civil society organizations. First, we show the consolidation of the LGBTIQ+ rights constellation in Brazil and Mexico as remarkable examples. We then show some advances made in other countries such as Ecuador, Chile, and Colombia.

97 *Duque v Colombia* (n 61) para 104; IACHR, 'Recognition of the Rights of LGBTI Persons' (n 94) para 37.

98 Inter-American Convention against All Forms of Discrimination and Intolerance (adopted 5 June 2013, entered into force 20 October 2022) art 7; IACHR, 'Recognition of the Rights of LGBTI Persons' (n 94) para 38.

99 IACHR, 'Violence against Lesbian, Gay, Bisexual, Trans and Intersex Persons in the Americas' (12 November 2015) para 1; Inter-American Convention against All Forms of Discrimination and Intolerance (n 98) art 7; IACHR, 'Recognition of the Rights of LGBTI Persons' (n 94) para 39.

100 Pablo Saavedra Alessandri, 'A Broader Look at the Transformative Impact of the Inter-American Court of Human Rights' Decisions' in Armin von Bogdandy and others (eds), *The Impact of the Inter-American Human Rights System. Transformations on the Ground* (Oxford University Press 2024) 537–563, 550.

For the purposes of this chapter, it is important to highlight that, just as there is divergence in the recognition of LGBTIQ+ rights across different countries in Latin America, there are also varying levels of interaction between the Inter-American system and the domestic legal frameworks of these states.[101] Even so, although the legal recognition of rights within the Latin American states differs,[102] there is a trend towards the consolidation of a common LGBTIQ+ law in the region. This trend is framed as the slow formation of a LGBTIQ+ *ius commune* in the region.[103] To understand its formation, we have already shown the path of LGBTIQ+ rights in the jurisprudence of the IACtHR and the IACHR. In this subsection, we show the multilevelled legal interactions between some national legal systems that actively engage with the LGBTIQ+ Inter-American established law.

The use of the Advisory Opinion within the Brazilian state has been outstanding. Brazilian judicial authorities have employed the Inter-American Court's Advisory Opinion to substantiate various decisions. For example, the Brazilian Federal Supreme Court (STF) has actively used Advisory Opinion OC-24/17 to advance LGBTI+ legal protections. In 2018, the STF ruled on the rights of transgender individuals to change their names and gender markers in the civil registry in the cases of ADI 4.275 and RE 670.422. The Court determined that these changes should not be contingent on surgical or hormonal treatments, aligning with the Inter-American Court's Advisory Opinion OC-24/17, which advocates for administrative and non-invasive processes for altering gender identity records.

In 2019, the STF addressed issues related to homotransphobia. In case MI 4.733, the Court acknowledged the unconstitutional delay in legislative action and applied the provisions of Law 7.716/1989, which addresses discrimination based on race, colour, ethnicity, religion, or national origin, to cases involving sexual orientation and gender identity, pending new legislation. Similarly, in case ADO 26, the Court declared legislative omission unconstitutional and extended the application of the same law to acts of homotransphobia. Borges Martins, in his recent research on the consolidation of an LGBTIQ+ *ius*

[101] Ximena Fuentes Torrijo, 'La evolución de la relación normativa entre el Sistema Interamericano de Derechos Humanos y los sistemas jurídicos nacionales' (2021) 19 *International Journal of Constitutional Law* 1207.

[102] Antonio Moreira Maués and others, 'Judicial Dialogue Between National Courts and the Inter-American Court of Human Rights: A Comparative Study of Argentina, Brazil, Colombia and Mexico' (2021) 21 *Human Rights Law Review* 108–131.

[103] Flávia Piovesan and others, 'Impact of the Inter-American Human Rights System on the Protection of the LGBTI+ Population' (2022) 67 *Revista da Faculdade de Direito UFPR* 153.

*commune* in Brazil, asserts that openness to the Inter-American system functioned as a mechanism to legitimize the criminalization of homotransphobia in this specific case.[104] Both decisions followed the standards on sexual orientation and gender identity established in the Advisory Opinion OC-24/17.

In 2020, the STF made several important rulings regarding LGBTI+ issues. In case ADI 5.543, the Court declared unconstitutional the provisions that prohibited blood donations from homosexual individuals, due to their discriminatory nature and violation of human dignity. In cases ADPF 457 and ADPF 461, the STF invalidated legislation prohibiting the dissemination of educational materials related to gender and sexual orientation. Minister Fachin, in the blood donation case, referenced the ACHR, while the rulings on educational matters also cited Advisory Opinion OC-24/17.

Moreover, it is worth examining the role of the National Council of Justice (CNJ) as the judiciary's primary administrative body, shaped by the influence of decisions from both the country's Constitutional Court and the IACtHR.[105] The CNJ fosters LGBTI+ judicial policies through dialogic governance and a commitment to open justice. Over a decade of consistent decisions has shaped the CNJ's approach to promoting sexual and gender diversity through dialogue with various branches of government and civil society, significantly impacting the lives of LGBTIQ+ individuals in Brazil.

In 2022, the CNJ published a report on discrimination and violence against the LGBTI+ population, introducing the *Registro de Ocorrência Geral de Emergência e Risco Imminente à Comunidade LGBTQIA+ (Rogéria Form)* to protect vulnerable sexual and gender groups. This form was developed through collaboration among justice system members, social movements, and LGBTI+ associations, following CNJ Ordinance 181/2021. In March 2023, Resolution 492 was passed, requiring all Brazilian judiciary bodies to adopt a gender perspective in their rulings, with the aim of eliminating gender stereotypes and discrimination based on sexual orientation or gender identity.

As demonstrated by prominent scholars, although the history of the relationship between domestic law and international law has evolved over the years, there is now a clear openness to Inter-American law, which is reflected in the constellation of rights protection for the LGBTIQ+ population in Brazil by

104 Dilermando Aparecido Borges Martins, 'Diálogos entre sistemas de direitos humanos e a proteção da População LGBTQIAPN+: construindo um ius commune Interamericano para criminalizar a homotransfobia' (Doctoral Thesis, Universidade Federal do Paraná 2024).

105 Ravane Soares D' Oliveira, 'Julgamento com perspectiva de gênero no poder judiciário e experiência em Corumbá' (Masters thesis, Fundação Universidade Federal de Mato Grosso do Sul 2024).

various institutions.[106] Some critical voices remain sceptical about the ability of adjudicatory bodies to achieve equality for marginalized groups in Brazil.[107] The Brazilian judiciary has engaged in extensive social dialogue, fostering the consolidation of a genuine community of practice dedicated to defending LGBTIQ+ rights in the country. Through the evolution of constitutional jurisprudence supporting LGBTIQ+ rights, the judiciary has implemented policies aimed at ensuring access to these rights for LGBTIQ+ individuals in Brazil. This reflects the tangible socio-legal impact resulting from ongoing dialogue with the Inter-American human rights system.

Mexico is another example of the transformative impact of the Advisory Opinion. As a federal country, the regulation of family and personal matters in this country falls under the jurisdiction of individual states. In this context, Jalisco was the first state to comply with the *Ius Commune* mandate, conducting conventionality control and ordering modifications to its Civil Code regulations through a governor's decree.[108] This decree allowed individuals under the age of 18 to access procedures for recognizing their self-perceived gender identity. Subsequently, other state legislatures reformed their laws to extend this right to minors.[109] Likewise, Advisory Opinion OC-24/17 has been used by the Supreme Court of Justice of the Nation as a critical foundation in rulings declaring unconstitutional the age requirement for accessing administrative procedures for the recognition of self-perceived gender identity.[110]

It is important to emphasize that this progress would not have been possible without the joint efforts of civil society and public human rights organizations,

[106] Flávia Piovesan and Julia Cortez da Cunha Cruz, 'A Multi-level Process: Compliance with International Human Rights Law in Brazil' in Rainer Grote and others (eds), *Research Handbook on Compliance in International Human Rights Law* (Edward Elgar Publishing Limited 2021).

[107] Juliano Zaiden Benvindo, *The Rule of Law in Brazil: The Legal Construction of Inequality* (Bloomsbury Publishing 2022).

[108] Estado de Jalisco, 'Acuerdo del Gobernador Constitucional del Estado de Jalisco, mediante el cual se modifica el reglamento del Registro Civil del Estado de Jalisco', *Periódico Oficial*, 22 Sección II (29 October 2020) https://vlex.com.mx/vid/acuerdo-dielag-acu-071-851260040 (jalisco.gob.mx).

[109] According to the *Report of the Asociación Civil por las Infancias Transgénero 2018–2023*, in Mexico City, Oaxaca, Morelos and Sinaloa this procedure is contemplated thprough administrative channels (p[ 11–12). Available: https://infanciastrans.org/wp-content/uploads/2024/01/5-AÑOS-DE-INFANCIASTRANS.pdf.

[110] Actions of Unconstitutionality: 45/2021, 73/2021, 132/2021, 174/2021, 43/2022, and 72/2022. To consult the judgments, visit: https://bj.scjn.gob.mx/busqueda?q=%22infancias%20trans%22&page=1&indice=sentencias_pub.

as happens in other countries.[111] These groups have played a vital role in the reception and application of Inter-American standards for the recognition and defence of the human rights of trans children and adolescents. Organizations such as the *Asociación Civil por las Infancias Trans en México*, founded in 2018, have supported families across the country in obtaining recognition of their trans children's gender identities. Cooperation with public human rights institutions empowered to file unconstitutionality actions has been essential in consolidating these achievements, ensuring that the legal framework aligns with international human rights standards. The interaction between civil society and state institutions through law, particularly through the pressure to align domestic law with Inter-American standards, is a significant aspect of the impact of Inter-American LGBTIQ+ protection. Therefore, civil society must be understood as a central actor in the local legal constellations that form the larger Inter-American LGBTIQ+ *ius commune*.

Regarding the political rights of LGBTIQ+ individuals, the dialogue between Mexico's highest electoral court and its regional and specialized chambers has also been driven by social organizations and LGBTIQ+ human rights defenders, who have invoked OC-24/17 as a pivotal legal reference.[112] This dialogue consists of 49 judgments. This legal framework has not only protected LGBTIQ+ rights but has also paved the way for greater inclusion in the country's political life, ensuring that diversity in gender and sexual orientation is recognized and respected throughout the electoral system. When examining each judgment and its connection to Advisory Opinion OC-24/17, several categories emerge. Most judgments pertain to identity and personal

---

[111] See: Paromita Pain (ed), *Global LGBTQ Activism: Social Media, Digital Technologies, and Protest Mechanisms* (Routledge 2024); Lucas Lixinski, 'Rights Litigation Piggybacking: Legal Mobilization Strategies in LGBTIQ International Human Rights Jurisprudence' (2020) 31 *Florida Journal of International Law* 273.

[112] To consult the judgments in which OC-24/17 has been mentioned, please visit the following link: BuscaTE.

autonomy,[113] affirmative measures and their interpretation,[114] equality and non-discrimination,[115] or the understanding of gender identity,[116] with some cases addressing multiple categories.

After reviewing the extended uses of the Advisory Opinion in Brazil and Mexico, it is also important to highlight the impact of this international instrument in other Latin American countries. For instance, in Ecuador, on 12 June 2019,[117] the Constitutional Court ruled that the Advisory Opinion constitutes a binding interpretation of the ACHR and is part of Ecuador's constitutional block.[118] Consequently, the Constitution (Article 67, which defines marriage as a union between a man and a woman) must be interpreted in accordance with the Advisory Opinion, thereby extending marriage rights to same-sex couples. Additionally, provisions of the Civil Code have been amended to reflect this change.[119]

---

113 See: *Judgment SM-JDC-0102-2018* (6 April 2018) Electoral Tribunal of the Judicial Branch of the Federation (ETJBF); *Judgment SUP-JDC-0304-2018* (21 June 2018) ETJBF; *Judgment SUP-JDC-1011-2021* (8 December 2021) ETJBF; *Judgment SUP-REC-0323-2023* (28 February 2024) ETJBF; *Judgment SRE-PSC-0006–2023* (2 February 2023) ETJBF; *Judgment SM-JDC-00212022* (30 March 2022) ETJBF; *Plenary agreement SUP-REP-0081-2022-Acuerdo1* (10 June 2022) ETJBF; *Judgment SUP-JDC-0951-2022* (14 September 2022) ETJBF; *Judgment SM-JDC-0396-2020* (15 January 2021) ETJBF; *Judgment SUP-REC-0277-2020* (29 December 2020) ETJBF; *Judgment SUP-JDC-1109-2021* (13 August 2021) ETJBF.

114 See: *Judgment SUP-JDC-0186-2024* (22 March 2024) ETJBF; *Judgment SX-JRC-0028-2023* (28 November 2023) ETJBF; *Judgment ST-JDC-0150-2023* (5 December 2023) ETJBF.

115 See: *Judgment SX-RAP-0041-2024* (19 March 2024) ETJBF; *Judgment SUP-REP-0346-2022* (6 July 2022) ETJBF; *Judgment SUP-REC-0584-2021* (5 June 2021) ETJBF; *Judgment SM-AG-0016-2023* (23 August 2023) ETJBF; *Judgment SUP-REC-0368-2024* (22 May 2024) ETJBF.

116 See: *Judgment SUP-JDC-0304-2018* (21 June 2018) ETJBF; *Judgment SUP-JDC-0951-2022* (14 September 2022) ETJBF; *Judgment SUP-JDC-1117-2022* (28 September 2022) ETJBF; *Judgment SM-JDC-0396-2020* (n 113); *Judgment SRE-PSC-0006-2023* (n 113).

117 *Judgment No 10-18-CN 'Matrimonio entre personas del mismo sexo'* (12 June 2019) Constitutional Court of Ecuador, http://doc.corteconstitucional.gob.ec:8080/alfresco/d/d/workspace/SpacesStore/4a2e4469-9d31-4ec9-b7d1-cd9c6022d2cc/0010-18-cn-19_sen.pdf?guest=true.

118 *Judgment No 1 1-18-CN/19 'matrimonio igualitario'* (1 July 2019) Constitutional Court of Ecuador, https://portal.corteconstitucional.gob.ec/Seguimiento/11-18-CN-19.pdf.

119 *Judgment No 10/18-CN/19 'Matrimonio entre personas del mismo sexo'* (12 June 2019) Constitutional Court of Ecuador, https://international.vlex.com/vid/

Chile followed suit on 10 March 2022, by enacting Law 21.400, which amended several legal instruments to regulate same-sex marriage on equal terms.[120] This law was a crucial tool in combating LGBTIQ+ discrimination in the country, as the Chilean judiciary had previously not followed the IACtHR's decision.[121] In Bolivia, the parliament has been called upon to introduce regulations to implement the Advisory Opinion into national law.[122]

The Colombian Constitutional Court has cited the Advisory Opinion in several cases since its publication.[123] In some instances, the Court refers to the Advisory Opinion merely to adopt legal definitions. However, in other cases, the Court uses the Advisory Opinion to advance LGBTIQ+ protections and legitimize a transformative constitutional position on a very contested social topic. For example, the Court has used the Advisory Opinion to bolster economic, social, and cultural rights for the transgender population, including the right to parental leave,[124] anti-discrimination protection in the workplace for transgender individuals,[125] and pension rights for trans women.[126] Notably, these decisions are either constitutionality decisions or unification of criteria decisions, both of which have broader interpretative impact in the Colombian legal system compared to individual case rulings.

---

ecuador-corte-constitucional-sentencia-874196547.

120 Ley No 21.400 Modifica diversos cuerpos legales para regular, en igualdad de condiciones, el matrimonio entre personas del mismo sexo (2021) Diario Oficial de la Republica de Chile, https://www.diariooficial.interior.gob.cl/publicaciones/2021/12/10/43124-B/01/2055451.pdf.

121 See: *Constitutional Court Ruling No 7774-2019* (4 June 2020) Constitutional Tribunal of Chile, https://www.pucv.cl/uuaa/site/docs/20200810/20200810205743/ficha_stc_rol_n__7774_2019.pdf.

122 Procuraduría General del Estado, 'Análisis Jurídico Especializado No 04/2024' (2024) https://www.procuraduria.gob.bo/ckfinder/userfiles/files/PGE-WEB/_Opinion/OPE202404G.pdf.

123 It is important to note that Colombia's Constitutional Court issued a controversial decision (C-030 of 2023) in which the Court distanced itself from recognizing conventionality control. However, this decision has been disregarded by the same Court, demonstrating that it was not a generalized stance but rather a specific case. In decisions subsequent to this ruling, there are frequent references to the Inter-American system, which are used to support the Court's positions, as shown in this subsection. See also Judgments C-408/23 and T-188/24.

124 *Judgment C-324/23* (23 August 2023) Colombian Constitutional Court, https://www.corteconstitucional.gov.co/relatoria/2023/c-324-23.htm.

125 *Judgment SU-067/23* (16 March 2023) Colombian Constitutional Court, https://www.corteconstitucional.gov.co/relatoria/2023/SU067-23.htm#_ftnref216.

126 *Judgment SU-440/21* (9 December 2021) Colombian Constitutional Court, https://www.corteconstitucional.gov.co/relatoria/2021/SU440-21.htm.

In Colombia, the use of the Advisory Opinion has been accompanied by social and legal mobilization. In case T-376/17, the Colombian Ombudsman invoked the Advisory Opinion in its intervention before the Constitutional Court. Similarly, in case T-447/19, the NGO Colombia Diversa used the Advisory Opinion to support its stance in a case concerning the right to identity for transgender individuals. In a constitutionality ruling on the legal concept of family, three non-state actors – namely the Office of the UN High Commissioner for Human Rights in Colombia, Dejusticia, and Colombia Diversa – intervened, referencing the Advisory Opinion. The use of the Advisory Opinion in strategic litigation shows the circulation and impact of this decision on domestic jurisdictions.

The process of Inter-Americanization is also evident in the area of identity rights for transgender individuals. For instance, the impact of Advisory Opinion OC-24/17 on the recognition of name and gender identity changes in identity documents and civil registries has been profound. In Ecuador, the 2016 Organic Law on Identity and Civil Data introduced procedures to replace the 'sex' field with 'gender' on identity cards and allowed amendments to names on birth certificates and other official documents.[127] In Uruguay, a 2019 law for trans individuals affirms that every person has the right to freely develop their personality in accordance with their gender identity, irrespective of biological, genetic, anatomical, or other characteristics.[128]

Advisory Opinion OC-24/17 exemplifies the transformative impact such opinions can have on social realities, empowering various actors.[129] While this research does not aim to establish a direct relationship between judicial decisions and the social realities of the LGBTIQ+ population, it is evident that legal recognition exerts a significant social impact by enhancing legitimacy and providing effective tools for the defence of human rights. It has led to significant legal and social changes across Latin America, influencing national legislation and court rulings to better protect LGBTIQ+ individuals and address systemic discrimination. As a result, many countries in the region have adopted progressive measures such as same-sex marriage and legal gender recognition, aligned with broader efforts to address structural deficits from a regional constitutionalism perspective. As in other areas regarding human

127 See: Ley orgánica de gestión de la Identidad y Datos Civiles (4 February 2016) Registro Civil Ecuador, https://www.igualdadgenero.gob.ec/wp-content/uploads/2021/01/LEY-ÓRGANICA-DE-GESTIÓN-DE-LA-IDENTIDAD-Y-DATOS.pdf.

128 Ley No 19684 Integral para Personas Trans (29 April 2018) https://www.impo.com.uy/bases/leyes/19684-2018 art 1.

129 Saavedra Alessandri, 'A Broader Look at the Transformative Impact of the Inter-American Court of Human Rights' Decisions' (n 100) 552.

rights protection, the advancement is not linear nor uniform, as shown not only by scholars but also by the very organs of the Inter-American system.

Authorities in national jurisdictions have also begun to apply other advisory opinions of the IACtHR which address the intersection of LGBTQ+ rights with social, economic, cultural, and environmental rights, such as AO-29 and AO-27. For example, the Colombian Constitutional Court has invoked both AO-24 and AO-27 to resolve cases involving LGBTIQ+ individuals in labour law contexts.[130] National policies, such as the Brazilian National Council of Justice's Resolutions No 348 and No 366, which regulate detention conditions for LGBTIQ+ individuals, have been influenced by Advisory Opinions OC-24/17 and OC-29/22. Similarly, the Colombian Constitutional Court has invoked both advisory opinions to establish high standards of protection for LGBTIQ+ detainees.[131]

While a trend towards the progressive recognition of LGBTIQ+ rights is evident in the region, there are exceptions. For instance, in its judgment 676/2020, issued on 3 November 2020, the Peruvian Constitutional Court chose not to apply Advisory Opinion OC-24/17.[132] Similarly, in Panama, the legal status of the Inter-American Court's advisory opinions, including OC-24/17, remains contested. On 16 February 2023, the Panamanian Supreme Court ruled that the advisory opinions of the IACtHR, including OC-24/17, cannot serve as binding precedents in national law, citing the need to preserve state sovereignty.[133] Other human rights protection constellations in the region have faced similar challenges and tensions.[134] As with any legal or social progress, these processes are subject to resistance from actors who oppose their transformative momentum. Nevertheless, the Inter-American system has managed to expand its spheres of protection even amidst these challenges.

---

[130] See for example: *Judgment SU-067/23* (16 March 2023) Colombian Constitutional Court, https://www.corteconstitucional.gov.co/relatoria/2023/SU067-23.htm#_ftnref216.

[131] *Judgment T-321/23* (22 August 2023) Colombian Constitutional Court, https://www.corteconstitucional.gov.co/relatoria/2023/t-321-23.htm.

[132] A minority of judges held that Peru had to follow the standard established in the AO 24/14 based on the doctrine of conventionality control.

[133] *Judgment of 16 February 2023* (2023) Supreme Court of Justice of the Republic of Panama 36.

[134] See, for example, the controversy around the Fontevecchia Case: Laura Clerico, 'La Enunciación Del Margen De Apreciacion: Fontevecchia 2017 Desde Los Margenes' (2018) 7 *Derechos En Accion* 295. A general overview of the tensions within and surrounding the IAHRS can be found in Jorge Contesse, 'Resisting the Inter-American Human Rights System' (2019) 44 *Yale Journal of International Law* 179.

In this subsection, we have mapped the appropriation of the Advisory Opinion by national judicial and governmental institutions, often in conjunction with the influence of social movements. It is important to recognize that the impact of the Inter-American system extends beyond state authorities, as civil society organizations and local human rights defenders use Inter-American jurisprudence to advance their demands for protection.[135] Although tracking local applications of this jurisprudence can be challenging due to the need for specific and complex interdisciplinary methodological tools, we have highlighted the role of social movements in specific cases, demonstrating the transformative impact of Inter-American law in legal mobilization by civil society organizations.

Countries like Argentina, Brazil, Colombia, and Uruguay had progressive legislation protecting LGBTIQ+ rights even before the publication of the Advisory Opinion, with social-legal mobilization playing a critical role in shaping the legal response. Considering this is important for understanding the argument about the community of practice discussed earlier. Legal mobilization by social movements, particularly the LGBTIQ+ movement, demonstrates how complex social interactions build a community of practice characterized by a shared language and common values that impact, create, recreate, and reinforce Inter-American standards. In this sense, it is also important to note that the process of Inter-Americanization cannot be fully understood without tracing bottom-up interactions with the law.[136]

## 4 CONCLUDING REMARKS

Based on the idea that transformation is not a fixed fact, but a constant, continuous, and fluctuating process,[137] the Inter-American system and its institutions must continue with the arduous task of seeking a common understanding of human rights in the Inter-American legal space. By focusing on the constellation of rights related to the LGBTIQ+ community, it is clear that the impact of the Inter-American system extends to various actors within the community of practice, as well as to the different processes these actors undertake.

---

135 See: Pain, *Global LGBTQ Activism: Social Media, Digital Technologies, and Protest Mechanisms* (n 111); Goodale, *Reinventing Human Rights* (n 24).

136 Morales Antoniazzi and Krsticevic, 'NGOs: a Critical Link to Understanding and Strengthening Compliance of International Decisions' (n 22) 485–508.

137 Rene Urueña and Stephania Yate Cortes, 'Creating the Narrative of Human Rights Impact in Latin America' in Armin von Bogdandy and others (eds), *The Impact of the Inter-American Human Rights System: Transformations on the Ground* (Oxford University Press 2024) 199–216.

We use the concept of 'constellation' to refer to the specific realm of LGBTIQ+ rights, drawing on this image as an illustrative example. The notion of a constellation allows us to 'describe the multiple jurisdictional relationships interwoven in a social conflict brought to the legal realm by specific actors'.[138] Building on previous work, this chapter employs the constellation metaphor to demonstrate that within a legal protection framework, 'legal elements originate from multiple centres of production, are transformed locally, and even influence legal interpretations on other scales, such as national or regional'.[139] This process can be observed in the Inter-American dialogue among social movements, national courts and institutions, and the organs of the IAHRS.

Transformations could be recorded on three axes: from non-protection to regulation, from a condemnatory judgment to a progressive jurisprudential line, and from the first challenges to the future horizons of protection. For example, in 2001, the Netherlands was the only country in the world to legalize same-sex marriage.[140] Today, more than 30 countries, including 11 Latin American countries, have followed suit.[141] The impact of the decisions of Tribunals has risen. For instance, in 1988, Ireland became the first country to be condemned by the ECtHR for criminalizing homosexual practices (*David Norris v Ireland*), a violation of Article 8 of the European Convention on Human Rights.[142] The case was led by the politician and activist David Norris, who played a pivotal role in decriminalizing homosexuality in the country. Less than thirty years later, in 2015, Ireland became the first country to legalize same-sex marriage through a popular referendum, with 62% of voters supporting marriage equality.[143] Nowadays, the ECtHR has issued more than 70 decisions on the rights of LGBTIQ+ individuals.[144] This elevated number is representative of the role of Courts regarding LGBTIQ+ rights.

---

138 Carolina Bejarano Martínez, 'Gente de Mar: Expansión urbana, luchas étnico-territoriales y jurisdicciones contingentes en Cartagena de Indias' (Doctoral Thesis, Universidad de los Andes 2024) 65.

139 ibid.

140 ILGA World Databank, 'Country: The Netherlands' (ILGA, 2024) https://database.ilga.org/netherlands-lgbti (accessed 24 September 2024).

141 ILGA World Databank, 'Legal Frameworks: Same-Sex Marriage and Civil Unions' (ILGA, 2024) https://database.ilga.org/same-sex-marriage-civil-unions (accessed 24 September 2024).

142 *Norris v Ireland* App No. 10581/83 (ECtHR, 26 October 1988).

143 Henry McDonald, 'Ireland becomes first country to legalise gay marriage by popular vote', *The Guardian* (Dublin, 23 May 2015) https://www.theguardian.com/world/2015/may/23/gay-marriage-ireland-yes-vote.

144 Paul Johnson, 'LGBT People, the Council of Europe, and the European Court of Human Rights' in Andreas R. Ziegler and others (eds), *The Oxford Handbook of LGBTI Law* (Oxford University Press 2024).

Similarly, since its first decision on the issue, the IACtHR has rapidly advanced toward the consolidation of an LGBTIQ+ *ius commune*. Over time, the IACtHR has developed a line of jurisprudence that increasingly protects the rights of LGBTI+ individuals. In its first case related to LGBTI+ issues, *Atala Riffo*, the Court concluded that 'the scope of the right to non-discrimination due to sexual orientation is not limited to the fact of being a homosexual *per se*, but includes its expressions and the ensuing consequences in a person's life project'.[145] The right to self-determination has since been elaborated in a broader and more inclusive manner, now encompassing the right to identity and its relationship with human dignity, the right to private life, and the principle of personal autonomy (Articles 7 and 11 ACHR).[146] Additionally, sexual orientation, identity, and gender expression are recognized as protected categories under Article 1.1.[147] The protection of LGBTI+ individuals is increasingly normatively anchored and understood as a distinct protective category within the American Convention. With the rich judicial development following *Atala Riffo v Chile*, the IACtHR shows a clear tendency to broaden the rights of this community.

Being an instrument of direct interpretation of the ACHR, and thus not bound to a specific case, the Advisory Opinion has played a crucial role in the process of the inter-Americanization of LGBTIQ+ rights across domestic jurisdictions. The Advisory Opinion OC-24/17 has significantly influenced the jurisprudence of the IACtHR, establishing new concepts such as sexual orientation, identity, and gender expression as protected categories under Article 1.1. A broader trend can also be observed across the IACtHR's advisory opinions: while the first opinion related to LGBTIQ+ individuals (OC-24/17) set forth general provisions, subsequent opinions have provided more nuanced protections. For example, Advisory Opinion OC-27/21 addresses (among other topics) LGBTIQ+ discrimination in the workplace, and OC-29/22 emphasizes the need for special measures for LGBTIQ+ individuals deprived of liberty.

Furthermore, the Advisory Opinion OC-24/17 has significantly influenced LGBTIQ+ national legal frameworks in Latin America, which shows the impact of the IAHRS beyond the individual cases and its compliance. For instance, in Brazil it led to rulings allowing transgender individuals to change

[145] *Atala Riffo and Daughters v Chile* (Reparations and Costs) IACtHR Series C No 239 (24 February 2012) para 133.

[146] *Pavez Pavez v Chile* (Merits, Reparations and Costs) IACtHR Series C No 449 (4 February 2022).

[147] *Gender Identity, and Equality and Non-Discrimination of Same-sex Couples*, Advisory Opinion 24/17, IACtHR Series A No 24 (15 November 2017); *Vicky Hernández and Others v Honduras* (Merits, Reparations and Costs) IACtHR Series C No 422 (26 March 2021).

gender markers without medical interventions and extended anti-discrimination laws to homotransphobia. Mexico also saw reforms, with minors able to change gender markers and federal courts ruling age restrictions unconstitutional. Ecuador, Chile, and Colombia advanced marriage equality and labour protections. However, resistance persists in countries like Peru and Panama. Despite challenges, OC-24/17 has driven major legal reforms, promoting greater equality and recognition of gender diversity across the region.

The sustained impact of the IACtHR's decisions exemplifies the transformative potential that international bodies can have when their rulings lead to tangible shifts in societal practices and legal frameworks. This dynamic illustrates how the concept of transformative impact – the capacity to effect structural change through legal mechanisms – is fundamental to the ongoing expansion and protection of LGBTIQ+ rights in the region. Furthermore, it underscores the broader influence of the IAHRS, as it not only enforces legal standards but also fosters societal transformations towards greater equality and non-discrimination.

At the same time, it is important to recognize that significant gaps remain in the protection of LGBTIQ+ rights. Panama's refusal to comply with the Advisory Opinion highlights how fragile the impact can be when states choose not to follow through. In such cases, it may become necessary to seek support from the international community, particularly the UN. A notable example is the UNDP's assistance in establishing the National Observatory on the Human Rights of LGBTIQ+ Persons in Panama, which underscores the role of international organizations in promoting compliance and safeguarding rights.

Access to justice is a fundamental principle of democratic societies, as it ensures that all individuals, particularly historically marginalized groups such as LGBTIQ+ people, can assert their rights fairly and effectively. In Panama, the National Observatory on the Human Rights of LGBTIQ+ Persons has been established to document discrimination and human rights violations while supporting informed policy-making processes.[148] Despite advancements in that area, a UNDP survey conducted in 2023[149] indicates that a significant

[148] Juana Cooke, 'Access to Justice, a Reality for All: Panama's National Observatory of Human Rights of LGBTIQ+ People' (*United Nations Development Programme*, 3 September 2024) https://www.undp.org/latin-america/blog/access-justice-reality-all-panamas-national-observatory-human-rights-lgbtiq-people (accessed 24 September 2024).

[149] US AID/UNDP, 'Dashboard LGBTQ+: Análisis sobre vulnerabilidades y violencia a la población LGBTQ+' (*Infosegura*, 2013) https://infosegura.org/dashboard-0 (accessed 24 September 2024).

number of LGBTQI+ individuals continue to face discrimination,[150] and are often deterred from pursuing legal action due to deep-seated mistrust of the justice system.[151] This initiative represents a concrete step towards realizing the commitments of the United Nations 2030 Agenda, which aims to leave no one behind and prioritize attention to disadvantaged groups.

While the impact of the advisory opinion is significant, and the progress in legal and institutional protection in countries like Costa Rica, Argentina, Mexico, Brazil, and Colombia is undeniable, it is important to acknowledge that many challenges still remain for the LGBTIQ+ population in our region. One of the main challenges that remains is, undoubtedly, the fight against the criminalization of LGBTIQ+ individuals. Currently, nine countries in the Anglophone Caribbean continue to criminalize consensual same-sex activities between adults by maintaining colonial-era legislation.[152] The presence of such laws conveys to society that these practices are inherently wrong, fostering hostility, violence, and attacks against the LGBTIQ+ community. The second major challenge is the rise of authoritarian populism in the region. Authoritarian populists frequently propagate homophobic and transphobic narratives that are grounded in intolerance.[153]

A third challenge comes from conservative religious groups that, under the banner of religious freedom, seek to undermine the rights of the LGBTIQ+ population. The IACHR consistently emphasizes the principles of equality and non-discrimination as the foundation for overcoming these challenges, including in relation to the exercise of religious freedom.[154]

---

150 Almost 30% of respondents stated that they had been violated in their rights or felt that their rights were violated in the previous 12 months due to their sexual orientation or gender identity.

151 Only 7% of respondents sought legal assistance to prosecute the perpetrators and successfully obtained it.

152 E.g. in Jamaica, the Offences Against the Person Act from 1864 is still in place that punishes 'the abominable crime of buggery'. See: ILGA World Databank, 'Legal Frameworks: Criminalisation of Consensual Same-sex Sexual Acts' (ILGA, 2024) https://database.ilga.org/criminalisation-consensual-same-sex-sexual-acts (accessed 24 September 2024).

153 See: Michael Rios, 'Argentina once led on LGBTQ rights. After 4 lesbians are set on fire, critics blame rising intolerance on Milei's government' *CNN World* (Atlanta, 6 July 2024) https://edition.cnn.com/2024/07/06/americas/argentina-lgbtq-milei-fire-deaths-intl-latam/index.html; Mauricio Albarracín, 'Atacar a las personas LGBTIQ+ hace parte del manual autoritario' (*Human Rights Watch*, 7 September 2022) https://www.hrw.org/es/news/2022/09/07/atacar-las-personas-lgbtiq-hace-parte-del-manual-autoritario (accessed 24 September 2024).

154 IACHR, 'Estudio sobre libertad de religión y creencia' (10 September 2023) OEA/Ser.L/V/II Doc. 384/23.

The guarantees of non-repetition ordered in the most recent case on the rights of LGBTIQ+ individuals ruled by the Inter-American Court reflect both the scale of the challenges and the transformative potential of the *ius commune*.[155] For instance, in the case of *Olivera Fuentes v Peru*, the IACtHR recognizes that states must adopt specific human rights policies aimed at combating discrimination against LGBTIQ+ individuals, as general anti-discrimination policies are insufficient. This specific order, although requested by the petitioners and the Commission, will have a transformative impact on the legal protection of the Peruvian LGBTIQ+ community more broadly.

Moreover, in the same case, the Court acknowledges that institutional legal culture presents obstacles to the protection of LGBTIQ+ rights. Therefore, the Court orders the state to develop, within one year, a comprehensive educational plan on sexual and gender diversity, equality, non-discrimination, gender perspective, and human rights for LGBTIQ+ individuals in the context of consumer relations. It is worth remarking that the IAHRS continues spreading its influences on a wide range of legal areas like, in this case, the area of consumption. It also mandates that this plan be incorporated into training courses for administrative and judicial authorities and other bodies related to law enforcement. Additionally, within the same timeframe, a legal reasoning manual on Inter-American standards in cases of discrimination against LGBTIQ+ individuals must be created.[156]

Through these measures, the Court seeks to bridge the gap between advances in legal protection and national legal cultures. As Saavedra affirms, 'guarantees of non-repetition can often transform structural problems that caused the violations'.[157] The non-repetition guarantees in the case of *Olivera Fuentes v Peru* illustrate the impact of the *ius commune* in promoting democratic societies based on respect for sexual and gender diversity and non-discrimination. These non-repetition guarantees, as well as the general LGBTIQ+ rights constellations this chapter traces, show clearly that 'the impacts of the Inter American

---

155 See: Nicolás Buitrago-Rey and others, 'Specificity in the Inter-American Court of Human Rights' 16 (2024) *Journal of Human Rights Practice* 754; Londoño Lázaro, María Carmelina and Hurtado Mónica, 'Las Garantías De No Repetición En La Práctica Judicial Interamericana y Su Potencial Impacto En La Creación Del Derecho Nacional' (2017) 50 *Boletín Mexicano de Derecho Comparado* 725; Londoño Lázaro and María Carmelina, *Las Garantías De No Repetición En La Jurisprudencia Interamericana: Derecho Internacional Y Cambios Estructurales Del Estado* (Universidad de La Sabana, Tirant lo Blanch 2014).

156 *Olivera Fuentes v Peru* (n 85) para 153.

157 Pablo Saavedra Alessandri, 'The Role of the Inter-American Court of Human Rights in Monitoring Compliance with Judgments' (2020) 12 *Journal of Human Rights Practice* 178, 179.

System of Human Rightsgo beyond mere compliance. Inter-American norms penetrate domestic legal reasoning in domestic courts, parliaments, and administrative agencies, thus creating in effect a wider Inter-American legal space that is relied upon by actors and victims throughout the region'.[158]

Although there are significant challenges to the protection of LGBTIQ+ rights, we can draw inspiration from the formula proposed by Kathryn Sikkink in her analysis of human rights advancements: indignation, coupled with hope, drives emancipatory actions, demonstrating the human capacity to transform realities.[159]

---

158 Urueña, 'Compliance as Transformation' (n 3) 246.

159 Kathryn Sikkink, *Evidence for Hope: Making Human Rights Work in the 21st Century* (Princeton University Press 2018).

# 9. Urgent measures and Indigenous peoples' territorial rights in the Inter-American system

**Daniel Cerqueira**

## 1 INTRODUCTION

The Inter-American Court of Human Rights (IACtHR) may issue provisional measures, and the Inter-American Commission on Human Rights (IACHR, or the Commission) may issue precautionary measures, when an individual or collective group is in imminent danger of irreparable harm. These urgent measures[1] have saved the lives, the physical integrity, and other fundamental rights of thousands of human rights defenders, prisoners, persons with serious illnesses who lack adequate treatment, journalists, witnesses in criminal proceedings, prosecutors and judges facing threats, and members of Indigenous and tribal peoples, among others.

Until 2011, the IACHR had a well-established practice of granting precautionary measures to suspend administrative or judicial decisions that could cause irreparable harm to Indigenous territories. Typically, they asked states to refrain from certain actions until the IACHR could issue a final decision on the merits of a related case in dispute. The adoption of a new institutional practice in 2011 led the IACHR to limit the scope of the precautionary measures

[1] The expression 'urgent measures' is used in this chapter to qualify the precautionary, provisional, or interim measures indicated by an international organ. This expression should not be confused with the 'urgent measures' that may be taken by the Presidency of the IACtHR prior to the decision on a request for provisional measures by its plenary, in accordance with Article 27(6) of the Court's Rules of Procedure. This provision states that: 'If the Court is not sitting, the Presidency, in consultation with the Permanent Commission and, if possible, with the other Judges, shall call upon the State concerned to adopt such urgent measures as may be necessary to ensure the effectiveness of any provisional measures that may be ordered by the Court during its next period of sessions'.

in favour of Indigenous and tribal peoples to the protection of their lives and physical integrity, with very few exceptions.

Since provisional measures are usually requested by the IACHR when a state fails to comply with its precautionary measures, the Commission's new approach has prevented the IACtHR from assessing the adequacy of provisional measures to protect Indigenous and tribal territories. This chapter examines the criteria of both organs of the Inter-American system when deciding on urgent measures in favour of Indigenous peoples, with a special focus on their territorial rights. The term 'Indigenous territorial rights' refers to the free use of their ancestral lands and natural resources, in accordance with their own traditions.

Following this introduction, the second section explains basic concepts with regard to provisional and interim measures under international human rights law, and how they are regulated in the United Nations and regional systems. The third section summarizes the Inter-American standards and special safeguards to Indigenous and tribal territories. Section 4 describes the circumstances in which the Inter-American Commission and Court have granted urgent measures to protect the rights of Indigenous and tribal communities. This section highlights the negative impacts of the IACHR abandonment of a well-established practice of requesting states to suspend decisions that could cause irreparable harm to Indigenous territorial rights.

The final section discusses possible ways to improve the protection of Indigenous territorial rights in the Inter-American system, consisting of (1) reinstating the urgent measures mechanism in exceptional circumstances, and (2) prioritizing the processing of contentious cases based on allegations of significant and irreparable harm to Indigenous and tribal lands.

## 2 URGENT MEASURES UNDER INTERNATIONAL HUMAN RIGHTS LAW

### 2.1 United Nations and Regional Human Rights Systems

Provisional and interim measures have been defined as orders that preserve certain rights under dispute and that safeguard the jurisdiction of an international tribunal. Article 41(1) of the Statute of the International Court of Justice (ICJ) establishes its faculty to 'indicate … any provisional measures which ought to be taken to preserve the respective rights of either party'.[2]

[2] Similarly, Article 41 of the Statute of the Permanent Court of International Justice establishes that: '[t]he Court shall have the power to indicate, if it considers that circumstances so require, any provisional measures which ought to be taken to reserve the respective rights of either party'. Article 25 of the Statute of

Most of the United Nations (UN) treaty bodies,[3] the European Court of Human Rights (ECtHR) and the organs of the African Human Rights System have included in their rules of procedure the power to grant provisional or interim measures, using language similar to Article 41(1) of the ICJ Statute.

The European Convention on Human Rights and its Protocols lack a specific provision authorizing the ECtHR (and the former European Commission of Human Rights) to grant interim measures. Rule 39(1) of the Rules of Procedure of the ECtHR is the only normative source of this faculty in the European System.[4]

Rule 100 of the Rules of Procedure of the African Commission on Human and Peoples' Rights (ACHPR) establishes the faculty to indicate provisional measures.[5] Similarly, Rule 59 of the Rules of Procedure of the ACHPR acknowledges its authority to adopt provisional measures 'in case of extreme

---

the International Tribunal for the Law of the Sea states that: 'the Tribunal and its Seabed Disputes Chamber shall have the power to prescribe provisional measures'.

[3] The treaty bodies are the committees of independent experts in charge of monitoring the implementation of the human rights treaties adopted by the UN General Assembly. See: OHCR, 'Treaty Bodies' (OHCHR, 2024) https://www.ohchr.org/en/treaty-bodies.

[4] Rule 39(1) of the ECtHR Rules of Court reads as follows: 'The Chamber or, where appropriate, its President may, at the request of a party or of any other person concerned, or of its own motion, indicate to the parties any interim measure which it considers should be adopted in the interests of the parties or of the proper conduct of the proceedings before it'. See: ECtHR Rules of Court (2023), Rule 39(1) https://www.echr.coe.int/documents/d/echr/rules_court_eng. Burbano Herrera and Hayek explain that the ECtHR has resorted to interim measures mostly in three situations: (1) imminent expulsion or extradition, (2) imminent enforcement of the death penalty, and (3) protection of the health of detainees. Interim measures have also been indicated in the context of contentious cases alleging arbitrary or illegal eviction of vulnerable individuals, the right to housing, the right to a fair trial in criminal proceedings, etc. See: Clara Burbano Herrera and Yves Haeck, 'Interim Measures in the Case Law of the European Court of Human Rights' (2003) 21 NQHR 631. See also: Clara Burbano Herrera and Yves Haeck, 'Staying the Return of Aliens from Europe through Interim Measures: The Case-law of the European Commission and the European Court of Human Rights' (2011) 13 *European Journal of Migration and Law* 31, 32–33.

[5] The ACHPR has granted provisional measures to protect the right to life and personal integrity and, to a lesser extent, other rights such as freedom of expression, the right to family, and the territorial rights of Indigenous peoples. See: *Zimbabwe Lawyers for Human Rights & Associated Newspapers of Zimbabwe v Zimbabwe* App No. 284/03 (ACHPR, 3 April 2009) paras 11–12 and 28; *Amnesty International v Zambia* App No. 212/98 (ACHPR, 5 May 1999); *Centre for Minority Rights Development (Kenya) and Minority Rights Group International*

gravity and urgency and where necessary to avoid irreparable harm to persons' and 'pending determination of the main application'.[6]

Unlike the Inter-American system – where most of the urgent measures are indicated without a contentious case, the UN, European, and African human rights systems have no stand-alone interim or provisional measures; i.e., these measures must be requested in the context of a pending case.

## 2.2 Inter-American Human Rights System

The Inter-American human rights system (IAHRS) was established as a by-product of the Organization of American States (OAS), with the adoption of the American Declaration of the Rights and Duties of Man in April 1948.[7] It is composed of two organs, the IACHR and the IACtHR. Created in 1959, the IACHR[8] is composed of seven members elected by the OAS General Assembly, who perform their duties independently of any government. Its mandate is to promote respect for human rights in the Americas through the examination of individual complaints,[9] on-site visits, and thematic and country reports. It is also entitled to grant precautionary measures and request provisional measures

*on behalf of the Endorois Welfare Council v The Republic of Kenya* App No. 276/2003 (ACHPR, 4 February 2010).

6 For a detailed analysis of this issue, see: Gino J. Naldi, 'Interim Measures of Protection in the African System for the Protection of Human and Peoples' Rights' (2002) 2 *African Human Rights Law Journal* 1.

7 American Declaration of the Rights and Duties of Man, OAS Res XXX, adopted by the Ninth International Conference of American States (1948), reprinted in Basic Documents Pertaining to Human Rights in the Inter-American System, OEA/Ser L V/II.82 Doc 6 Rev 1 at 17 (1992).

8 For an overview of the role of the IACHR since its creation in 1959, see: Robert K. Goldman, 'History and Action: The Inter-American Human Rights System and the Role of the Inter-American Commission on Human Rights' (2009) 31 *Human Rights Quarterly* 856, 857–8. For a more detailed account of the historical background of the IAHRS, see: Francisco-José Quintana, 'The (Latin) American Dream? Human Rights and the Construction of Inter-American Regional Organisation (1945–1948)' (2023) 25 JHIL 560–591.

9 With the adoption of the first Statute of the IACHR in 1959, the member states of the OAS entrusted the IACHR with the mission of promoting awareness of human rights, making recommendations to governments for the adoption of progressive measures in favour of human rights, preparing studies, and serving as an advisory body to the OAS in this field.

from the IACtHR, to submit cases to this tribunal, and to serve the OAS as an advisory body.[10]

Adopted in 1969, the American Convention on Human Rights (ACHR) established the IACtHR, an autonomous judicial body whose purpose is to apply and interpret the ACHR. It is composed of seven judges elected by the state parties to the American Convention. It can issue advisory opinions regarding the interpretation of the Convention and any other human rights instrument. At the request of the IACHR or on its own initiative, the Court may issue provisional measures to prevent irreparable harm to the rights of persons in serious and extremely urgent situations.[11]

### 2.2.1 Provisional measures of the Inter-American Court of Human Rights

Article 63(2) of the American Convention establishes that:

> In cases of extreme gravity and urgency, and when necessary to avoid irreparable damage to persons, the Court shall adopt such provisional measures as it deems pertinent in matters it has under consideration. With respect to a case not yet submitted to the Court, it may act at the request of the Commission.

These measures serve both a precautionary function, in the sense of preserving the *status quo* of a claim pending adjudication, and a protective function, as they seek to avoid irreparable harm to persons. [12]

---

[10] See: American Convention on Human Rights (adopted 22 November, entered into force 18 July 1978) OAS Treaty Series No. 36, 1144 UNTS 123, Chapter VII. For an overview of the IACHR's main functions from its creation until 2014, see: Daniel Cerqueira and Katya Salazar, 'The Functions of the Inter-American Commission on Human Rights Before, During, and After the Strengthening Process: Striking a Balance between the Desirable and the Possible' in Due Process of Law Foundation and others (eds), *The Inter-American Human Rights System – Changing Times, Ongoing Challenges* (DPLF 2015).

[11] ACHR, Chapter VIII. As of September 2024, 23 out of 35 the OAS member states have ratified the ACHR, of which 20 accept the IACtHR's jurisdiction.

[12] This dual function has been explained by the IACtHR as follows:

> The precautionary character is related to the framework of international contentious cases, as provisional measures intend to preserve the rights potentially at risk until the controversy is resolved. Their goal is to ensure the integrity and effectiveness of the decision on merits, and to avoid infringement of the rights under consideration, which could render innocuous or have an effect on the *effet utile* of the final decision. Provisional measures therefore allow the State in question to comply with the final decision, and, if applicable, to implement the reparations ordered. With

The IACtHR has stressed the following difference between the provisional measures under domestic procedural law and international human rights law:

> The purpose of provisional measures in domestic legal systems (domestic procedural law) in general, is to preserve the rights of the parties to a dispute, thereby ensuring that execution of the judgment on the merits is not obstructed or otherwise prejudiced by their actions *pendente lite*. Under the International Law of Human Rights, urgent and provisional measures serve a further purpose, which is to protect fundamental human rights, thereby avoiding irreparable harm to persons.[13]

For several decades, the Inter-American Commission had exclusive *locus standi* to request provisional measures from the IACtHR. In 2003, the Court amended its Rules of Procedure to allow alleged victims and their representatives to submit this type of request in the context of contentious cases already under its jurisdiction.[14]

---

> regards to the protective character, the Court has indicated that provisional measures become a true jurisdictional guarantee of a preventive nature as they protect human rights, to the extent that they seek to avoid irreparable damages to persons.

See *Four Ngöbe Indigenous Communities and their Members v Panama*, Provisional Measures (28 May 2010) para 3. Internal quotation marks have been removed from the original text.

13 *Case of Lysias Fleury*, Provisional Measures (7 June 2003) para 7. The paragraphs cited in the text are repeated in several other decisions on provisional measures indicated by the IACtHR. See: e.g., *Indigenous People of Sarayaku v Ecuador*, Provisional Measures (6 July 2004) paras 5–6; *Persons Imprisoned in the Dr Sebastião Martins Silveira Penitentiary in Araraquara, São Paulo*, Provisional Measures (30 September 2006) para 4.

14 Following this amendment, Article 27 of the IACtHR Rules of Procedure now reads as follows:

Article 27. Provisional Measures

1. At any stage of proceedings involving cases of extreme gravity and urgency, and when necessary to avoid irreparable damage to persons, the Court may, on its own motion, order such provisional measures as it deems appropriate, pursuant to Article 63(2) of the Convention.
2. With respect to matters not yet submitted to it, the Court may act at the request of the Commission.
3. In contentious cases before the Court, victims or alleged victims, or their representatives, may submit to it a request for provisional measures, which must be related to the subject matter of the case.
4. The request may be submitted to the Presidency, to any Judge of the Court, or to the Secretariat, by any means of communication. In every case, the recipient of the request shall immediately bring it to the attention of the Presidency.

With respect to the requirements set forth in Article 63(2) of the American Convention, the IACtHR has indicated that 'gravity' must be extreme, 'that is, at its most intense or elevated degree'.[15] Urgency means that the risk of threat requires an immediate response. Regarding the irreparability, the Court has stated that 'there must be reasonable probability that the damages will occur, and it must not involve assets or legal interests that can be repaired'.[16]

Most of the provisional measures adopted by the IACtHR aimed at protecting the life and personal integrity of individuals,[17] particularly those facing threats and detainees subjected to inhumane conditions of detention.[18] A

---

5. The Court, or if the Court is not sitting, the Presidency, upon considering that it is possible and necessary, may require the State, the Commission, or the representatives of the beneficiaries to provide information on a request for provisional measures before deciding on the measure requested.
6. If the Court is not sitting, the Presidency, in consultation with the Permanent Commission and, if possible, with the other Judges, shall call upon the State concerned to adopt such urgent measures as may be necessary to ensure the effectiveness of any provisional measures that may be ordered by the Court during its next period of sessions.
7. The monitoring of urgent or provisional measures ordered shall be carried out through the submission of reports by the State and the filing of observations to those reports by the beneficiaries of the measures or their representatives. The Commission shall submit observations to the State's reports and to the observations of the beneficiaries of the measures or their representatives.
8. When the Court considers it appropriate, it may require from other sources of information any relevant data on the matter that would permit it to assess the gravity and urgency of the situation and the effectiveness of the measures. To that end, it may also require expert opinion and any other report that it considers appropriate.
9. The Court, or its Presidency if the Court is not sitting, may convene the Commission, the beneficiaries of the measures or their representatives, and the State to a public or private hearing on provisional measures.
10. In its Annual Report to the General Assembly, the Court shall include a statement concerning the provisional measures ordered during the period covered by the report. If those measures have not been duly implemented, the Court shall make such recommendations as it deems appropriate.

[15] *Four Ngöbe Indigenous Communities and their Members v Panama* (n 12) 8.

[16] *Four Ngöbe Indigenous Communities and their Members v Panama* (n 12) para 9–10.

[17] IACtHR, 'Sistematización de las resoluciones sobre medidas provisionales emitidas por la Corte Interamericana de Derechos Humanos (Arts. 63.2 de la Convención Americana sobre Derechos Humanos y 27 del Reglamento de la Corte Interamericana)' https://www.corteidh.or.cr/docs/Sistematizacion.pdf.

[18] Clara Burbano Herrera and Yves Haeck, 'The Use of Transformative Provisional Measures by the Inter-American Court of Human Rights: Toward a Tangible Impact' in Armin von Bogdandy and others (eds), *The Impact of the*

limited number of measures sought to protect these along with other rights, such as the right to family[19] and legal guarantees.[20] On a few occasions, the Court ordered states to stay domestic proceedings or to preserve rights whose violation would impair its own jurisdiction[21] or the ability of the Commission[22] to provide adequate reparations in a final decision on the merits of a contentious case. Most of these precedents relate to the suspension of the death penalty, one to the suspension of extradition proceedings,[23] and another to the suspension of a sentence against a journalist convicted of defamation.[24]

### 2.2.2 Precautionary measures of the Inter-American Commission on Human Rights

The faculty to adopt precautionary measures was originally established in the 1980 Rules of Procedure of the Commission,[25] in the chapter on the individual complaint mechanism. Since the amendment of the IACHR Rules of Procedure in October 1996,[26] it has been regulated in a separate chapter, which

*Inter-American Human Rights System: Transformations on the Ground* (Oxford University Press 2024).

[19] *Case of Haitian and Haitian-Origin Dominican Persons in the Dominican Republic*, Provisional Measures (18 August 2000) para 5.

[20] *Case of Ivcher-Bronstein (Peru)*, Provisional Measures (21 November 2000) paras 1–2.

[21] *Case of Tyrone DaCosta Cadongan (Barbados)*, Provisional Measures (2 December 2008). In this case, the Commission had issued precautionary measures to suspend the execution of the death penalty against Mr Tyrone DaCosta in order not to impede the processing of his case before the organs of the Inter-American system. After reaching a final decision on the merits of the case, the Commission submitted it to the jurisdiction of the IACtHR and requested provisional measures, which were initially granted by the President of the Court on 4 November and ratified by its plenary on 2 December 2008.

[22] *Case of La Nación Newspaper (Costa Rica)*, Provisional Measures (23 May, 7 and 8 September 2001, and 26 August 2002), in which the IACtHR granted provisional measures when the contentious case was still under the jurisdiction of the Commission and pending a final decision on the merits by this body. Under the same circumstances, see the provisional measure concerning the suspension of the death sentences in the *Case of James and Others* (Trinidad and Tobago). Order of 25 May 1999, decision para 2(b).

[23] *Wong Ho Wing v Peru*, Provisional Measures (28 May 2010).

[24] *Case of La Nación Newspaper (Costa Rica)*, Provisional Measures (21 May 2001).

[25] Rules of Procedure of the Inter-American Commission on Human Rights (1980) OEA/SER.L/V/II.49, para 26.

[26] IACHR Rules of Procedure (1996) OEA/SER.L/V/II.93, para 29.

seems to reflect the IACHR's practice of granting these measures either in connection with or independently of an individual complaint.

The Inter-American Convention on Forced Disappearance of Persons codifies the authority of the IACHR to issue precautionary measures,[27] which demonstrate the general practice of the OAS member states to acknowledge the binding nature of such measures.[28]

The vast majority of the precautionary measures granted by the IACHR over the past 25 years have been issued outside the context of a contentious case. Although they sought to protect a wide range of rights under the ACHR and other Inter-American instruments, the IACHR has increasingly limited these measures to situations of serious risk of irreparable harm to the life and physical integrity of persons.

## 3 INDIGENOUS TERRITORIAL RIGHTS UNDER THE INTER-AMERICAN STANDARDS

The case law of the IACtHR emphasizes the special relationship between the cultural integrity and identity of Indigenous peoples and other fundamental rights.[29] According to the IACHR's doctrine, this relationship 'extends beyond the settlement of specific villages to include lands that are used for agriculture, hunting, fishing, gathering, transportation, cultural and other purposes'.[30] The IACtHR has also stated that the traditional territory and its natural resources

---

[27] Article XIII of the Inter-American Convention on Forced Disappearance of Persons states that: 'For the purposes of this Convention, the processing of petitions or communications presented to the Inter-American Commission on Human Rights alleging the forced disappearance of persons shall be subject to the procedures established in the American Convention on Human Rights and to the Statute and Regulations of the Inter-American Commission on Human Rights and to the Statute and Rules and Procedure of the Inter-American Court of Human Rights, including the provisions on precautionary measures'.

[28] The IACtHR has pointed out that the principle of good faith and the effectiveness of the Inter-American human rights system require states to respect its precautionary measures. See: *Case of James and Others (Trinidad and Tobago)*, Provisional Measures (26 September 2001).

[29] *Yakye Axa Indigenous Community v Paraguay* (Merits, Reparations and Costs) IACtHR Series C No. 125 (17 June 2005) para 131.

[30] *Maya Indigenous Communities of the Toledo District v Belize*, Report No. 40/04, Case 12.053 (12 October 2004) paras 129 and 155. See also: IACHR, 'Access to Justice and Social Inclusion: The Road towards Strengthening Democracy in Bolivia' OEA/Ser.L/V/II (28 June 2007) para 297.

are the condition for the material subsistence of Indigenous peoples and inherent to their spiritual values and cultural identity.[31]

According to the IACHR, 'ancestral cemeteries, places of religious meaning and importance, and ceremonial or ritual sites linked to the occupation and use of physical territories constitute an intrinsic part of the right to cultural identity'.[32] The IACtHR has stated that the 'possession of their traditional territory is indelibly recorded in their historical memory, and their relationship with the land is such that severing that tie entails the certain risk of an irreparable ethnic and cultural loss, with the ensuing loss of diversity'.[33]

In the 2012 *Case of the Kichwa Indigenous People of Sarayaku v Ecuador*, the IACtHR highlighted the link between the right to collective property and the cultural integrity of Indigenous peoples. According to the IACtHR, 'the right to cultural identity is a fundamental right – and one of a collective nature – of the Indigenous communities, which should be respected in a multicultural, pluralistic and democratic society'.[34]

## 3.1 Special Safeguards to Indigenous Territorial Rights

The IACtHR has defined property as the material things that can be possessed,[35] the rights incorporated in a person's patrimony,[36] and the intangible things that can have value.[37] This right is enshrined in Article 21 of the ACHR and Article XXIII of the American Declaration. Although these provisions do not mention Indigenous and tribal peoples, the organs of the IAHRS have stressed that both the private property of individuals and communal property of the Indigenous

---

31 *Sawhoyamaxa Indigenous Community v Paraguay* (Merits, Reparations and Costs) IACtHR Series C No. 146 (29 March 2006) para 118; *Yakye Axa Indigenous Community v Paraguay* (n 29) 135.

32 IACtHR, 'Indigenous and Tribal Peoples' Rights over their Ancestral Lands and Natural Resources' (30 December 2009) OEA/Ser.L/V/II, para 160.

33 *Yakye Axa Indigenous Community v Paraguay* (n 29) para 216.

34 *Kichwa Indigenous People of Sarayaku v Ecuador* (Merits and Reparations) IACtHR Series C No. 245 (27 June 2012) para 217.

35 *Perozo and Others v Venezuela* (Preliminary Objections, Merits, Reparations, and Costs) IACtHR Series C No. 195 (28 January 2009) para 399; *Ivcher Bronstein v Peru* (Merits, Reparations and Costs) IACtHR Series C No. 74 (6 February 2001) para 122; *Salvador-Chiriboga v Ecuador* (Preliminary Objections and Merits) IACtHR Series C No. 179 (6 May 2008) para 55.

36 *'Five Pensioners' v Peru* (Merits, Reparations and Costs) IACtHR Series C No. 98 (28 February 2003) para 102.

37 *Salvador-Chiriboga v Ecuador* (n 35) 55.

communities are protected under Articles 21 of the American Convention[38] and XXIII of the Declaration.[39]

According to the Inter-American case law, the property rights of Indigenous and tribal peoples over their territories derive from customary land tenure, rather than from formal recognition.[40] In this sense, while states have an obligation to title and demarcate the traditional territories,[41] the exercise of collective property rights is not to be conditioned on these acts.[42]

When the property claims of Indigenous peoples collide with private property acquired in good faith by third parties, the IACtHR has examined whether the restriction to the communal property is justified. Its jurisprudence indicates that the right to collective property may be restricted if the state follows a pre-established law, if the restriction is necessary to achieve a legitimate aim, and if it is strictly proportional. In carrying out this test, the IACtHR has concluded that the ancestral land encompasses a broader concept linked to the cultural integrity of Indigenous peoples, the material subsistence of their members, and their very existence as an organized group.[43]

In line with the wording of Article 16(4) of International Labour Organization (ILO) Convention No. 169,[44] the IACtHR has maintained that when a state justifies the impossibility of restoring a traditional territory, it must compensate the Indigenous community with lands equivalent in size and quality. Compensation must be carried out under the consent of Indigenous peoples concerned 'in accordance with their own mechanism of consultation, values, customs and customary law'.[45]

---

38 *Yakye Axa Indigenous Community v Paraguay* (n 29) 143.

39 *Mary and Carrie Dann v United* States, IACHR Report No. 75/02, Case 11.1140 (27 December 2002) paras 44–52.

40 *Mayagna (Sumo) Awas Tingni Community v Nicaragua* (Merits, Reparations and Costs) IACtHR Series C No. 79 (31 August 2001) para 140(a).

41 *Saramaka People v Suriname*, IACHR (28 November 2007) 115; *Yakye Axa Indigenous Community v Paraguay* (n 29) 143.

42 *Saramaka People v Suriname* (n 41) 115; *Mayagna (Sumo) Awas Tingni Community v Nicaragua* (n 40) para 153; *Yakye Axa Indigenous Community v Paraguay* (n 29) 215; *Moiwana Community v Suriname* (Preliminary Objections, Merits, Reparations and Costs) IACtHR Series C No. 124 (15 June 2005) para 209.

43 *Yakye Axa Indigenous Community v Paraguay* (n 29) 147.

44 This provision states that '[w]hen such return is not possible ... these peoples shall be provided in all possible cases with lands of quality and legal status at least equal to that of the lands previously occupied by them, suitable to provide for their present needs and future development. Where the peoples concerned express a preference for compensation in money or in kind, they shall be so compensated under appropriate guarantees'.

45 *Yakye Axa Indigenous Community v Paraguay* (n 29) 151.

In brief, the Inter-American jurisprudence establishes the following special guarantees for Indigenous territorial rights: (1) traditional tenure of a territory entails the same effect as a title of domain; (2) it also entitles the Indigenous community to request the official recognition and title of property; (3) Indigenous peoples involuntarily displaced from their traditional lands do not lose their property rights; (4) the acquisition of traditional lands by third parties in good faith does not circumvent the obligation of states to restore them to the members of the Indigenous community; and (5) when the impossibility of restoring the traditional lands is fully justified, the Indigenous community has the right to obtain lands similar in size and quality or to choose another form of compensation.[46]

The IACtHR has indicated that the special safeguards for Indigenous and tribal territories cannot be interpreted as a general prohibition on the concession of economic activities.[47] In addition to the requirements generally applied to the restriction of the right to property (legality, necessity, and strict proportionality), the restriction resulting from such a concession must not jeopardize

---

[46] In the *Case of the Xucuru Indigenous People and its members v Brazil*, the IACtHR summarised the following special safeguards for the collective property of Indigenous peoples over their traditional territories: (1) the traditional possession of Indigenous peoples over their lands has the same effects as the title of full ownership granted by the State; (2) traditional possession grants the Indigenous peoples the right to require official recognition of ownership and its registration; (3) members of Indigenous peoples who, for reasons beyond their control, have left or lost possession of their traditional lands maintain the right to ownership of such lands, even without legal title, except when those lands have been legitimately transferred to third parties in good faith; (4) the State must delimit, demarcate, and grant collective title to the lands of the members of the Indigenous communities; (5) members of Indigenous peoples who, involuntarily, have lost the possession of their lands, and these have been transferred legitimately to third parties in good faith, have the right to recover them or to obtain other land of the same area and quality; (6) the State must ensure the effective ownership of the Indigenous peoples and refrain from taking actions that could result in agents of the State itself, or third parties acting with its acquiescence or tolerance, adversely affecting the existence, value, use, or enjoyment of their territory; (7) the State must ensure the right of the Indigenous peoples to control effectively and be owners of their territory without any type of external interference by third parties; and (8) the State must ensure the right of the Indigenous peoples to the control and use of their territory and natural resources [...].

See: *Xucuru Indigenous People and its members v Brazil* (Preliminary Objections, Merits, Reparations and Costs) IACtHR Series C No. 346 (5 February 2017) para 117.

[47] *Saramaka People v Suriname* (n 41) 126.

the cultural integrity of the community and its subsistence as an organized group.[48] To achieve this objective, states must carry out a free and informed consultation prior to authorizing economic enterprises that affect Indigenous and tribal territories.[49] In addition, states must ensure that the affected communities receive fair benefits from these activities and that no concession is granted until an independent and technically qualified entity, acting under the supervision of the state, has conducted an assessment of the social and environmental impact of the project.[50]

With regard to large-scale projects with a deep impact on Indigenous territories, the IACtHR has established the obligation to obtain the mandatory consent of the affected communities, in accordance with their customs and traditions.[51] The Inter-American Commission has developed this obligation further, emphasizing concrete guidelines for determining when an investment project can be labelled as 'large-scale'. These guidelines include the magnitude of the project, the extent and intensity of its impact on the territory, and the human and social consequences of the activity. In this regard, the IACHR has concluded that 'industrial mining' and the exploitation of hydrocarbons

---

48 ibid para 128, quoting *Länsman and Others v Finlandia* App No. 511/1992, UN Doc CCPR/C/52/D/511/1994 (8 November 1994) para 9(4).

49 For a comprehensive study of the Inter-American standards on the right to consultation and participation of Indigenous and tribal peoples in the decisions that affect their interests and territory see: IACHR, 'Indigenous and Tribal Peoples' Rights over their Ancestral Lands and Natural Resources' (n 32) Chapter IX.

50 *Saramaka People v Suriname* (n 41) 129.

51 ibid paras 134–7, citing Economic and Social Council (ESC), 'UN Report of the Special Rapporteur on the situation of human rights and fundamental freedoms of Indigenous people, Rodolfo Stavenhagen, submitted in accordance with Commission resolution 2001/65' (Fifty-ninth session) UN Doc E/CN.4/2003/90 (21 January 2003) paras 2 and 66; and United Nations Committee on the Elimination of Racial Discrimination (UNCERD), 'Consideration of Reports submitted by States Parties under Article 9 of the Convention, Concluding Observations on Ecuador' (Sixty-second session, 2003) UN Doc CERD/C/62/CO/2 (2 June 2003) para 16. It is important to mention that in the previous case of *Awas Tingni* the IACtHR indicated that as a state party to the ILO Convention No. 169, Nicaragua had the obligation to perform a prior consultation with the members of this community. In the case of *Saramaka People v Suriname* (n 41), whereby Suriname had not ratified ILO Convention No. 169, the IACtHR concluded that the obligation to obtain a previous, free, and informed consent derives from the American Convention and other instruments that constitute the international *corpus juris* on the rights of Indigenous peoples.

are concrete examples of large-scale activities that require the mandatory consent of the Indigenous and tribal peoples affected.[52]

# 4 INDIGENOUS PEOPLES' RIGHTS AND URGENT MEASURES IN THE INTER-AMERICAN SYSTEM

## 4.1 Precautionary Measures

Most of the precautionary measures granted by the IACHR in situations involving risks for Indigenous and tribal peoples have sought to protect the life and physical integrity of their members.[53]

By 2011, the IACHR had issued a significant number of precautionary measures, in the form of injunctions, to suspend domestic decisions that could cause irreparable harm to Indigenous communities and their territorial rights. Almost all of these measures were linked to a pending contentious case, and they sought to preserve the rights of the beneficiaries until the organs of the Inter-American system had the opportunity to adopt a final decision on the merits of the case. The only two exceptions to this approach occurred in July 2006, with the precautionary measure in favour of the Sitio El Rosario-Naranjo Maya Community in Guatemala, and in April 2011, with the precautionary measure regarding the Belo Monte hydroelectric dam, in Brazil.

The following subsections summarize the main aspects of the precautionary measures in favour of Indigenous and tribal peoples over the past 25 years.[54] Subsection 4.1.1 deals with precautionary measures that protect the life, physical integrity, and other related rights of Indigenous peoples, outside the scope of a contentious case. This is the most common situation in which the IACHR has granted and continues to grant precautionary measures to members of Indigenous and tribal peoples. Section 4.1.2 examines the precautionary measures that intend to suspend domestic proceedings that could affect Indigenous territorial rights, as an injunctive measure related to a contentious

[52] IACHR, 'Indigenous Peoples, Afro-Descendant Communities, and Natural Resources: Protection of Human Rights in the Context of Extraction, Exploitation, and Development Activities' (31 December 2015) paras 185–93.

[53] The summary of the precautionary measures cited in this subsection was taken from the information available at the IACHR's web page: www.cidh.oas.org/medidas.eng.htm.

[54] The precautionary measures adopted after March 2013 contain a serial number, both in the resolution and in the precautionary measure (PM) registry. Older precautionary measures do not contain either of these serial numbers on the IACHR's webpage, and their identification is made by the date of issuance and the name of the beneficiary community.

case. Section 4.1.3 analyzes the two precedents in which the IACHR requested the suspension of a domestic decision outside the scope of a case.[55]

### 4.1.1 Precautionary measures protecting the lives and physical integrity of Indigenous and tribal peoples

Most of these precautionary measures relate to threats, killings, and other acts of violence against members of Indigenous and tribal peoples. Many of them involve illegal armed groups, particularly in Colombia and Mexico. In some cases, the IACHR has concluded that the risk of irreparable harm is linked to the efforts of communities to obtain legal recognition of their lands or to their opposition to large-scale projects.

Some of the precautionary measures described in this subsection refer to the conditions of detention, torture, and lack of adequate medical care for Indigenous prisoners, particularly in Nicaragua. When the beneficiaries are Indigenous persons who are also human rights defenders, the IACHR usually requests states to 'ensure that they can perform their work as human rights defenders without being subject to threats, harassment, or any other act of violence'.[56]

A smaller group of precautionary measures has been granted in the context of serious environmental damage caused by oil spills and harmful chemicals on Indigenous territories. In this scenario, the IACHR usually requests the state to stop the source of contamination, to provide the necessary medical examination and treatment, to clean up the affected areas, and to ensure adequate food and sanitation for the beneficiaries.

In recent years, the IACHR has added a standard sentence to some precautionary measures concerning Indigenous peoples, calling for 'culturally appropriate measures to protect the life and personal integrity' and to 'agree upon the measures to be adopted with the beneficiaries and their representatives, taking into account the importance of safeguarding the cultural identity of the proposed beneficiaries'.[57]

---

[55] For an analysis of how the IACHR has incorporated an intercultural approach in recent decisions on precautionary measures in favour of Indigenous peoples, see Antonia Urrejola and Elsy Curihuinca Neira, 'Indigenous Rights in the Inter-American System: The Application of Precautionary Measures from a Culturally Appropriate Perspective' in Armin von Bogdandy and others (eds), *The Impact of the Inter-American Human Rights System: Transformations on the Ground* (Oxford University Press 2024).

[56] See, e.g., Resolution No. 19/24, PM 73-24 – Thirteen members of the La Plata Bahía Málaga Community, Colombia.

[57] ibid.

Several measures protecting Indigenous communities have been issued under Article 25(3) of the IACHR's Rules of Procedure, which establishes that precautionary measures 'may be of a collective nature to prevent irreparable harm to persons due to their association with an organization, a group, or a community with identified or identifiable members'.[58] Indigenous and tribal communities, as well as persons deprived of their liberty in a particular detention centre, are the most common group to which the IACHR grants precautionary measures under Article 25(3) of its Rules, without the need to identify the individual beneficiaries.[59] However, the IACHR requires information that is precise enough to identify the beneficiaries in a given geographical area.

Between January 2003 and January 2025, the IACHR granted 76 precautionary measures[60] to protect the life and personal integrity of Indigenous and tribal communities as a collective group, their leaders, or their individual members.[61] A small number of these measures required states to

---

58 Krsticevic and Reggiardo, 'Artículo 25' (2023) *Comentario al Procedimiento ante el Sistema Interamericano de Derechos Humanos* 108 and 109.

59 Prior to the 2013 amendment, the IACHR granted several collective precautionary measures to other non-Indigenous groups, such as human rights organizations, peasant and rural communities, media outlet workers, etc. Since 2013, the IACHR has adopted the general practice of granting measures in favour of the individual members of these groups rather than the organization, community, or entity to which they belong.

60 It was not until March 2013 that the IACHR began to publish a resolution on the precautionary measures granted. Therefore, there is no mention of a resolution number for those measures issued between 2010 and 2012. On the other hand, the IACHR did not add serial numbers to the measures issued before 2008, due to which they are referred to in this chapter by means of the date of adoption and the names of the beneficiaries.

61 These precautionary measures are the following: Res. No. 77/24 – Steadman Fagot Muller, Nicaragua; Res. No. 28/24 – Members of the Tapeba Indigenous People of Caucaia, Brazil; Res. No. 34/24 – Sonia Chilgueso Dagua, Diana Montilla Moreno, and their families, Colombia; Res. No. 19/24 – Thirteen members of the La Plata Bahía Málaga Community, Colombia; Res. No. 13/24 – Selected families of the native Kichwa community Santa Rosillo de Yanayacu, Peru; Res. No. 12/24 – Cindy Vanessa Arenas Fernández and her family, Colombia; Res. No. 11/24 – J. Santos Rosales Contreras and twelve other members of the Nahua indigenous community of Ayotitlán, Mexico; Res. No. 83/23 – Tolupan indigenous members of the Movimiento Amplio por la Justicia y la Dignidad, Honduras; Res. No. 60/23 – Nancy Elizabeth Henriquez James, Nicaragua; Res. No. 59/23 – Brooklyn Rivera Bryan, Nicaragua; Res. No. 41/23 – Indigenous Carib Community of Chinese Landing, Guyana; Res. No. 27/23 – Álvaro Alcides Crespo Hernández and his daughter, Colombia; Res. No. 25/23 – Members of the Pataxó Indigenous People located in the Barra Velha and Comexatibá

Indigenous Lands in the state of Bahia, Brazil; Res. No. 20/23 – D.R.Z., D.A.B.A., A.C.L. and I.C.L., Nicaragua; Res. No. 10/23 – Members of the Boa Hora III/ Marmorana Quilombola Territory, Brazil; Res. No. 70/22 – Jhon Anderson Ipia Bubu, Colombia; Res. No. 59/22 PM 449-22 – Identified members of the 'União dos Povos Indígenas do Vale de Javari', Brazil; Res. No. 50/22 – Members of the Guapoy´s community of the Guarani Kaiowá Indigenous People, Brazil; Res. No. 5/22 – Families of the Río Murindó and Río Chageradó Reservations of the Embera Eyábida Indigenous People, Colombia; Res. No. 105/21 – Families from the Mixteca Indigenous communities of Guerrero Grande and Ndoyonuyuji, et al., Mexico; Res. No. 53/21 – Yiner Hernán Quiguantar Cortés, Colombia; Res. No. 35/21 – Tsotsil Indigenous families from twelve communities in the municipality of Aldama, Chiapas, Mexico; Res. No. 32/21– Seven pregnant women of the Wichí ethnic group, Argentina; Res. No. 1/21 – Members of the Guajajara and Awá Indigenous Peoples of the Araribóia Indigenous Land, Brazil; Res. No. 94/20 – Munduruku Indigenous People, Brazil; Res. No. 81/20 – Members of the Indigenous Community of Santa Clara de Uchunya et al., Peru; Res. No. 67/20 – Poqomchi' Mayan Indigenous Families of Washington and Dos Fuentes communities, Guatemala; Res. No. 44/20 – Quilombo Rio dos Macacos Community, Brazil; Res. No. 35/20 – Members of the Yanomami and Ye'kwana Indigenous Peoples, Brazil; Res. No. 47/19 – Guyraroká community of the Guarani Kaiowá Indigenous People, Brazil; Res. No. 33/19 – Quelvin Otoniel Jimenez Villalta, Guatemala; Res. No. 7/19 – Indigenous persons of the Pemon ethnic group in the San Francisco de Yuruaní, Venezuela; Res. No. 67/18 PM 807-18 – Yaku Pérez Guartambel, Ecuador; Res. No. 53/18 – Authorities and members of the Siona (ZioBain) Indigenous people's reservations Gonzaya and Po Piyuya, Colombia; Res. No. 15/18 – Tsotsil Indigenous communities in Chalchihuitán and Chenalhó, Mexico; Res. No. 13/18 – Tsotsil Indigenous persons displaced from the Puebla communal land and members of the Ku'untik Center for Human Rights, Mexico; Res. No. 1/18 – Lucila Bettina Cruz and her family, Mexico; Res. No. 30/17 – Julio César Vélez Restrepo et al., Colombia; Res. No. 4/1 – Víctor Vásquez, Honduras; Res. No. 32/16 – Members of the Otomí-Mexica Indigenous Community of San Francisco Xochicuautla, Mexico; Res. No. 46/15 – Ana Miran Romero and Others, Honduras; Res. No. 37/15 – Members of the communities 'Esperanza, Santa Clara, Nicaragua; Res. No. 15/15 P – Cruz Sánchez Lagarda and others, Mexico; Res. No. 29/14 – Prudencio Ramos Ramos and others, Mexico; PM 131/12 – Hernán Henry Díaz, Colombia; PM 60/12 – Members of the Triqui Indigenous Community in the San Pedro River Valley, San Juan Cópala, Putla de Guerrero, Oaxaca, Mexico; PM 255/11 – Nasa people of Toribio, San Francisco, Tacueyo, and Jambalo Reservations, Colombia; PM 61/11 – Members of the Awá Indigenous People of the Departments of Nariño and Putumayo, Colombia; PM 404/10 – Qom Navogoh Indigenous Community of 'La Primavera,' Argentina; PM 355/10 – 21 Families of the Nonam Community of the Wounaan Indigenous People, Colombia; PM 17/10 – Inhabitants of the community of Omoa, Honduras; PM 208-10 – Estela Ángeles Mondragón, Mexico; PM 347/09 – Members of the El Nogalito (Lule) community

take the necessary actions to ensure the safe return to their communities of beneficiaries displaced by acts of violence.[62]

Some older precautionary measures include a general request to protect 'the community's special relationship with its territory', in addition to the protection of the life and personal integrity of its members.[63]

There is a single precautionary measure outside the scope of a contentious case whereby the IACHR requested the prevention of irreparable harm to the life and physical integrity of the beneficiaries with a more specific order to demarcate an Indigenous territory. Adopted on 4 August 2010, the precautionary measures granted to the Mixteca Indigenous community of Lázaro Cárdenas in Oaxaca, Mexico, requested the Mexican state to 'remove the risk

---

of Tucumán Province, Argentina; PM 61/11 – Members of the Awá Indigenous People of the Departments of Nariño and Putumayo, Colombia; PM 255/11 – Nasa people of Toribio, San Francisco, Tacueyo, and Jambalo Reservations, Colombia; PM 355/10 – 21 Families of the Nonam Community of the Wounaan Indigenous People, Colombia; PM 197/10 – 135 Inhabitants of San Juan Copala, Mexico; PM 102/10 – Inhabitants of the Mixteca Indigenous Community of Lázaro Cárdenas, Putla, Oaxaca, Mexico; PM 12/09 – Community of Alto Guayabal-Coredcito of the Emberá People, Colombia; PM 290/09 – Jesús Tecú Osorio and his family, Guatemala; PM 301/08 – Leaders of the Indigenous Regional Council of Cauca (CRIC) and their Advisers, Colombia; (August 20, 2007) – Marcos Bonifacio Castillo, member of the Garifuna Community of Punta Piedras, Honduras; (November 27, 2006) – The Union of Guarayo Native Peoples (COPNAG), Bolivia; (November 7, 2005) – Aura Lolita Chávez Ixcaquic, Guatemala; (March 11, 2005) – Tacana Indigenous Community of Miraflores, Riberalta, Bolivia; (January 14, 2005) – Obtilia Eugenio Manuel et al, Mexico; (December 6, 2004) – Indigenous Peoples Ingaricó, Macuxi, Wapichana, Patamona and Taurepang in Raposa Serra do Sol, Roraima State, Brazil; (October 14, 2004) – Holmes Enrique Fernández, Jorge Salazar and other members of the Cauca Association of Persons Displaced from the Naya, Colombia; (September 27, 2004) – Raúl Javier Gatica Bautista, Mexico; (September 23, 2004) – Women leaders of the Wayúu Indigenous people, Colombia; (August 17, 2004) – Community of San Mateo de Huanchor, Peru; (February 27, 2004) – Leonidas Iza, Ecuador; (October 3, 2003) – Amílcar Mendez, Guatemala; (October 2, 2003) – Members of 15 cabildos and resguardos of the Pijao Indigenous people, Colombia; (September 24, 2003) – Kankuamo Indigenous people, Colombia; (August 11, 2003) – Rosalina Tuyuc, Guatemala; (May 5, 2003) – Members of the Sarayaku Indigenous community.

62 See, e.g., Resolution No. 13/24, PM 1109-23 – Selected families of the native Kichwa community Santa Rosillo de Yanayacu, Peru.

63 This language was included, for example, in the precautionary measure issued on 5 May 2003, in favour of the members of the Sarayaku Indigenous people in Ecuador; on 24 September 2003, to the Kankuamo Indigenous peoples in Colombia; and on 4 February 2005, to the Wiwa Indigenous people of Colombia.

factors tied to the demarcation of lands'[64] claimed by the beneficiary community. Although this precedent did not elaborate on the protection of territorial rights, it made clear that the root cause of the violence faced by the beneficiaries was a land dispute with another Indigenous community, and that Mexico should address this issue to reduce the risk of irreparable harm to the lives and physical integrity of the beneficiaries.

*Protection of life and personal integrity in the context of eviction and displacement*

Between January 2001 and January 2025, the IACHR granted 12 precautionary measures to Indigenous and tribal peoples at risk of violent displacement or eviction from their territories. These measures do not address concrete territorial rights and are limited to the protection of life, physical integrity, and, to a lesser extent, freedom of movement.[65]

Most of these measures were aimed at alleviating the humanitarian conditions caused by the enforcement of eviction orders. Five precedents requested the states concerned to enable the beneficiary community or its individual members to return to their traditional lands under safe conditions.[66] The precautionary measures issued on 26 September 2001, in favour of the Yakye Axa Indigenous Community in Paraguay, are the only precedent ever granted outside the context of a contentious case that combines the protection of the life and personal integrity with the suspension of a judicial eviction order.

---

[64] PM 102/10 – Inhabitants of the Mixteca Indigenous Community of Lázaro Cárdenas, Putla, Oaxaca, Mexico.

[65] These measures are the following: Res. No. 28/24 – Members of the Tapeba Indigenous People of Caucaia, Brazil; Res. No. 62/23 – Triqui families from the Community of Tierra Blanca Cópala who have been displaced to the neighbouring community of Yosoyuxi Copala, Mexico; Res. No. 43/18, PM 44-18 – Maya Q'eqchi' community La Cumbre Sa'kuxhá, Guatemala; Res. No. 7/18, PM 872-17 – Maya Q'eqchi' community Nueva Semuy Chacchilla, Guatemala; Res. No. 3/18, PM 860-17 – Indigenous families of the Chaab´il Ch´och' community, Guatemala; PM 255/11 – Nasa people of Toribio, San Francisco, Tacueyo, and Jambalo Reservations, Colombia; PM 121/11 – 14 Q'echi Indigenous Communities of the Municipality of Panzós, Guatemala; PM 321/10 – Rapa Nui Indigenous People, Chile; PM 355/10 – 21 Families of the Nonam Community of the Wounaan Indigenous People, Colombia; PM 118/09 – Naso Indigenous People of the Bocas del Toro Region, Panama; (October 12, 2004) – Indigenous Community Kelyenmagategma of the Enxet People, Paraguay; (September 26, 2001) – Yakye Axa Indigenous Community, Paraguay.

[66] These precedents are: Resolution No. 28/24, Resolution No. 62/23, PM 255-11, PM 355-10 and Indigenous Community Kelyenmagategma of the Enxet People.

*Protection of life and physical integrity of voluntary isolated communities*

By January 2025, the IACHR had issued three precautionary measures to Indigenous communities in voluntary isolation. Although their main purpose was to protect the lives and physical integrity of the beneficiaries, they also asked the states concerned to guarantee the intangibility of the territories inhabited by self-isolated communities. Their unique situation of vulnerability seems to justify precautionary measures aimed at preventing the intrusion into their territory, which could lead to violent clashes, the spread of deadly diseases, and, ultimately, the extermination of these communities. The content of the precautionary measures adopted under this approach can be outlined as follows:

Resolution No. 4/16 PM 54-13 – Matter of communities in voluntary isolation of the Ayoreo Totobiegosode People, Paraguay

On 3 February 2016, the IACHR granted precautionary measures to protect these communities in voluntary isolation; to avoid deforestation; to create a mechanism to protect and prevent third parties from entering their lands; and to elaborate specific protocols, based on international standards, to avoid unwanted contact with the beneficiaries.

Indigenous peoples of Mashco Piro, Yora, and Amahuaca, Peru

On 22 March 2007, the IACHR granted precautionary measures and asked Peru to prevent irreparable harm to the life and personal integrity of these communities, resulting from the illegal logging and the presence of third persons in their territories.

Tagaeri and Taromenami Indigenous peoples, Ecuador

On 10 May 2006, the IACHR granted precautionary measures for these peoples in voluntary isolation. Members of the Taromenami tribe were allegedly murdered on 26 April 2006, during reprisals linked to illegal logging in the Yasuní Park. Ecuador was asked to protect the territory inhabited by the beneficiaries from third party invasions.

In addition to these three precedents, a fourth precautionary measure was granted in April 2011 in the *Belo Monte* case regarding Brazil, aimed at protecting the intangibility of self-isolated Indigenous peoples and the life and physical integrity of several other contacted communities. This precedent is discussed in subsection 4.1.2, as it contains additional elements that go beyond the scope of the three measures described in this subsection.

### 4.1.2 Precautionary measures requesting the stay of domestic decisions, adopted in the context of a contentious case

From the mid-1990s until early 2011, the IACHR issued eight precautionary measures ordering the suspension of large-scale projects in Indigenous peoples' territories. These orders are similar to injunctive measures in domestic procedural law, as well as interim/provisional measures indicated by other international adjudicative bodies. The Commission's eight precedents can be summarised as follows:

*PM 269/08 – Members of the Lof Paichil Antriao Community of the Mapuche Indigenous People, Argentina*

> On 6 Apri 2011, the IACHR granted precautionary measures for the members of the Lof Paichil Antriao community of the Mapuche Indigenous people, who faced a risk of irreparable harm stemming from acts of harassment and of the destruction of their sacred place known as a Rewe, due to a large-scale project construction underway in their territory. The request alleged that while the Rewe is currently being protected by a domestic legal measure, the members of the community had not been able to access the site to practise their rituals. The IACHR asked Argentina to adopt the necessary measures so that the protective legal measure to prevent alteration of the Rewe is not lifted until the IACHR has ruled on the merits of Petition 962-08. The IACHR also requested the State to ensure effective compliance with the aforementioned legal measure.

*PM 105/11 – Communities of the Kuna of Madungandí and Emberá of Bayano Peoples, Panama*

> On 5 Apri 2011, the IACHR granted precautionary measures for the Kuna of Madungandí and Emberá of Bayano peoples, in Panama. The measure was connected to Case 12.354, whose Admissibility Report No. 58/09 had been approved on 21 April 2009. The request alleged that in February and March of 2011 there were massive intrusions into the territories of the Kuna of Madungandí and Emberá of Bayano Indigenous reserve. It asserted that colonists violently seized and destroyed primary forests used by the Indigenous communities to ensure their food supply. The IACHR requested Panama to protect the ancestral territory of the Kuna of Madungandí and Emberá of Bayano peoples from intrusions by third parties and from the destruction of their forests and crops, until such time as it adopts a final decision on the merits of Case 12.354.

*PM 395-09 – Maho Indigenous Community, Suriname*

> On October 27, 2010, the IACHR granted precautionary measures for the inhabitants of the Maho Indigenous Community, in Suriname. The request alleged that since 1990 third parties have been encroaching upon the land reserved for the Maho Community in 1971. It also maintained that the invaders destroyed the community's crops and threatened its members. The IACHR asked Suriname to ensure

the presence of the Maho Community in the land that was reserved for them, free from incursions from third persons, until it adopts a decision on the merits of an individual complaint filed along with the request for precautionary measure.

## *PM 260-07 – Communities of the Maya People (Sipakapense and Mam) of the Sipacapa and San Miguel Ixtahuacán Municipalities in the Department of San Marcos, Guatemala*

On 20 May 2010, the IACHR adopted precautionary measures for the members of 18 communities of the Maya Indigenous people in Guatemala. In November 2003 the Ministry of Energy and Mines granted the Montana company a licence to mine for gold and silver for 25 years in the municipalities of Sipacapa and San Miguel Ixtahuacán. The petitioners alleged that mining began without a prior, complete, free, and informed consultation with the affected communities. The mining allegedly produced serious consequences for the life, personal integrity, environment, and property of the affected Indigenous people. Guatemala was asked to suspend the operations of the project and to implement effective measures to prevent environmental contamination, until such time as the IACHR adopts a decision on the merits of the petition associated with the request for precautionary measures. It was also asked to decontaminate the water sources of the beneficiary communities and to ensure their members access to water fit for human consumption and to begin a health care and assistance program for the beneficiaries.

## *PM 56/08 – Ngöbe Indigenous Communities and Others, Panama*

On 18 June 2009, the IACHR granted precautionary measures for members of the Indigenous communities of the Ngöbe people. The request alleged that a 20-year concession was granted to a company to build hydroelectric dams along the Teribe-Changuinola River. One of the dams would flood an area inhabited by four Ngöbe Indigenous communities. The petitioners alleged that the lands affected by the dam are part of their ancestral territory, used to carry out their traditional hunting and fishing activities. The IACHR requested Panama to suspend the construction until it adopts a final decision on a related contentious case. The IACHR also asked Panama to guarantee the free circulation, life, and physical integrity of the members of the Ngöbe community, and to prevent acts of violence or intimidation. As explained below, on 19 January 2010, the IACHR requested provisional measures on this matter, but the IACtHR dismissed the request.

## *Garifuna Community of San Juan, Honduras*

On 7 July 2006, the IACHR granted precautionary measures for the Garifuna community of San Juan, in Honduras. The situation of this Indigenous community *vis-à-vis* the conflicts related to ownership of their ancestral lands was the subject of a petition being processed by the IACHR. The IACHR asked Honduras to adopt the necessary measures to protect the lives and personal integrity of the leaders of the community, to protect the right to ownership of said lands, and to suspend the implementation of any judicial or administrative action that could affect the rights derived from the beneficiary community's ancestral property, until such time as it adopts a final decision with respect to Petition 674-06.

*Garifuna Community of Triunfo de la Cruz, Honduras*

On 28 April 2006, the IACHR granted precautionary measures for the Garifuna community of Triunfo de la Cruz, in Honduras. The situation of this Indigenous community *vis-à-vis* the conflicts related to ownership of their ancestral lands was the subject of a petition being processed by the IACHR. Honduras was asked to suspend the implementation of any judicial or administrative action that could affect the rights derived from the beneficiary community's ancestral territory, until such time as the bodies of the Inter-American system adopt a final decision with respect to the contentious case.

*Mercedes Julia Huenteao and Others, Chile*

On 1 August 2003, the IACHR granted precautionary measures in favour of five Pehuenche Indigenous women in Chile. The individual complaint associated with the request alleged that the state was carrying out a project to install a hydroelectric dam that would adversely affect the ancestral territory inhabited by the proposed beneficiaries. Chile was asked to abstain from undertaking any action that would modify the *status quo* of the matter until such time as it could adopt a decision on the merits of the case. The Commission also requested Chile to avoid or suspend any judicial or administrative action that would imply the displacement of the beneficiaries from their traditional land. On 11 March 2004, the IACHR approved a friendly settlement report in this case.

This list shows a consistent practice of issuing precautionary measures to preserve Indigenous territorial rights. April 2011 was the last time that the IACHR followed this practice, as explained in the following subsection.

### 4.1.3 Precautionary measures requesting the suspension of domestic decisions in the absence of a related contentious case

There are only two precedents under this category, the most controversial of which took place in April 2011. It refers to the precautionary measure granted to suspend the construction of a hydroelectric dam on the Xingu River in Brazil, one of the country's largest, located in the heart of the Amazon forest. This project, known as Belo Monte, had a devastating impact on a number of Indigenous communities whose physical and cultural existence depends on the conservation of the Xingu River's basin and its wildlife. The IACHR asked Brazil to suspend the approval of the project, even though there was no underlying petition or case under its jurisdiction. This decision went beyond the scope of the eight precedents described in the previous subsection, all of which were framed as injunctions to ensure the *effet utile* of a future decision on the merits of a related contentious case.

The second precedent dates from July 2006, in an atypical circumstance in which the Government of Guatemala did not oppose the adoption of precautionary measures. These are the main aspects of this second precedent.

*Maya Sitio El Rosario-Naranjo Community, Guatemala*
On 14 July 2006, the IACHR granted precautionary measures in favour of the Sitio El Rosario-Naranjo Community, identified as an archaeological monument and sacred place for those who practice Mayan spirituality. According to the request, the area of El Rosario-Naranjo had been titled to private actors who began to build a housing project and commissioned a study that proposed a significant reduction of the Indigenous sacred land. The Guatemalan Supreme Court declared that the construction in El Rosario-Naranjo would interfere with Mayan religious and social celebrations and ordered the construction to stop. However, this ruling was not complied with. After being notified by the IACHR on the request for precautionary measures, the Guatemalan government stressed that there was nothing to prevent the IACHR from intervening, given the disregard for the Supreme Court's ruling by private actors. Considering this, the Inter-American Commission asked the state of Guatemala to take the necessary measures to suspend any housing project in the Rosario-Naranjo Archaeological Center.

Given the government's endorsement and other unique circumstances surrounding this decision, it can be concluded that the Belo Monte precautionary measure regarding Brazil is the only precedent in which the IACHR has requested the suspension of a domestic decision affecting Indigenous territorial rights outside the scope of an underlying contentious case. The legal justification for this decision is as follows:

*PM 382/10 – Indigenous Communities of the Xingu River Basin, Pará, Brazil*
On 1 April 2011, the IACHR granted precautionary measures to 10 Indigenous communities living in the Xingu River basin in the state of Pará, Brazil, as well as to communities in voluntary isolation in the area. It was alleged that the lives and physical integrity of the beneficiaries were at risk due to the construction of the Belo Monte hydroelectric dam in the region. Brazil was asked to suspend the permitting process for the Belo Monte project until it (1) conducts a prior consultation – free, informed, in good faith, culturally appropriate, and with the aim of reaching an agreement – with each of the affected Indigenous communities that are beneficiaries of these precautionary measures; (2) ensure that the Indigenous communities have access to the project's social and environmental impact study, in an accessible format, including translation into the respective Indigenous languages; (3) adopt measures to protect the life and physical integrity of the members of the Indigenous peoples living in voluntary

isolation of the Xingu Basin, and to prevent the spread of diseases among them.[67]

On 29 July 2011, the IACHR modified its order, and requested that the State: (1) adopt measures to protect the life, health, and physical integrity of the members of the Indigenous communities who are in voluntary isolation; (2) ensure that the pending process of titling the ancestral lands of the Indigenous peoples of the Xingu Basin is completed soon; and (3) adopt effective measures to protect these ancestral lands from invasion and occupation by non-Indigenous people. The IACHR decided that the controversy over the alleged lack of prior consultation and consent has turned into a discussion on the merits of an individual complaint filed after the original decision of 1 April 2011, for which this aspect was removed from the precautionary measure.

The Belo Monte precedent triggered a sharp reaction from the Brazilian government at the time. The then-president, Dilma Rousseff, withdrew her ambassador to the OAS and froze all financial contributions to the organization.[68] Brazil's response fuelled a hostile diplomatic environment, led by other countries dissatisfied with certain decisions of the IACHR, such as Ecuador, Bolivia, and Venezuela.[69]

Created in 2011 by the OAS Permanent Council, the 'Special Working Group to Reflect on the Work of the Inter-American Commission on Human Rights with a view to Strengthening the Inter-American System for the Protection of Human Rights'[70] galvanized a kind of collective diplomatic catharsis against the IACHR. This process led the Inter-American Commission to make one of

---

[67] According to public information, the Belo Monte hydroelectric complex would be the third biggest in the world with a capacity to generate more than 11,000 GW of electricity every year. For more information on the Belo Monte hydroelectric plant see: Tom Phillips, 'Brazil to build controversial Belo Monte hydroelectric dam in Amazon rainforest', *The Guardian* (London, 2 February 2010) www.guardian.co.uk/environment/2010/feb/02/brazil-amazon-rainforest-hydroelectric-dam.

[68] For a detailed account of the Brazilian government's response to the Belo Monte's precautionary measures, see: Amazon Watch, 'Brazil Green Lights Controversial Amazon Dam, Steamrolling Environmental Laws and Human Rights' (*Amazon Watch*, 1 June 2011) http://amazonwatch.org/news/2011/0601-brazil-green-lights-controversial-amazon-dam.

[69] For a detailed description of the effects of the diplomatic turmoil against the IACHR that took place between 2011 and 2013 and its impact on how the Inter-American body changed its institutional policies, see: Cerqueira and Salazar, 'The Functions of the Inter-American Commission on Human Rights Before, During, and After the Strengthening Process' (n 10) 129.

[70] OAS, 'Report of the Special Working Group to Reflect on the Workings of the Inter-American Commission on Human Rights with a view to Strengthening

the most comprehensive changes to its Rules of Procedure and institutional policies in its history.[71] By acceding to several demands of dissatisfied governments, the IACHR managed to avoid a more dangerous move towards a reform to inter-state instruments, such as the American Convention and its Statute.

Although the so-called strengthening process was triggered by several factors that went beyond the IACHR's practice on precautionary measures, it forced this body to limit the situations in which it grants such measures. Article 25 of its Rules of Procedure was significantly modified, introducing additional procedural requirements and stricter rules for granting these measures.[72] Clearly, one of the consequences of the 'strengthening process' was the IACHR's new practice of refraining from issuing precautionary measures to suspend large-scale projects in Indigenous and tribal territories, even when they are related to contentious cases alleging foreseeable, serious, and irreparable harm. This change has deprived hundreds of peoples and communities of an important tool to protect their territorial rights at the IAHRS.

### 4.2 Provisional Measures of the Inter-American Court of Human Rights

Compared to the IACHR's precautionary measures, the IACtHR has issued far fewer provisional measures concerning Indigenous peoples.[73] As of January 2025, the Inter-American Court had granted eight measures, all of which are

the Inter-American System for the Protection of Human Rights' (13 December 2011) OEA/Ser.G, GT/SIDH-13/11 rev. 2.

[71] See: IACHR Resolution 1/13, 'Reform of the Rules of Procedure, Policies and Practices' http://www.oas.org/en/iachr/mandate/strengthening.asp.

[72] During the strengthening process, some ambassadors and the Secretary-General of the OAS challenged the very binding nature of the precautionary measures, suggesting that this faculty should be regulated through an inter-state instrument, such as the IACHR Statute or the American Convention, and not by the Rules of Procedure of the Commission. Some of these statements are available in Portuguese at: http://g1.globo.com/brasil/noticia/2011/05/comissao-da-oea-deve-revisar-decisao-sobre-belo-monte-diz-secretario-geral.html.

[73] Unlike the IACHR, the IACtHR publishes resolutions rejecting provisional measures requests. There are four resolutions of this kind, related to the rights of Indigenous peoples. These are: *Case of the Tagaeri and Taromenane Indigenous Peoples v Ecuador* (Order of 18 October 2022); *Case of two girls of the Taromenane indigenous people in voluntary isolation v Ecuador* (Order of 31 March 2014); *Case of Garífuna Community of Barra Vieja regarding Honduras* (Order of 14 October 2014); *Case of Four Ngöbe Indigenous Communities and its members regarding Panama* (Order of 28 May 2010).

limited to protecting the right to life and personal integrity of Indigenous peoples.[74]

Most of these precedents were adopted in the context of acts of violence, many of which were committed by illegal armed groups and other non-state actors. Only one precedent relates to the situation of Indigenous persons deprived of their liberty (*Matter of four Mayangna Indigenous in Nicaragua*) and two relate to the situation of Indigenous peoples displaced from their traditional lands. In some measures concerning the forcible displacement of Indigenous communities, the states concerned were ordered to 'protect the territorial integrity and cultural identity' and to protect 'the rights to life and personal integrity of the [beneficiary communities …] ensuring the safety of their belongings and crops abandoned in the communities during their displacement, and the necessary measures for their safe return'.[75]

In the case of the Indigenous people of Kankuamo in Colombia, the IACHR had requested the Inter-American Court to adopt provisional measures to '[p]rotect the life and the integrity of persons of the members of the Kankuamo Indigenous people in the Sierra Nevada de Santa Marta, and respect their cultural identity and their special relationship with their ancestral territory'.[76] The IACtHR granted such measures and added a more specific order to protect the right to freedom of movement and to ensure that the displaced beneficiaries could safely return to their ancestral lands.[77]

---

74 These provisional measures are: *Matter of four Mayangna Indigenous persons deprived of liberty regarding Nicaragua* (Order of 27 June 2023); *Matter of Members of the Miskitu and Mayangna Indigenous Peoples of the North Caribbean Coast regarding Nicaragua* (Order of 27 June 2023); *Matter of members of the Yanomami, Ye'kwana and Munduruku Indigenous Peoples regarding Brazil* (Order of 1 July 2022); *Matter of members of the Choréachi Indigenous Community regarding Mexico* (Order of 25 March 2017); *Matter of Members of the Miskitu Indigenous Peoples of the North Caribbean Coast regarding Nicaragua* (Order of 1 September 2016); *Matter of Kichwa Indigenous People of Sarayaku regarding Ecuador* (Order of Human Rights of 6 July 2004); *Matter of Indigenous Community Kankuamo regarding Colombia* (Order of 5 July 2004); *Case of the Mayagna (Sumo) Awas Tingni Community v Nicaragua* (Order of 6 September 2002).

75 See, e.g.: *Members of the Miskitu and Mayangna Indigenous Peoples of the North Caribbean Coast regarding Nicaragua*, Extension of Provisional Measures (Order of the Inter-American Court of Human Rights of 27 June 2023 and initial Order of provisional measures of 1 September 2016).

76 *Case of Kankuamo (Colombia)*, Provisional Measures (Order of 5 July 2004) considering para 1.

77 ibid paras 1 and 3. The cited requests were reiterated by the IACtHR in its order of 3 April 2009.

On 15 June 2004, the Commission made a similar request for provisional measures to protect the lives, personal integrity and special relationship of members of the Kichwa Indigenous people of Sarayaku to their territory in Ecuador.[78] After addressing the alleged arbitrary detentions, shootings, beatings, threats, and roadblocks within the Sarayaku territory, the IACtHR called on Ecuador to:

> adopt, forthwith, the measures necessary to protect the life and integrity of person of the members of the Kichwa Indigenous community of Sarayaku and of those who represent and defend them in proceedings ordered before the authorities … [and] to guarantee the right to freedom of movement of the members of the Kichwa community of Sarayaku.[79]

The Kankuamo and Sarayaku precedents combine a general order to protect life and physical integrity with a more specific order to protect the special safeguards of Indigenous territories. It should be noted that the subsidiary protection of territorial rights in these precedents was not framed as an injunction, i.e., they did not order the suspension of decisions of a state that could cause irreparable harm. The only request for provisional measures in which the IACHR asked the Court to do so is the *Matter of Four Ngöbe Indigenous Communities and their Members regarding Panama*, which was ultimately rejected by the Court.

On 19 January 2010, the IACHR submitted this request to the IACtHR, claiming that Panama had failed to comply with its 18 June 2009 precautionary measures.[80] The IACtHR dismissed the request on the grounds that the Commission failed to prove several aspects of its claim, such as:

a. the alleged death threats or acts of police repression against the leaders of certain communities, given that there is no precise data after August 2009, that is, after the start of the agreements between the State, the company and the communities;
b. the problems that would result from the deforestation methodology currently implemented, as well as with regards [sic] to the flood that would affect the resettlement of the community's members;

---

[78] *Case of Pueblo Indigena Sarayaku (Ecuador)*, Provisional Measures (Order of 6 July 2004) considering para 1.

[79] ibid paras 1 and 2. In its orders of 17 June 2005 and 4 February 2010, the Court reiterated the provisional measures and, additionally, called upon the Ecuadorian state to 'promptly and effectively remove the explosive material buried in the territory where said community is settled'.

[80] *Case of Four Ngöbe Indigenous Communities and their Members v Panama*, Provisional Measures (Order of 28 May 2010) para 1.

c. the apparent conformity expressed by several members of the Indigenous communities in relation to the lands offered and, in certain cases, already granted for their resettlement;
d. [...]
e. the alleged restrictions to freedom of movement and to the traditional mobility of the members of the Ngöbe community, considering the lack of claims regarding the manner in which the deforestation is performed, and in relation to that recently reported by the State on Changuinola River.[81]

The IACtHR pointed out that some of the arguments raised by the Commission 'seemed to refer to the merits of the case', such as the allegation that agreements were signed by leaders of the community under coercion and that the communities were subjected to restrictions on their freedom of movement within their territory. In assessing these allegations, the Court emphasized that in a request for provisional measures, 'it cannot consider any argument that is not strictly related with the extreme gravity, urgency and need to avoid irreparable damages to individuals [and] any other issue should be resolved within the respective contentious case'.[82]

In its analysis of the urgency of the situation, the Court noted that the Commission had received an individual complaint in favour of the Ngöbe communities on 7 March 2008, but did not file the request for provisional measures until almost two years later, on 19 January 2010. The IACtHR concluded that 'the Inter-American Commission should proceed with greater speed on the decision on this petition. On the contrary, there would be an inconsistency in that the urgency claimed to request provisional measures does not imply an urgent consideration regarding the assessment of merits of the petition'.[83]

Although the Court's resolution on the *Ngöbe communities matter v Panama* is not clear on whether provisional measures are an appropriate mechanism to suspend decisions with significant impacts on Indigenous territories, it does include a very high threshold of corroboration for the proposed beneficiaries and their representatives.

---

81 *Case of Four Ngöbe Indigenous Communities and their Members v Panama* (n 80) considering para 11.

82 ibid, considering para 13.

83 ibid, considering para 16.

# 5 POSSIBLE STEPS TO IMPROVE THE PROTECTION OF INDIGENOUS PEOPLES' TERRITORIAL RIGHTS IN THE INTER-AMERICAN SYSTEM

According to the current approach of the IACHR, the allegations concerning Indigenous territorial rights are outside the scope of the precautionary measure's mechanism and are intrinsically tied to an analysis on the merits of a contentious case.[84] A recent resolution on the precautionary measure granted to the Indigenous Carab communities in Guyana summarizes this position as follows:

> [...] both applicants and State have presented arguments regarding the recognition of land ownership in favour of the proposed beneficiaries and the extension of rights derived from it, as well as the legality of the mine exploitation by third parties [...] *the IACHR adverts that they require an analysis of (sic) merits to determine possible violations of the American Declaration of the Rights and Duties of Man and therefore, fall outside the scope of the present precautionary measures procedure.* As indicated above, this is better suited to be addressed by the Petition and Case system. The analysis that follows relates exclusively to the alleged serious and urgent situations presenting a risk of irreparable harm, which can be resolved without making any determinations on the merits.[85]

This reasoning is problematic, since there is no need to anticipate a conclusion on the merits of a case in dispute in these urgent measures framed as an injunction. The IACHR could issue this type of measure – as it did until 2011 – and then conclude that the alleged violations raised in the contentious case were not substantiated. The underlying petition or case could also be dismissed for failure to comply with the admissibility requirements set forth in Article 28 of its Rules of Procedure. The logical consequence of the dismissal of the petition either on admissibility or on the merits would be the lifting of the precautionary measures previously granted.

Depending on the magnitude of the harm that the state's decision may cause, the rejection of a precautionary measure may render the reparations adopted

---

[84] See, e.g., IACHR Resolution No. 83/23, PM 416-13 – Tolupan indigenous members of the Movimiento Amplio por la Justicia y la Dignidad (Broad Movement for Justice and Dignity), Honduras, para 54; and IACtHR Resolution 88/2021, Precautionary Measures Nos 405-09, 112-16, 405-09, and 112-16, *Case of Berta Isabel Cáceres, her family unit, members of COPINH and Others v Honduras*, para 80.

[85] IACHR Resolution No. 41/23 PM 196-23, Indigenous Carib Community of Chinese Landing, Guyana, para 49. The italicized text has been added to the original version.

on the merits moot. This is particularly true in situations involving large-scale extraction of natural resources. As explained previously, Inter-American standards acknowledge the special relationship of Indigenous and tribal peoples to their ancestral territories, which is a prerequisite for the exercise of other fundamental rights, including their physical and cultural integrity.[86] Simply put, the IACHR has excluded the protection of these rights from the precautionary measure mechanism without any reasonable explanation as to how they could be redressed if the state proceeds with certain large-scale projects.

The flaws in the current IACHR's reasoning are also evident when we evaluate the precautionary measures of an injunctive nature that are regularly granted to suspend state decisions in other circumstances. The IACHR has granted several measures of this type, for instance, to stay the enforcement of death penalties, when there is a related contentious case pending a final decision. The purpose of these measures is to preserve the Commission's jurisdiction over a petition or case, since the reparations established for potential human rights violations will not be achieved if the proposed beneficiary/alleged victim is ultimately executed.[87] Despite the various factual and legal

---

86 In the matter of the Guapoy´s community of the Guarani Kaiowá Indigenous People regarding Brazil, the IACHR outlined these standards as follows: '[...] in the case of indigenous peoples, the lack of access to land and natural resources can lead to conditions of misery for the indigenous communities concerned, since the lack of possession of and access to their territories prevents them from using and enjoying the natural resources they need to provide themselves with the goods necessary for their subsistence. The foregoing impacts on the conditions for a dignified life, given that for indigenous peoples, the lack of access to their ancestral territory causes them suffering, and damages the preservation of their ways of life, customs and language'. See: IACHR Resolution No. 50/2022, PM 517-22, Members of the Guapoy´s community of the Guarani Kaiowá Indigenous People regarding Brazil, 2 October 2022, para 35.

87 Strictly speaking, the death penalty does not violate Inter-American standards per se in those countries – such as the United States and some Caribbean nations – that have not ratified the American Convention and its Optional Protocol on the Abolition of the Death Penalty. However, in virtually all the merits reports on death penalty cases – most of which involve the United States – the Commission has concluded that either the method of execution, the domestic process, or both, violate the guarantees protected by the American Declaration. Likewise, the merits reports adopted by the IACHR and the rulings issued by the IACtHR on cases related to large-scale projects in Indigenous territories have all established violations of fundamental rights related to the special relationship of Indigenous and tribal communities with their traditional territories, which has been the subject of serious harm. In this sense, it is worth asking whether the reparations established in these merits reports and judgments could not be implemented due to irreparable

differences between precautionary measures suspending the execution of the death penalty and those suspending state decisions with significant impact on Indigenous territories, they are equally grounded on the need to preserve the *effet utile* of the IACHR's jurisdiction.[88] In other words, they serve the precautionary more than the preventive function of the urgent measure mechanism.

In addition to the examples of the death penalty described here, the IACHR has granted a small number of precautionary measures of an injunctive nature in cases related to the international custody of minors[89] and to the enforcement of extradition orders that violate the prohibition of *non-refoulement*.[90] These precedents are in line with the practice of other supranational human rights bodies and with the general principles of domestic procedural law.

According to the general principles of procedural law, the party seeking an injunction must satisfy two requirements: the *fumus boni iuris* ('smoke of good right') and the *periculum in mora* ('danger in delay'). The first requirement means that the request to preserve a legal situation is linked to the existence of a right protected by the applicable law. The second means that the

---

damage to the traditional territories of the Indigenous peoples or communities concerned. Although this question is not the subject of this chapter, it would support the argument presented here that the reparations established in a final judgment in a contentious case may be meaningless if the organs of the Inter-American system do not order the suspension of certain state decisions that have a significant impact on traditional lands.

[88] Every single resolution on precautionary measures adopted by the IACHR in the last five years includes the following standard paragraph, which emphasizes the uniqueness of this type of 'injunctive precautionary measure' linked to a pending contentious case: 'Regarding their precautionary nature, these measures have the purpose of preserving a legal situation while under consideration by the organs of the Inter-American system. They aim to safeguard the rights at risk until the petition pending before the Inter-American system is resolved. Their object and purpose are to ensure the integrity and effectiveness of an eventual decision on the merits and, thus, avoid any further infringement of the rights at issue, a situation that may adversely affect the useful effect (*effet utile*) of the final decision. In this regard, precautionary or provisional measures enable the State concerned to comply with the final decision and, if necessary, to implement the ordered reparations.'

[89] See, e.g., IACHR Resolution No. 7/17 PM 68/17, Youth Panambí, Paraguay.

[90] See, e.g., *Wong Ho Wing v Peru*, Provisional Measures 10/09. This precedent gave rise to a provisional measure issued by the Inter-American Court. See: *Wong Ho Wing v Peru*, Provisional Measures (Order of 28 May 2010). It should be noted that in this precedent, the Court dismissed the case in question in its judgment on the merits, for which the provisional measures were lifted a few months after their adoption. Again, this is a normal practice of any judicial body authorized to issue precautionary/interim measures.

available evidence corroborates an imminent risk of infringement to that right. The adoption of precautionary measures to suspend state decisions that could cause irreparable harm to Indigenous territories requires a *prima facie* analysis of the existence of a *fumus boni iuris*, which is an adjudicative exercise utterly different from a prejudgment on the merits of a case.

In this sense, the complex and sometimes hostile diplomatic environment in which the IACHR exercises its mandate, and not the existence of legal constraints, seems to be the reason why the protection of Indigenous territorial rights was excluded from the precautionary measure mechanism back in 2011. While the political consequences of the IACHR's decisions go beyond the scope of this chapter, it is worth concluding with a legal path that could reinstate at least part of the approach abandoned in 2011.

Precautionary measures should be adopted when a *prima facie* assessment of the information indicates that the consent of Indigenous or tribal peoples whose territories are at risk of imminent irreparable harm has been violated. As described previously, there is a well-established rule in international human rights law that establishes the consent of such peoples when the authorization of certain economic activities has a profound impact on their cultural identity and physical subsistence. Articles 10 and 29(2) of the United Nations Declaration on the Rights of Indigenous Peoples uphold this rule, for example, with regards to the storage of hazardous materials on Indigenous lands or to decisions that could lead to their forced displacement. The IACHR has gone even further, explicitly adding industrial mining and hydrocarbons extraction to the list of activities that cannot be authorized without the consent of Indigenous and tribal peoples. The denial of precautionary measures in this type of situation would render the reparations in a related contentious case unachievable, especially if the decision on the merits is made several years after the filing of the complaint.

In light of the above, the IACHR should adopt a twofold practice consisting of: (1) granting precautionary measures to suspend large-scale projects with significant impacts on Indigenous territories until it issues a decision on the merits of the related case; and (2) prioritizing the processing of contentious cases that allege imminent irreparable harm to Indigenous territorial rights. With regard to the first suggestion, the IACHR should request information that establishes, with a *prima facie* standard of proof, that the concessions in question are those in which the Inter-American jurisprudence requires the mandatory consent of the Indigenous peoples or communities that suffer a potential impact.

As to the second suggestion, given the length of years and even decades that a petition can take at the IAHRS,[91] the decision to prioritize should be made on a broader basis and not only when the Commission decides to issue precautionary measures. This practice would correct a troubling omission in Resolution 4/23, which establishes the IACHR's policies for prioritizing petitions and cases that meet certain criteria. Adopted in December 2023, this resolution describes several examples of matters that merit expedited processing, such as international disputes over the custody of minors, deportation, or extradition when there is a risk of torture, lack of medical care for persons deprived of their liberty, etc.[92] Unfortunately, the resolution omitted the risk of significant harm to Indigenous and tribal territories from the list of circumstances justifying priority processing.

# 6 CONCLUSIONS

Although the IAHRS is the supranational system with the most advanced standards on Indigenous territorial rights, the current practice of its organs makes it virtually impossible to protect these rights through precautionary and provisional measures. Despite this limitation, some specific allegations related to the adverse impacts of large-scale projects in Indigenous and tribal lands are still addressed by the Court and, in particular, by the Commission. These include the protection of the life and physical integrity and, in some cases, the health of the communities as a whole or of their individual members, in the following circumstances:

- Threats, criminalization, and other acts of violence in retaliation for an Indigenous community's efforts to obtain legal recognition of its traditional territories and to defend its natural resources.
- Serious environmental degradation, such as oil spills and the presence of toxic substances in traditional lands, with a lack of access to adequate food, sanitation, and medical care.
- Forcible evictions and other forms of displacement. In a small number of these cases, states were requested to take the necessary measures to allow the affected community or individual members to return to their lands under safe conditions.

---

[91] See: Fernando Basch and others, 'La efectividad del sistema interamericano de protección de derechos humanos: Un enfoque cuantitativo sobre su funcionamiento y sobre el cumplimiento de sus decisiones' (2010) 7 SUR 9. See also: Camilo Sánchez, 'Una década de peticiones y casos ante la CIDH' (2021) 23 *Aportes* 28.

[92] IACHR Resolution 4/23 – Doc. 329 Prioritization Policy for Petitions and Cases, 20 December 2023, para 2.

- Trespass and acts of violence, usually committed by illegal miners, loggers, and other non-state actors, in areas inhabited by Indigenous peoples in voluntary isolation.

While the precautionary and provisional measures remain accessible in these circumstances, the protection of Indigenous territorial rights has been excluded from these mechanisms since 2011, clearly due to political rather than legal constraints. This new approach has had a significant negative impact on Indigenous and tribal communities, which require a rapid response from the Inter-American bodies when their territories are at risk of irreparable harm.

It should be noted that the provisional measures of the Inter-American Court are usually requested by the IACHR when a state fails to comply with its precautionary measures. The last and only time that the IACHR requested this type of provisional measure was in the *Matter of the Four Ngöbe Indigenous Communities and their Members*, regarding Panama, in January 2010. Although the IACtHR rejected the request, it made no mention of the unsuitability of the provisional measures mechanism to prevent irreparable harm to Indigenous territorial rights. The Court could not reconsider this legal issue unless the IACHR modifies the approach inaugurated in 2011 and makes a new request for provisional measures.

This chapter concludes that the IACHR should reinstate the adoption of precautionary measures to suspend large-scale projects in exceptional circumstances that fall under the states' mandatory obligation to obtain the consent of Indigenous and tribal peoples. Finally, it should prioritize the processing of petitions and cases in which the alleged facts involve the risk of irreparable harm to their traditional territories, since they are indispensable to the exercise of rights such as physical subsistence and cultural integrity, the violation of which cannot be remedied.

# 10. Concluding remarks: impact is a rich concept that encompasses a variety of dimensions

**Clara Burbano Herrera and Yves Haeck**

The aim of this volume is to provide a range of analytical perspectives for assessing the impact of the Inter-American human rights system (IAHRS). This regional human rights framework has gained increasing significance due to several factors, including the breadth of human rights it safeguards, its dynamic and evolving interpretation of these rights, the obligations it imposes on states, and its interactions with domestic actors. As a result, there is a pressing need for more in-depth academic research on the system's impact, both within domestic contexts and beyond the scope of human rights institutions.[1]

This volume compiles the work of fifteen scholars who have written eight contributions. These contributions present a range of perspectives on the interpretation, definition and conceptualization of 'impact,' with a specific emphasis on the IAHRS. Several of these contributions focus on theoretical and methodological frameworks that delineate an impact model and point to the challenges of measuring impact (Engstrom; Ragone and Nocera; Urueña and Yate Cortes; Burbano Herrera, Haeck and Verwohlt-Hansen). A number of scholars have directed their attention towards the multifaceted nature of impact, meticulously unpacking its constituent elements, pledges and constraints (Engstrom; Ragone and Nocera; Urueña and Yate Cortes; Burbano Herrera, Haeck and Verwohlt-Hansen; Parra Vera and Trespalacios-Leal).

[1] This chapter wad developed by the authors within the framework of the Programme for Studies on Human Rights in Context at Ghent University (Belgium), and funded by the European Research Council (ERC) Grant Agreement No 101044852, as part of the ERC Project *IMPACTUM* and the Research Fund at Ghent University. Views and opinions expressed are, however, those of the authors only and do not necessarily reflect those of the European Union, the European Research Council Executive Agency, nor Ghent University. Neither the European Union nor the granting authority can be held responsible for them.

Some authors have suggested that measuring impact can be challenging, as it is a variable result of analysis that can vary depending on the specific situation. Therefore, it may not be feasible for researchers to assess all the potential features of impact (Burbano Herrera, Haeck and Verwohlt-Hansen). Other scholars have analyzed the multiple ways in which Inter-American law impacts practices, structures, and social outcomes both within and beyond the Inter-American human rights system by providing reflections on impact, focusing on specific countries such as Brazil, Colombia and Mexico (Morales Antoniazzi and Bejarano; Cerqueira; Boti Bernardi and Roriz; Parra Vera and Trespalacios-Leal) and specific groups such as: victims of the internal armed conflict in Colombia (Parra Vera and Trespalacios-Leal); Indigenous peoples (Boti Bernardi and Roriz; Cerqueira); LGBTQI+ people (Morales Antoniazzi and Bejarano); and people deprived of their liberty (Burbano Herrera, Haeck and Verwohlt Hansen). Each of these scholars provides an in-depth reflection on the concept in the specific context of the Americas, with the exception of Ragone and Nocera, and Morales Antoniazzi and Bejarano, who also provide a comparative analysis with reference to the European Court of Human Rights (ECtHR). The following lines will reflect on five aspects that most authors agree on to understand impact:

1. Impact as distinct from compliance;
2. Impact that can be categorized into various types;
3. Impact as the result of the dynamics between IAHRS bodies and domestic actors;
4. Political dynamics and context behind decision-making that influence impact; and
5. The importance of addressing victims in impact analysis.

## 1 IMPACT AS DISTINCT FROM COMPLIANCE

There is consensus among the contributors that the IAHRS exerts effects that extend beyond the specific case in question. The authors clearly differentiate between the concepts of impact and compliance. Particularly noteworthy is Engstrom's assertion that the IAHRS exerts effects that extend beyond those traditionally associated with enforcement and rule compliance models. Ragone and Nocera further posit that 'each legal system tends to construct a sphere of influence that is different from that of the usual intended recipients'. This is particularly evident in a legal system that aims to protect fundamental rights. Indeed, modern international courts are institutions whose systemic function is no longer limited to settling disputes between two or more parties. In this context, the activity of international human rights systems is not limited to the resolution of judicial disputes, since the systems also integrate a range of activities whose nature and analysis are more complex than the purely judicial perspective could provide. Morales and Bejarano explain that they use the term 'impact' as a more extensive analytical prism than 'compliance' to elucidate the dynamics of human rights protection in the Americas. While the concept of impact has been explored by scholars with various nuances, collectively they indicate a shift in focus from mere state compliance with judicial orders to a broader conceptualization of impact. This broad scope includes advances in the protection of human rights within the IAHRS and the uses of Inter-American standards by civil society groups. Urueña and Yate Cortes emphasize that the role of aesthetics in the Inter-American Court of Human Rights's (IACtHR) narratives is crucial in shaping the perception and impact of human rights discourse. These narratives have an aesthetic dimension in that they engage readers not only through legal argumentation but also by immersing them in a particular representation of events. Finally, Burbano Herrera, Haeck and Verwohlt-Hansen posit that impact and compliance are two distinct concepts. Nevertheless, the two concepts are interconnected, with impact having a close relationship with both compliance and non-compliance. According to them, the concept of compliance is closely associated with the actions undertaken by the state in question, to comply with the urgent measures requests issued by the human rights body. By contrast, the concept of impact is related to the effects of the decision on the beneficiary and beyond the beneficiary of the urgent measures.

## 2 IMPACT CAN BE CATEGORIZED INTO VARIOUS TYPES

The contributors propose the identification of various categories of impact. For instance, Ragone and Nocera propose three distinct types of impact arising from the case law of two regional human rights bodies: (1) 'ordinary impact' (or 'natural impact'), which refers to the influence exerted by the decisions of the IACtHR and/or ECtHR on all national judges and courts within the same region; (2) 'conformative impact' on non-judicial institutions, which pertains to the influence of both the ECtHR and IACtHR on state non-judicial institutions, particularly in relation to their interactions with parliaments and legislative bodies; and (3) 'systemic-transformative impact', which describes the effect on actors who are not embedded in judicial or institutional public organizations, but who are part of society. Burbano Herrera, Haeck and Verwohlt-Hansen propose a multi-layered framework to understand how impact may vary across society and from different perspectives. They distinguish between (in)direct and symbolic impacts, and outline the micro-level, meso-level and macro-level of analysis. They also recognize that impact may occur over various timeframes—short, medium and long term—and that its manifestation may differ depending on the point in time at which it is assessed. In a similar vein, Parra Vera and Trespalacios-Leal acknowledge the expanding body of literature on the impact of decisions made by the IAHRS's organs, within which different categories have been developed, such as instrumental, structural and symbolic impact.

## 3 IMPACT AS THE RESULT OF THE DYNAMICS BETWEEN IAHRS BODIES AND DOMESTIC ACTORS

It is contended that domestic actors play a crucial role in driving the impact of the system. In this regard, the impact of the IAHRS can be understood as a process that is iterative, interactive and dynamic (Engstrom; Boti Bernardi and Roriz; Morales Antoniazzi and Bejarano; Burbano Herrera, Haeck and Verwohlt-Hansen). The authors argue that the context-sensitivity and responsiveness of the Inter-American system have facilitated a comprehensive understanding of the circulation, appropriation and application of Inter-American standards among Latin American human rights actors (Engstrom, Morales Antoniazzi and Bejarano; Boti Bernardi and Roriz; Ragone and Nocera; Parra Vera and Trespalacios-Leal). Moreover, the normative and institutional evolution of the IAHRS since its establishment has progressively intensified interactions between the system and domestic legal frameworks, political processes and actors (Engstrom, Morales Antoniazzi and Bejarano). Engstrom emphasizes that an essential aspect of impact can be found in the dynamic interplay between various actors, underscoring the importance of dialogue and flexibility, as well as the ongoing experimentation with strategies for effective human rights implementation. Furthermore, Engstrom proposes a theory of institutional effectiveness centred on patterns of interaction, highlighting the potential for long-term impact through dynamic causal pathways that emerge over time. The authors contribute to the discussion of impact by conceptualizing it as a constantly evolving description of reality performed by the IACtHR. They analyze how the IACtHR constructs and modulates representations of violence, victims and justice, and how this influences how these realities are understood and internalized by the community of practice (Urueña and Yate Cortes).

## 4 THE POLITICAL DYNAMICS AND CONTEXT BEHIND DECISION-MAKING INFLUENCE IMPACT

To attain a more comprehensive understanding of the impact of the IAHRS, it is essential to consider the political context in which decisions are made. Boti Bernardi and Roriz, and Cerqueira argue that impact analysis must integrate an examination of the micro-dynamics of decision-making, which includes the specific bureaucratic politics within human rights bodies as well as their interactions with civil society groups and states. This holistic approach facilitates a deeper understanding of both the nature and substance of decisions made by human rights institutions. Furthermore, Boti Bernardi and Roriz emphasize that, in addition to analyzing how international human rights decisions are received and implemented in particular countries, it is crucial to 'open the black box' of human rights bodies themselves to gain insight into how and why they act in the way they do. The authors assert that the Inter-American Commission on Human Rights (IACHR) recommendation in favour of demarcating Indigenous lands in the *Yanomami v Brazil case* was the result of several factors. These included the high level of motivation and technical knowledge of the complainants, who were also able to utilize their transnational connections to engage systematically with the IACHR. This enabled them to leverage direct political and legal advocacy before both the Commissioners and IACHR staff. The ensuing impacts of this case were not confined solely to the specific issues at hand, but also had broader implications for the future jurisprudence of the IACHR. In a similar vein, Cerqueira contends that political factors, rather than legal constraints, have had a detrimental effect on the protection of Indigenous territorial rights through the adoption of precautionary measures. The author argues that there is compelling evidence indicating that the safeguarding of Indigenous territorial rights has been excluded from precautionary measures since 2011. This exclusion is believed to stem from political pressure exerted by certain states, particularly Brazil, which opposed IACHR decisions regarding precautionary measures. As a result, the IACHR has refrained from issuing precautionary measures to halt large-scale projects in Indigenous and tribal territories, even in cases where there were contentious allegations of foreseeable, serious and irreparable harm. This shift has effectively denied a significant number of individuals and communities an essential tool to protect their territorial rights within the IAHRS. Cerqueira maintains that, although the IAHRS upholds some of the most sophisticated standards for Indigenous territorial rights, the current operational practices of its bodies render it almost impossible to protect these rights through urgent measures.

## 5 THE IMPORTANCE OF ADDRESSING VICTIMS IN IMPACT ANALYSIS

All contributors highlight the significance of engaging with the victims of human rights violations. Ragone and Nocera assert that, overall, both the IACtHR and the ECtHR have influenced both institutional and non-institutional actors at the domestic level, promoting greater awareness of human rights and contributing to the spread of a form of constitutional pluralism.

Urueña and Yate Cortés argue that the narratives of the IACtHR play a crucial role in constructing and shaping representations of victims, which, in turn, influence the reception and impact of human rights discourse throughout Latin America. They examine how the IACHR formulates the image of the victim, at times reinforcing conventional understandings of vulnerability, while at other times challenging simplistic binary representations of victimhood and responsibility. This process involves recognizing a diverse range of victims and considering the broader political and structural contexts surrounding each case. Indeed, the IACtHR has acknowledged narratives that transcend the dichotomy of opposing categories such as 'good' and 'evil'. From a different perspective, Burbano Herrera, Haeck and Verwohlt-Hansen propose a theoretical and analytical framework which calls for the inclusion of voices from those deprived of liberty, their surrounding environments, state authorities and members of human rights organisations in the analysis. They recommend the adoption of decolonial methodologies throughout the research process, recognizing the distinct challenges faced by individuals deprived of liberty within various prison systems and governmental regimes across Latin America. Parra Vera and Trespalacios-Leal offer a comprehensive analysis of the impact of Inter-American jurisprudence on the decisions made by the Colombian Constitutional Court (CCC) and the Special Jurisdiction for Peace (JEP) regarding the optimal protection of the rights of victims of systematic violence. They argue that the jurisprudence of the IAHRS compelled the negotiators of the Colombian peace agreement to prioritize the maximization of justice. The CCC stipulated that all benefits must be contingent upon the fulfilment of victims' rights. Furthermore, by providing a platform for victims who had previously been silenced by the ordinary justice system, the JEP has facilitated restorative dialogue between victims and perpetrators, thereby redefining the parameters of justice for egregious crimes within the broader context of peacebuilding. Parra Vera and Trespalacios-Leal, in particular, present an analysis of the innovative transitional justice strategy implemented in Colombia following the peace agreement. They view this strategy as an illustration of the impact of the IAHRS, especially through the dialogues between tribunals on how best to safeguard the rights of victims of systematic violence.

## 6 CONCLUSION

In conclusion, this volume offers a comprehensive exploration of the diverse and multifaceted impact of the IAHRS. Through the contributions of diverse scholars, it underscores the challenges involved in defining, measuring and assessing impact. The wide array of perspectives, encompassing theoretical frameworks, practical applications and specific regional case studies, provides significant insights into how the IAHRS influences both legal frameworks and societal outcomes across the Americas. Despite the difficulties in fully capturing its extensive effects, the volume highlights the importance of ongoing academic research into the system's impact, especially concerning marginalized groups and specific national contexts.

We extend our sincere gratitude to the contributors for their invaluable work in shaping this volume. We trust that readers will find this book both enlightening and thought-provoking, and that it will serve as a catalyst for further academic discussion and research on the IAHRS and its impact.

# Index

Printed and bound by CPI Group (UK) Ltd, Croydon, CR0 4YY

17/06/2026

14902650-0004